The Austrian Legal System

Two week loan

Ma

Zitiervorschlag: *H. Hausmaninger,* Austrian Legal System[2] (2000)

Die Deutsche Bibliothek – CIP-Einheitsaufnahme

Hausmaninger, Herbert:
The Austrian Legal System / Herbert Hausmaninger. –
2., rev. and enl. ed.. – Wien : Manz; TheHague ;
London ; Boston : Kluwer Law Internat., 2000
ISBN 3-214-00247-3 (Manz)
ISBN 90-411-1480-7 (Kluwer)

Printed in Austria

Copublished by Kluwer Law International
P.O. Box 85889
2508 CN The Hague, The Netherlands

Sold and distributed in Austria by
MANZ'sche Verlags- und Universitätsbuchhandlung AG
Kohlmarkt 16
1014 Wien, Austria

Sold and distributed in the USA and Canada by
Kluwer Law International
675 Massachusetts Avenue
Cambridge, MA 02139, USA

Sold and distributed in all other countries by
Kluwer Law International
Distribution Centre
P.O. Box 322
3300 AH Dordrecht, The Netherlands

© 2000 MANZ'sche Verlags- und Universitätsbuchhandlung GmbH
A-1014 Kohlmarkt 16
Telefon: (01) 531 61-0
eMail: verlag@MANZ.at
World Wide Web: www.MANZ.at
Druck: Novographic Druck G.m.b.H., 1230 Wien

For Elisabeth

For Elisabeth

Preface

This book is a first attempt to present a broad range of aspects of Austrian law and legal culture in English for the purpose of comparison with other legal systems. Within the European Civil law tradition, Austrian law together with German and Swiss law belongs to the Germanic legal family. It shares fundamental features as well as numerous details of its legal system with the law of its neighbors, but it has also developed interesting ideas of its own. In 1995, Austria joined the European Union and thus became subject to an extensive layer of European Community law. It is fascinating to observe a process of interaction, harmonization and unification of European law, in which elements of Common and Civil law blend on the supra-national level and, at the same time, profoundly influence individual national systems. In this process, Austria will not only learn from foreign legal experience, but will also have an opportunity to make creative legal contributions to a growing body of European law.

My primary goal is to introduce foreign readers to some of the basic elements of the Austrian legal system, including history and political context, sources and interpretation of law, legal education, and actors and roles in the legal process. Special attention will be given to such distinctive features of Austrian legal culture as the Administrative and the Constitutional Court, the protection of civil rights, criminal procedure, and the Civil Code. This focus is intended to facilitate the foreign observer's comparison with essential elements of his own legal system. But Austrian students and practitioners, too, may find this approach helpful when it comes to explaining their law to others. In describing Austrian law, I have generally used American rather than English legal concepts and terminology, not only because of my personal experience in teaching comparative law in American law schools, but also on account of the growing importance of American law in a perspective of globalization of legal science and legal practice.

The book's contents are selective rather than comprehensive, but they will hopefully convey a sufficiently clear picture of some of the defining characteristics of Austrian law. Comparative observations will be made sparingly in order to keep the focus on Austria. Individual chapters may be read out of order, they are self-contained, which accounts for some repetitions.

My work could not have been accomplished without the help and encouragement of several collaborators and friends. *Dr. Richard Gamauf, Dr. Viktor Mayer-Schönberger, Mag. Doris Vater-Dannhäuser, Mag. Verena Haas, Mag. Alessandra Melloni* and *Dieter Swoboda* of the University of Vienna Law School greatly assisted me in collecting and arranging information, Professors *Patrick R. Hugg* (New Orleans) and *Paul B. Stephan* (Charlottesville, Virginia) read versions of the manuscript and made many useful suggestions. *Eric L. Palmquist* and *Gabriel B. Pellathy* of the Cornell Law School provided valuable editorial help. I owe all of them profound gratitude. For errors, omissions and opinions the full responsibility remains my own.

Vienna, March 1998   *Herbert Hausmaninger*

Preface to the Second Edition

The quick absorption of the Austrian Legal System by the legal community provides the opportunity to submit a substantially revised and enlarged second edition only two years after the first. New chapters have been added on private law (including family, property, succession, contract, and tort law), labor law, and civil procedure. Revisions and additions were made in particular to account for recent changes in the political system, in Austria's relations with the EU, and in legal education and legal professions. All other chapters were updated to reflect the latest developments.

Once again, I am grateful to more persons than I can name for providing useful criticism and advice. I wish to single out, however, the major contributions made by my associates at the University of Vienna Law School: *Dr. Richard Gamauf, Mag. Verena Haas, Dr. Fritz Popp, Mag. Barbara Steininger,* and *Mag. Dieter Swoboda.* Very special thanks also go to Professor *Patrick R. Hugg* (Loyola Law School, New Orleans) who again read the entire manuscript, and to three experts in Vienna whose helpful comments greatly improved individual chapters: Professor *Helmut Koziol* (Private Law), Judge *Michael Schwab* (Criminal Procedure), and Professor *Theodor Tomandl* (Labor Law).

Vienna, July 2000   *Herbert Hausmaninger*

Contents

Chapter 1
Political History

Chapter 2
The Constitution, Sources, and Interpretation of Law

Chapter 3
The Political System

Chapter 4
Austria and the European Union

Chapter 8
Constitutional Review

Chapter 9
Fundamental Rights

Chapter 10
Criminal Procedure

Chapter 11
Austrian Civil Procedure

Abbreviations

ABGB	*Allgemeines Bürgerliches Gesetzbuch* (Austrian General Civil Code)
ALR	*Allgemeines Landrecht für die Preussischen Staaten* (Universal Territorial Law for the Prussian States)
ASVG	*Allgemeines Sozialversicherungsgesetz* (General Social Insurance Act)
ATS	Austrian Schilling(s)
BG	*Bezirksgericht* (District Court)
BGB	*Bürgerliches Gesetzbuch* (German Civil Code)
BGBl	*Bundesgesetzblatt* (Federal Law Gazette)
B-VG	*Bundes-Verfassungsgesetz* (Federal Constitution)
BVG	*Bundesverfassungsgesetz* (Federal Constitutional Law)
CFSP	Common Foreign and Security Policy
dRGBl	*deutsches Reichsgesetzblatt* (German Imperial Law Gazette)
EC	European Community (Communities)
ECHR	European Convention of Human Rights
ECSC	European Coal and Steel Community
EEA	European Economic Area
EEC	European Economic Community
EFTA	European Free Trade Association
EU	European Union
EuGRZ	*Europäische Grundrechte-Zeitschrift*
FPÖ	*Freiheitliche Partei Österreichs* (Austrian Freedom Party)
FS	*Festschrift*
GAL	*Grüne Alternative* (Green Alternative)
GDP	Gross domestic product
GDR	German Democratic Republic
GS	*Gedächtnisschrift*
HGB	*Handelsgesetzbuch* (Commercial Code)
JAP	*Juristische Ausbildung und Praxisvorbereitung*
JBl	*Juristische Blätter*
JRP	*Journal für Rechtspolitik*
KPÖ	*Kommunistische Partei Österreichs* (Communist Party of Austria)
LG	*Landesgericht* (Regional Court)
LIF	*Liberales Forum* (Liberal Forum)
NATO	North Atlantic Treaty Organization
OECD	Organization for Economic Cooperation and Development
OEEC	Organization for European Economic Cooperation
OGH	*Oberster Gerichtshof* (Supreme Court)
ÖJZ	*Österreichische Juristenzeitung*
OLG	*Oberlandesgericht* (Court of Appeals)
ÖVP	*Österreichische Volkspartei* (Austrian People's Party)
ÖZÖR	*Österreichische Zeitschrift für öffentliches Recht*
ÖZP	*Österreichische Zeitschrift für Politikwissenschaft*
RGBl	*Reichsgesetzblatt* (Imperial Law Gazette)
SEA	Single European Act
SPÖ	*Sozialistische/Sozialdemokratische Partei Österreichs* (Socialist or Social Democratic Party of Austria)
StGB	*Strafgesetzbuch* (Criminial Code)

StPO	*Strafprozeßordnung* (Criminal Procedure Code)
TEU	Treaty of the European Union
UN	United Nations
UVS	*Unabhängiger Verwaltungssenat* (Independent Administrative Panel)
VdU	*Verband der Unabhängigen* (Association of Independents)
VerfGG	*Verfassungsgerichtshofgesetz*
VfSlg	*Sammlung der Erkenntnisse und wichtigsten Beschlüsse des Verfassungsgerichtshofes*
WEU	Western European Union
ZfRV	*Zeitschrift für Rechtsvergleichung*
ZGB	*Zivilgesetzbuch* (Swiss Civil Code)
ZÖR	*Zeitschrift für öffentliches Recht*
ZPO	*Zivilprozeßordnung* (Civil Procedure Code)

Chapter 1
Political History

I. Introduction

Modern Austria is a small state at the crossroads of Central Europe.[1] Its present territory of 32,377 square miles (83,856 square kilometers) and its population of approximately 8.1 million (1999) are the product of the dismemberment of the Austro-Hungarian Monarchy (the multinational Habsburg Empire) as a result of World War I in 1918. Ninety-eight percent of the present Austrian population is German-speaking. Small communities of ethnic Hungarians and Croats live in Burgenland, Slovenes live in southern Carinthia. 756,500 inhabitants or nine percent of the total population are foreign nationals, mostly from the former Yugoslavia and Turkey.[2] 78 percent of the population is Roman Catholic, five percent is Protestant (mostly Lutherans), four percent belongs to other denominations, and nine percent is without religious affiliation.[3]

II. Austria as Part of the Holy Roman Empire

For almost one thousand years, most of the territories making up today's Republic of Austria were part of the Holy Roman Empire of the German Nation that was formed by Charlemagne (crowned in Rome in 800 A.D.) and his successors. Austria's role began as and continued to be that of a fortified bulwark in the East against recurrent Magyar and later Ottoman (Turkish) invasions.[4] The Habsburgs became dukes of Austria, the northeastern part of the present republic, towards the end of the thirteenth century. Over time they skilfully added to their possessions, including Bohemia and Hungary in 1526. All of these territories maintained their separate identities and were united only by the person of the king or prince. Members of the Habsburg dynasty ruled Germany as Roman Emperors with brief intermissions until 1806. While central power had always been weak in that Empire, after the Thirty Years' War (1618–48), which was essentially a rebellion of Protestant princes and towns against the Catholic Emperor, the component parts, including the hereditary Habsburg lands, obtained *de facto* sovereignty. Austria began to play an independent role as a great power in European politics, often in confrontations

---

[1] Austria borders eight countries: Germany, the Czech Republic, Slovakia, Hungary, Slovenia, Italy, Switzerland and Liechtenstein.

[2] Almost one-half of them live in Vienna, where they constitute 17.5 percent of the population (cf. Berlin 13%, Paris 13%, London 20%).

[3] Four percent provides no information.

[4] Vienna was besieged unsuccessfully by Turkish armies in 1529 and 1683.

with Prussia, the other leading German state. Habsburg rulers like Maria Theresia (1740–80) and her son Joseph II (1780–90) conducted sweeping legal and administrative reforms in their territories.

III. The Habsburg Monarchy 1806–1918

A. The Breakup of the Holy Roman Empire

The French Revolution of 1789 posed a serious threat to the established European monarchies. They responded by forming political and military alliances. Beginning in 1792, twenty-three years of confrontation or outright war ensued between Austria and France. Austria suffered its first major defeats at the hands of the young French general Napoleon Bonaparte in 1797, resulting in the loss of the Netherlands and Lombardy. Later battles led to further losses, and even to two brief French occupations of Vienna in 1805 and 1809. When Napoleon transformed the French political system into a hereditary monarchy on May 18, 1804, Francis II, the elected Habsburg Roman Emperor of the German Nation, adopted the additional title of Hereditary Emperor of Austria on August 10 of that year. When in 1805 and 1806 the majority of German princes had joined the Rhine Confederation (*Rheinbund*) under Napoleon's protectorate, Francis II, under pressure from Napoleon, renounced his function of Roman-German Emperor on August 6, 1806, thus putting a formal end to the fragmented Holy Roman Empire, which for some time had existed in name only.

B. "Pre-March 1848" Austria and the German Confederation (*Deutscher Bund*)

After a grand coalition under Austrian leadership (including Russia, England and Prussia) had defeated Napoleon, the German states in 1815 formed the *Deutsche Bund*, a loose confederation of sovereign countries, not a federal state. The German Confederation had only one organ, the Confederate Assembly (*Bundesversammlung*), which consisted of representatives instructed by their governments. The Assembly met in Frankfurt and was presided over by Austria. Most member states were hereditary monarchies with antiliberal and antidemocratic tendencies. The purpose of the German Confederation was limited to protecting the external and internal security of Germany and maintaining the independence and inviolability of the individual German states. The revolutionary movements of 1848 temporarily changed the character of the Confederation: 585 elected deputies convened as the *Deutsche Verfassunggebende Nationalversammlung* (German National Constituent Assembly) and adopted a bill of rights and an all-German constitution. But the revolutions were quickly subdued and the Confederation returned to its previous condition. Its future was doomed by the escalating rivalry between Prussia and Austria, both of which aspired to the leading role. When in 1866 Prussian troops occupied the Duchy of Holstein, then administered by Austria, the

German Confederation supported Austria by imposing military sanctions on Prussia. Austria, however, was defeated by the Prussian army on the battlefield of Königgrätz. The subsequent peace treaty of Prague ended the German Confederation.

C. From the Revolution of 1848 to the Constitutional Reforms of 1867

The February 1848 uprising against the royal French government in Paris triggered revolutions all over Europe. In Austria, the March 1848 revolution had both a democratic-liberal element, which demanded civil rights and popular participation in government, and a social component urging reforms in the face of hardships brought on by the industrial revolution. Especially outside the German territories, a strong push was made for national autonomy. After initial concessions by the government and work on a liberal constitution, uprisings in Vienna, Hungary, and Austrian territories in Italy were crushed with military force, and a period of neo-absolutism followed from 1849 to 1860. The humiliating defeat of Austria inflicted by Sardinia and France in northern Italy (1859) led to domestic reforms under the long reign of Emperor Francis Joseph (1848–1916). In 1867, a succession of constitutional experiments that had started in 1860 culminated in a constitutional compromise (*Ausgleich*) with Hungary, granting the latter virtual independence in a loosely structured personal union of Austrian Emperor and Hungarian King (a Dual Monarchy with very few common affairs). But this arrangement occurred only after another military defeat, this time against Prussia at Königgrätz in 1866, had ended Austria's role in Germany.

For the Austrian part of the Monarchy, the 1861 Constitution was amended by State Fundamental Laws (*Staatsgrundgesetze*) providing for an upgraded parliament, judicial independence, and important fundamental rights, such as equality before the law, freedom of speech, press, assembly, etc. This "December Constitution" of 1867 remained in force until the end of the monarchy in 1918.[5] It ultimately proved unable to contain the conflict of nationalities, in particular the pressures of Poles and Czechs – opposed by German liberals – for autonomy similar to that obtained by the Hungarians in 1867. In combination with other factors, such as slow industrialization and lack of liberal-democratic traditions, these national tensions led to the rapid collapse of the Empire in 1918.

D. World War I and the Dismemberment of the Austro-Hungarian Empire

In the course of the withdrawal of the Ottoman Empire from the Balkans, Austria had occupied the former Turkish provinces of Bosnia and Her-

---

[5] Its Bill of Rights is still part of Austrian constitutional law, see *infra* Chapter 2 (The Constitution, Sources, and Interpretation of Law), II.B.

cegovina in 1878. Their annexation by Austria in 1908 deepened hostility on the part of Serbia, which strove vigorously for the unification of all southern Slavs. When Archduke Francis Ferdinand, heir designate to the Austrian throne, was assassinated in Sarajevo on June 28, 1914, by a young Bosnian Serb nationalist, Austria accused Serbia of instigating the murder and declared war on Serbia on July 28. Austria's ally, Germany, within a few days declared war on France and Russia, which were joined in an alliance with Britain. Austria entered this First World War (1914–18) militarily ill-prepared and under incompetent leadership. It became a military satellite to Germany and lost its capability to effect domestic reform. With the death of Emperor Francis Joseph in 1916, the multinational empire lost an essential unifying link. When the United States entered in the war in 1917, that nation supported secessionist national ambitions in the Austro-Hungarian Monarchy because they were viewed as expressions of democratic liberation movements. President Woodrow Wilson's Fourteen Points of January 8, 1918, encouraged national self-determination and led to declarations of independence by Poles, Czechs and southern Slavs during the month of October, even before the war had ended in an armistice on November 3, 1918.

IV. The First Republic (1918–1933)

On October 30, 1918, the German-speaking deputies to the *Reichsrat* (Imperial Council, the parliament of the Austrian part of the Dual Monarchy) in Vienna, left behind by all others, proclaimed an independent state *Deutsch-österreich* (German-Austria). On November 11, 1918, Emperor Charles, who had succeeded Francis Joseph in 1916, withdrew from participation in the government (without formally abdicating). One day later, the self-proclaimed National Assembly declared German-Austria a democratic republic and a component part of the recently formed German republic, demonstrating that not even the "founding fathers" of the new republic believed in its viability. It claimed control over all former Habsburg territories that had a German majority, including German-speaking areas of Bohemia and Moravia. The new state was faced with formidable economic, social, and political problems. The breakup of the Monarchy had caused economic disruption. Austrian industry lost its markets and suppliers. Communist groups worked towards a revolutionary change of the system, while conservative provinces attempted to break away from Socialist-dominated Vienna. In a constitutional assembly elected in February of 1919, the Social Democrats (*Sozialdemokraten*) held 69 of 165 seats, the conservative Christian-Socials (*Christlichsoziale*) 63, the German Nationals (*Großdeutsche*) 26. A federal constitution went into effect for the Republic of Austria on October 1, 1920. It concentrated political power in the parliament.

Article 88 of the peace treaty of Saint Germain, signed between Austria and the victorious Allies on September 10, 1919, forbade Austria to join Germany and to use the name "German-Austria." It also denied Austria the incorporation of German-speaking areas of Bohemia and Moravia. Italy was

given the German-speaking territory of South Tirol (beyond the Brenner Pass).
Border questions with Hungary and a newly-formed Yugoslav state were set-
tled by referendum in 1920.

New elections after the adoption of the Constitution gave a relative
majority to the Christian-Socials. The Social Democrats went into opposition
and remained there throughout the First Republic. They had a huge electorate
in the industrial labor force of the city of Vienna, which comprised one-third
of the Austrian population and received the status of a separate *Land* (province
or state) in 1922. They transformed Vienna into a showcase of social reform
(public transport, housing, kindergartens, etc.). The radical Marxist rhetoric of
the Socialists prevented the Communists from achieving political influence.
The Christian-Socials drew support from Roman Catholic farmers and conservative city dwellers (including civil servants, white-collar workers, middle-
class merchants and craftsmen), many of whom were still monarchists at heart.
But a sizeable number of the urban middle class also voted for the German
Nationals and other (smaller) parties of the national spectrum. The inability of
the two major parties either to gain absolute majorities or to form a coalition
led to a succession of no fewer than 20 unstable and short-lived coalition governments of the Christian-Socials with smaller parties between 1920 and 1934.

Inflation threatened the country with financial collapse in 1922. But
by 1926 economic recovery had been achieved due to a League of Nations
loan and tight international budgetary supervision. Yet political democracy
was unable to develop due to the ideological rigidity and "camp mentality"
(*Lagerdenken*) of the political groups, each of which profoundly distrusted the
aims of the others and prepared for the worst. In particular, the Socialists
armed and trained a paramilitary *Schutzbund* (Defense League), and the conservatives formed the *Heimwehren* (Home Guards), which regularly demon-
strated against each other. In one confrontation in 1927, two people were accidentally shot by rightist war veterans, who were subsequently acquitted by a
Vienna jury. A demonstration organized by the Socialists on July 15, 1927, led
to the burning down of the Palace of Justice and to the killing of more than a
hundred people in a confrontation with police.

Heimwehr demands to strengthen the executive led to compromise
amendments to the Constitution in 1929 that upgraded the powers of the President. However, political distrust remained. The world economic crisis, with
the crash of Austria's largest bank in May of 1931, left more than 600,000
(30% of the labor force) unemployed in February of 1933. This strengthened
the ranks of Socialists and National Socialists ("*Nazi*") and the general tendency to seek authoritarian rather than democratic solutions.

The last democratic parliamentary elections on November 9, 1930,
once again produced no stable majorities in the National Council, and a succession of coalition governments was unable to prevent radical political confrontation outside of parliament. The conflict between conservatives and Socialists gained an added dimension with the strengthening of Austrian National
Socialists after Adolf Hitler's assumption of power in Germany on January 30,
1933.

V. The Authoritarian Christian Corporate State (1934–38)

On March 4, 1933, in a political situation in which the government controlled only one seat more than the opposition in parliament, a dispute erupted in the National Council concerning the outcome of a vote it had taken. As a result of the disagreement, all three presidents resigned. The Rules of the National Council did not provide for that contingency. The government interpreted the move as a "self-elimination" of the parliament and began to rule by means of executive decrees based *pro forma* on an obsolete and irrelevant War Economic Emergency Act (*Kriegswirtschaftliches Ermächtigungsgesetz*) of 1917.

On the same questionable legal foundation the government quickly suspended the Constitutional Court which could have nullified such governmental actions as unconstitutional. On February 12, 1934, a civil war broke out in Vienna and other industrial regions. After four days of fighting, the Socialist paramilitary forces (*Schutzbund*) were subdued by the Federal Army and Christian-Social paramilitary forces (*Heimwehren*). Some of the Socialist leaders managed to flee the country, many were arrested, and several were executed. In April 1934, the government adopted a new constitution, abolishing parliamentary democracy and replacing it with an authoritarian "Christian Corporate State" (*christlicher Ständestaat*), which some labeled a clerico-fascist dictatorship. The ideological underpinnings of this model had been provided by the papal encyclical *Quadragesimo anno* (1931). The Christian-Social Patriotic Front (*Vaterländische Front*) was to function as the only legitimate political movement.

On July 25, 1934, the Austrian Federal Chancellor Engelbert Dollfuß was murdered by National Socialists attempting to seize power. His successor, Kurt Schuschnigg, made belated and futile attempts to restore cooperation with the Socialist opposition. When Italy's Fascist dictator Benito Mussolini, who had politically supported Dollfuß, shifted his alliance from Austria to Germany in 1936, Schuschnigg came under increasing pressure by Hitler to install a government friendly to Germany. Finally, in total international isolation, Schuschnigg took the desperate step of ordering a referendum for March 13, 1938, to decide whether Austria should remain independent or join Germany. To prevent this plebiscite, Hitler ordered the German army to Austria on March 12 and incorporated Austria into the German Reich the next day. Foreign powers, attempting to avoid a confrontation with Hitler at that time, accepted this incorporation (*Anschluß*) without protest.

VI. Occupation by Hitler's National Socialist Germany (1938–45)

A sham plebiscite held on April 10, 1938, produced an overwhelming majority for the *Anschluß*. Austria became part of Germany. Austrian politicians and the entire Jewish population were ruthlessly persecuted by Hitler's terror machine. Those who were unable to seek exile abroad were arrested and put into concentration camps. On September 1, 1939, World War II broke out with Hitler's invasion of Poland. Subsequently, Austrians served as soldiers in the German armed forces.

More than 65,000 Austrian Jews were killed in the period of German domination. In 1938, an estimated 185,000 people of Jewish faith had lived in Austria. In 1951 their number was 11,000. At least 2,700 non-Jewish Austrians were executed for resistance to the Nazi regime, while 32,000 more died in prisons and concentration camps. Approximately 107,000 Austrians died as soldiers in the war; 76,000 more Austrian soldiers were still reported as missing in action as late as in 1955. More than 24,000 civilians died as a result of air-raids and during the invasion by Allied troops at the end of the war.

VII. The Second Republic

A. Allied Occupation (1945–55)

1. Political and Legal Framework

When Hitler's opponents began to plan the post-war geography of Europe, the reestablishment of Austria as a free and independent state became one of the declared war aims of the Allied Powers. In Moscow on November 1, 1943, they issued the following Declaration:

"The Governments of the United Kingdom, the Soviet Union and the United States of America are agreed that Austria, the first free country to fall victim to Hitlerite aggression, shall be liberated from German domination.

"They regard the annexation imposed upon Austria by Germany on March 15th, 1938, as null and void. They consider themselves as in no way bound by any changes effected in Austria since that date. They declare that they wish to see reestablished a free and independent Austria, and thereby to open the way for the Austrian people themselves, as well as those neighboring states which will be faced with similar problems, to find that political and economic security which is the only basis for lasting peace.

"Austria is reminded, however, that she has a responsibility, which she cannot evade, for participation in the war on the side of Hitlerite Germany, and that in the final settlement account will inevitably be taken of her own contribution to her liberation."

Although originally this Declaration may have had the primary intent of encouraging Austrian resistance to Hitler, in later conferences, especially at Yalta in February 1945, the three Allied Powers agreed on specific measures regarding the reestablishment of Austria, including the demarcation of four future occupation zones.

In early April 1945, Soviet troops entered Austria from the south and east and assumed control of the Eastern part of Austria. The three Western powers (liberated France had acceded to the Moscow Declaration) did not enter their occupation zones until the beginning of May. On April 21, 1945, Soviet officers brought 74-year-old Karl Renner, head of the Austrian government after World War I and a well-known Austro-Marxist theoretician, from his home in Gloggnitz to Vienna and permitted him to form a coalition government for all of Austria. Upon his arrival in Vienna, Renner was surprised to learn that political parties had already been founded (or re-founded) and a municipal administration was already functioning. The two major parties, the *Österreichische Volkspartei* (*ÖVP*, Austrian People's Party, successor to the Christian-Socials) and the *Sozialistische Partei Österreichs* (*SPÖ*, Socialist Party of Austria, the former Social Democrats) were at that time joined by a third coalition partner, the *Kommunistische Partei Österreichs* (*KPÖ*, Communist Party of Austria). The Communists, however, left the government in 1947 and were soon reduced to political insignificance.

On April 27, 1945, a Provisional Government of Austria formed in Vienna proclaimed the re-establishment of Austria as a democratic republic. On May 1, 1945, the government adopted a Provisional Constitution and a Constitutional Law on the Re-establishment of Rule of Law in Austria. The latter annulled statutes and regulations enacted after March 13, 1938, in so far as they were incompatible with the existence of a free and independent Austrian state, contradicted the legal consciousness of the Austrian people, or contained typical expressions of Nazi ideology. Other German legislation introduced in Austria during that period (e.g., the Commercial Code of 1897 and the Marriage Act of 1938) remained in force. The government was immediately recognized by the Soviets, and by October 20, 1945, it had also gained recognition by the Western Allies, who had initially feared that the Soviets had installed a puppet regime. Under a First Control Agreement concluded by the four occupying powers on July 4, 1945, the Austrian government could act only under the instructions of the Allied Council. A Second Control Agreement of June 28, 1946, somewhat modified the rule of the four High Commissioners (Allied Council) and their apparatus (Allied Commission), but Austrian constitutional laws still required the written approval of the Allied Council, and all Austrian statutes and treaties entered into force only after a period of 31 days during which they could be vetoed by the Allied Council. The Council could also demand repeal or amendment of any legislative or administrative measure.

After the recognition of one government for all of Austria, the four occupying powers consented to free and secret elections in the whole country, in which the Communists suffered a disastrous defeat. On November 25, 1945, the *ÖVP* won 85 of the 165 seats and thus the absolute majority in the National Council (the lower house of Parliament). 76 seats went to the *SPÖ*, and only four seats to the Communists. On December 19, 1945, when the newly elected Parliament met, the Constitution of 1920/1929 again went into effect. Yet Austria did not gain full sovereignty until the conclusion of the "State Treaty"[6] between Austria and the four Allied Powers in 1955.

---

[6] It is not called the "Peace Treaty" because technically Austria had not been at war, but "incapacitated" under German occupation.

The political and legal position taken by the Austrian government to-wards the 1938 *Anschluß* with Germany was expressed in an "occupation theory." Accordingly, Austria had not been annexed and become an integral part of the German *Reich*, but had continued to exist as a separate state, whose freedom of action had been temporarily blocked by German occupation. Thus Austria was not subject to liability under international law for wrongs committed by the German *Reich* during that period. On the contrary, Austria was one of the first victims of Hitlerite aggression. This "victim theory" disregarded the active participation of many Austrians in the Nazi regime and for a long time prevented a meaningful discussion of the involvement of Austrians in the Holocaust as well as adequate measures of restitution to and compensation of victims.

2. Domestic Politics: Political System and Economic Recovery

a. Political Cooperation

Politicians of the two major parties, many of whom had jointly suffered in German concentration camps or exile, decided to bury their past conflicts and to make a new beginning, working together in the interest of Austrian reconstruction. The Austrian People's Party moved away from its former program of political Catholicism, and the Socialist Party relinquished its radical "Austro-Marxism." Moderate politicians of both parties cooperated in reviving the economy, establishing a democratic system, and pressing for Austria's independence.

One major problem was "denazification" (*Entnazifizierung*). Almost 700,000 Austrians had joined Hitler's National Socialist Party (*NSDAP*). These former Nazis were now forced to register, were deprived of political rights (above all the right to vote) and were excluded from the civil service and some other professional activities. People's Courts (*Volksgerichte*) were established to prosecute war criminals and leading Nazi party functionaries in a summary procedure. Most people resented these measures, and regarded them as the victors' revenge against those who had lost the war. The Cold War that broke out between the Soviet Union and the West in 1945 encouraged a quick reintegration of "less incriminated" (*minderbelastete*) former Nazis into the political system. They were given the right to vote in 1947, and even "incriminated" (*belastete*) Nazis were amnestied in 1948. Both major parties attempted to attract these "reintegrated" voters, thus encouraging the population in general to shut their eyes rather than turn their minds to the past. In 1949, an Association of Independents (*Verband der Unabhängigen* or *VdU*), 80% of whom were former Nazis, ran for Parliament and obtained 16 seats. In 1955 it was succeeded by the Austrian Freedom Party (*Freiheitliche Partei Österreichs* or *FPÖ*).

After the Communists had left the three-party government in 1947, the two major parties embarked on a virtually unopposed coalition that was to last for twenty years. Initially, the First Republic "camp mentality" persisted among large groups of party loyalists. With time, however, party membership became less strongly rooted in ideological conviction or family tradition, and was instead based on simple political opportunism. The two parties had the huge state administration, including nationalized industries, banks, transport, communication, media, schools and hospitals under their control and patronage. Party membership became essential for finding a job, an apartment, and various other benefits. The system became increasingly rigid and politicized. The balance of power of the two parties was maintained by a coalition committee (*Koalitionsausschuß*) enforcing a coalition pact with strict discipline in a rubber-stamp parliament. In this framework, politics became a process of vetoes and compromises, and a principle of *Proporz* (proportional job placement) led to overstaffed and duplicative administrative mechanisms. Most decisions in economic and social policy were taken de facto by a party-controlled "social partnership" (*Sozialpartnerschaft*)[7] between employers' associations and labor unions. These decisions were subsequently ratified by legislative enactments in parliament. This social partnership avoided the economic losses suffered in other countries as a result of open labor conflicts, including strikes, which were virtually unknown in Austria. The bargaining process proved to function successfully even in subsequent periods of single-party governments.

b. Economic Reconstruction

In 1945, the final year of the war, Austria suffered tremendous economic damage through aerial bombardment and invading Allied ground troops. In Vienna alone, 80,000 apartments were destroyed. Transportation and food supply collapsed. Hundreds of thousands of German and other refugees moving into Austria from central and eastern Europe exacerbated the situation. Occupation costs devoured one-third of the 1946 federal budget. The Soviet troops systematically stripped their zone of industrial production equipment and shipped it back to their country as "reparations."

In this situation, Austrian politicians resorted to a large-scale nationalization of energy resources and basic industries in order to save them from the Soviets, and also because massive private investment could not be expected. This nationalized industry became the motor of economic revival in the 1950s and 1960s. From 1947 onwards, wage and price agreements between employers' organizations and labor unions prevented inflation and permitted the formation of capital. The most important impetus, however, was provided by the Marshall Plan (European Recovery Program or ERP), in the course of which 16 European states created the Organization for European Economic Cooperation (OEEC, Paris 1948) and Austria received 962 million dollars from the U.S., out of which power stations, steel works, highways, and other large projects were completed and the modernization of economic infrastructure could be accomplished.

---

[7] See *infra* Chapter 3 (The Political System), II.D.

3. Austria's Position in International Relations

As early as 1945, the Cold War had started due to the different ideological positions of the Communist Soviet Union on the one side and the democratically-oriented states under the leadership of the United States on the other side. Austria, located between the two blocs, was of strategic interest to both of them.

Despite rigid control over its occupation zone in eastern Austria and generous support to the Austrian Communist Party, the Soviet Union was unable to attain direct influence over Austria. Soon after Stalin's death in 1953, the Soviet leadership under Nikita Khrushchev developed a new foreign policy aimed at creating and influencing a third bloc of non-aligned nations, particularly among the developing countries. Especially in case of geographical proximity, neutral states could form a useful buffer zone around the "Socialist Camp." This view led the Soviet Union to promote neutrality in general and the idea of a neutral Austria in particular. It was to play an important role in the negotiations leading to the State Treaty of 1955.

B. The State Treaty and Neutrality (1955)

In 1953, Austria proposed to the Soviet Union to make an official commitment to military neutrality in order to break the deadlock in negotiations concerning the State Treaty. At the Berlin conference of the Allied Powers in February 1954, the Soviet Union suggested the insertion of a provision of non-alliance for Austria into the State Treaty. This proposal, which would have amounted to Austria's contractual neutralization, was rejected by the Western powers. They were reluctant to accept a neutral wedge formed by Switzerland and Austria between the northern and southern tiers of NATO, and they also feared a precedent for the solution of the German question – reunification under neutrality, or separate statehood for the Federal Republic and the German Democratic Republic and their integration into the rival blocs.

When an Austrian government delegation promised in Moscow on April 15, 1955 ("Moscow Memorandum"), to issue a declaration which would internationally commit Austria to permanent neutrality according to the Swiss model, the Soviet delegation accepted this proposal and no longer insisted on a special provision in the State Treaty itself. The Western Allies grudgingly accepted Austria's gentlemen's agreement with the Soviet Union and signed the State Treaty of Vienna on May 15, 1955. Austria was re-established as a sovereign, independent and democratic state (art. 1), but any future *Anschluß* with Germany was forbidden (art. 4). In article 6 of the treaty, Austria promised to observe human rights, and article 7 defined the rights of Slovenian and Croatian minorities living in Austria. Pursuant to the "Moscow Memorandum," Austria adopted permanent neutrality in the Federal Constitutional Law on Neutrality of October 26, 1955, after the last foreign soldier had left Austrian soil.[8]

Austria notified its new status as permanently neutral state to all states with which it maintained diplomatic relations. The express or tacit recognition by them created an international obligation for Austria to maintain its neutrality in the future. Austria was admitted to the United Nations on December 14, 1955, and it joined the Council of Europe on August 16, 1956.

C. Austrian Politics 1955–2000

1. Domestic Development

The stabilizing effect of the grand coalition of the two major parties formed after the Communists had left the government in 1947 was instrumental in accomplishing the economic reconstruction of the country and in gaining Austria's independence, but it eventually outlived its usefulness. In 1966, the *ÖVP* formed the first single-party government of the Second Republic. It initiated a phase of modernization and democratization, including a more meaningful role of parliament and the development of a critical public opinion. This process continued and deepened in the following years of Socialist government under Chancellor Bruno Kreisky (1970–1983). Profound reforms, in particular of the educational system and of criminal and family law, often reflected more of a liberal, rather than a Socialist agenda. But in many respects, generous social welfare benefits were provided in an economically prosperous phase between 1968 and 1974. These benefits were continued during the economic decline triggered by the oil crisis of 1973, resulting in a rapidly rising government debt. Nationalized industries and other sectors of the economy and administration were used to create and support jobs, regardless of economic efficiency. Despite massive subsidies from the state budget, they could no longer be maintained in the 1980s. Growing structural unemployment exacerbated social problems, such as xenophobia and other irrational fears, as well as a growing disaffection with politics, leading to a loss of confidence in the Socialist government.

In 1983, Bruno Kreisky's Socialist government lost its absolute majority. Kreisky's successor, Fred Sinowatz, formed a "small" coalition with the *FPÖ* under Norbert Steger. The government struggled against political scandals, the further decline of nationalized industries, and growing ecological pressures. In 1986, Kurt Waldheim was elected Federal President. Fred

---

[8] *BGBl* 1955/211: "Article I,

"1. For the purpose of the lasting maintenance of her independence externally, and for the purpose of the inviolability of her territory, Austria declares of her own free will her perpetual neutrality. Austria will maintain and defend this with all means at her disposal.

"2. For the securing of this purpose in all future times, Austria will not join any military alliances and will not permit the establishment of any foreign military bases on her territory."

Sinowatz resigned and was succeeded by Franz Vranitzky as Federal Chancellor. When the liberal Norbert Steger was replaced by the nationalist Jörg Haider as chairman of the *FPÖ*, Vranitzky dissolved the coalition. In the subsequent elections of November 1986, the *FPÖ* doubled its vote to more than nine percent, and the environmentalists (Greens) moved into Parliament for the first time with nearly five percent.

Kurt Waldheim, a career diplomat, had served as *ÖVP* Minister of Foreign Affairs and later as Secretary General of the UN, and enjoyed much support in Austrian public opinion. When he ran for President in 1986, the *SPÖ*, which had previously monopolized this office and feared losing it, provided the press with information alleging Waldheim's membership in Nazi organizations and accusing him of falsification of his war activities in his official biography. It turned out that he had indeed been a member of National Socialist organizations and served as an intelligence officer in the German Army in the Balkans. He tried to save face by denial and claiming memory lapses. Charges by the World Jewish Congress and foreign media that Waldheim participated in war crimes were rebutted in international investigations by lawyers and historians. While the conflict concerning his war years isolated Waldheim internationally and he could not accomplish his promise to be an active president, it had the salutary effect of leading to a broad discussion of Austrians' role under National Socialism and encouraged the country to finally come to honest terms with this part of its history.

The parliamentary elections of 1986, 1990, 1994, and 1995 were invariably followed by "grand" coalitions of the *ÖVP* and the *SPÖ* under Socialist Chancellor Franz Vranitzky. They led to a process of normalization that brought Austria closer to conditions in other West European states. Government influence on the economy diminished and efforts were made gradually to privatize the nationalized industries. The budget deficit no longer permitted state intervention in order to maintain jobs and to stimulate the economy. The social partnership began to lose its halo as the guarantor of economic prosperity and social security. Today, conflicts can no longer be resolved by traditional means. Increasing ecological awareness, critical citizens' initiatives, and movements against industrial projects pose new challenges to the established parties and their political system.

A part of the new social movements supports the Greens, but the most dramatic political impact was produced by Jörg Haider, whose plausible criticism of the "old parties" and an aggressive populist style hitherto absent from Austrian politics proved to be immensely successful, increasing the *FPÖ* vote from less than five percent in 1983 to more than 22 % in 1994. Subsequently, parts of the *ÖVP* continued to speculate about forming a coalition with Haider, whereas the *SPÖ* desperately tried to prevent the loss of core working class voters to him. In 1993 Haider's nationalist course led to a split with his party's liberal wing, which founded a new party, the Liberal Forum (*Liberales Forum*). Friction among the partners of the government coalition led to new elections in 1995 (producing little political change) and ultimately the resignation of Chancellor Vranitzky in January 1997. His successor, Viktor Klima, was obviously chosen by his party in hopes of stemming the rising pro-Haider tide. Yet he ultimately proved incapable of initiating the necessary drastic reforms. During his tenure, the coalition was in agony, mostly due to the *SPÖ*'s reluctance to cut back excesses of the welfare state.

2. Foreign Affairs

In the 1960s, the former Austrian Foreign Minister and later Chancellor Bruno Kreisky widened the content of Austrian neutrality. He claimed that permanent neutrality required Austria to maintain freedom of action in its economic relations with third states, including the right to suspend or even terminate economic agreements in the event of armed conflicts. In particular, Austria had to take certain preparations in times of peace to assure supplies in wartime. As a consequence, for more than 30 years Austria's permanent neutrality and membership in the European Economic Community (EEC) were held to be incompatible. One obstacle was seen in the long-term political goals pursued by the European Communities, another in article 113 of the EEC Treaty (now article 133 TEC), which authorizes the adoption of economic sanctions (including a unilateral embargo on the export of war material against one belligerent party) by majority vote of the EEC Council. Another important consideration in this context was the Soviet Union's opposition to Austria's membership in the EEC, which to the Soviets represented the European economic pillar of NATO. The Soviet understanding of neutrality thus included a restriction of Austria's treaty-making power that had not been explicitly provided for by prior agreement with Austria. But from the very beginning, Austria took Soviet warnings very seriously, and approached the question of EEC membership with great caution.

In 1961, the Soviet Union addressed an *aide-memoire* to the Austrian government in which Austria's intended negotiation of an association agreement under article 238 of the EEC Treaty (now art. 310 TEC) was declared incompatible with the status of permanent neutrality. Nevertheless, Austria's aim was to take part in a long-term process of development of the western European economic region. With the establishment of the EEC, the other members of the Organization for European Economic Cooperation (OEEC),[9] among them the neutral states Austria, Switzerland and Sweden, feared that the customs union would discriminate against them. Therefore, seven western European non-EEC states, Austria included, founded the European Free Trade Association (EFTA) in 1960. Concerns about neutrality were resolved by the escape clause of article 18.[10]

---

[9] In 1960, the OEEC was transformed into the OECD (Organization for Economic Cooperation and Development).

[10] Article 18 (1): "Nothing in this Convention shall prevent any Member State from taking action which it considers necessary for the protection of its essential security interests, where such action ... is taken in time of war or other emergency in international relations."

The scope of the EFTA Treaty was very limited. It applied only to free trade in industrial goods, but not – as did the Treaty of Rome that created the EEC – to agriculture, transport, labor, capital, technology and services. Decisions only could be taken unanimously. For these reasons, the EFTA could not meet the expectations of many of its members. In 1973, the United Kingdom, the strongest EFTA member, Denmark, and the Republic of Ireland left the EFTA and joined the EEC. In the same year, each of the six remaining EFTA members, including Austria, concluded bilateral trade treaties with the EEC. On July 22, 1972, a free-trade agreement between the EEC and each EFTA-state was signed. These treaties mainly concerned industrial free trade and governed trade relations between the EFTA nations and the EEC until 1994.

On January 1, 1994, a treaty of partnership between the EFTA and the EU created a European Economic Area, extending the "four freedoms" of the EC to EFTA partners (but not including the bulk of agricultural production and not creating a customs union), with Austria as a member on the EFTA side. But Austria had already applied for EC (later EU) membership[11] as early as July 17, 1989, when it had become clear that the Soviet Union would no longer block this move. The Treaty of Accession of Austria to the EU was signed on June 24, 1994, and went into effect on January 1, 1995.

The end of the Cold War had a far-reaching impact on Austria's political position in Europe. With the fundamental changes in the former Soviet Bloc between 1989 and 1991, Austria's neutrality lost much of its foreign policy function. This process led to a more restrictive interpretation of the duties arising from neutrality by Austrian scholars and politicians. Today Austrian participation in measures to ensure peace either within the framework of the UN or within other systems of collective security is considered fully compatible with permanent neutrality status.

On February 3, 1995, Austria joined the NATO Partnership for Peace. The coalition government of *SPÖ* and *ÖVP* remained divided on the question of full NATO membership. The Socialists to this day cling to a concept (ideology?) of neutrality, although Austria's eastern neighbors Hungary, the Czech Republic, and Poland in 1999 joined a newly-defined NATO, one which has assumed a more political than military role. Foreign Minister Wolfgang Schüssel (*ÖVP*) urged a decision on Austria's security options in early 1998, suggesting that the Austrian people would approve full cooperation in NATO as well as in the Western European Union (WEU), the still underdeveloped defense mechanism of the European Union, provided that neither foreign troops nor nuclear arms will be stationed in Austria. He failed to reach agreement with the *SPÖ*.

---

[11] Regarding terminology see note 1 in Chapter 4 (Austria and the European Union).

D. The 1999 Elections and Austria's New Center-Right Government

The parliamentary elections of October 3, 1999, reflected popular insecurity and fear triggered by profound economic and social transformation processes of European integration and globalization. The benevolent paternalism of the old coalition parties was no longer capable of fully satisfying its clients. The opposition parties *FPÖ* and Greens came across as more authentic and credible. The *SPÖ*, although remaining the strongest party, dropped to 33.2% of the vote and lost six of its previously 71 seats in the 183 member Parliament. The *FPÖ* came in second (gaining 11 seats), the *ÖVP*, holding its former strength, dropped to third place (only 415 votes behind the *FPÖ*), each capturing 26.9% of the vote and 52 seats. The Greens obtained 14 seats (gaining five), the Liberals were wiped out.

In subsequent attempts to form a viable government, the conservative *ÖVP* made a bona fide effort to enter into yet another coalition with the Social Democrats, provided that these would agree to a stronger move toward pension and welfare reform, restructuring of the health care system, privatization of public enterprises, etc. But the *SPÖ* was unable to make even modest reforms palatable to its labor union wing, and was unwilling to give up the Finance Ministry to the *ÖVP* or an independent expert. It had politically ostracized the *FPÖ* under the leadership of Jörg Haider, whereas at least parts of the *ÖVP* had kept lines of communication open. On February 4, 2000, the *ÖVP* ultimately decided to form a government with Haider's Freedom Party, against strong opposition from the Federal President and multiple threats and warnings at home and abroad. It assumed a high risk, yet in fact had little choice. The alternative would have been new elections most likely strengthening Haider at the expense of other parties.

Prior to the formation of this new government, on January 31, the Portuguese Presidency of the European Union sent a strong message to Austria: "The Governments of the XIV Member States will not promote or accept any bilateral official contacts at political level with an Austrian Government integrating the *FPÖ*. There will be no support in favor of Austrian candidates seeking positions in international organizations. Austrian Ambassadors in European capitals will only be received at a technical level." This step by the EU is unprecedented and has no formal legal basis. The EU governments have tried to explain their actions in terms of grave concern for the maintenance of European values. Yet the imposition of illegal sanctions without due process seems to violate the very values it claims to defend. It is also likely to be counterproductive, leading not only to a backlash in Austria that may further strengthen Haider, but also doing long-term damage to the credibility of the European Union in the eyes of smaller member states and accession candidates. These states will justifiably fear future examples of authoritarian EU interference in their domestic affairs, and will thus be reluctant to transfer more power or relinquish veto rights in the process of transforming the EU from an economic to a political union.

Eleven of the 15 EU member states are governed by Socialists who commiserated with the *SPÖ*'s loss of power and were willing to support it from outside. They, but also a number of European conservative parties, feared that rightist populism rampant in their own countries and cutting into their voter reservoirs would otherwise be encouraged and become generally acceptable. Most of the furor thus seemed domestically motivated (and internationally orchestrated by French diplomacy). Austrian and foreign anxiety about rightist populism is understandable. Yet apocalyptic visions of resurgent fascism are not. The EU is entitled to voice its concern, and to send a strong message that Austria's future actions will be carefully observed and that violations of human rights will not be tolerated. Prospective boycott and quarantine, however, are clearly unwarranted.

Austria has stable democratic institutions and processes. At the same time, it needs to develop a more sophisticated political culture, with more political education and rational dialog instead of destructive opposition. The present crisis may be helpful in several ways. It may lead to a normalization of the *FPÖ* when its governmental responsibility will lock it into democratic and human rights commitments. There may be a turning away of voters from a governing *FPÖ* once it becomes obvious that it cannot deliver on excessive promises made as an opposition party. Austria may in the future experience a more regular turnover in government, a departure from obsolete political illusions like neutrality and an overblown welfare state. The new government may prepare the ground for a more mature democratic society in Austria and more sensitive political processes in the future integration of Europe.

Literature

See also the literature cited in Chapter 3 (The Political System).

General

Baltl, H., Kocher, G., Österreichische Rechtsgeschichte (9th ed. 1997)
Brauneder W., Lachmayer, F., Österreichische Verfassungsgeschichte (7th ed. 1998)
Federal Press Service (ed.), Austria: Facts and Figures (2000)
Hoke, R., Österreichische und deutsche Rechtsgeschichte (2nd ed. 1996)
Sandgruber, R., Ökonomie und Politik: Österreichische Wirtschaftsgeschichte vom Mittelalter bis zur Gegenwart (1995)
Wolfram, H., (ed.), Österreichische Geschichte (12 vols. since 1994; see in particular the volumes by *Sandgruber, Rumpler* and *Hanisch* cited *infra*)
Zöllner, E., Geschichte Österreichs: Von den Anfängen bis zur Gegenwart (8th ed. 1990)

The Habsburg Monarchy

Kann, R. A., History of the Habsburg Empire 1526–1918 (1974)
Mason, J., The Dissolution of the Austro-Hungarian Empire, 1867–1918 (2nd ed. 1997)
Rumpler, H., Eine Chance für Mitteleuropa: Bürgerliche Emanzipation und Staatsverfall in der Habsburgermonarchie (1997)

Taylor, A. J. P., The Habsburg Monarchy 1809–1918 (repr. 1990)
Wandruszka, A., Urbanitsch, P. (eds.), Die Habsburgermonarchie 1848–1918 (vols. 1–6, 1973–1993)

The Republic

Albrich, T. et al. (eds.), Österreich in den Fünfzigern (1995)
Berchtold, K., 1918–1933: Fünfzehn Jahre Verfassungskampf (1998)
Bischof, G., Austrian Historical Memory and National Identity (1997)
Bischof, G., Pelinka, A. (eds.), Austria in the New Europe (1992)
Bischof, G. (ed.), The Kreisky Era in Austria (1994)
Bischof, G., Pelinka, A., Karlhofer, F. (eds.), The Vranitzky Era in Austria (1999)
Bottomore, T. B. (ed.), Austro-Marxism (1978)
Brauneder, W., Deutsch-Österreich: die Republik entsteht (2000)
Dachs, H. et al. (eds.), Die Politiker. Karrieren und Wirken bedeutender Repräsentanten der Zweiten Republik (1995)
Dachs, H. et al. (eds.), Geschichte der österreichischen Bundesländer seit 1945 (10 vols. since 1997)
Davy, U. (ed.), Nationalsozialismus und Recht: Rechtssetzung und Rechtswissenschaft in Österreich unter der Herrschaft des Nationalsozialismus (1990)
Federal Press Service (ed.), Austria Documentation: The First Republic 1918–1938 (1988)
Good, D. F., Wodak, R. (eds.), From World War to Waldheim: Culture and Politics in Austria and the United States (1999)
Gruber, H., Red Vienna. Experiment in Working Class Culture 1919–1934 (1991)
Hanisch, E., Der lange Schatten des Staates. Österreichische Gesellschaftsgeschichte im 20. Jahrhundert (1994)
Jelavich, B., Modern Austria: Empire and Republic 1800–1980 (1987)
Kennedy, D., Specht, L., Austria and the European Communities, Common Market Law Review 26 (1989) 615
Parkinson, F., Conquering the Past. Austrian Nazism Yesterday & Today (1989)
Segar, K. (ed.), Austria in the Thirties: Culture and Politics (1991)
Sieder, R. et al. (eds.), Österreich 1945–1995: Gesellschaft, Politik, Kultur (2nd ed. 1996)
Steininger, R., Gehler M. (eds.), Österreich im 20. Jahrhundert (2 vols., 1997)
Stourzh, G., The Origins of Austrian Neutrality, in *A. T. Leonhard (ed.)*, Neutrality. Changing Concepts and Practices (1988) 35
Stourzh, G., Um Einheit und Freiheit: Staatsvertrag, Neutralität und das Ende der Ost-West-Besetzung Österreichs 1945–1955 (4th ed. 1998)
Sully, M. A., A Contemporary History of Austria (1990)
Tálos, E. et al. (eds.), Austrofaschismus. Beiträge über Politik, Ökonomie und Kultur 1934–1938 (4th ed. 1988)
Tálos, E. et al. (eds.), NS-Herrschaft in Österreich 1938–1945 (1988)

Chapter 2

The Constitution, Sources, and Interpretation of Law

I. The Constitution

A. Constitutional Development

Modern Austrian constitutional history began in 1848, the year of European revolutions. Up to that point, the constitutional ideas of the French Revolution of 1789 and the American independence movement had been successfully suppressed by the absolute monarchies of continental Europe. After the resignation of Austrian State Chancellor Klemens Prince of Metternich, the chief architect of that autocratic system, in March 1848, a series of Austrian constitutions up to 1867 mark the path towards constitutional monarchy. Defeat in World War I (1914–1918) led to the dismemberment of the Austro-Hungarian Monarchy and the revolutionary formation of a new state called "German-Austria" (*Deutschösterreich*). The Emperor withdrew and a republic was proclaimed.

The peace treaty of St. Germain in 1919 fixed the boundaries of the new state, gave it a new name, *Österreich* (Austria), and prohibited it from merging with Germany. On October 1, 1920, a constitutional convention adopted a new Federal Constitution (*Bundesverfassungsgesetz, B-VG*), which was amended in 1925 to implement the separation of powers between the Federation and the *Länder*, and again in 1929 to strengthen the presidential element. This constitution remained in force until 1934, and was readopted in 1945.

Between 1934 and 1938, Austria was under authoritarian rule instituted by the Christian-Social Chancellor Engelbert Dollfuß, who had dissolved parliament and created a "Christian corporate state" under a Constitution adopted in April 1934 on the questionable legal basis of the 1917 War Emergency Act. From 1938 to 1945, Austria was part of the German *Reich* under Adolf Hitler.

In 1945, Austria was occupied by the victorious Allies (the U.S., the U.S.S.R., Great Britain and France). By a constitutional act of May 1, 1945, the Constitution of 1920 as amended in 1929 was re-established. But Austria did not regain its sovereignty until ten years later in the State Treaty of Vienna (1955). In 1995, Austria joined the European Union.

B. Constitutional Principles

The Austrian Constitution is not rigid, but rather flexible, i.e., easily amended. Any legislative rule may be raised to constitutional rank simply by designating it as a "constitutional provision" (*Verfassungsbestimmung*) and passing it by a two-thirds majority in the National Council (*Nationalrat*, the lower house of Parliament). Unlike in Germany, the rule need not be incorporated in the text of the Constitution. Thus, aside from more than 40 amendments inserted into the text of the constitutional document, there exist approximately 1,000 constitutional provisions "floating" outside the Constitution proper, many of them hidden in unexpected places, making Austrian constitutional law more complex than necessary.

The Austrian Constitution contains several principles that are usually referred to as "fundamental" or "structural principles" (*Baugesetze*) of the Federal Constitution. A substantial alteration of any one of them would be considered a "total revision" (*Gesamtänderung*), which could only be effected by a constitutional amendment passed in Parliament and subsequently approved by popular referendum (Const. art. 44 (3)). Most scholars agree on the following six fundamental principles: the democratic, the republican, the federal, the separation of powers, the liberal, and the rule of law principles.[1]

1. The Democratic Principle

According to article 1 of the Constitution, Austria is a democratic republic, whose law emanates from the people. On this provision rests a system of indirect parliamentary democracy, which is detailed in the Constitution and supported by the Political Parties Act of 1975. Article 1 of the latter (ranking as a constitutional provision) declares the existence and the plurality of political parties to be essential components of the Austrian political system. Currently, four political parties are represented in the Austrian Parliament.

Although Austrian democracy is basically indirect, i.e., implemented by elected representatives of the people, procedures of direct democracy, such as public consultation, popular initiative, and referendum have been developed more fully in recent years.[2]

2. The Republican Principle

The republican principle is included in article 1 of the Constitution together with the democratic principle. It has little positive content, but should be understood in its historical context, as the rejection of the previous political system, the monarchy. Any change in government in the direction of a constitutional monarchy would represent a "total revision" subject to popular refer-

---

[1] In Germany, constitutional amendments must be passed by two-thirds majorities in both the *Bundestag* and the *Bundesrat*. They must be included in the Basic Law as modifying or supplementing its text. Under article 79 (3) of the Basic Law, the most fundamental provisions, namely, the division of the Federation into *Länder* and their participation in the legislative process, or the principles laid down in articles 1 (protection of human dignity and human rights) and 20 (democratic and social federal state, separation of powers, rule of law) may not be amended.

[2] The German Basic Law is very restrictive on this point. See *infra* Chapter 3 (The Political System), note 2.

endum. To reinforce this principle, the Constitution (art. 60 (3)) prohibits members of the Habsburg family from running for the office of Federal President.

3. The Federal Principle

Article 2 (1) of the Constitution reads: "Austria is a federal state." The Federation (*Bund*) is composed of nine autonomous member states (*Länder*) – Burgenland, Carinthia, Lower Austria, Upper Austria, Salzburg, Styria, Tirol, Vorarlberg and Vienna. The *Länder* have limited legislative powers, some executive powers, but no separate court systems. They cooperate in the legislative activity of the Federation (*Bund*) by means of an institution akin to a second house of Parliament, the Federal Council (*Bundesrat*), and they participate in the administration of federal law through their own bureaucracies (*mittelbare Bundesverwaltung*).[3]

4. Separation of Powers

The separation of powers principle is not expressly named in the Constitution, but some of its aspects appear in formulations like "judicial and executive power shall be separated on all levels" (Const. art. 94) or "the legislative power of the Federation is exercised by the National Council jointly with the Federal Council" (Const. art. 24). But the Austrian Constitution also contains elements of concentration of power in parliament, to a large extent subordinating the executive branch to the legislative.[4] A system of checks and balances encompasses parliamentary control of the executive, the right of administrative authorities to pass regulations, and a special system of judicial review of administrative acts.[5]

5. The Liberal Principle

The liberal principle finds expression in a series of fundamental rights and freedoms developed under the influence of political liberalism and designed to protect the individual against unwarranted state influence.[6]

6. Rule of Law

The notion of a state under the rule of law finds formal expression in the legality principle of article 18 (1) of the Constitution[7] and in the competencies of the Constitutional Court[8] and the Administrative Court[9] to supervise the

---

[3] See the detailed discussion *infra* Chapter 3, V.

[4] Cf. article 18 (1): "The entire public administration may only be conducted on the basis of statutes."

[5] See the discussion of legislative bodies in Chapter 3, and Chapters 6 to 8 on the courts.

[6] Chapter 9 (Fundamental Rights).

[7] See *supra* note 4.

[8] *Infra* Chapter 8 (Constitutional Review).

[9] *Infra* Chapter 7 (Administrative Adjudication).

constitutionality and legality of all state action. It is also reflected in the existence of independent courts adjudicating civil and criminal matters.[10] From an originally more formal concept, the principle has been developed in a more substantive direction under the influence of fundamental rights and freedoms.

II. Sources of Austrian Law

A. Hierarchy of Norms

Austrian law is primarily statutory law. There is very little room for customary law. Judge-made law is not recognized as formal precedent. Nevertheless, the jurisprudence of the supreme courts provides important guidelines for law application. Legal science has a significant indirect influence on lawmaking and implementation.

Austrian legal theory distinguishes between general norms containing more or less abstract rules that are directed at groups (e.g., constitutional law, statutes, regulations), and individual norms containing specific (concrete) rulings addressed to individuals (e.g., judgments of courts, administrative rulings). The eminent constitutional law scholars Adolf Merkel (1890–1970) and Hans Kelsen (1881–1973) developed a "hierarchy of norms" (*Stufenbau der Rechtsordnung*), at the top of which is constitutional law (*Verfassungsrecht*) which determines the scope of "ordinary" legislation (*einfaches Gesetzesrecht*, statutory law). Statutes may be specified in more detail by administrative regulations (*Verordnungen*), and ultimately applied to individual cases by administrative rulings (*Verwaltungsbescheide*) or court judgments (*Gerichtsurteile*).

A legal norm may only be abrogated by norms of equal or higher rank in this hierarchy. But a lower norm which contradicts a higher norm will generally be applied until it is nullified by the Constitutional Court. As far as norms of the same level are concerned, a more recent norm overrides an existing enactment (*lex posterior derogat priori*), and a special provision abrogates the general (*lex specialis derogat generali*).

B. Constitutional Law

Austrian law distinguishes between constitutional law and ordinary statutes, and within constitutional law itself there exists a higher layer of "structural principles." The adoption of constitutional law requires a higher quorum in the National Council (one-half of the deputies present, two-thirds of them voting in favor)[11] and the express designation as "constitutional law" (*Verfassungsgesetz*) or "constitutional provision" (*Verfassungsbestimmung*). Essential changes affecting one of the structural principles (*supra* I.B) require approval by a subsequent popular referendum.

---

[10] *Infra* Chapter 6 (The Courts).
[11] On the limited powers of the Federal Council see *infra* Chapter 3, V.

Rules of substantively "constitutional" character (*materielles Verfassungsrecht*), such as the fundamental structure of state organization and the regulation of the lawmaking process, are generally – though not always – enacted as constitutional law in the formal sense (*formelles Verfassungsrecht*). But many other legal provisions have also been passed in the form of constitutional laws or constitutional provisions merely in order to provide them with greater protection against subsequent change.[12] The form of constitutional law is also chosen (or misused) in order to immunize a provision against nullification by the Constitutional Court. This has even happened after the Court had declared an ordinary statute unconstitutional. The Parliament simply re-enacted it with a two-thirds majority and labeled it "constitutional law," thus withdrawing it from judicial control of constitutionality. The most important sources of Austrian constitutional law are:

– the Federal Constitution (*B-VG*) of 1920 as (frequently) amended;
– pre-Constitutional legislation as adopted in constitutional rank by article 149 of the Constitution (e.g., the State Fundamental Law on the General Rights of Citizens of 1867);
– special constitutional laws (e.g., the Federal Constitutional Law of October 26, 1955, on Austria's Neutrality);
– international treaties with constitutional rank (e.g., the European Convention on Human Rights);
– constitutional provisions in ordinary legislation (e.g., art. 1 Political Parties Act 1975) or in international treaties (e.g., several articles of the State Treaty of 1955).

Austrian constitutional law is exclusively written law. The existence of customary law on the constitutional level has been generally denied, arguing that it would lead to legal uncertainty. The fragmentation of Austrian constitutional law has led to frequent demands for recodification, at least of particularly important areas such as fundamental rights (*Grundrechte*). Yet despite considerable preparatory work, no political consensus could be achieved concerning substantive aspects, mostly due to the different ideological orientations of the major political parties. Political energy seems to be lacking even for a merely technical reform.

C. European Union Law[13]

As a consequence of Austria's accession to the EU (effective January 1, 1995), all EU legislation, whether adopted before or after that date, is binding on Austria. EU law is supranational law, which according to a theory developed by the European Court of Justice (Costa v. ENEL, 1964) takes precedence over Austrian law, including Austrian constitutional law. But member states (including Austria) do not generally recognize this supremacy with

---

12 E.g., the basic structure of the educational system.
13 See *infra* Chapter 4 (Austria and the European Union).

regard to their fundamental constitutional principles. They claim that Community law violating the "core" of their constitutions would be null and void.[14]

To the extent that EU law overrides or determines Austrian law, the latter no longer provides a basis for the Austrian Constitutional Court to assess the constitutionality or legality of Austrian provisions. When European law applies, the European Court of Justice has a monopoly of interpretation in order to ensure its uniform application throughout the Community. But to the extent that the Austrian legislator still enjoys discretion (e.g., in implementing an EC directive), he is subject to dual control, including the right of the Constitutional Court to judge conformity with Austrian constitutional law that possibly restricts this discretion. This control applies to regulations and rulings of Austrian administrative authorities as well.

In the case of a conflict with EC law, all Austrian courts and administrative authorities must disregard a national law that conflicts with EC law and have to apply the latter. As the European Court of Justice held in Simmenthal II (1978), the supremacy of EC law is to be understood as precedence in application. Incompatible national law is neither annulled nor is it void, but may not be applied to the case in point. Austria's accession to the EU ended the previous monopoly of the Constitutional Court to examine statutes and regulations (which until that time had to be applied by all regular Austrian courts and administrative authorities).

D. Federal Law and *Land* Law

Austria is a federal state. Articles 10 to 15 of the Federal Constitution regulate the separation of legislative and executive powers between the Federation (*Bund*) and the member states (*Länder*). Four categories exist: 1) exclusive *Bund* legislation and execution; 2) *Bund* legislation and *Länder* execution; 3) fundamental legislation by the *Bund*, enabling legislation and execution by the Länder; and 4) exclusive *Länder* legislation and execution. Although the *Länder* enjoy residual powers in areas not expressly assigned to the Federation, the latter exercises the most important powers as enumerated in article 10 of the Constitution.[15]

Unlike the German Basic Law,[16] the Austrian Constitution contains no supremacy clause in favor of federal law. Federal and *Länder* statutes have the same rank. Thus, if one legislature enacts a statute that violates the constitutional distribution of powers, it remains valid until annulled by the Constitutional Court.

---

[14] Cf. *infra* Chapter 9, V.B.
[15] See *infra* Chapter 3, V.
[16] Article 31: "Federal law shall override *Land* law."

E. Statutory Law

1. General Observations

Austria is a *Gesetzesstaat* ("statutory state"). The Constitution establishes statutes passed by the democratically elected legislature as the primary source of law. The other branches of government (executive and judiciary) exercise the subordinate activities of *Vollziehung* (implementation of statutes). All executive-administrative action requires a statutory base, and administrative regulation is permissible only within narrowly defined statutory limits. This concentration of lawmaking in the legislature leads to its overburdening, and Parliament is under constant pressure to address urgent needs.

The bulk of Austrian legislation consists of *ad hoc* reactions to perceived problems. Yet the preparatory process in each instance may take years of struggle to achieve compromise, only to culminate in a hectic final phase producing a hasty and imperfect formulation. With the rising number of statutes, their quality has visibly declined. Legislators anxious to please clients in various interest groups bow to their last minute wishes, permitting them to fill in details that often have originated in contradictory ideas or models. There is waning respect for solid scholarly preparation, internal consistency, and careful legislative draftsmanship. Casuistic compromise not only obscures underlying principles by accident, but frequently keeps the law opaque on purpose, thus delegating the task of clarification to the courts. And quite often it remains uncertain whether gaps in legal regulation were intentional or due to legislative negligence.

2. Codification

In many important areas statutory law has been codified, i.e., the subject matter has been arranged systematically and comprehensively in a separate code. Examples of this civil law tradition (which reaches back into the 18th century, cf. the five "big" French codes) are the Civil Code (*Allgemeines Bürgerliches Gesetzbuch, ABGB* 1811), the Civil Procedure Code (*Zivilprozeßordnung, ZPO* 1895), the Commercial Code (the German *Handelsgesetzbuch, HGB* 1897, introduced in Austria in 1938), the Criminal Code (*Strafgesetzbuch, StGB* 1974) and the Criminal Procedure Code (*Strafprozeßordnung, StPO* 1975, originally 1873). Today, codification has little chance in ideologically disputed areas. Thus, for instance, there exists no labor law code. A major part of social legislation, however, has been codified in the General Social Insurance Act (*Allgemeines Sozialversicherungsgesetz, ASVG*). Over time, some codifications may lose to ancillary laws their function of clear and comprehensive regulation (as in the case of the *ABGB*) or they may become confusingly complex through frequent amendment (as in the case of the *ASVG*). Technical clarification occasionally occurs through re-publication (as with the *StPO*).

3. Publication

Statutes and other general norms become effective only upon appropriate publication. Unless the statute to be enacted specifies a different (earlier or later) date, it becomes effective on the day following its publication in the Federal Law Gazette (*Bundesgesetzblatt, BGBl*). In 1995, the *BGBl* contained no fewer than 8,548 pages. As of January 1, 1997, it is published in three parts: I. Statutes, II. Regulations and III. Treaties.[17] Special publication organs exist for *Länder* statutes. Rights acquired under previous legislation, as well as the effect of retroactive legislation, are subject to the equal protection clause of the Constitution as interpreted by the Constitutional Court. But there is no general constitutional barrier against retroactive legislation. Retroactive criminal law is excluded by article 7 of the European Human Rights Convention, unless the act has already been criminal under generally acknowledged principles of civilized nations.

4. Ignorance of the Law

Properly published statutory law is applied even if the persons affected have no knowledge of it. Ignorance of the law, however, does not automatically amount to fault. The legislature frequently makes detailed amendments to existing statutes without restating the revised text, making it increasingly difficult to know the most up-to-date versions. Courts determine whether in the specific circumstances knowledge of a legal provision could be reasonably expected. The standard applied in these cases is strict. Foreign drivers on Austrian roads, for instance, are under a duty to inform themselves about Austrian traffic laws. Occasionally the Constitutional Court has struck down statutory law as unconstitutional in cases where it was too difficult to locate or too difficult to understand.

F. International Treaties

The general rules of international law (i.e., customary law) are automatically incorporated into Austrian federal law under article 9 (1) of the Constitution. International treaties may be a source of domestic law under article 50. They are concluded by the Federal President acting on proposals by the Federal Government. If their character is political, or if they change or supplement statutory law, the approval of the National Council is required. The National Council may decide that the treaty is non-self-executing, i.e., needs to be implemented by additional legislation. The rank of treaty provisions in domestic law is determined by their content. If it is a matter of constitutional regulation, it is transformed into Austrian law on the level of constitutional law, subject to the requirements for constitutional amendment.

---

17 In 1999, part I contained 1,558, part II 3,505, and part III 1,301 pages.

G. Administrative Regulations

According to article 18 (2) of the Constitution, every administrative authority (*Verwaltungsbehörde*) may within its sphere of authority enact regulations (*Verordnungen*) that are based on statutory law. The rank of a regulation is lower than that of a statute. It may not contradict a statute, nor may it be enacted without a statutory base. It may only flesh out an existing statute with more detail, giving administrative authorities a limited opportunity to tailor abstract statutory provisions to specific needs or to regulate their implementation, without encroaching upon the rights of the legislature. Otherwise regulations may be annulled by the Constitutional Court. Like statutes, regulations do not become effective without publication, in either the Federal Law Gazette or in special publication organs of the authorities concerned.

In exceptional circumstances and within narrow limits, the Constitution authorizes the Federal President and *Land* Governors to issue emergency regulations (*Notverordnungen*), which have the force to alter existing statutory law.

H. Collective Agreements and Charters

Apart from statutes and regulations enacted by state organs, other general norms may be of considerable importance to a large number of people. The "normative parts" of collective agreements (*Kollektivverträge*) concluded by organizations of employers (primarily the Economic Chamber) and organizations of labor (primarily the Austrian Federation of Labor Unions)[18] concerning questions of labor law, such as labor conditions and minimum wages, have quasi-statutory force. They are binding beyond the contracting partners on all employees of a certain sector of the economy. But contractual exceptions in favor of individuals or groups of employees remain possible. The Federal Settlement Office (*Bundeseinigungsamt*) at the Federal Ministry of Economic Affairs and Labor may extend a specific agreement to similar employment relations not yet governed by a collective agreement. It thereby acquires the rank of a charter (*Satzung*) and quasi-statutory effect for the employment relations concerned.

I. Custom

Customary law arises from a general practice over time, which is founded on a conviction of legal obligation (*opinio iuris*). Although some public law scholars deny the existence of customary law altogether because the Constitution does not mention it as a source of law, this extreme position is not generally shared. There is agreement, however, that no customary law exists on the constitutional level. Customary law is expressly recognized in article 4

---

[18] On this "social partnership" see *infra* Chapter 3, II.D and Chapter 15 (Labor Law), IV.

of the Fourth Introductory Ordinance to the Commercial Code. Private law scholars unanimously confirm its existence as well as its rarity.

Court or administrative "custom" (*Gerichtsgebrauch, Verwaltungsbrauch*) consists of practices which are not founded in written law, yet are regularly observed. Deviation from constant practice without good reason to the detriment of a party may be considered "arbitrary" and thus a violation of the constitutional equal protection clause.[19]

J. Court Judgments and Administrative Rulings

1. Judgments

Continental legal systems generally recognize no theory of judicial precedent and *stare decisis*. Article 12 *ABGB* expressly limits judicial decisions to individual cases, permitting judges in theory to disregard previous practice. But in the interest of legal certainty, stability and predictability, as well as equal protection, it is agreed that a firm line of decisions should not be abandoned without good reason. Supreme Courts thus maintain uniformity and continuity in their decisionmaking, and their decisions are viewed as guidelines by lower courts and authorities. This jurisprudence or consistent court practice (*Gerichtsgebrauch*) may be seen as creating customary law which grants legitimacy to "judicial adaptation of the law" (*richterliche Rechtsfortbildung*). Since courts are bound by the statute, they may not overtly disregard it. It is, at least in theory, not the task of the courts to correct unsatisfactory statutory provisions. Yet imaginative scholars and judges, frustrated by legislative inactivity, frequently find ways of creative interpretation that amount to *de facto* judicial lawmaking.

Some decisions of the Austrian Supreme Court (*Oberster Gerichtshof, OGH*) are taken by an enlarged panel (*verstärkter Senat*) of 11 judges. These are called upon to consider deviations from constant jurisprudence or to clarify principles that have not been consistently applied by different panels of the Court. Their decisions are binding on regular five-member panels. Similar rules apply to the Administrative Court.

Two types of decisions of the Constitutional Court have formal legal force beyond the case at hand: 1) when the Court acts as "negative legislator" by annulling unconstitutional law, and 2) when the Court, at the request of the Federal Government or a *Land* Government, passes a decision concerning their respective legislative or executive powers. These decisions are published like statutes.

2. Rulings

In 1925, the laws governing administrative procedure were codified, and a uniform type of ruling (*Bescheid*) was created for all administrative ac-

---

[19] On the equal protection clause see *infra* Chapter 9, III.F.

tion *vis-à-vis* individuals. All "sovereign" administrative decisions (*hoheitliche Erledigungen*) must use this legal form of ruling because it provides the basis for a system of legal protection (remedies). A ruling must meet a number of formal requirements. It must, for instance, be in writing and it must be served on the parties. Rulings may create, clarify, or change legal relationships and specific duties. Like court judgments, administrative rulings may enter into legal force, and they may be challenged by regular procedures within the administrative hierarchy and may be brought before an Independent Administrative Panel.[20] After the exhaustion of these appeals, a complaint may be filed in the Administrative Court or in the Constitutional Court.

A ruling is usually preceded by a formal procedure. In exceptional cases, administrative authorities may act without prior procedure. They may impose "measures of immediate administrative instruction and compulsion" (*unmittelbare verwaltungsbehördliche Befehls- und Zwangsakte*), when an imminent danger or a threat to the public order does not permit a regular legal process to run its course. Such measures include, for example, the temporary seizure of a driver's license, the towing of a vehicle, the search of premises, or the arrest of a person. All of these actions are subject to a subsequent review of their legality by an Independent Administrative Panel.

K. Scholarly Doctrine

A primary function of legal science is to analyze and explain the law, viewing it in systematic context and understanding it as a cohesive whole. Scholars point out difficulties of interpretation as well as gaps in legal enactments, and suggest solutions to problems or warn of their consequences. Legal scholarship examines legislation and court decisions, criticizes deficiencies and contradictions, and through its systematic writings (textbooks, commentaries) as well as *ad hoc* analysis (law review articles, expert opinions) influences both the legislative and the judicial process. Generally speaking, scholarly dialogue functions better with the judiciary than with the legislature. Judges are more appreciative of the orientation provided by academics than are politicians, who are often too impatient or too arrogant to look for careful scholarly preparation of their legislative initiatives.

III. The Legal System

The Roman law distinction between public law and private law is still very influential in the civil law tradition, providing a fundamental structural element of the entire legal system. In Austrian law, this distinction affects above all the competence of different organs to implement legal rules, in particular whether a rule is to be applied by an administrative authority subject to instructions of superiors (*Verwaltungsbehörde*) or by an independent court (*Gericht*). In case of doubt, private law matters are adjudicated by the ordinary

---

[20] *Infra* Chapter 7 (Administrative Adjudication).

courts, public law matters by administrative authorities (and only as a last resort by specialized supreme courts, namely, the Administrative Court and the Constitutional Court). Although legislation occasionally assigns specific matters to specific bodies, it does not provide a general definition of the distinction. In its attempt to devise a plausible theory, legal scholarship emphasizes as the governing aspect for qualifying a legal relationship as "public" the participation in it of a subject equipped with sovereign power (*Hoheitsgewalt*) in the exercise of that power. For example, if the state expropriates land, it acts in that sovereign capacity; if it buys land like a private person, the contract is subject to private law.

Public law includes constitutional law, administrative law, criminal law and all procedural law. Private law consists of general private law (property, contract, tort, family, succession) and special private law areas that have been spun off over time, such as commercial law, corporate law, securities, intellectual property, competition, and parts of labor law. Whereas public law is characterized by subordination to decisions made by authorities who may interfere with individual rights due to their sovereign power, private law is subject to the principle of autonomy of equal partners contractually to shape their relations (within certain limits imposed by law).

IV. Interpretation of Law

A. Introduction

Even the most careful legislative drafting cannot entirely avoid contradictory, ambiguous, or simply unclear formulations. Moreover, the legislator may in his choice of language insufficiently provide for situations that require legal regulation. Guidelines for statutory interpretation and gapfilling are occasionally supplied by the legislator himself, but appropriate principles will at any rate be developed by legal scholars and by the judges who have to apply these legislative enactments. The Austrian Constitution does not prescribe a specific method of interpretation either for itself or for other sources of Austrian law. The principles of interpretation used by the courts have instead developed out of the interpretive rules incorporated in articles 6 and 7 of the Austrian Civil Code (*ABGB*) of 1811.[21] They reflect legal scholarship of the time. Although originally designed for the interpretation of private law, these principles now are applied throughout the entire legal system.

---

[21] Article 6: "No other interpretation may be given to a statute in its application than the one that is apparent from the plain meaning of the words in their context and from the clear intention of the legislator."

Article 7: "When a case cannot be decided on the basis of the words or the natural meaning of a statute, the judge must look to the solutions laid down by the statutes for comparable cases and to the reasons underlying other related statutes. Should the matter still remain doubtful, it must be decided by the judge by applying the principles of natural law to the conscientiously collected and carefully evaluated facts of the case."

In two specific areas, however, certain modifications have been deemed necessary. Like other nations, Austria prohibits the use of analogy to the detriment of the defendant in criminal law, thus assuring a high level of legal certainty and predictability in that area. A comparable need for certainty and stability has prompted the creation of a special interpretive methodology for the distribution of competencies between the Federation and the *Länder* (*Kompetenztatbestände*) of the Austrian Constitution. It is a "petrification theory" (*Versteinerungstheorie*) based on original meaning at the time the constitutional regulation became effective in 1925.

B. Methodological Schools

The general development of interpretive methods in Austria has taken place under the influence of two opposing methodological schools: "Conceptual jurisprudence" (*Begriffsjurisprudenz*) and sociological jurisprudence or "jurisprudence of interests" (*Interessenjurisprudenz*). The former limits interpretation to the logical deduction of legal consequences from general rules as applied to specific facts. The latter criticizes this approach as being too mechanical, rigid and formal. While logical deduction may be adequate as far as the "core" meaning of legal concepts is concerned, the hard questions arising in the "periphery" of meaning can only be answered by looking at the conflicting interests the rule tries to regulate.

The now prevailing younger version of this "jurisprudence of interests," the so-called "value-oriented jurisprudence" (*Wertungsjurisprudenz*), acknowledges the strengths and weaknesses of both these approaches. It does not focus on raw interests of human beings that are affected by a legal rule, but rather on the selection and evaluation of these interests by the legislator. Such valuations are derived both from a philosophical investigation of the idea of law in an abstract sense (*Rechtsidee*) and from a more sociological endeavor to discern the values of the specific legal community in question. A consensus concerning these values develops over time. Typically, conceptions of values are first introduced into an academic legal debate where they are tested and refined. Once they have proven their merits, they become permanent tools for the interpretation and application of the norm concerned in judicial practice. Thus, statutory law is enriched by generally accepted legal decisions and academic reasoning in an interpretive process that reflects value-oriented reasoning, rather than mechanical logical deduction.

C. Methods of Interpretation

A number of specific methods have been devised to facilitate the process of interpretation:

Literal (grammatical) interpretation examines the actual words and grammatical structure used in a legal text to discern its possible meaning. Depending on the nature of the rule to be interpreted, it will explore the ordinary or a more technical meaning used by the legislator. The latter will be governing in areas in which the law uses words referring to specific legal concepts or terms of trade. Literal interpretation will often suffice when the situation affected falls into the "core area" of the concept to be interpreted. Beyond this area, other methods will have to be employed, but literal interpretation will in any case provide the outer limits of any interpretive process by establishing what could possibly be meant (or no longer be meant) by the words at issue. Depending on the result reached within this range, one speaks of a "restrictive", "strict" or "extensive" interpretation.

Systematic-logical interpretation analyzes the meaning of a rule by looking at its context within the statute or even the entire legal system. An important variant of this method is interpretation in conformity with the Constitution. If a statute may be interpreted in different ways, those that conflict with the Constitution are not to be considered. The Constitution itself is subject to systematic interpretation in conformity with its "structural principles." Furthermore, EU law requires that national law be interpreted in conformity with European Union law.

Historical interpretation considers the original intent of the legislator when enacting the norm. It may be discovered in various legislative materials, for example, explanations accompanying legislative drafts and parliamentary debates. They are irrelevant if they are unclear, contradictory or obviously opposed to the text of the statute.

Objective-teleological interpretation explores the objective purpose of a rule in the light of goals to be achieved by the respective regulation. It poses the question what a contemporary legislator would have in mind were he to formulate a similar rule given similar factual circumstances. This method permits the judge to adjust obsolete rules (which no longer correspond to existing conditions) or valuations to current needs and perceptions.

Comparative analysis of similar statutes from other jurisdictions may serve an auxiliary function in identifying possible underlying values, which may have been overlooked in the application of traditional interpretive methods.

There is no clear ranking order among these methods of interpretation; they must not be applied mechanically, one after the other, but they are to be jointly considered and weighed in each individual case.[22] In the case of a conflict whether to interpret a statute in accordance with legislative intent at the time of enactment or in accordance with needs and perceptions at the time of application, Austrian courts clearly have given preference to the latter method over the former.

---

[22] A "flexible system" approach of weighing and balancing various factors was suggested by W. Wilburg, *Entwicklung eines beweglichen Systems im Bürgerlichen Recht* (1950), cf. The Development of a Flexible System in the Area of Private Law [trans. H. Hausmaninger, 2000]. It has become rather influential in and beyond Austrian legal scholarship.

D. Gapfilling

Gaps (*lacunae*) in the law are either intentional (the legislator wanted to refrain from legal regulation) or unintentional. In the case of unintentional incompleteness of the law (as judged by looking at the entire legal system) the gap has to be filled by the court: In order to be consistent (often in the light of the requirements of the constitutional equal protection clause), the legislator would have had to regulate the problem.

In Austria, gaps are in general filled by the use of analogy. This may take place on either of two levels: 1) statute-oriented analogy (*Gesetzesanalogie*) applies the legal consequence of an existing statutory regulation to a similar non-regulated situation that is subject to the same valuation; 2) system-oriented analogy (*Rechtsanalogie*) takes a more general approach: Several existing rules viewed together permit the establishment of a principle that may be applied to the non-regulated situation.

If a gap cannot be filled by way of analogy, article 7 *ABGB* (*supra* note 22) provides for the application of "principles of natural law" (*natürliche Rechtsgrundsätze*). This formula points to the most general values underlying the legal system. There has been a long and arduous scholarly debate on the content, structure and reach of these principles, and judicial reference to them is rare.

Occasionally, a statute will be over-inclusive, regulating more than what was intended by the legislator. In such cases, a teleological reduction may take place, and the statute will not be applied to cases which are covered by its wording but not by its intent.

E. Constitutional Interpretation

In principle, the general methods of interpretation also apply to constitutional law. But the abstract character of many constitutional provisions may create special problems. An older theory viewed the Constitution exclusively as a procedural framework for the political process or "rules of the game." Considering legislative supremacy and judicial restraint, constitutional law was viewed as being strictly formal, requiring literal interpretation and historical understanding or original intent. A "petrification theory" (*Versteinerungstheorie*), which still applies to the distribution of competencies between the Federation and the *Länder* today, claims that constitutional concepts must be understood in the sense they had at the time they became effective (1925). But in important areas of constitutional interpretation, in particular the application of human rights, this formal "reductionist" style was abandoned by legal scholarship in the 1960s and replaced with a theory of value-oriented substantive (i.e., teleological) interpretation, which was ultimately (since the 1980s) also adopted by the Constitutional Court in a number of important fields of its jurisprudence. Yet literal interpretation continues to persist in other areas, and the coexistence of several methods makes Constitutional Court decisions difficult to predict.

Literature

See also Appendix 6 (A Note on Legal Research).

The Constitution

Adamovich, L. K. et al., Österreichisches Staatsrecht (vol. 1, 1997; vol. 2, 1998)
Blaustein, A. P., Flanz, G. H., Constitutions of the Countries of the World I (Austria: release 1998-1, *trans. G. H. Flanz*)
Federal Press Service (ed.), Austria Documentation: Austrian Federal Constitutional Laws (selection, 1995)
Funk, B., Einführung in das österreichische Verfassungsrecht (9th ed. 1996)
Heller, K., Outline of Austrian Constitutional Law (1989)
Korinek, K., Holoubek, M. (eds.), Österreichisches Bundesverfassungsrecht (loose-leaf commentary, 6 vols. since 1999)
Mayer, H., Das österreichische Bundesverfassungsrecht. Kurzkommentar (2nd ed. 1997)
Novak, R., Wieser, B., Zur Neukodifikation des österreichischen Bundesverfassungsrechts (1994)
Öhlinger, T., Verfassungsrecht (4th ed. 1999)
Österreichische Parlamentarische Gesellschaft (ed.), 75 Jahre Bundesverfassung (1995)
Pernthaler, P., Allgemeine Staatslehre und Verfassungslehre (2nd ed. 1996)
Schäffer, H. (ed.), Österreichische Verfassungs- und Verwaltungsgesetze (loose-leaf edition, 2000)
Schäffer, H., Austria, in *Karpen, U. (ed.)*, Legislation in European Countries (1996) 53
Schäffer, H., Melichar, E., Sources of Law in the Republic of Austria, in *Kourilsky, C. et al. (eds.)*, The Sources of Law. A Comparative Empirical Study (1982) 17
The Austrian Federal Constitution (*trans. C. Kessler*, 2nd ed. 1983)
Walter, R., Mayer, H., Bundesverfassungsrecht (9th ed. 2000)
Walter, R., Zur Neukodifikation des österreichischen Bundesverfassungsrechts 1/2 (1994)
Wieshaider, W., Gewohnheitsrecht als Rechtsquelle des österreichischen Bundesverfassungsrechts, ÖJZ 1997, 481
Winkler, G., Verfassungsrecht und Verfassungsrechtsdenken, in Verfassungstag 1991 (1992)

Sources

Antoniolli, W., Koja, F., Allgemeines Verwaltungsrecht (3rd ed. 1996)
Griller, S., Verfassungsfragen der österreichischen EU-Mitgliedschaft, ZfRV 1995, 89
Holzinger, G., Zu den Auswirkungen der österreichischen EU-Mitgliedschaft auf das Rechtsschutzsystem der Bundesverfassung, FS Winkler (1997) 351
Koja, F., Einführung in das öffentliche Recht (1998)
Kucsko-Stadlmayer, G., Der Vorrang des EU-Rechts vor österreichischem Recht, ecolex 1995, 338
Mayer, H., Die Verordnung (1977)
Mayer-Maly, T., Rechtskenntnis und Gesetzesflut (1969)
Obwexer, W., Niedermühlbichler, H., Das EU-Recht in der österreichischen Rechtsordnung, ecolex 1995, 145
Öhlinger, T., Der Stufenbau der Rechtsordnung (1975)
Öhlinger, T., Der völkerrechtliche Vertrag im staatlichen Recht (1973)
Öhlinger, T., Methodik der Gesetzgebung: Legistische Richtlinien in Theorie und Praxis (1982)

Öhlinger, T., Unmittelbare Geltung und Vorrang des Gemeinschaftsrechts und die Auswirkungen auf das verfassungsrechtliche Rechtsschutzsystem, FS Rill (1995) 359

Öhlinger, T., Verfassungsfragen einer Mitgliedschaft zur Europäischen Union: ausgewählte Abhandlungen (1999)

Öhlinger, T., Potacs, M., Gemeinschaftsrecht und staatliches Recht: die Anwendung des Europarechts im innerstaatlichen Bereich (1998)

Pernthaler, P., Die neue Doppelverfassung Österreichs, FS Winkler (1997) 773

Raschauer, B., Allgemeines Verwaltungsrecht (1998)

Ress, G. (ed.), Entwicklungstendenzen im Verwaltungsverfahrensrecht und in der Verwaltungsgerichtsbarkeit – Rechtsvergleichende Analysen zum österreichischen und deutschen Recht (1990)

Schäffer, H. (ed.), Gesetzgebung und Rechtskultur (1987)

Thun-Hohenstein, C., Das Verhältnis zwischen österreichischem Recht und dem Recht der europäischen Union (1995)

Walter, R., Der Aufbau der Rechtsordnung (2nd ed. 1974)

Wiederin, E., Bundesrecht und Landesrecht (1995)

Winkler, G., Der Bescheid (1956)

Winkler, G., Schilcher, B. (eds.), Gesetzgebung: Kritische Überlegungen zur Gesetzgebungslehre und zur Gesetzgebungstechnik (1981)

System

Bydlinski, F., System und Prinzipien des Privatrechts (1996)

Rill, H. P., Zur Abgrenzung des öffentlichen und privaten Rechts, ÖZÖR XI (1961) 457

Interpretation

Bydlinski, F., Fundamentale Rechtsgrundsätze: Zur rechtsethischen Verfassung der Sozietät (1988)

Bydlinski, F., in Rummel, Kommentar zum allgemeinen bürgerlichen Gesetzbuch (2nd ed. 1990) ad §§ 1, 2, 6 and 7

Bydlinski, F., Juristische Methodenlehre und Rechtsbegriff (2nd ed. 1991)

Korinek, K., Zur Interpretation von Verfassungsrecht, FS Walter (1991) 363

Mayer-Maly, T., Die natürlichen Rechtsgrundsätze als Teil des geltenden österreichischen Rechts, GS Marcic (1983) 853

Potacs, M., Auslegung im öffentlichen Recht. Eine vergleichende Untersuchung der Auslegungspraxis des Europäischen Gerichtshofs und der österreichischen Gerichtshöfe des öffentlichen Rechts (1994)

Rüffler, F., Richtlinienkonforme Auslegung nationalen Rechts, ÖJZ 1997, 121

Schäffer, H., Jahnel, D., Constitutions: Interpretation and Interpreters, ZÖR 1996, 19

Schäffer, H., Kriterien juristischer Auslegung, FS Rill (1995) 595

Schäffer, H., Verfassungsinterpretation in Österreich: Eine kritische Bestandsaufnahme (1971)

Stelzer, M., Das Wesensgehaltsargument und der Grundsatz der Verhältnismäßigkeit (1991)

Wilburg, W., The Development of a Flexible System in the Area of Private Law (*trans.* H. Hausmaninger, 2000)

General and Comparative Works

Alexy, R., A Theory of Legal Argumentation (1989)

Canaris, C.-W., Larenz, K., Methodenlehre der Rechtswissenschaft (4th ed. 2000)

Kelsen, H., Pure Theory of Law, 2nd ed. 1960 (*trans. M. Knight,* 1967)
MacCormick, D. N., Summers, R. S., Interpreting Statutes – A Comparative Study (1991, including *Alexy, R., Dreier, R.,* Statutory Interpretation in the Federal Republic of Germany, *ibid.* 73)
Mayer-Maly, T., Rechtswissenschaft (5th ed. 1991)
Müller, F., Juristische Methodik (7th ed. 1997)
Tomandl, T., Rechtsstaat Österreich: Illusion oder Realität (1997)
Walter, R., Schwerpunkte der Reinen Rechtslehre (1992)
Winkler, G., Wertbetrachtung im Recht und ihre Grenzen (1969)
Zippelius, R., Einführung in die juristische Methodenlehre (7th ed. 1999)

Chapter 3
The Political System

I. Introduction[1]

The Austrian government is essentially based on the principle of indirect or representative democracy. In regular intervals, the people elect deputies to parliament, and in theory the parliament controls the government. The Austrian system of parliamentary democracy follows the British model of concentration of power in parliament rather than the American model of separation of legislative and executive powers. Whereas in Germany this concentration is counterbalanced by the rather extensive powers of the *Länder*, the Austrian federal government is highly centralized.

In the exercise of all state functions on all levels (with the sole exception of an independent judiciary), political parties play a vital role. Their leaders compete in parliamentary elections and as a result form a government that de facto dominates the parliament. Because over many years two major parties (*SPÖ* and *ÖVP* – see *infra* II.B) became so deeply entrenched in all aspects of public life, Austria has been called a party state (*Parteienstaat*). Parties and government in turn depend on major economic interests as institutionalized in powerful organizations (e.g., the Economic Chamber of Austria and the Austrian Labor Union Federation). These organizations form a "social partnership" (*Sozialpartnerschaft*)[2] which interacts as a sort of "side-government" (*Nebenregierung*) with a strong tenured bureaucracy and elected officials in all important legislative and executive matters. This corporate element has prompted scholars to label Austria a "chambers" or "associations state" (*Kammer- oder Verbändestaat*).

After decades of "grand coalitions," or at least socio-economic consensus of the two major parties (*SPÖ* and *ÖVP*), the resulting stagnation has led to mounting criticism, mostly expressed by new political groups, demanding broad and deep systemic change: privatization of nationalized industries, reduction of numbers and privileges of civil servants, reduction of politicians' salaries,[3] reduction of social benefits (in cases of unemployment, sickness, old

---

[1] The following chapter describes the legislative and executive institutions and processes of Austrian government (see the chart in Appendix 2). The judiciary will be treated in later parts of the book, see Chapter 6: The Courts; Chapter 7: Administrative Adjudication; Chapter 8: Constitutional Review. The description is based on the constitutional framework, but also takes political reality into account.

[2] See *infra* II.D.

[3] In May 1997, Parliament adopted a new "pyramid" of – in some instances drastically reduced – salaries for political functionaries (to be regularly adjusted to inflation), for instance:
– Federal President 280,000 ATS per month

age, etc.) which can no longer be financed, redefinition of federalism, protection of the environment, fulfillment of the economic convergence and stability criteria for the new European currency, and re-evaluation of Austria's neutrality and security needs (including accession to NATO). The governing elites will have to respond to a growing disaffection of the people with the traditional political mechanism. In recent elections this dissatisfaction has led to abstentions as well as a considerable protest vote, with the result that in 2000 the *SPÖ* had to leave the government for the first time since 1970. Under economic pressure to shrink an oversized bureaucracy and privatize nationalized industries, party patronage is now undergoing a painful downsizing process. The social partnership's and the government's leeway in economic and social policy-making is drastically curtailed by the EU. It is safe to assume that the Austrian political system has embarked on a process of profound transformation.

II. Democracy

A. Elements of Direct Democracy

Austria, like the U.S. and most European states, has fundamentally opted for a political system of indirect or "representative" democracy. The people decide periodically through elections how their government should operate. Political parties play a major role in the process of interest articulation and interest aggregation, and in the election of popular representatives. Yet there are also avenues of more direct input and immediate participation by the people in the political decision-making process. The Austrian Constitution specifies three instruments of direct democracy: referendum (*Volksabstimmung*), popular initiative (*Volksbegehren*), and public consultation (*Volksbefragung*).[4]

1. Referendum (*Volksabstimmung*)

Under article 43 of the Constitution, a referendum is a national plebiscite concerning the enactment of a specific statute. It is held after the adoption

---

- Federal Chancellor 250,000
- Federal Minister 200,000
- *Land* Governor 200,000 (maximum)
- Deputy to the National Council 100,000
- Deputy to the Federal Council 50,000.

[4] Based on fears concerning the influence of demagoguery on the popular will (the Nazi experience in the Weimar republic), the German Basic Law of 1949 restricted the exercise of direct democracy like referendum and initiative to questions of territorial change. In 1996, the proposed merger of the *Länder* Berlin and Brandenburg was defeated in a popular referendum under Basic Law article 29. But the constitutions of the various German *Länder* provide for all three instruments of direct democracy. Switzerland, on the other hand, has a long and unbroken history of direct popular participation on both the federal and cantonal levels.

of the statute by the Parliament. The positive result of a referendum is binding. If the majority of participating voters has approved the statute, it will be signed into law by the Federal President. The Austrian Constitution distinguishes mandatory and optional referendums.

a. Federal Level

A mandatory referendum is one that must be held if the Federal Constitution is to be affected by a "total revision." This is the case when one of its fundamental principles is to be altered.[5] Such a referendum has been held only once in Austria's history, namely, when constitutional changes necessitated by Austria's accession to the European Union were submitted to popular approval on June 12, 1994. The result was surprisingly clear, two in three Austrians voted in favor of membership.[6]

An optional referendum can be initiated by the legislature after a statute has passed the parliamentary process but has not yet been submitted to the Federal President for signature. One-third of the members of either the National or the Federal Council may bring a motion to this effect. The motion is carried by a simple majority in the *Nationalrat*. If a majority of voters rejects the respective statute, it may not be formally enacted.[7]

b. *Land* Level

Some *Länder* constitutions mandate a referendum concerning a specific statute if a significant number of voters (e.g., 7,500 in Tirol; 15,000 in Burgenland and 50,000 in Lower Austria) have petitioned for it.

An optional referendum may be initiated by a *Land* parliament concerning any statute that has been adopted but not yet promulgated.

Some *Länder* constitutions also provide for optional referendums to be held on the municipal level. Such plebiscites have become increasingly popular and have come to cover a broad range of issues, in particular regarding building permits for large housing or other construction projects (e.g., sewage treatment plants or power lines).

2. Popular Initiative (*Volksbegehren*)

The popular initiative is a formal request by the public to introduce a matter for legislative action in the Parliament.

---

[5] Cf. *supra* Chapter 2 (The Constitution, Sources, and Interpretation of Law), I.B.

[6] The present government plans to introduce a mandatory referendum for cases when a popular initiative (*Volksbegehren* – see *infra* 2.a) is signed by 15% of the electorate.

[7] This is disputed by several authors. Under a special act of parliament, a referendum was held in 1979 on the question of whether Austria should produce nuclear energy. A 51% majority of negative votes prevented completion of Austria's only nuclear power plant in Zwentendorf.

a. Federal Level

It requires a petition signed by at least one per mill of the inhabitants (approximately 8,000). Voters then may sign the initiative during a period of seven days. If at least 100,000 signatures have been collected, the *Nationalrat* must formally discuss the matter ahead of all other scheduled topics. But it will not be obligated to respond to the request in substance. Thus far, 24 popular initiatives have been conducted on the federal level since 1964.[8]

b. *Land* Level

The *Volksbegehren* is part of all *Länder* constitutions. Usually, a certain number of signatures obligates the *Landtag* (*Land* parliament) to discuss the matter (e.g., 50,000 in Lower Austria; five percent of the voters in Vienna). In Burgenland, Lower Austria, Styria, Tirol, and Vorarlberg, the initiative may also be taken by *Gemeinden* (municipalities) – if a certain number of them sign an initiative, the *Landtag* must formally debate the matter. In some *Länder* (e.g., Vorarlberg and Styria), a popular initiative supported by a significant number of voters not only obligates the *Land* parliament to discuss but also compels it to schedule a referendum concerning the requested statute.

3. Public Consultation (*Volksbefragung*)

The public consultation was devised for the limited purpose of aiding the legislature in exploring public sentiment. It is the weakest of the three instruments of direct democracy. It was incorporated into the Federal Constitution as article 49b in 1988. A special Public Consultation Statute (*Volksbefragungsgesetz* 1989) spells out the procedure. The *Volksbefragung* is a tool of the *Nationalrat* (National Council), which may decide by a majority vote to put a specific question concerning a "matter of fundamental importance" subject to federal legislation to the people. Citizens may then participate in a voting process similar to a national election or referendum. But contrary to a referendum, a consultation does not have a binding effect but only an advisory character. Parliament retains complete independence in its decisionmaking process.

a. Federal Level

A federal *Volksbefragung* may only be conducted concerning a legislative issue of nation-wide importance. Elections, or matters of executive or judicial decision-making, cannot become subject to a public consultation. To date, there have been no federal *Volksbefragungen*.

---

[8] The five most recent concerned women's equality, genetic engineering (April 1997), the introduction of a common European currency (EURO, November 1999), the use of nuclear power in Austria (November 1997) and more financial support for families (September 1999).

b. *Land* Level

Public consultation statutes in Austrian *Länder* occasionally differ from the federal model. In Styria and Tirol, public consultations concerning legislative matters may be initiated by the executive, and in the same *Länder* and in Vorarlberg, legislatures may initiate consultations concerning executive matters. In 1996, the *Land* government of Tirol asked the people to approve an initiative to host the 2006 Winter Olympics to Innsbruck. It was resoundingly defeated.[9]

B. Political Parties

1. The Party System

Article 1 of the Political Parties Act of 1975 has the rank of a constitutional provision. It defines the role of parties in the context of the political system by assigning them the following key function: "(1) The existence and plurality of political parties are essential components of the democratic system of the Republic of Austria. (2) The tasks of the political parties include their participation in the policy-making process."[10]

Political parties may be freely formed in Austria,[11] but the revival of National Socialism is prohibited.[12] For this reason, the right-wing National Democratic Party (*NDP*) was outlawed by the Constitutional Court in 1987.

Since 1960, a comprehensive system of party financing by the state has been developed. Initially, the state supported the parliamentary caucuses, then it funded the political education efforts of the parties as conducted in their respective academies. Since 1975, the party organizations themselves have received funds from the state. Since 1987, every party with five or more deputies in Parliament receives an annual minimum amount of three million ATS plus (depending on its voting strength in the most recent elections) a share in a total sum of more than 100 million ATS.

---

[9] In Styria, the only public consultation to date was held in 1990 concerning a number of environmental issues. Since only 17% of the electorate participated, its impact was limited.

[10] Cf. article 21 (1) of the German Basic Law: "The parties shall help form the political will of the people. They may be freely established. Their internal organization shall conform to democratic principles. They shall publicly account for the sources and use of their funds and for their assets."

[11] More than 700 of them are formally registered at this time, but only four are represented in parliament.

[12] This prohibition is not only contained in the Prohibition Act (*Verbotsgesetz*) and the Political Parties Act (*Parteiengesetz*), but also in the State Treaty (*Staatsvertrag*). Austria is thus under an international obligation in this respect. The German prohibition is broader, cf. article 21 (2) of the Basic Law: "Parties which by reason of their aims or the conduct of their adherents seek to impair or do away with the free democratic basic order or threaten the existence of the Federal Republic of Germany shall be unconstitutional. The Federal Constitutional Court shall rule on the question of unconstitutionality."

Many deputies are professional politicians, temporarily relieved of their duties as civil servants or employees of interest groups and party organizations. Some continue to work in these positions part-time. In the past, deputies often maintained their outside employment *pro forma* and drew double salaries. Parties determine who may run for electoral office and enforce party discipline throughout the discussion and voting process in parliament. As independent candidates are not able to muster sufficient financial support, there are none in parliament today.

At present, four parties are represented in the National Council: the Social Democrats (*Sozialdemokratische Partei Österreichs, SPÖ*), the Austrian People's Party (*Österreichische Volkspartei, ÖVP*), the Freedom Party (*Freiheitliche Partei Österreichs, FPÖ*) and the Green Alternative (*Grüne Alternative, GAL*, since 1986).

2. The Succession of Governments

1945 – 47	All-Parties Government (*ÖVP, SPÖ, KPÖ*[13])
1947 – 66	Grand Coalition (*ÖVP, SPÖ*; 87–97% parliamentary support)
1966 – 70	*ÖVP* Government (51%)
1970 – 71	*SPÖ* Minority Government (49%)
1971 – 83	*SPÖ* Government (51–52%)
1983 – 87	Small Coalition (*SPÖ, FPÖ*; 56%)
1987 – 2000	Grand Coalition (*SPÖ, ÖVP*; 63–86%)
2000 –	Small Coalition (*ÖVP, FPÖ*; 56%)

As of October 1999, the distribution of seats in Parliament, as compared with the previous elections in 1995, is as follows: *SPÖ* 65 (-6); Freedom Party 52 (+10); *ÖVP* 52 (=); Greens 14 (+5); Liberals 0 (-9).

Austria had a Socialist Federal Chancellor from 1970 to 2000. In recent times, ideological differences between the two traditional major parties have eroded. There is no longer the "camp mentality" (*Lagerdenken*) of the First Republic, where recruitment and voting patterns conformed to social classes (Christian-Socials: farmers, merchants, white-collar workers, civil servants; Social Democrats: blue-collar workers). Today both *SPÖ* and *ÖVP* attempt to project a broad popular appeal, espousing similar topics and goals. In February 2000, *ÖVP* and *FPÖ* formed a center-right government under an *ÖVP* Federal Chancellor.

---

[13] *Kommunistische Partei Österreichs* (Communist Party).

3. The Parties

a. The Social Democratic Party of Austria (*Sozialdemokratische Partei Österreichs, SPÖ*)

Founded in 1874 as *Sozialdemokratische Arbeiterpartei Österreichs*, the party served as a platform for integration of the most important leftist ideological currents. This task was accomplished by Victor Adler from 1888 to 1889. The party then quickly grew into a mass movement, winning general and equal suffrage for men in 1907,[14] and moving into Parliament as the strongest single caucus.

From 1918 to 1920, the party formed a coalition with conservative parties, then went into opposition, adopting a new party program in 1926, the *Linzer Programm*, which served as the ideological base of Austro-Marxism. This ideology aimed at constructing a socialist society within the bounds of law by means of winning a parliamentary majority. But it kept the option of establishing a dictatorship were the bourgeoisie to resist by illegal means.

When the Christian-Social Federal Chancellor Engelbert Dollfuß dismissed parliament in 1934, the Social Democratic Party was outlawed. It was refounded in 1945 as *Sozialistische Partei Österreichs*. In 1991, it was renamed *Sozialdemokratische Partei* in order to express a political "movement toward the center."

In the 1980s, the party had almost 600,000 members and thus commanded the largest membership by far among all Austrian parties, but in recent years it has been losing members to the tune of 25,000 per annum.[15] It also has been losing voters, dropping from two million in 1990 to 1.5 million in 1999. It has traditionally drawn its strength from blue-collar workers, as well as inhabitants of Vienna and other big cities. But some of the working class voters have defected to the *FPÖ*, which projects itself as a populist "movement of emancipation from an outmoded political system." Thus, the *FPÖ* commands a majority among Vienna street car drivers and policemen, a traditionally 100% Socialist voter reservoir. In the 1999 national elections, 47% of all workers voted for the *FPÖ*. On the other side of the spectrum, the *SPÖ* has clearly been losing leftist-liberal urban intellectuals to the small opposition groups Green Alternative and Liberal Forum. In the 1994 national elections, the *SPÖ* dropped from 42.8% to under 35% of the vote, capturing only 65 of the 183 seats in Parliament and failing to reach a two-thirds majority together with its coalition partner, the *ÖVP*. In 1995, new elections became necessary because the smaller coalition partner *ÖVP* demanded more drastic budgetary savings. The voters provided the *SPÖ* with an increase in seats (re-equipping the renewed coalition government with the two-thirds majority necessary to enact constitutional amendments), but municipal and European Union elections in 1996 produced severe losses. In Vienna city elections the *SPÖ* for the first time failed to reach its traditional absolute majority and had to

---

[14] Women obtained the right to vote in 1918.
[15] It dropped to under 400,000 members in 2000.

enter into a coalition with the *ÖVP*. In the elections to the European Parliament, the Socialists for the first time in nationwide elections since 1966 came in second behind the *ÖVP*. In the 1999 elections to the Austrian Parliament they regained the first place, but dropped to 33.2% of the popular vote. In 2000 the party found itself in the opposition role for the first time in 30 years. It has embarked on internal reform and ideological repositioning.

b. The Austrian People's Party (*Österreichische Volkspartei, ÖVP*)

When the *ÖVP* was founded in 1945, it took great pains to distance itself from its tainted pre-war forerunner, the Christian-Social Party. The *ÖVP* quickly emphasized allegiance to democracy and the Austrian nation, and it downplayed its former overt religious affiliation. It was able to broaden its appeal beyond its traditional voter reservoir of active Catholics, farmers, merchants, civil servants, and other white-collar workers. Yet a certain continuity in the party's personal and ideological makeup remained. One persistent problem has been the fragmentation of the party into *Bünde* (Federations) representing interests that are often difficult to reconcile: the Farmers' Federation, the Workers' and Employees' Federation, and the Employers' Federation. The spectrum of opinion in the *ÖVP* ranges far and wide on most economic, social, and ecological questions. One serious problem of the *ÖVP* is the frequent conflict between interests pursued by the federal party center and the strong *Länder* organizations.

During the first 25 years of the Second Republic, the *ÖVP* functioned as the senior partner in "grand coalitions" and as the first party to govern alone from 1966 to 1970. It was the major opposition party from 1970 to 1987, and from then on until 1999 governed as the junior partner in a coalition with the *SPÖ*. Voter identification in national elections has been slipping from 48.3% in 1966 to 26.9% in 1999. The party's declining voter strength is in part due to the dwindling number of farmers, small businessmen, and Catholics, in part due to the difficult position of the party as junior partner in a grand coalition. In the 1996 elections to the European Parliament, the *ÖVP* enjoyed a temporary success, but later developments showed declining voter sympathy. The party slipped to the third place (415 votes behind the *FPÖ*) in the 1999 elections to the Austrian Parliament. Having formed a center-right government with the *FPÖ* in February 2000,[16] it hopes to contain the *FPÖ*, profiting from the "chancellor bonus" and previous government experience. Voter approval may, however, be difficult to gain in the face of necessary, yet painful social and economic reforms.

c. The Freedom Party of Austria (*Freiheitliche Partei Österreichs, FPÖ*)

In 1955, the *FPÖ* was founded as successor to the *VdU (Verband der Unabhängigen)*, an "Association of Independents" established in 1949 as a

---

[16] See *supra* Chapter 1 (Political History), VII.D.

reservoir of disgruntled liberal and national voters, with a voter potential of 10%.[17] Initially isolated and often stigmatized as "nationalist,"[18] it began in the mid-sixties to emphasize liberal ideas in order to become politically more acceptable. Between 1983 and 1986, it entered into a government coalition with the *SPÖ*, but in this period its vote dropped to five percent. In 1985, a new leader, Jörg Haider, shaped the party into a nationalist movement on the right of the political spectrum. Thanks to his charisma and skill, Haider commands extremely loyal vassals at the party base who have permitted him to remove all political rivals and ideological opponents within the party. His electoral success has been spectacular, rising to 26.9% of the vote on the national level in 1999 and making heavy inroads into traditional voter reservoirs of both the *SPÖ* and the *ÖVP*. Today the *FPÖ* holds the first place in one *Land* (Carinthia) and the second place on the federal level as well as in two other *Länder* (Vienna and Vorarlberg). A major part of Haider's impact can be attributed to protest voters who appreciate his motto to "attack rather than compromise" and who support his scathing criticism of pork barrel projects, "social partnership," party domination of society, and politicization of the bureaucracy. In addition, Haider has been pursuing populist policies playing on popular fears, in particular with an anti-EU and anti-foreigner thrust. Haider's rhetoric induced unsuccessful domestic and international attempts to prevent the *FPÖ's* participation in the Federal Government. In February 2000, the *FPÖ* formed a coalition government with the *ÖVP*. Haider resigned his party chairmanship on May 1, yet continues a critical populist stance as Governor of Carinthia, while Vice-Chancellor Susanne Riess-Passer, his successor in the party leadership, will attempt to project a more moderate style and to position the *FPÖ* as a responsible partner in the Federal Government.

d. The Green Alternative (*Grüne Alternative, GAL*)

The Green Alternative was formed in 1986 from various smaller green parties that had arisen out of popular initiatives, civic groups, and protest movements (environmentalists, pacifists, anti-nuclear groups, etc.) dating back to the seventies. It commands a small core membership, but enjoys a large and fluctuating reservoir of supporters. It presents itself as a pro-democratic, social-minded, and minority-conscious protest party. The Greens have the largest proportion of female deputies of all parties. Their greatest success (and at the same time frustration) has been the fact that other parties have frequently appropriated issues and solutions developed by the Greens. The party has not yet overcome strong internal divisions on questions such as Austria's membership in the EU, as well as oscillations between pragmatism and fundamentalism. The Greens appeal to mostly young, educated city-dwellers. They won 7.4%

---

[17] According to its own statistics, 80% of the *VdU's* voters were former National Socialists who had not yet been integrated into other parties.

[18] "National" in Austria traditionally has the meaning "All-German national," emphasizing German culture and often aiming for political union.

of the vote in the 1999 general elections; opinion polls in July 2000 gave them up to 12%.

e. The Liberal Forum (*Liberales Forum, LIF*)

Five *FPÖ* deputies, led by Heide Schmid, resigned from Haider's Freedom Party in 1992 to form a separate parliamentary caucus (later party) emphasizing the liberal (economic and social), as opposed to the national, tradition. In its economic liberalism (free enterprise), the new party seeks to rival the *ÖVP*, while in its support of social liberalism (separation of church and state, equality for homosexuals, liberalization of drug control), it seeks to attract Green and *SPÖ* voters. The party approves membership in the EU and competes with the Greens in its appeal to urban intellectuals and young people. It captured 5.5% of the vote in the 1995 national elections, but was less successful in subsequent regional elections. In 1999, it received only 3.65% of the national vote and therefore dropped out of Parliament. A political comeback of the Liberal Forum is not likely.

f. The Communist Party of Austria (*Kommunistische Partei Österreichs, KPÖ*)

The Communist Party was a member of the first governing coalition approved by the Allied occupation forces (from 1945 to 1947). It then assumed the role of a radical opposition party, receiving 4.4% of the vote and three seats in Parliament. As a result of the Hungarian Revolution of 1956 it lost much support, and it has held no parliamentary seats since 1959. Today it is politically insignificant, receiving only 0.48% of the popular vote in 1999.

C. The Electoral System

Austrian citizens who are above the age of 18 and who are not excluded on account of a criminal conviction[19] enjoy a general,[20] equal,[21] immediate,[22] personal[23] and secret right to vote. Every Austrian above the age of 21 who has the right to vote may stand for election. Austria's electoral system is based on the principle of proportional representation of contending political parties in parliament. In other words, the number of votes cast for a party in principle determines the number of its seats in parliament. There are no single-member districts, and no principle of "winner takes all." But in May 1993, modifications were introduced that sought to achieve more contact between the voters and the deputies and more personality-oriented candidate selection.

---

[19] Anyone receiving a final sentence of more than one year of imprisonment for an intentional crime is disenfranchised until six months after completion of the sentence.

[20] All men obtained the right to vote in 1907, women in 1918.

[21] All votes must have equal weight.

[22] There is no electoral college.

[23] No voting through authorized agents.

This new system provides for a distribution of National Council seats on regional, *Land,* and federal levels, and prevents excessive fragmentbation by means of a four percent clause.

To this end, Austria was organized into one federal, nine *Land,* and 43 regional electoral districts.[24] Every voter may cast one vote for a particular party and two preferential votes for candidates belonging to the same party:[25] one for a candidate on the regional level, and one for a candidate on the *Land* level. A candidate may run on both a regional and a *Land* list.

The 183 seats of the National Council are first distributed according to population in the 43 regional districts. Seats won by a party in the regional district according to the principle of proportional representation will foremost be filled with candidates who have achieved a high number (approximately 25,000) of preferential votes. Seats not filled and votes remaining go to the *Land* district, where only parties (and candidates with preferential votes) winning a seat in a regional district (*Grundmandat*) or achieving at least four percent of the vote nation-wide may participate.[26] The same formula applies to the third step on the federal level.

This complex voting system[27] causes considerable delay in the publication of final results. The procedure is not well understood, and preferential voting is underutilized. It has not yet produced any effect on the outcome of elections.

D. Interest Groups and Social Partnership

Most Austrian interest groups are more or less closely linked to either the *SPÖ* or the *ÖVP*. On the one hand, all parties seek to maintain a variety of voluntary auxiliary organizations for the purpose of political penetration of society. This spectrum of subgroups includes youth, student, senior citizen, sport, and cultural organizations. Even powerful lobbies like automobile clubs are party-oriented. On the other hand, lobbies and interest groups can only achieve their goals in Austria's party-dominated political system (*Parteienstaat*) if they keep close contact with one or the other party, and function as pressure groups within their respective "camps."

---

[24] There are two districts each in Burgenland and Vorarlberg; three in Salzburg; four in Carinthia; five each in Tirol and Upper Austria; seven each in Vienna and Lower Austria; and eight in Styria.

[25] In the German electoral system, one-half of the members of the *Bundestag* are elected in single-member districts. The voters cast their first vote for a district candidate, and the candidate with the greatest number of votes wins the seat in parliament. The second vote goes to a *Land* party list and determines the number of seats that party will have in parliament under the principle of proportional representation. Voters may choose to give this vote to a party different from the one of their district candidate.

[26] The German threshold is 5% of the second votes cast nationwide or three seats gained in first-vote districts.

[27] Austrians abroad may also vote in embassies and consulates; even a vote in the presence of one (Austrian) witness will suffice.

Economic interest groups play a key role in the political process. Some of them are organized by federal statute as official representative organs of special interests. These Chambers (*Kammern*), for example, the regional and federal Economic Chambers (*Wirtschaftskammern*) and the Chambers of Labor (*Kammern für Arbeiter und Angestellte*), are public law corporations with mandatory membership and regulatory autonomy. Others are organized as associations (*Vereine*), e.g., the Austrian Labor Union Federation (*Österreichischer Gewerkschaftsbund, ÖGB*) or the Association of Austrian Industrialists (*Vereinigung Österreichischer Industrieller*). These institutional interest groups are closely linked to the major political parties and are powerful actors in the political process. The Austrian "party state" thus acquired characteristics of a "chambers" or "associations state." In a "social partnership" that was started after World War II and fully developed in the 1960s and 1970s, these chambers and associations functioned as a veritable side-government.

This social partnership (*Sozialpartnerschaft*) is one of the most remarkable, perhaps even unique features of the Austrian political system.[28] It was created as a mechanism of cooperation between the social groups that controlled capital and labor. Representatives of four employers' and employees' organizations (the Economic Chamber of Austria and the Presidents' Conference of the *Länder* Chambers of Agriculture on the employers' side; the Austrian Labor Union Federation and the Chambers of Labor on the employees' side), together with the Federal Government, determined economic and social policy. This partnership functioned for many years as a comprehensive network of contacts with a minimum of formal institutionalization. Its main organ, the *Paritätische Kommission* (Joint Commission), was founded in 1957 with subcommittees on prices and wages, and a board for economic and social questions. The Commission has no legal foundation, no office, and no staff. Its decisions are gentlemen's agreements reached unanimously. They are observed and implemented because of mutual confidence. Numerous working groups provide regular or *ad hoc* contact between the social partners and the government ministries, facilitating the preparation of decisions. The social partners also enjoy a legal right to examine and comment on all legislative drafts by the government. Many leading representatives of the social partnership are at the same time party functionaries and/or deputies in the parliament.

In recent times the influence of this corporate element of the Austrian political system has been weakened for several reasons – structural and budgetary problems, the loss of power and patronage by the two major parties, and a legitimacy crisis of interest groups that have relied on mandatory membership.[29] While Austria's accession to the European Union lowers the influence

---

[28] In the words of Vienna political scientist Peter Gerlich, "it cannot be explained to a foreigner, but need not be explained to a native."

[29] The Austrian Labor Union Federation suffered a drop in membership from 1,535,000 in 1996 to 1,465,000 in 2000.

of interest groups on the national level, it may lead to a new and important role for such groups on the European level.[30]

III. The Legislature

A. The National Council (*Nationalrat*)

1. Organization

In the structure of federal states, the legislature customarily consists of two chambers of parliament, one of which represents the constituent parts or member states of the Federation. The Austrian Constitution, however, rather than speaking of two chambers or houses of one parliament, refers to two distinct representative bodies (art. 24: "The legislative power of the Federation is exercised by the National Council jointly with the Federal Council").[31] Given the comparatively weak powers of the Federal Council (*infra* B), it would not seem incorrect for most purposes to refer to the National Council alone as "the Parliament."

The National Council functions as the central decision-making organ of Austria's parliamentary democracy. It is composed of 183 deputies elected for a four-year term by the people on the basis of equal, direct, secret, and personal franchise. As a result of the election of October 1999, four parties are represented in Parliament. Their respective strength is as follows:

- Social Democrats: 65 (1995, 71; 1994, 65; 1990, 80), 33.2% of the popular vote
- Freedom Party: 52 (42, 42, 33), 26.9%
- People's Party: 52 (52, 52, 60), 26.9%
- Green Alternative: 14 (9, 13, 10), 7.4%.

The National Council elects from among its members a President, currently Heinz Fischer of the *SPÖ,* as well as a Second President, Thomas Prinzhorn of the *FPÖ,* and a Third President, Werner Fasslabend of the *ÖVP.* Together with the party whips, the three presidents form a steering committee (*Präsidialkonferenz*) to organize the work of Parliament. Should the Federal President be disabled for more than 20 days, the three presidents of the National Council collectively perform the functions of the head of state.

2. Functions

The main activities of the National Council are: a) legislation, b) participation in administration, and c) control of administration.

---

[30] See ECOSOC *infra* Chapter 4, VI.A.

[31] The situation is similar in Germany – the *Bundestag* (Federal Diet) functions as the central representative organ of parliamentary democracy, the *Bundesrat* (Federal Council) represents *Länder* interests on the federal level.

a. Legislation

The National Council enacts between 100 and 140 statutes per annum. A bill may be introduced in either of the following ways:

— as an initiative by at least five members of the National Council;
— as a proposal by the Federal Government (government draft);
— as a proposal by the Federal Council;
— as a popular initiative signed by at least 100,000 voters.

In everyday political practice, only government drafts (*Regierungs-vorlagen*) and deputies' initiatives (*Initiativanträge*) are of any importance. The former account for 65–70% of all draft legislation and are usually prepared by the ministerial bureaucracies. Prior to their approval in the Council of Ministers, they are subjected to a process of examination and comment by other ministries and interest groups.

Government parties occasionally use the deputies' initiative to abbreviate the legislative process by excluding the examination procedure. Internal matters of parliament, such as rules of procedure and deputies' immunity, also are usually introduced as deputies' initiatives. In coalition governments, one partner may resort to a deputies' initiative if the other partner is reluctant to join an agreement, but parts of the opposition might cooperate in enacting a desirable law. The opposition frequently uses the deputies' initiative to introduce legislative drafts that highlight its own positions, contrasting them with the government program. Occasionally single deputies will become active when the government does not move.

In a so-called "first reading," bills are usually referred to the appropriate committee. The committee after its deliberations reports the draft law for a "second reading" (i.e., a debate in the plenum). A subsequent "third reading" will only correct more or less formal details. A statute may be adopted if at least one-third of the deputies are present and more than one-half of the votes validly cast are in favor of the bill.

Prior to 1986, when only three parties were represented in the National Council, more than 75% of all legislation was adopted unanimously. This percentage dropped to 41% when a fourth party, the Greens, entered Parliament that year.

Constitutional amendments require the presence of one-half of the deputies and the consent of two-thirds of the votes cast. They must be expressly designated as "constitutional laws" or "constitutional provisions." Amendments affecting a fundamental principle of the Constitution ("total revisions") must be submitted to a popular referendum.

Legislative drafts adopted by the National Council must be submitted to the Federal Council.[32]

---

[32] For the continuation of the legislative process see *infra* B.2.

b. Participation in Administration

In addition to various informal ways of exerting influence and pressure on the Federal Government, the National Council possesses the following formal participatory rights:

- the parliamentary resolution, which gives political, legally non-binding advice to the government;
- the right to adopt the budget; in addition, the Finance Minister must submit quarterly reports to the National Council;
- participation in concluding international treaties; if these are of a political nature or if they change or supplement legislation, they require the approval of the National Council (about 40 instances per year);
- participation of the Main Committee (*Hauptausschuß*) in the adoption of certain government regulations (e.g., the determination of postal rates);
- other consultative activities, including the discussion of fundamental political questions in the National Defense Council, the Foreign Policy Council, and the Council for Problems of European Integration; and
- nomination of three members and two substitute members of the Constitutional Court for appointment by the Federal President.

c. Control

Measures to control the executive are predominantly used by the opposition. They include the vote of no-confidence in the government, the question period, committees of investigation, examination of the reports of the Board of Audit and the People's Advocates' Office, and the debates on the budget and the annual fiscal report. Written questions submitted by individual deputies to members of the government are the most important device. There have been no fewer than 6,000 of these questions between 1986 and 1990. If five deputies so demand, a question must be answered in the same meeting of the National Council ("urgent question"). This instrument is increasingly used by the opposition to present its own views in question form, attempting to publicly embarrass the government through high media coverage. Whereas a total of 31 urgent questions were asked between 1986 and 1990, this number was already exceeded during the following two-year period.[33]

B. The Federal Council (*Bundesrat*)

1. Organization

The duty of the Federal Council is to represent *Länder* interests in the legislative process of the Federation. The number of its members is newly determined after every census. At present it comprises 64 members according to the following principles of representation: the most populous *Land* sends

---

[33] The most recent figures are 30 in 1995, 25 in 1996, 17 in 1997, 15 in 1998 and 12 in 1999.

twelve delegates, while every other *Land* has a proportionally lower number of delegates, but at least three. The political composition of the *Bundesrat* changes with every *Land* election. In July 2000, the *ÖVP* had 27, the *SPÖ* 22, and the *FPÖ* 15 seats. The members are not directly elected, instead they are deputized by the respective *Land* parliament (*Landtag*) according to a principle of proportional representation that grants at least one seat to the party ranking second in the *Landtag*.[34] *Land* governors have the right to participate in the deliberations of the Federal Council.

2. Functions

The most important function of the Federal Council is its participation in the legislative process of the Federation, where it is supposed to act in the interest of the nine member states. However, it is by no means an equal or active partner of the National Council.

As a rule, there are three courses of action available to the Federal Council after receiving a legislative draft which has been adopted by the National Council:[35]

— expressly decide not to object to it;
— do nothing and simply let the eight-week period allotted for its reaction pass; or
— raise a reasoned objection, which has the character of a not very strong suspensive veto.

The National Council may react to an objection raised by the Federal Council by reiterating its original position. This decision (*Beharrungsbeschluß*) requires merely a higher number of deputies to be present (i.e., at least one-half of the total number), but no higher level of approval than a simple majority. Between 1983 and 1986, the Federal Council made 47 objections, and the National Council countered with 44 reiterations. From 1986 to July 2000, there were only two objections and no reiteration. The explanation is as simple as political – in the earlier period, a conservative-dominated Federal Council opposed the socio-liberal coalition majority in the National Council. In the latter period, the conservatives had formed a coalition government with the Socialists.

If the Federal Council makes no objection or if its suspensive veto is overriden by the National Council, the Federal Chancellor submits the law to the Federal President. The President certifies with his signature that the law has been enacted according to the proper constitutional procedure. The statute will then be published by the Federal Chancellor in the Federal Law Gazette.

---

[34] The German Federal Council (Basic Law arts. 50–53) consists of 68 *Länder* delegates. Depending on its population, each of the 16 German *Länder* has between three and six delegates or votes. They are appointed, instructed, and recalled by the respective *Land* governments, i.e., political minorities in the *Länder* are not represented. Votes of a *Land* may only be cast as a bloc.

[35] See *supra* A.2.a.

Unless the statute itself specifies a different date, it will enter into force on the day after publication.

The Federal Council has no right to object to the dissolution of the National Council, the budget, the issuing of government bonds, or to the sale of government property.

The Federal Council has an absolute veto power in only two instances. First, constitutional provisions restricting the jurisdiction of the *Länder* require the assent of the Federal Council, with one-half of the members present and a two-thirds majority of the votes cast. Second, constitutional provisions affecting the Federal Council itself require the assent of a majority of deputies from at least four *Länder* in the *Bundesrat*.

Although the Federal Council has a number of participatory rights (including the right to nominate members to the Constitutional Court) and control functions, most of its rights are weak, because no sanctions (for example a vote of no-confidence) are available to the Council. The limited rights of the Federal Council have been debated for many years, with proposals ranging from enhancing the powers of the institution to abolishing it altogether. In recent years, the Federal Council was accorded the right of legislative initiative and the right to hold question periods, but these rights are rarely used. The shadow existence of the Federal Council in political practice may be explained by the fact that the *Länder* have found other – more effective – ways of safeguarding their interests and maintaining their influence, e.g., informally via the central party secretariats and in a more formal way through the Liaison Office of the *Länder* and the Governors' Conferences.[36]

C. Other Organs

1. The Federal Assembly (*Bundesversammlung*)

The Federal Assembly is composed of the members of the National Council and the Federal Council. It has very limited functions, namely, to

---

[36] Note that the German *Bundesrat* plays a more important role in the federal legislative process. Laws drafted by the Federal Government are first submitted to the *Bundesrat*, which states its position within six weeks, frequently proposing additions and alternatives from the viewpoint of *Länder* which will have to implement these federal statutes. The Federal Government then writes a counterproposal and submits all materials to the *Bundestag*. After enactment of the statute by the *Bundestag*, it returns to the *Bundesrat*. If the latter is dissatisfied, it may within three weeks call for a conference committee (*Vermittlungsausschuß*), which may make recommendations. If there is no agreement in this committee, the *Bundesrat* may issue a veto (*Einspruch*), forcing the *Bundestag* to reconsider the bill. Under article 77 of the Basic Law, the *Bundesrat* generally enjoys a suspensive veto, which may be overridden by the *Bundestag* with a simple or a two-thirds majority (depending on the majority with which the veto was passed in the *Bundesrat*). The *Bundesrat* has an absolute veto concerning matters of special importance to the *Länder* (e.g., state finances, state administrative agencies). *De facto*, 60% of federal statutes require the consent of the *Bundesrat*. Amendments to the constitution require a two-thirds majority in both houses.

witness the induction of the Federal President into his office, or to impeach the Federal President, or to adopt a declaration of war.[37]

2. The Board of Audit (*Rechnungshof*)

a. Organization

The Board of Audit is an auxiliary organ of the legislature for the purpose of financial control of the administration. Its forerunners include the *Hofrechenkammer* (Court Accounting Chamber) of Maria Theresia (1761) and the *Oberste Rechnungshof* (Supreme Board of Audit) of the Constitution of 1867, which was subordinate to the Emperor.[38]

The Board is a strictly monocratic institution under a President elected by the National Council. His current term of office is 12 years. He may not be reelected, but may be prematurely recalled. Between 1964 and 1992, two deputies from the opposition Freedom Party (Jörg Kandutsch 1964–80, Tassilo Broesigke 1980–92) functioned as Presidents. In 1992, the previous Vice-President, Franz Fiedler (*ÖVP*), was elected because the government coalition could not agree on an opposition candidate.

The President of the Board of Audit wields substantial power. He determines the organization of the Board and nominates its employees, or submits binding nominations to the Federal President. The employees are civil servants who are bound by the instructions of the President. He alone selects the administrative institutions or state enterprises targeted for review. He also may determine the content of the examination reports.

The Board may examine the activities of thousands of public employees.[39] Its staff, however, is surprisingly small (indeed much too small), and only 178 of 320 employees have higher education, mainly in law.

b. Functions

The Board of Audit is primarily an organ of the Federation and examines the entire federal administration (i.e., the ministries, other agencies, and public enterprises in which the Federation alone or jointly with other public entities holds a majority interest). Austria still has a considerable nationalized industry as well as government owned or controlled banks, postal and railroad services, radio and TV networks, hospitals, social insurance institutions, etc. Recipients of state subsidies are also subject to review by the Board of Audit. In addition, the Board examines the financial affairs of the

---

[37] The German *Bundesversammlung* (Federal Convention) consists of the members of the *Bundestag* and an equal number of members elected by the *Landtage* (*Land* parliaments) on the basis of proportional representation. Its only function is to elect the Federal President.

[38] The German Basic Law (art. 114 (2)) provides for a similar institution.

[39] A few years ago, they numbered more than 750,000. But due to massive (and ongoing) privatization, the 1997 figures were 247,000 (2000: 212,000) federal and 300,000 employees of the *Länder* and municipalities.

Länder, their institutions and economic enterprises, and all municipalities with more than 20,000 inhabitants.

c. Efficacy

The Board may make recommendations for improving efficiency, thrift, and expediency, but it cannot enforce them. Only the competent ministers may take appropriate organizational measures. But strong parliamentary interest by the opposition and public discussion in the media may put sufficient pressure on the administration to take criticism seriously and implement the Board's proposals. In recent years many details from draft reports have been leaked prior to publication. Often this was due to fears by Board employees that their findings would be weakened or suppressed by political intervention. Advance publication of preliminary findings, yet to be discussed with the examinee, is illegal, and occasionally undermines the authority of the Board in cases where the institution being examined subsequently succeeds in rebutting the criticism of the Board.

Reform proposals focus on increasing the number of qualified personnel on the Board, and establishing independent examination panels to strengthen the Board's autonomy.

3. The People's Advocates' Office (*Volksanwaltschaft*)

a. Organization

This institution was created in 1977 in keeping with the idea of the Scandinavian "ombudsman," in order to reduce the feeling of impotence on the part of the individual citizen when facing the state bureaucracy.[40] This is a federal office designed to aid the legislature in controlling the administration. It consists of three members from the three strongest parties in Parliament, at present Christa Krammer (*SPÖ*), Ingrid Korosec (*ÖVP*) and Horst Schender (*FPÖ*). They serve for six years and rotate as chairperson each year. They may be reelected once, and are independent and irremovable. Decisions are made collectively, unless the Advocates agree to distribute matters for individual decision-making. Each Advocate has a staff of six or seven assistants.

b. Functions

The *Volksanwaltschaft* examines complaints filed by citizens or legal entities alleging maladministration by the Federation in cases where there is no legal recourse available or where all legal remedies have been exhausted. *Länder* may transfer the authority to examine their *Land* administration to the federal *Volksanwaltschaft*, and most have done so. But they also may establish their own Offices, as Tirol and Vorarlberg have done. The *Volksanwaltschaft* also may become active *ex officio*. It must be assisted by all federal, *Land* and

---

[40] There is no equivalent in the German Basic Law.

municipal agencies, which must provide information and allow inspection of their records. If it determines that a complaint is justified, the Office issues a recommendation to the competent administrative agency, which must act upon the recommendation within eight weeks or explain its refusal to act. The complainant is informed of the investigation's outcome and the action taken.

The People's Advocates' Office submits an annual report to the National Council. There is an average of 4,000 complaints per year, mostly in areas concerning social security, police and taxes.

IV. The Executive

A. The Federal President (*Bundespräsident*)

The Austrian system of government, like the French, represents a combination of the English parliamentary model (characterized by concentration rather than separation of powers) and the American model of presidential democracy. The Austrian system is more heavily influenced by the parliamentary model, while the French leans more strongly towards the presidential.

1. Structure of the Presidency

The Austrian President (*Bundespräsident*) is the head of state but not the chief executive. The latter function is exercised by the Federal Chancellor (*Bundeskanzler*), who leads the executive branch of government. The Federal President is directly elected by the people, and his minimum age is 35 (the youngest incumbent having been 60). His period of office is six years, and he may be reelected for one consecutive period. To be elected, a candidate needs more than one-half of the valid votes. If necessary, a run-off between the two leading candidates is held within 35 days of the first round.

There are two procedures by which the period of office of the President can be prematurely terminated, but neither method has been employed yet:

a. Impeachment for culpable (including negligent) violation of the Constitution. The charge is brought by the Federal Assembly (i.e., the members of the National Council and the Federal Council in a joint session). The decision is taken by the Constitutional Court, the sanction is loss of office.[41]

b. Recall by popular referendum. The National Council may request the Federal Assembly to call for a referendum to oust the Federal President. If this referendum fails to achieve a majority in favor of removal, the President is considered to be reelected for another term and the National Council is dissolved.

---

[41] The German Basic Law provides for impeachment by the *Bundestag* or the *Bundesrat* (with a majority of two-thirds of the members) and trial in the Constitutional Court for wilful violation of the Constitution or federal law (art. 61).

The President enjoys immunity from criminal prosecution unless extradited by the Federal Assembly. In this case, conviction by a criminal court for an intentional crime results in the loss of office. The Austrian President's immunity has never been lifted. To ensure the President's independence, there are strict rules of incompatibility – he may not conduct any other professional activity, or belong to any political representative body, or exercise any function in a political party.

In case of absence or temporary disability of the President, his functions can be exercised for a maximum of 20 days by the Federal Chancellor. After this period, the three presidents of the National Council jointly exercise the functions of the presidency. In case of permanent incapacitation of the Federal President as a result of illness, death, resignation, conviction, or recall, the three presidents of the National Council jointly exercise presidential functions,[42] and the Federal Government orders new elections to be held immediately.

2. Powers

In general, every act of the President must be based on a proposal by the Federal Government or a Federal Minister authorized by the Federal Government. The President may not deviate from these proposals, yet he is under no obligation to act. There are several important instances in which the President may act without proposal:

– Appointment and dismissal of the Federal Chancellor.
– Dismissal of the entire Federal Government.
– Certification that federal statutes have been adopted according to the rules of the Constitution. Constitutional theory is split on the question of whether this is a purely notarial function or one that includes the right, or even the duty, to examine the substance of a statute as to its constitutionality.[43]
– Supreme command of the armed forces.[44]

The following functions are exercised by the Federal President upon the proposal of the Federal Government or other organs:

– He represents the Republic under international law. This includes, in particular, the accreditation of foreign diplomatic and consular representatives, the appointment of Austrian representatives abroad, and the conclusion of international treaties.

---

[42] In Germany they are exercised by the President of the *Bundesrat*.

[43] Under German doctrine, the President has the right and the duty to refuse signature and publication if he has serious doubts concerning procedural or substantive constitutionality of the act.

[44] The situation is complex. In some cases the President may give orders to the Minister of Defense without being bound by proposals, but in most cases the Federal Government makes binding proposals.

– He dissolves the *Nationalrat*, but he may do this only once for the same reason; the Federal Government is obligated to secure the convocation of the newly elected National Council within 100 days.
– He appoints and dismisses the Vice-Chancellor or individual Federal Ministers at the request of the Federal Chancellor.
– He appoints high-level civil servants, including judges, army officers, and university professors.
– He awards titles, honors, medals, etc.
– He grants pardons.
– He orders the execution of judgments of the Constitutional Court upon the Court's request.
– He calls sessions of the National Council.
– He orders referendums.
– He has the right to issue emergency regulations (*Notverordnungen*). "In order to avert an obvious and irreparable danger to the public" (Const. art. 18 (3)), the President may issue temporary law-amending regulations, if the National Council cannot be convened in time. In order to act, the President requires a proposal of the Federal Government based on the assent of a permanent subcommittee of the National Council. An emergency regulation may not violate constitutional law and may not result in a permanent financial burden on the Federation, the *Länder*, municipalities, or individual citizens. It must not lead to the sale of state property, nor may it interfere with rent protection or labor and social law. The regulation must be submitted to the National Council, which is to be convened as soon as possible.

The Federal President commands a relatively small staff and a very limited budget. Whereas 692 employees work in the Federal Chancellor's Office, among them 126 university graduates, the presidential staff comprises only 65 individuals, including 15 university graduates.

3. Political Role

Until November 1918, the Austrian head of state was the Emperor. According to article 1 of a State Fundamental Law of 1867, he was considered "hallowed, inviolable, and unaccountable." In the discussion concerning the first republican constitution, the Socialists opposed the idea of a strong president elected by the people. They wanted the chairman of parliament to exercise the function of head of state. As a compromise, the Constitution of 1920 provided for a strong parliament and a weak president. The latter was not elected by the people, but by parliament, and all presidential acts required a proposal by the Federal Government. In the constitutional amendments of 1929, the governing Christian-Socials imposed a stronger presidency on the opposition Socialists. In its present form, the office contains contradictory elements that permit different interpretations and implementation.

Regarding his legal powers and his political potential, the Austrian Federal President stands between his weaker German colleague[45] and the stronger French presidency. His democratic legitimacy, based on direct popular election, and some of his constitutional rights (e.g., the appointment and dismissal of the Federal Chancellor and the dissolution of parliament) confer considerable political power on him. He is functionally linked with the three traditional state powers in a system of checks and balances, and he may interact with them as a fourth power or mediator.

Austrian Presidents have traditionally shown considerable political restraint by not only avoiding open conflict with the government but by leaving virtually all initiative to the latter, supporting its program in public and foregoing any exercise of the constitutional power of their own office. They have seen their primary mission in protecting social peace and in seeking political compromise and cooperation. One explanation for the limited exercise of presidential powers may be found in the traditional political system in which the leaders of the two dominant political parties developed a domination of the government over the parliament and formed a "chancellor democracy." Parliamentary elections are styled as "chancellor plebiscites," the respective party leader governs with a stable parliamentary majority, and for the office of President the parties invariably have chosen (and the people have elected) a respectable "elder statesman" figure without political ambitions of his own.

There are unquestionable advantages in a policy of restraint on the part of the Federal President. For example, the President is viewed by the public as a symbol of unity, stability, and continuity. In the past, the Austrian President was widely considered to be an impartial, independent moral authority standing above partial communities and interests. He was able to personalize and project important aspects of political culture, and served as a model of integrity and style.

Critics of such a static, symbolic exercise of the presidency wanted to see more than a "substitute emperor" devoting most of his time to ceremonial appearances. They called for a defender of the Constitution and legality, who would not confine himself to the function of a "state notary." Indeed, no President has ever refused his signature under an act of parliament. These critics also demanded that the President go beyond delivering Sunday sermons as a "state preacher" and that he act as more than just an "authority in reserve" to handle potential state crises. The President, they argued, should develop an active, not merely reactive, relationship with the government, and should re-

---

[45] The Basic Law of 1949 reduced the strong position of the President under the Weimar Constitution (popular election, seven-year term of office, commander-in-chief of the armed forces, right to appoint the Chancellor and to issue emergency decrees), because in the exercise of his broad powers, President Paul Hindenburg had aided the establishment of the Nazi dictatorship. Today, the German *Bundespräsident* is elected for five years by the *Bundesversammlung* (see *supra* note 37), is no longer commander-in-chief, merely nominates the *Bundeskanzler* (Federal Chancellor) for election in the *Bundestag*, and has only very limited emergency powers.

gard his constitutional powers as a mandate to participate in a dynamic process of molding Austrian political reality.

In response to this criticism, the uninterrupted succession of Socialist presidents since 1945 was upset in 1986 by the election of Kurt Waldheim, a former Austrian diplomat, Minister of Foreign Affairs, Secretary General of the UN, and the candidate of the conservative opposition. Ironically, the first presidential candidate to campaign for a more active role became virtually immobilized due to the debate concerning his role in World War II and *de facto* lost most foreign policy functions of the head of state to the Federal Chancellor.

In the spring of 1992, Thomas Klestil, a little known but highly ambitious career diplomat, was elected Federal President on the conservative ticket. He had managed to project himself as an independent who would form an active counterpart to the coalition government, especially to the Socialist Federal Chancellor. His slogan, "Power needs to be controlled," was hugely successful. One year after his election, Klestil had extraordinary public approval rates of more than 85% and had become the favorite politician of the republic. He was reelected to a second six-year term in 1998 with a majority of 63.4%.

In his first year in office, Klestil was unusually active in the realm of foreign affairs, conducting a large number of official visits and speeches abroad as well as in Vienna, mainly to promote Austria's membership in the EU. There also was hardly any question of domestic policy about which he did not offer his views. In the exercise of his constitutional powers, he delayed authorizing the appointment of several high-ranking civil servants and judges, because he was more certain of their political than of their professional qualifications. He ultimately accepted these nominations, but not without asking parliament and the government to develop more objective selection criteria in the future. On occasion, Klestil also delayed signing federal statutes of questionable substantive constitutionality, thus sending a signal to the political and legal communities.

The President's political ambitions were massively opposed by the Federal Chancellor and his Social Democratic Party, who insisted that the political responsibility of the government was exclusively to the parliament. But there even have been high-ranking politicians of the People's Party who considered a constitutional amendment to restrict the powers of the President.[46]

Some observers maintain that in the present four-party system, with no party controlling an absolute majority, the role of the Federal President in forming the government and thus his political power and responsibility has become too strong, leading to serious confrontations between the President and the Chancellor in their leadership ambitions. There have not only been

---

[46] One such amendment was passed in 1994, surprisingly without any public or scholarly debate, pursuant to which the President lost his right to choose members of the Constitutional Court from lists of three submitted by the National Council or Federal Council.

suggestions to limit the President's powers, but even to abolish the presidency altogether in order to return to the pure parliamentary democracy of 1920.

After the parliamentary elections of October 3, 1999, President Klestil clearly favored a continuation of the previous *SPÖ/ÖVP* coalition, reminding the *ÖVP* of its "historic political responsibility." After the *SPÖ* had broken off negotiations with the *ÖVP*, he asked Acting Federal Chancellor Klima (*SPÖ*) to form a minority government. When these attempts had failed, he reluctantly appointed a coalition government of *ÖVP* and *FPÖ*, headed by Federal Chancellor Schüssel (*ÖVP*). Before taking this step he forced the two party leaders Schüssel and Haider to sign a declaration containing commitments to democracy and European integration as well as a condemnation of the Holocaust. President Klestil also refused to appoint two *FPÖ* candidates for cabinet positions. Yet he was ultimately unable to prevent the formation of a government which had a majority in parliament, unless he would risk further growth of the *FPÖ* in new elections.

B. The Federal Government and Administration

Except for matters reserved to the Federal President (*Bundespräsident, supra* IV.A), the guidance of federal administration is entrusted to the Federal Chancellor (*Bundeskanzler*), the Vice-Chancellor (*Vizekanzler*) and other Federal Ministers (*Bundesminister*). Together they form the Federal Government (*Bundesregierung*), chaired by the Federal Chancellor. The latter is appointed by the Federal President, whose power in this respect is not subject to any legal restraints but is limited politically by the fact that the Federal Government must enjoy the confidence of the National Council (*Nationalrat*). Traditionally, the Federal President asks the leader of the strongest parliamentary party to form the government. The other members of this government are appointed by the President as proposed by the Chancellor.

The Constitution does not list the ministries or determine the number of ministers. Aside from the Chancellor and Vice-Chancellor, only the Minister of Finance is expressly mentioned. Since 1973, the ministries and their powers have been listed in a – frequently amended – special Federal Ministries Act (*Bundesministeriengesetz*). The legislature may assign the execution of legislative acts either to the collective organ Federal Government, to a specific Federal Minister acting as monocratic organ, or to several ministers acting in conjunction with one another. Most executive matters are dealt with by individual ministers.

1. The Federal Government (*Bundesregierung*)

In the present coalition government, the Austrian People's Party (*ÖVP*) is represented by Federal Chancellor Wolfgang Schüssel and five ministers.[47] The Freedom Party (*FPÖ*) is represented by Vice-Chancellor and Minister for Public Service and Sports Susanne Riess-Passer and five ministers.[48]

Matters reserved to the Federal Government as a whole include:

- submission of legislative drafts and reports to the National Council;
- proposals to the Federal President;
- objections to legislative enactments of the *Länder*;
- petitions to the Constitutional Court;
- activities concerning elections, calling parliament into session, and adoption of emergency regulations.

In political practice, the Federal Government makes only unanimous decisions. According to constitutional doctrine, unanimity is legally required, and a Minister who feels he cannot agree must resign. In the exercise of its powers, the Federal Government is not bound by the instructions of any other state institution. However, it must observe the law and is politically accountable to the Federal President, who may dismiss the Federal Chancellor or the entire Federal Government at any time, and to the National Council, which may at any time and without any special reason pass a vote of no-confidence and thereby force the Federal Chancellor to dismiss an individual Federal Minister, or compel the Federal President to dismiss the entire Federal Government.[49]

In the case of the dismissal or resignation of the Federal Government, the Federal President appoints an acting government consisting of members of the previous government or high-ranking civil servants.

2. Federal Ministers (*Bundesminister*)

Within their areas of authority, Federal Ministers act as supreme executive organs. They are not bound by any instructions, including those of the Federal Chancellor. But the Federal President must dismiss any Federal Minister on the proposal of the Federal Chancellor. On a proposal by the National Council, Federal Ministers may be impeached in the Constitutional Court for

---

[47] Benita Ferrero-Waldner (Foreign Affairs), Martin Bartenstein (Economic Affairs and Labor), Ernst Strasser (Interior), Elisabeth Gehrer (Education, Science, and Culture), and Wilhelm Molterer (Agriculture and Forestry, Environment and Water Management).

[48] Karl-Heinz Grasser (Finances), Michael Schmid (Traffic, Innovation, and Technology), Elisabeth Sickl (Social Security and Generations), Herbert Scheibner (Defense). Dieter Böhmdorfer (Justice) is not a party member but for many years served as legal advisor to the *FPÖ*.

[49] Under article 67 of the Basic Law, the German Federal Chancellor may be removed only by a "constructive" vote of no-confidence, i.e., if the *Bundestag* simultaneously elects a successor (whom the Federal President must appoint). The position of the German Federal Chancellor was strengthened in the Basic Law of 1949 while that of the Federal President was weakened, both in reaction to the Weimar Constitution that had facilitated the establishment of Hitler's Nazi dictatorship in 1933.

culpable violation of the law. If found guilty, they must be dismissed by the Federal President. Federal Ministers may be (but do not have to be) deputies. As deputies they enjoy immunity from criminal prosecution. Members of the Federal Government must present themselves to the National Council and have the right to attend and be heard in all deliberations of the National Council and its committees.

State Secretaries (*Staatssekretäre*) may be attached to Ministers in order to assist them in their work and represent them in Parliament.[50] They are appointed and dismissed like Ministers, and they are legally bound by the latter's instructions. They are not members of the Federal Government in the legal sense, but they participate in cabinet meetings without the right to vote. In the political practice of coalition governments, State Secretaries have in the past frequently exercised "surveillance" of a Minister of the other party as their main function. Today each party in government has two State Secretaries, some to control Ministers of the other party, others to assist Ministers of their own party in managing particularly important portfolios.[51]

3. The Federal Chancellor (*Bundeskanzler*)

The Federal Chancellor heads his own ministry, the Federal Chancellor's Office (*Bundeskanzleramt*), and chairs the Federal Government as first among equals. The Vice-Chancellor functions as his deputy. Unlike the German Chancellor, the Austrian Federal Chancellor has no legal power to lay down policy guidelines.[52] His leadership is based more on his political position, as the head of his political party, than on constitutional law. His authority is supported by a high degree of centralization and discipline of political parties and their deputies in Parliament.

The Federal Chancellor's Office functions as a super-ministry for political planning, coordination, and information. The trend towards the personalization of politics is encouraged by the media, to which the Federal Chancellor has preferred access. This allows him to create his specific political style ("Chancellor democracy"), to project himself as an arbiter and unifier, and to transform parliamentary elections into "Chancellor plebiscites." His government dominates parliament, where his supporters defend the government's position against a critical but powerless opposition. Ministers of the Chancel-

---

[50] Germany has two types of State Secretaries. The *Parlamentarische Staatssekretäre* (Parliamentary State Secretaries) must be members of parliament. They are nominated by the Federal Chancellor and appointed by the Federal President. The *beamtete Staatssekretäre* are non-tenured civil servants at the top of the public service hierarchy in the ministries.

[51] Franz Morak (*ÖVP*, Federal Chancellery), Alfred Finz (*ÖVP*, Finances), Mares Rossmann (*FPÖ*, Economic Affairs and Labor), Reinhart Waneck (*FPÖ*, Social Security and Generations).

[52] Cf. article 65 of the German Basic Law: "The Federal Chancellor shall determine, and be responsible for, the general policy guidelines. Within the limits set by these guidelines, each Federal Minister shall conduct the affairs of his department autonomously and on his own responsibility."

lor's party are *de facto* accountable to him; the Chancellor himself is considered to be directly responsible to the people in the following general election.

Even a strong Federal Chancellor is, however, subject to certain rules of internal party democracy, and in a coalition government he must share power with a more or less influential political partner. Internal power constellations have thus far reserved nominations for ministerial appointment to important groups (e.g., for a Socialist Minister of Social Affairs to the Labor Union Federation, for a conservative Minister of Agriculture to the Farmers' Association, etc.).

4. The System of Administration

The Austrian Constitution does not differentiate between executive (governmental) and administrative functions. Government (*Regierung*) is considered part of administration (*Verwaltung*). Both of them are viewed as implementation (*Vollziehung*) of legislation and strictly determined by the latter.[53] Administration is a function of the state that affects most aspects of life of an individual or society. It may take the form of instructions or prohibitions (planning and policing functions, collection of taxes, etc.), but also of services provided by the state, such as financial grants to the arts and education, agriculture, or the operation and supervision of social insurance and pension systems, public transportation, and utilities. Administration is typically carried out by civil servants who do not enjoy judicial independence but are subject to the orders and instructions of their superiors in a hierarchical system headed by elected or appointed politicians.

5. The Bureaucracy

The structure of public administration and public service in Austria has strong historical roots in the enlightened absolutism of Maria Theresia (1740–80) and Joseph II (1780–90), who created a civil service loyal to the Emperor in his struggle against the privileges of the feudal aristocracy. Civil servants like the military had ranks and titles and wore uniforms. Their attitude towards the population was authoritarian or at least paternalistic. Some of this administrative style and attitude still prevails. The transition to rule of law in 1867 and after, and in particular the "legality principle" governing all public administration under article 18 (1) of the Constitution of 1920, requires public servants to have extensive knowledge of the law. This has led to a still more or less intact "lawyers' monopoly" (*Juristenmonopol*) in the higher ranks of the Austrian bureaucracy.

Public service is subject to the principles of legality (*Gesetzesgebundenheit*) and obedience (*Weisungsgebundenheit*), i.e., hierarchical subordination to the orders and instructions of superiors. Public servants work in two categories: *Beamte* (civil servants) and *Vertragsbedienstete* (employees under

---

[53] Article 18 (1): "The entire public administration may only be exercised on the basis of statutes."

private law contract). Appointment as a civil servant entails a special relationship between the official and the state. There is a duty of loyalty based on professional ethics, including honesty and accuracy in accomplishing tasks, objectivity, and impartiality. This ethos has, however, been eroding. As a result, the public generally perceives bureaucrats as pedantic formalists, who lack initiative and courage, and enjoy undeserved privileges. *Beamte*, for example, have a claim to life-long alimentation by the state. After a probationary period, they enjoy tenure (*Pragmatisierung*),[54] they may not be dismissed without cause,[55] and they may not even be transferred to other positions.[56] They retire at age 65 with 80% of their last salary.[57]

Recruitment and promotion of civil servants became subject to blatant political patronage during the Grand Coalition of 1946–66, and party penetration of the public service is still very high despite a more objective selection procedure introduced in 1989. Today, top positions are filled for limited periods (e.g., five years). Reappointment is based on satisfactory performance. The number of federal employees dropped from 300,000 in 1993 to 212,000 in 2000, mainly as a result of the railroad system being removed from the federal budget in 1994.

Unlike the German or American system of administration, the Austrian system has no political appointees assuming certain high-level positions in the bureaucracy for a limited time, subject to political change at the top of the respective departments. But all Austrian Ministers invariably attempt to recruit and promote civil servants from pools of loyal political supporters. Since 1960, Ministers have maintained small personal secretariats for which they could recruit personnel from outside the tenured federal bureaucracy.

Reforms have become imperative to increase the efficiency, service orientation, and managerial quality of the Austrian public service. In difficult negotiations with the civil servants' union, the government has so far succeeded only partially in its aims to reduce tenure and pensions, provide mobility, insert incentives into rigid salary scales, improve training, and emphasize performance evaluation.

6. *Privatwirtschaftsverwaltung*

The Federal Government or its members also perform leading or coordinating functions in the so-called "private economic administration" (*Pri-*

---

[54] In 1997, approximately 50% of all public servants (64% of federal civil servants) were tenured.

[55] But there is disciplinary accountability for culpable violation of official duties (reprimand, fines of up to five months' salary, dismissal). Abuse of official power may constitute a crime (art. 302 of the Criminal Code).

[56] A *Beamtenschutzgesetz* (Law for the Protection of Civil Servants) passed in 1969 marks the high point of union power, producing an extraordinary loss of flexibility on the part of the government. Reform proposals to be implemented in the near future envisage drastic reductions in tenured civil service positions.

[57] Pension reforms introduced in 1997 provide for gradual reductions aiming at a harmonization of Austria's numerous retirement schemes.

vatwirtschaftsverwaltung) of the Federation. This is an area of administration in which the state operates public enterprises (e.g., nationalized industries), grants subsidies, and finances public projects. The Government enters contractual relationships rather than acting in its sovereign capacity, and because of its political weight, substantially influences this sector. However, the possibilities of individual legal protection and parliamentary control are as yet underdeveloped in this area.

7. Perspectives

During the last years of the *SPÖ/ÖVP* coalition, the Federal Government, which forms the hub of the political system, developed remarkable independence from party secretariats, the bureaucracy, and even from the traditional "side-government" (*Nebenregierung*) of employers' and employees' associations, the "social partnership" (*Sozialpartnerschaft, supra* II.D). This emancipation process is likely to continue. But like any coalition government it accumulated considerable potential for conflict and more than usual wear and tear, which lent itself to skilled and populist exploitation on the part of the opposition, in particular the *FPÖ*.

The *ÖVP/FPÖ* government appointed on February 4, 2000 faces the difficult task of implementing highly unpopular yet overdue reforms of the social and economic system, with painful cutbacks in expenditures required by EU demands for drastic budget consolidation and national debt reduction. Such reforms must include profound changes in the health care and pension schemes, reduction of the bureaucracy, further deregulation and liberalization of the markets, and continuation of the privatization of public enterprises. The government is confronted with vigorous opposition by the *SPÖ*, the *ÖVP's* former partner in government, without whose cooperation many problems cannot be solved, because they require constitutional amendment and thus a two-thirds majority in Parliament. Besides, the government will have to help the EU find an exit strategy from the sanctions it rashly and unlawfully imposed on Austria to discourage the formation of a center-right government (see *supra* Chapter 1, VII.D).

V. Federalism

A. History

The current federal structure prescribed by the Austrian Constitution has its roots in the Habsburg Monarchy, the predecessor of the modern republic. The Austro-Hungarian Empire had been a conglomerate of territories essentially linked only by the person of the ruler. Despite centralist tendencies under absolute monarchs in the eighteenth century (Maria Theresia and Joseph II), the territories had continued to maintain their historically based individualism, as well as a measure of autonomy.

On October 21, 1918, after the dismemberment of the Austro-Hungarian Monarchy as a consequence of the defeat in World War I, a Provisional National Assembly in Vienna proclaimed the establishment of the *Republik Deutschösterreich* (Republic of German-Austria). In the territories claimed by the new republic, however, state power was still being exercised by *Länder* parliaments elected during the time of the Monarchy. Some *Länder* adopted new constitutions and intended to secede. Tirol, for instance, sought to prevent the cession of South Tirol to Italy by creating a "free state," while Vorarlberg planned to join Switzerland. In Salzburg (and partly in Tirol) there was a tendency to join Germany.

On October 29, 1918, State Chancellor Karl Renner demanded that all *Länder* issue statements of adhesion to the Republic, and by November 1, most German-speaking *Länder* had declared their intent, based on that of their people, to join the new state. These declarations were formally accepted by the government in Vienna. A subsequent statute, however, did not establish a federal state, but only a somewhat decentralized unitary state. There were several reasons for this approach. First, the question of joining Germany had remained unresolved. The Austrian government, which intended to join Germany, thought that this *Anschluß* could be accomplished more easily by a more centralized Austrian state. In the peace treaty of Saint Germain signed in 1919, however, Austria was forbidden to join Germany, and subsequently German-Austria was renamed the Republic of Austria. Second, the young republic had serious economic difficulties. For these reasons, the Social Democratic Party advocated a unitary state. This viewpoint was also influenced by the fact that the Christian-Social Party was dominant in the *Länder* outside Vienna.

The Constitution of October 1, 1920, represents a compromise between the Social Democrats and the Christian-Socials, in which the Social Democrats accepted some federal elements on the condition that a unified economic area and uniform social legislation be imposed. A genuine federal state was achieved through the constitutional amendments of 1925. In Western Europe, only Belgium, Switzerland, Germany and Austria are federal states. Of these four countries, Austria is the least decentralized.

B. The Federal Model of the 1920 Constitution

Article 2 of the Constitution states: "(1) Austria is a federal state. (2) The federal state is formed by the autonomous *Länder* Burgenland, Kärnten, Niederösterreich, Oberösterreich, Salzburg, Steiermark, Tirol, Vorarlberg, Wien." The territory of the Austrian state is identical with the territories of these nine *Länder*; there is no federal district (like Washington, D.C.) which is separate from *Länder* territory. According to constitutional theory, the federal principle is regarded as one of the fundamental structural principles of the

Constitution, which may be altered not by ordinary constitutional amendment, but only by means of an additional popular referendum (Const. art. 44 (3)).[58]

Such a referendum was held for the first (and to this date only) time on June 12, 1994, in the context of Austria's accession to the EU. Membership in the European Union *inter alia* affects the federal principle of the Austrian Constitution. As a direct effect of Austria's accession to the EU, the *Länder* suffered a loss of autonomy, since EU legislation (especially regulations) becomes automatically effective in the sphere of *Länder* legislation.

The federal principle has from the very beginning been comparatively weak and subject to many centralist tendencies in both the Constitution and in political reality. Contrary to the German Basic Law, which in article 31 provides that federal law overrides *Land* law, the Austrian Constitution contains no supremacy clause. Constitutional theory stipulates a system in which the Federation is on the same level as the *Länder*. According to Hans Kelsen, a leading constitutional theorist and architect of the Austrian Constitution, the Austrian legal system has three parts: federal law, *Land* law, and a body of law that forms a layer above the two. In practice there is a clear preponderance of federal law.

Whereas a typical federal state provides for a separation of powers regarding all three branches of government, Austrian *Länder* have no judicial powers.[59] As to legislation, all important powers are concentrated in the Federation.[60] The Constitution provides for *Länder* participation in the federal legislative process by means of the *Bundesrat* (Federal Council), a body similar to a second chamber of Parliament and composed of *Länder* representatives, but this has not been an effective instrument for safeguarding *Länder* interests.[61] In Austria, the most decentralized branch of government is the executive. The *Länder* administer not only their own law, but also implement important areas of federal law on behalf of the Federation.

Austrian *Länder* have only limited powers of taxation (including the power to collect taxes on real property, tourism, hunting, fishing, and advertising). Most of their financial resources are derived from revenue sharing (*Finanzausgleich*) with the Federation, in a constitutional framework, but subject to renegotiation of details every few years.

Although the legal autonomy of the *Länder* is weak, this does not prevent the citizens from identifying with their particular *Land* and even resorting to occasional acts of civil disobedience in response to federal measures. Particularly in western Austria, the distant Federal Government in

---

[58] Cf. the "eternity clause" of the German Basic Law in article 79 (3): "Amendments to this Basic Law affecting the division of the Federation into Länder, their participation in the legislative process ... shall be prohibited."

[59] In the U.S., complete court systems exist on the federal and on the state level. In Germany, *Länder* court systems enforce federal law under the supervision of federal supreme courts.

[60] This is similar in Germany, but different in the U.S.

[61] The situation is different in Germany, where the *Bundesrat* has much stronger powers.

Vienna is frequently considered to be an arrogant intermeddler. Unlike Germany,[62] Austria has placed all institutions of the central government in Vienna, and there is little recruitment of non-Viennese into these institutions (courts included).[63]

C. The Powers of the *Länder*

1. Legislation

a. Separation of Legislative Powers

The Federal Constitution recognizes four types of legislative authority:

- **Legislation and implementation by the Federation** (art. 10). This includes important matters like civil and criminal law, trade and industry, transportation, health, science, and defense.
- **Legislation by the Federation, implementation by the *Länder*** (art. 11). This includes areas such as citizenship and traffic police.
- **Basic (fundamental) legislation by the Federation, enabling legislation and implementation by the *Länder*** (art. 12). This includes land reform, electrical energy, and agricultural labor law.
- **Legislation and implementation by the *Länder*** (art. 15).[64] These residual powers are few, all important matters being assigned to the Federation. Exclusive *Länder* powers include land use, construction codes, and hunting laws.[65]

---

62 Where the Constitutional Court and the Federal Supreme Court sit in Karlsruhe, the Federal Labor Court in Erfurt, the Federal Social Court in Kassel, the Federal Administrative Court in Berlin (scheduled to move to Leipzig in 2002), and the Federal Tax Court in Munich. Although most legislative and executive bodies moved to Berlin in the year 1999, a number of ministries remained in Bonn.

63 There is a noticeable reluctance on the part of senior officials to move to Vienna, mostly because of the difficult housing situation there.

64 The German Basic Law establishes four types of legislative powers: exclusive federal legislation (an extensive list in art. 74), concurrent federal and *Land* legislative powers (which the Federation may exercise in case of need; see the even longer list in art. 72), federal framework or skeleton legislation (*Rahmenvorschriften*), and (unenumerated) residual legislative powers of the states (art. 70). With few exceptions, federal legislation is implemented by the *Länder* in their own right (art. 83). In some instances, *Länder* enforce federal law as agents of the Federation and subject to federal instructions (e.g., income and sales taxes, federal highways). Examples of direct federal administration include foreign affairs, national defense, and currency matters.

65 The German Basic Law, too, leaves very few matters as residual powers to the *Länder* (art. 70), e.g., education, culture, public health and safety, and the organization of *Land* and local government. But the Constitutional Court provides strong protection of this sphere.

Outside this structure of Federal and *Länder* authority, there are special rules for revenue sharing,[66] schools and a few other matters. The distribution of powers is safeguarded by the Constitutional Court.

b. Checks and Balances

Länder may influence federal legislation by virtue of a suspensive
veto in the *Bundesrat*. But the *Nationalrat* may override such veto by a simple
majority. The consent of the *Bundesrat* is required (absolute veto) where a
constitutional law would restrict *Länder* powers.

The Federal Government may object to *Länder* legislation which
jeopardizes federal interests. However, the *Land* parliament (*Landtag*) concerned may override this protest.

The Constitutional Court may be asked by the Federal or a *Land*
Government to determine whether an act of legislation or implementation falls
into its sphere of authority, and each may contest the constitutionality or
legality of the other's statutes and regulations.

c. Participation of the *Länder* and Municipalities in EU Legislation

EU legislation does not take into account the internal distribution of
powers between the Federation and the *Länder*. Only states, and not their
component parts, are members of the EU and participants in its legislative
processes. To at least partially compensate the *Länder* for their loss of power,
article 23d of the Austrian Constitution was inserted in 1994 and grants the
Länder certain participatory rights – the Federation is obligated to inform the
Länder immediately of all EU projects that affect their autonomy or other
interests. This allows the *Länder* to issue formal opinions on these matters.
The same applies to rights and interests of municipalities (art. 23d (1)).

A unanimous opinion by the *Länder* on matters affecting *Länder* legislation is binding on the Federation when negotiating and voting within the
EU. The Federation may depart from such an opinion only for compelling
reasons of foreign and integration policy. These reasons have to be notified to
the *Länder* (art. 23d (2)). In matters affecting *Länder* interests, the Federal
Government may delegate its seat on the European Council to a representative
nominated by the *Länder* (art. 23d (3)).

The *Länder* are obligated to implement EU legislation that affects
their powers. Should they fail to do so and this failure has been stated *vis-à-vis*
Austria by an EU court, the respective power devolves to the Federation (art.
23d (5)). *Länder* do not have standing to sue in the European Court of Justice.
Therefore, under a treaty between the Federation and the *Länder*, the Federation is obligated to bring an action at the request of a *Land* whose legislative
powers are affected by an unlawful action or omission by an organ of the EU.

---

[66] For Germany, cf. the special provisions in the Basic Law (arts. 104a–115).

2. Executive

In the sphere of implementation, there exists a functional separation of federal and *Land* administration. But only in exceptional areas are there separate federal agencies, such as federal police agencies or the internal revenue service. For the most part, federal administration is conducted as indirect or delegated federal administration (*mittelbare Bundesverwaltung*) by the *Landeshauptmann* (*Land* Governor) and *Land* agencies subordinated to him, especially district administrations (*Bezirkshauptmannschaften*). The *Landeshauptmann* has a dual role: on the one hand, he is a member and the chairman of the supreme organ of *Land* administration, the *Landesregierung* (*Land* Government), on the other hand, he also represents the federal administration and receives orders and instructions from the Federal Government or individual Federal Ministers. Politically, this may lead to conflicts of loyalty if he has to execute federal instructions he considers harmful to his own *Land*. There is no doubt that this system of delegated federal administration endangers the autonomy of the *Länder*. The latter gradually lose independent decision-making authority and tend to become mere enforcement organs of the Federation.

Apart from their powers under constitutional law, the Federation and the *Länder* may conduct activities as subjects under private law. This "private economic administration" (*Privatwirtschaftsverwaltung*) includes the administration of federal and *Land* property, the management of public enterprises, and various activities for which private law forms have been chosen for the purpose of circumventing the constitutional separation of powers. Thus, both the Federation and the *Länder* grant subsidies in the form of private law contracts in areas in which they could not act by means of public law rulings or decrees. This leads not only to an erosion of powers but also to a lack of due process guarantees and state liability which would normally arise from public action. A frequent example of this subversion is the creation of private law corporations which raise money in the capital market and construct roads or office buildings outside the limits of the state budget.

3. Judiciary

The *Länder* have no judicial powers. But a constitutional amendment in 1988 provided for Independent Administrative Panels in the *Länder*.[67] These are not courts, but their members enjoy quasi-judicial independence, and the panels qualify as tribunals under article 6 of the European Human Rights Convention. They may serve as a stepping stone towards a genuine administrative court system. Not all *Länder* aspire to this judicial control, however, and some are reluctant to assume the costs of such a court system.

D. Instruments of Coordination

The Constitution authorizes the conclusion of treaties between the Federation (*Bund*) and the *Länder*, and the *Länder* may also conclude treaties

---

[67] See *infra* Chapter 7.

among themselves concerning the exercise of their powers in order to better coordinate their activities.

In May 1998, the Federation and the *Länder* concluded two treaties concerning a consultation mechanism (*Konsultationsmechanismus*) about legislative action that would cause costs for the other party, and a stability pact (*Stabilitätspakt*) to meet EU criteria for public expenditures and deficit.

Informal means of communication and coordination are available through the Liaison Office of the *Länder* (*Verbindungsstelle der Bundesländer*) and regular conferences of governors[68] and civil servants, in particular for the purpose of discussing financial matters and questions arising from Austria's participation in the European Union. With respect to the latter, the *Länder* have established a special integration conference (*Integrationskonferenz der Länder, IKL*) and a permanent integration committee (*Ständiger Integratiosausschuß der Länder, SIL*).

E. The Municipalities

A third territorial entity below the level of the Federation and the *Land* is the municipality (*Gemeinde*). *Gemeinden* do not function merely as administrative units, but enjoy a (limited) sphere of autonomous self-government protected by the Constitution.[69] The organs of the municipalities (council, mayor) are democratically elected. Municipalities do not have legislative powers, but only administrative functions, which they exercise either as delegated jurisdiction on behalf of the Federation or on behalf of the *Länder*, or on their own autonomous authority. Municipal decisions in matters of delegated jurisdiction may be appealed to federal or *Land* organs. Within their own jurisdiction, municipalities are subject to a special legal supervision by the Federation or the respective *Land*. The municipalities' own powers include matters of local interest such as construction, fire, or market inspection and policing, ambulance service, etc. Municipalities may contest illegal interference with their powers by federal or *Land* authorities in the Constitutional Court.

In June 1994, the Federal Constitution was amended to permit the direct election of mayors subject to the provisions of the *Länder* constitutions. A number of *Länder* (Burgenland, Carinthia, Salzburg, Tirol, Upper Austria, and Vorarlberg) have already exercised this option.

F. Reform Tendencies

Länder politicians have frequently demanded the strengthening of *Länder* autonomy within Austria's federal structure. They have criticized the

---

[68] There are plans to anchor the Governors' Conference (*Landeshauptmännerkonferenz*) in the Federal Constitution.

[69] The German Basic Law also guarantees the autonomy of local government (art. 28 (2)), whereas the U.S. Constitution does not.

growing concentration of powers in the Federation in a process of small steps amounting to an unspectacular but serious erosion of the federal principle of the Constitution.

The *Länder* have repeatedly put forward lists of demands to reverse this trend, containing suggestions for transferring powers to them, for strengthening the *Bundesrat* and the position of the *Landeshauptmann*, and for improving the distribution of funds. Most *Länder* would also like to have their own courts, or at least genuine administrative courts. The establishment of such administrative courts, which are to replace the Independent Administrative Panels,[70] has been designated a legislative priority by the present government.

The *Länder* were understandably worried that they would suffer a loss of autonomy due to Austria's accession to the EU, because EU regulations become automatically effective in the sphere of *Länder* jurisdiction. *Länder* may also suffer an increase in local problems (transit traffic, environmental protection standards, and land purchase by foreigners).

A main concern among western *Länder*, particularly in Tirol, was the "sell-out" of land to foreigners for the construction of vacation homes. Tirol is one of the most densely populated areas in Europe.[71] Under article 70 of the Treaty of Accession to the EU, Austria was permitted to maintain its present restrictions of land purchase by foreigners for another five years. It may then impose national, regional, or municipal restrictions on secondary residences for reasons of social and economic planning and environmental protection, provided that these restrictions do not discriminate against citizens of EU member states.

Another serious problem which faces the western *Länder* in particular is transit highway traffic through Austria. Austria issues a limited number of "eco-points" to Austrian and foreign truck companies. Every trip through Austria "costs" a certain number of points. Trucks with lower emissions and quieter engines require fewer points. An annual reduction of points aims to reduce carbon dioxide emissions (60% by 2003) and to transfer traffic from road to rail. In February 1996, the tolls on the Brenner and Tauern highways were substantially raised. This revenue is expected to be higher than the amount necessary for the maintenance of these roads. Because this surplus may violate EU legislation, the Commission brought an action against Austria before the European Court of Justice in May 1998.

National Austrian environmental protection law may remain in force under EU rules as long as it does not discriminate against foreigners. The *Länder* had demanded that higher Austrian standards in areas like the labeling of chemicals, the use of asbestos, formaldehyde or mercury, as well as stricter car emission levels remain intact.

---

[70] See *infra* Chapter 7, II.

[71] 399 inhabitants per square kilometer, or even 583 in the summer time, as compared to 361 in the Netherlands.

The Federal Government successfully diffused tensions by involving the *Länder* in the negotiations preceding Austria's membership in the EU (position papers, experts' meetings, working groups, and participation of *Länder* representatives in the negotiations in Brussels). In 1992, an agreement between the Federation and the *Länder* provided the legal foundation for the participation of the *Länder* in this integration process. Many of its provisions were subsequently embodied in constitutional amendments adopted in 1992 and 1994 (see *supra* C.I.c). The Federation transferred jurisdiction in matters of administrative restriction of land use and conveyance to the *Länder* (Const. art. 10 (1) item 6, as amended in 1992) and granted the *Länder* and municipalities the right to prompt and comprehensive information, as well as the right to voice an opinion in all matters of European integration affecting their interests. The Federation is bound by unanimous decisions of the *Länder* in areas subject to their legislation.

Since 1989, a new distribution of powers between the Federation and the *Länder* has been under consideration. The proposal provides for the abolition of indirect federal administration, transferring it to the autonomous jurisdiction of the *Länder*. The federal legislature would be authorized to delegate its legislative power to the *Länder*. However, there are no plans to strengthen the *Bundesrat*. In recent years, several observers have suggested that the present federal structure is too costly and should, for instance, be reduced to three entities instead of nine. But these proposals appear to run against the general European trend of regionalization, which aims to bring government closer to the people.[72]

Literature

See also the literature cited in Chapters 1 (Political History) and 2 (The Constitution, Sources and Interpretation of Law).

General and Comparative Works

Bischof, G., Pelinka, A. (eds.), Austro-Corporatism (1996)
Dachs, H. et al. (eds.), Handbuch des politischen Systems Österreichs (3rd ed. 1997)
Ermacora, F. et al. (eds.), Föderalismus in Österreich (1970)
Fischer, H. (ed.), Das politische System Österreichs (3rd ed. 1982)
Fitzmaurice, J., Austrian Politics and Society Today (1991)
Gerlich, P. et al., Corporatism in Crisis: Stability and Change of Social Partnership in Austria, Political Studies 36 (1988) 209
Good, D., From World War to Waldheim: Culture and Politics in Austria and the United States (1999)
Lauber, V. (ed.), Contemporary Austrian Politics (1996)
Luther, K. R., Pulzer, P. (eds.), Austria 1945–95: Fifty Years of the Second Republic (1998)

---

[72] Cf. the decentralization efforts of formerly highly centralized countries like Italy, France, and Spain.

Luther, K. R., Müller, W. C. (eds.), Politics in Austria: Still a Case of Consociationalism? (1992)
Mantl, W. (ed.), Politik in Österreich (1992)
Pelinka, A., Plasser, F. (eds.), The Austrian Party System (1989)
Pelinka, A., Austria: Out of the Shadow of the Past (1998)
Pelinka, A., Rosenberger, S., Österreichische Politik: Grundlagen – Strukturen – Trends (2000)
Schambeck, H. (ed.), Österreichs Parlamentarismus (1986)
Steiner, K. (ed.), Modern Austria (1981)
Steiner, K., Politics in Austria (1972)
Sweeney, J., Weidenholzer, J. (eds.), Austria: A Study in Modern Achievement (1988)

Monographs and Articles

Cerny, W. F., Parlament und Parteien (1994)
Dickinger, C., Der Bundespräsident im politischen System Österreichs (1999)
Karlhofer, F. (ed.), Die Zukunft der Sozialpartnerschaft: Veränderungsdynamik und Reformbedarf (1999)
Klecatsky, H., Pickl, V., Die Volksanwaltschaft (1989)
Kneucker, R., Austria, An Administrative State. The Role of Austrian Bureaucracy, ÖZP 2 (1973) 95
Koja, F., Der Bundespräsident und das Heer, JRP 1997, 15
Korinek, K. (ed.), Die Kontrolle wirtschaftlicher Unternehmungen durch den Rechnungshof (1986)
Mayer, H., Verfahrensfragen der direkten Demokratie, FS Schambeck (1994) 511
Öhlinger, T., Das Scheitern der Bundesstaatsreform, ÖJP 1995, 543
Pelinka, A. (ed.), EU-Referendum: Zur Praxis direkter Demokratie (1994)
Pernthaler, P., Der differenzierte Bundesstaat (1992)
Pernthaler, P., Hat die österreichische Bundesstaatsreform noch eine Zukunft? (1998)
Pernthaler, P. (ed.), Bundesstaatsreform als Instrument der Verwaltungsreform und des europäischen Föderalismus (1997)
Schäffer, H., Stolzlechner, H. (eds.), Reformbestrebungen im österreichischen Bundesstaatssystem (1993)
Schambeck, H., Regierung und Kontrolle in Österreich (1997)
Schambeck, H. (ed.), Bundesstaat und Bundesrat in Österreich (1997)
Sully, M., The Haider Phenomenon (1997)
Tomandl, T., Fürböck, K., Social Partnership: The Austrian System of Industrial Relations and Social Insurance (1986)
Welan, M., Das österreichische Staatsoberhaupt: Aufwertung oder Abwertung (3rd ed. 1997)
Welan, M., Neisser, H., Der Bundeskanzler im österreichischen Verfassungsgefüge (1971)
Wiederin, E., Bundesrecht und Landesrecht (1995)
Winkler, G., Rechtswissenschaft und Politik (1998)

Chapter 4
Austria and the European Union

I. The European Union

A. Introduction

The modern history of European integration begins at the end of World War II, when the states of Europe were motivated by a common interest in rebuilding a devastated continent. European unification was to prevent future wars in Europe and lead to constructive economic cooperation. The first step was taken by French Foreign Minister Robert Schuman and French businessman Jean Monnet. In 1950, they developed a concept for the fusion of the coal and steel industries of European countries, in particular France and Germany. Placing these industries under common control would preclude any state from independently preparing for war.

Today the European Union (EU) is a supranational association of 15 European countries. In 1951, Germany, France, Italy, Belgium, the Netherlands and Luxembourg first founded the European Coal and Steel Community (ECSC). In 1957, the original six members established the European Economic Community (EEC) as well as a European Atomic Energy Community (Euratom). They were joined by Denmark, Ireland and the UK in 1973, by Greece in 1981, by Spain and Portugal in 1986, and most recently, by Austria, Finland and Sweden in 1995. The EU is based on intergovernmental treaties through which the member states have granted important powers and functions to centralized institutions.

B. The Treaties

1. The Schuman Plan of 1950 led to the establishment of the European Coal and Steel Community (ECSC) by France, Germany, Italy and the Benelux countries (Treaty of Paris, 1951). It created four Community institutions: a High Authority (renamed Commission in the 1965 Merger Treaty, see *infra* 3.), a Council, an Assembly (Parliament), and a Court.

2. The same six states signed the two Treaties of Rome in 1957, founding the European Economic Community (EEC, which in 1992 was renamed "European Community" or EC) and the European Atomic Energy Community (Euratom). Each of the Communities was to have separate organs, including a Court of Justice, but it was agreed that a single court should serve all three of them. The Court of the ECSC became the Court of Justice of the European Communities. It has retained this name even after the formation of the European Union (EU) by the Maastricht Treaty of 1992.

3. Since the Merger Treaty, which established a Single Council and a Single Commission of the European Communities in Brussels in 1965, all three communities have been governed by the same institutions, but they have not been fused.

4. The Single European Act (SEA) of 1986 (effective as of July 1, 1987), which brought new powers to the EEC in the areas of environment protection as well as economic and social cohesion, made significant procedural amendments increasing the influence of Parliament in the law-making process and the use of qualified majority voting (rather than unanimity) in the Council, thus facilitating the rapid creation of the internal market. It also introduced the possibility of establishing a Court of First Instance to relieve the European Court of Justice of its increasing workload.

5. The European Union Treaty (TEU) was concluded on February 7, 1992, in Maastricht and entered into force on November 1, 1993. It established a European Union (EU) based on the European Communities and two additional "pillars" of interstate cooperation (Titles V and VI TEU).[1]

6. The Treaty of Amsterdam was signed on October 2, 1997, and went into effect on May 1, 1999 after ratification by all members. It envisages, *inter alia*, a coordinated strategy for employment and contains an Agreement on Social Policy. The Treaty strengthens citizens' rights and environmental, health, and consumer protection. Furthermore, it enhances the powers of the Commission President and expands the powers of the European Parliament. Instead of the previously exclusive intergovernmental decision-making in the areas of justice and home affairs, Community rules now apply regarding asylum, visas, immigration and control at external borders. Intensified police and judicial cooperation is to help combat criminal activities, especially terrorism, drug trafficking, and fraud. But the Treaty made little progress towards effective common foreign and security policy structures and postponed needed institutional reforms that are becoming increasingly urgent with the planned enlargement of the Union.

On January 1, 1999 stage three of economic and monetary union (EMU) as defined in the Treaty of Maastricht went into effect with the introduction of a common currency, the EURO.[2] The European Central Bank

---

[1] Note on terminology: In the TEU, the EEC and the EEC Treaty were renamed the EC (European Community) and EC Treaty. This is confusing, because EC also stands for European Communities (plural). The EU includes the EC, whose institutions, in particular the Commission of the European Communities, also handle affairs in Pillars II and III, or matters affecting all three pillars (Council of the European Union). There is as yet very little EU law, in contrast to EC law. The Treaty of Amsterdam provides a Consolidated Version of the TEU and the TEC. Citations in this book will be to this version. When appropriate, the original numbering of articles will be added in parenthesis.

[2] All member states had to meet strict economic criteria for admission to EMU: an inflation rate not higher than 1,5% of the average of the three lowest member state rates; long term interest rates no higher than 2% above the average of the three lowest; a budget deficit below 3% of GDP; and a total public debt of less than 60% of GDP.

started operations in Frankfurt. Eleven participating states[3] fixed the exchange rates between the EURO and their national currencies. The latter will be replaced by EURO notes and coins in 2002.

Institutional reform and enlargement are the two greatest present challenges to the EU. The Union needs to revise internal structures and processes before admitting a dozen or more new members. It is planned to increase areas of majority voting and provide a new weighting of votes in favor of big states in the Council of Ministers, to limit the number of Commissioners, and to find more flexible forms of cooperation within the framework of the EU, permitting stronger political integration of a "core"-Europe or "vanguard" (e.g., the Original Six, or the Euro Eleven) open for other members to join at different speeds. An Intergovernmental Conference is to submit specific proposals for treaty revision by December 2000 (Summit of Nice). After ratification of a new treaty by 2002, the EU should be prepared for the admission of new members, which can realistically not be expected before 2005.[4]

C. The Structure of the EU

The EU is both a structure and a process. As a structure, it unites "three pillars" under a "common roof." The first and strongest pillar is made up of the three European Communities.

1. The European Communities

The communities forming the First Pillar are supranational organizations to which the member states have delegated part of their sovereignty. They may make law which becomes immediately valid in the member states and supersedes national law. The Maastricht Treaty defined for them the goal of economic and monetary union. It also introduced new EC powers and a more active role of the EC in consumer protection, trans-European networks, public health, development cooperation, visa policy, industrial policy, education, and culture. The Treaty of Amsterdam added provisions on citizens' rights and employment.

2. Common Foreign and Security Policy

The Second Pillar envisages a common foreign and security policy based on intergovernmental cooperation with steps towards institutionalization. Organs acting for it are the European Council, the Council of the EU, the

---

[3] Britain, Denmark and Sweden opted out, Greece did not qualify (but will join in 2001).

[4] Negotiations with six candidates (Poland, Hungary, the Czech Republic, Slovenia, Estonia, Cyprus) were begun in March 1998. A second group of six candidates (Romania, Bulgaria, Slovakia, Latvia, Lithuania, Malta) was recognized in December 1999, with negotiations starting in February 2000. Turkey received candidate status in 1999, but no date for negotiations has been set.

European Parliament, and the Commission, assisted by a High Representative for Common Foreign and Security Policy.

3. Police and Judicial Cooperation in Criminal Matters

The Third Pillar envisages police and judicial cooperation in combating crime, in particular terrorism, trafficking in persons, drugs or arms, offenses against children, corruption, and fraud. A European Police Office (Europol) was established.

In the Second and Third Pillars, development of common policies follows the classic pattern of international law, depending on contractual relations elaborated ad hoc. Community organs acting for the Third Pillar are the Council, the Parliament, the Commission, and the Court of Justice.[5]

4. Horizontal Links

Under the "common roof" provided by the European Council, horizontal links are to hold the three pillars together. The European Council consists of the heads of state or government of the member states plus the Commission President. Assisted by the ministers for foreign affairs and an additional member of the Commission, it guides the development of the Union by means of political "impulses" and "targets."[6] According to article 3 (ex art. C) TEU, the Union has a "single institutional framework which shall ensure the consistency and the continuity of the activities carried out."

II. Legislative and Executive Institutions of the EU

A. The Council

The Council of the European Union, usually called Council of Ministers, is the principal governing body with ultimate political power. It sets policy and passes all major legislation. The Council is composed of one representative per member state, usually the minister most closely concerned with the business under discussion. For example, ministers of agriculture will convene to discuss agricultural policy formulation. Member states take six-month turns in the Council Presidency. Austria's first turn was in the second half of 1998.[7]

---

[5] The Treaty of Amsterdam transferred asylum and immigration matters from the Third to the First Pillar.

[6] Article 4 (ex art. D) TEU: "The European Council shall provide the Union with the necessary impetus for its development and shall define the general political guidelines thereof." It meets up to four times a year ("summits") under the chairmanship of the head of state or government of the member state which holds the Presidency of the Council of the European Union.

[7] It was followed by Germany and Finland in 1999, Portugal and France in 2000. The Presidency will be occupied by Sweden and Belgium in 2001, by Spain and Denmark in 2002, by Greece in the first semester of 2003.

Although some decisions require unanimity, for the most part, either simple majority voting is prescribed or (more frequently) a qualified majority. A system of weighting gives more populous states more votes than others. The Council's decisions are prepared by COREPER, the Committee of Permanent Representatives. This Committee is composed of the members states' ambassadors, who in turn rely on a multitude of working groups.[8]

B. The Commission

The European Commission is the Community's administration, or civil service. In addition, it plays an autonomous role in a number of quasi-political respects, and thus has no real equivalent on a national level. Seated in Brussels, it performs four main functions:

- It is responsible for promoting the interest of the Community as a whole. This includes representing the Community in international matters within the Community's powers, acting as a "guardian of the Treaties" and taking action against member states to enforce compliance with community law.
- It administers the legislation contained in the Treaty and elsewhere, either directly or through the administrations of member states.
- It has the right of legislative initiative, making proposals for action or legislation to the Council, thus functioning as a "motor of integration."
- It enacts legislation or adopts decisions which are legally binding on the addressees. It exercises powers conferred by the Council as well as autonomous decision-making power.

The Commission comprises 20 Members (Commissioners) who are appointed unanimously by the member states and hold office for five-year terms. Each appointment is subject to approval by the European Parliament; the term is renewable.[9]

The Commission has a staff of approximately 20,000 "Eurocrats" organized into general services, including a Secretariat General, a Legal Service, a Statistical Office, a Translation Service, and 24 sectorally based Directorates General (e.g., DG III Industry, DG IV Competition). The DGs are subdivided into Directorates and Units.

The Community has legal personality (art. 281 TEC, ex art. 210). The Commission represents the Community in proceedings with the member states and negotiates international agreements on behalf of the Community. These are then concluded by the Council (art. 300 TEC, ex art. 228), and are binding on the institutions of the Community and the member states.

---

[8] Actually, there are two Committees: COREPER II, composed of the member states' permanent representatives, and COREPER I, composed of their deputies.

[9] Romano Prodi, a former President of the Council of Ministers of the Italian Republic (1996–1998) was appointed President of the European Commission in September 1999. Under article 219 TEC: "The Commission shall work under the political guidance of its President."

C. The European Parliament

The functions of the European Parliament have in the past evolved very slowly towards equivalence with those of national parliaments. The parliaments of the member states have resisted the transfer of their own powers, thus producing a much debated "democratic deficit" in the Community. Since 1979, deputies have been directly elected for five-year terms, and the number of deputies is roughly proportionate to the population of the respective member states. At present there are 626 deputies, with Germany electing 99, the UK, Italy, and France 87 each, and so forth. There are 21 Austrian deputies, while Luxembourg has the smallest contingent with six. The grouping of deputies in the Parliament is according to party affiliation, not national origin.[10]

The European Parliament exercises principal functions in four major areas.[11]

Legislation. The European Parliament is not an independent legislative organ like a national parliament. It has traditionally played a consultative role. All legislative proposals were submitted to it for an advisory opinion. A complex cooperation procedure was introduced by the SEA in 1986. In selected areas (basically matters of the internal market), the Parliament could reject or amend the Council's "common position" on a legislative proposal by the Commission. Yet the Council retained the last word. A co-decision procedure was adopted by the Treaty of Maastricht in 1992. It gave the Parliament a veto power over matters such as culture, health, and research if negotiations with the Council failed. In 1997, the Treaty of Amsterdam mandated co-decision in many additional areas, making it the general rule. Parliament still cannot draft legislation, yet it may ask the Commission to do so, and it reaches many legislative compromises under the co-decision procedure.

Budget. The budget is prepared by the Commission and submitted to the Council. The Parliament has the right to approve or modify it. According to Article 272 (8) TEC (ex art. 203 (8)), the European Parliament – acting by a majority of its members and two-thirds of the votes cast – may reject the draft budget for important reasons and ask for a new draft to be submitted.

Appointment and Control. The nomination of the Commission President needs the assent of the European Parliament. Subsequently, the President designate and the other members of the Commission are subject to a confirmation vote. The Parliament may put questions to the Council and the

---

[10] Elections in June 1999: European People's Party 242 (1994: 201), Socialist Party of Europe 180 (214), Liberals 43 (42), Greens 37 (27), etc. Membership in the European Parliament is incompatible with membership in a national government or in the Commission. Voter turnout has been falling continually (1979: 63%, 1989: 58.5%, 1999: 49.4%) mostly due to a general deficit in voter information about the functioning of the EU. In the 1999 elections, the UK had the lowest voter turnout with 24% and Belgium the highest with 91%. Voter turnout in Austria was 49%.

[11] The European Parliament was the big winner of the 1997 Amsterdam Treaty, which enlarged the Parliament's power in a legislative co-decision procedure with the Council.

Commission. It may set up committees of inquiry, and it may sue the Commission or the Council before the Court of Justice for annulment of unlawful acts or for failure to act. Parliament may dismiss the Commission (not, however, single members) by a two-thirds vote of no confidence.[12]

The European Parliament appoints an Ombudsman, a kind of people's advocate as it was first introduced in Scandinavian countries and later successfully adopted by others. During his five-year term, his function is to receive and investigate European citizens'[13] complaints of maladministration by any Community body, except the Courts acting in their judicial roles. He has no power of enforcement, but may report and suggest remedies to Parliament.

External Relations. The Parliament must approve major international agreements of the EC with other states and international organizations. The accession of new members is subject to its assent.

D. The Court of Auditors

"Especially qualified" persons are to be appointed to the Court of Auditors in a manner similar to being appointed to the Court of Justice (*infra* IV.B). Their function is to provide a complete and independent check of the financial activities of all Community institutions and the organs established by these institutions, and on the expenditure of Community money in the member states, in collaboration with national auditing bodies.

E. Other Bodies

Within the framework of the EC, a growing number of organizations have legally recognized roles. They include the European Investment Bank, the European Monetary Institute, and the European Central Bank.[14] Another set of bodies is purely consultative, for example, the Economic and Social Committee (ECOSOC) and the Committee of the Regions (COR).

III. Sources of Community Law

A. Primary Legislation

European Community law has essentially the same features as national legal systems in that it creates enforceable rights and obligations which may be invoked through legal proceedings. A large number of provisions are immediately binding on individuals, in the same way that national law is binding on them.

---

[12] This has been threatened in the past, yet never exercised. In March 1999, the Comission headed by President Jacques Santer, rather than risking censure, collectively resigned over charges of mismanagement against individual Commissioners.

[13] Every citizen of a member state is at the same time a citizen of the EU.

[14] The European Central Bank determines and implements the monetary policy of the EC subject to the goal of price stability.

Sources of Community law to be interpreted and applied by the Court of Justice include the founding Treaties, as amended, that form the "constitution" of the Communities ("primary legislation"), as well as acts of various Community institutions, such as directives, regulations, and decisions of the European Parliament acting jointly with the Council (art. 249 TEC, ex art. 189, as amended by art. 8 TEU, ex art. G), of the Council acting alone, and of the Commission. Acts of general application (directives and regulations) are sometimes referred to as "secondary legislation." Other sources of Community law include the case law of the European Court of Justice, principles of law common to the member states, and international agreements adhered to either by the Community itself or by the member states generally, including the European Human Rights Convention (art. 6 TEU, ex art. F).

B. Regulations

Regulations are produced either by the Council (pursuant to the Treaty) or by the Commission (under powers delegated by the Council, art. 211 TEC, ex art. 155). They take the form of detailed legislation, which is binding and directly applicable in the member states (art. 249 TEC, ex art. 189).[15] As matters of criminal and civil enforcement are normally left within the realm of the member states, EU regulations may need to be supplemented in this respect by national provisions.

C. Directives

Directives are issued by the Council or by the Commission. They are binding on the Member States as to the result to be achieved, leaving to the individual countries the choice of form and methods (art. 249 TEC, ex art. 189). Implementing legislation and administrative action will usually follow. The European Court has held that directives may have direct effect,[16] creating rights which may be relied upon by litigants in proceedings before national courts, in particular when the member states have failed to implement a directive by the required date. The direct effect of a directive is subject to the condition that its provisions establish clear, precise, and legally complete obligations, leaving the judge no room for excessive political evaluation or discretion. Claims involving a directive with direct effect are vertical in nature, and may only be brought by an individual against the state, and not vice versa. Only regulations have horizontal effect, establishing rights and duties between individuals.

---

[15] In other words, they need not and must not be reenacted in national legislation.

[16] Case 41/74, Van Duyn v. Home Office (1974).

D. Decisions

Decisions are not general legislation but are specific acts (art. 249 TEC, ex art. 189); they are only binding on the addressee (member state, company in matters of competition policy, etc.), and may have direct effect.

E. Supremacy of EC Law

Community law that has direct effect takes precedence over national law. An inconsistent national provision is therefore automatically overruled by a Community provision. Any national legislation which is in fact incompatible with Community law should be repealed for the sake of good legal order, even though it is automatically superseded.[17] National legal systems, including courts and public authorities, are obligated to ensure the effectiveness of Community law by making proper remedies and procedures available to the litigant.

IV. The Court of Justice of the European Communities

A. Introduction

The principle of judicial control was implemented at the very outset of the process of European integration. The European Coal and Steel Community (ECSC) established in 1951 already included a court structure that was strongly influenced by the French administrative law tradition. In the Treaties of Rome (1957), founding the European Economic Community (EEC) and the European Atomic Energy Community, it was decided that each of the Communities should have a Court of Justice, but that a single court should serve all three. As a result, the Court of the ECSC became the Court of Justice of the European Communities. It retained this name after the formation of the European Union by the Maastricht Treaty (TEU) of February 7, 1992.

The Single European Act (SEA) of 1986 added new powers to the EEC and introduced the possibility of establishing a Court of First Instance. This Court was subsequently created in 1989 and attached to the Court of Justice in Luxembourg, relieving the European Court of Justice of a growing caseload.

Under article 220 (ex art. 164) of the EC Treaty, the European Court of Justice is to "ensure that in the interpretation and application of this Treaty the law is observed." It is to guarantee that the other Community organs act within the limits of their respective powers. Sources of Community law to be interpreted and applied by the Court of Justice include the founding Treaties that form the "constitution" of the Communities.

In the Second Pillar (Common Foreign and Security Policy) the jurisdiction of the Court is excluded, whereas the Treaty of Amsterdam has given

---

[17] Case 26/62, Van Gend en Loos v. Nederlandse Administratie der Belastingen (1963); Case 6/64, Flaminio Costa v. ENEL (1964).

the ECJ jurisdiction to review certain measures adopted under the Third Pillar (Police and Judicial Cooperation in Criminal Matters).

B. Composition and Organization of the Court of Justice

The European Court of Justice consists of 15 judges (art. 221 TEC, ex art. 165), one from each member state.[18] They are appointed for (renewable) six-year terms by the common accord of the member states. The Court is assisted by currently nine Advocates General "acting with complete impartiality and independence, to make, in open court, reasoned submissions on cases brought before the Court" (art. 222, ex art. 166). When the Court sits as a full court, a quorum of nine judges is required. In most cases, however, the Court sits in chambers of three or five judges. A written procedure precedes oral arguments.

C. The Court of First Instance

The Court of First Instance consists of 15 members, one from each member state, and usually sits in chambers of three or five judges. Initially, the Court was to handle three categories of cases: competition, application of the Coal and Steel Treaty, and staff cases. In 1993 and 1994, the Council transferred all cases brought by parties other than member states or Community institutions, including anti-dumping cases, to the Court of First Instance.[19] Decisions of the Court of First Instance may be appealed to the Court of Justice of the European Communities on points of law.

D. Jurisdiction of the Court of Justice

1. Actions Against Member States

Various proceedings may be brought against member states that violate their Community obligations. The most important of these are the following:

a. Article 226 TEC (ex Article 169), Commission sues member state

Under article 226 (ex art. 169), the Commission may sue a member state for the breach of obligations created by Community law. Such action involves three formal stages. In practice, the Commission takes a preliminary informal step of writing a letter to the member state, warning it of its breach

---

[18] When the number of Community members was even (e.g., six or twelve), an additional judge was appointed by agreement of the large member states or by drawing lots.

[19] Under the European Trade Mark Regulation of 1993, challenges to decisions of the Community Trade Mark Office (in Alicante, Spain) also come before the Court of First Instance.

and inviting its comments. In two out of three cases, this step leads to a satis-factory settlement of the issue.

If a settlement is not achieved, the Commission takes the first formal step, requesting that the state submit its observations on the alleged breach. If the Commission is not satisfied by the explanations offered by the member state, it delivers a "reasoned opinion". Approximately 90% of the cases termi-nate at this point, with the state correcting its breach.

In the second stage, the Commission brings the case before the Court. This is followed by the third stage, in which the Court issues an opinion. The Court's judgment is declaratory, neither depriving national law of its effect nor creating new law, but obligating the state to take appropriate measures of compliance. A failure to comply may lead to further proceedings under article 226. In practice, the need for such follow-up "prosecution" of the delinquent state has been relatively rare.

Yet under the Maastricht Treaty, based on a British proposal, the Commission was granted the right to petition the Court to impose a lump sum or penalty payments on the non-compliant member state (art. 228 TEC, ex art. 171).[20] Nearly all judgments of the Court have been implemented voluntarily, even though in some cases only after substantial delay.[21]

b. Article 88 TEC (ex art. 93), Commission sues member state when state aid distorts competition

When state aid distorts or threatens to distort competition within the Common Market, the Commission, after asking the parties to submit their comments, may render a decision demanding that the state abolish or alter the subsidy within a certain time limit. In cases of non-compliance, the Commis-sion, or any interested state, may directly refer the matter to the Court. This special procedure is more expeditious than the one under article 226 TEC (ex art. 169).[22] The Commission may ask the Court for an interim order (art. 243 TEC, ex art. 186).

---

[20] By December 1998, the Commission had applied for penalties under article 228 TEC 14 times (four times against Greece, three times each against Italy and Ger-many, twice against France, and once each against Belgium and Luxembourg). Most cases concerned violations of environmental law. On July 4, 2000, the Court for the first time imposed penalty payments, sentencing Greece to 20,000 EURO for each further day of non-compliance.

[21] In 1998, for example, the Commission issued 1,101 article 226 (ex art. 169) letters (1997: 1,461) and 675 reasoned opinions (1997: 334). It brought 123 actions in the Court under article 169. The Court almost without exception endorsed the view taken by the Commission. In 1999, the Court decided 46 cases under art. 226, and 162 new cases were brought before the Court. To this date, 21 actions for failure to fulfill obligations have been brought against Austria since its accession to the EU.

[22] The state, of course, also has the option of challenging the Commission's decision before the Court under article 230 (ex art. 173).

2. Effect of Judgments Against Member States

Judgments against member states are only declaratory, calling on the errant Community member to comply with its Treaty obligations. The Court has no power to annul national law. But it may, upon the request of the Commission, impose penalties for non-compliance after further proceedings under article 228 TEC (ex art. 171). The Court has no power to award damages against a member state to compensate those harmed by the infringement.

3. Judicial Review of Community Acts

The Treaties serve as a Constitution of the Community, defining the legislative and executive or administrative powers of Community institutions such as the Council and the Commission. The Court monitors the lawful implementation of these powers, thus exercising both constitutional and administrative jurisdiction. The most important actions brought in the Court are those to annul illegal Community acts (art. 230 TEC, ex art. 173).

All unlawful Community acts may be challenged by member states, the Council, or the Commission. These are the so-called "privileged applicants." The European Parliament and the European Central Bank may sue only for the purpose of protecting their prerogatives. Natural and legal persons may attack not only regulations and decisions that are addressed to them, but also regulations or decisions addressed to other persons which are of "direct and individual concern" to them as well. The Court has been anxious not to be flooded by such suits and makes it difficult to satisfy this test.

There are four grounds for annulment: lack of competence; violation of an essential procedural requirement; infringement of the EC Treaty or any rule of law relating to its application; and misuse of powers. They are derived from French administrative law and the jurisprudence of the French *Conseil d'Etat*. German and English law have influenced the further development of grounds for review. Procedural violations are frequently invoked, e.g., the failure to give sufficient reasons for the decision in question. The infringement of any rule of law relating to the relevant Treaty has been construed liberally by the Court, including general principles as recognized in international law or "general principles common to the laws of the member states," e.g., the principle of proportionality of administrative acts, of legal certainty, or of due process, and ultimately fundamental rights in general, which form, according to the Court, "an integral part of the general principles of law."

The Court has discretion to postpone the effects of annulment in order to enable Community organs to enact new valid law.

4. Preliminary Rulings

Community law is generally enforced by the national courts of the member states. But under article 234 TEC (ex art. 177), the European Court of Justice gives preliminary rulings concerning the interpretation of the Treaties and the validity and interpretation of Community acts. Courts or tribunals of last resort of member states must request a ruling of the European Court of Justice when such a question is raised in a case before them and they consider the resolution of this question necessary to enable them to render judgment. Other courts or tribunals may make such references.

Since the European Court of Justice enjoys a monopoly in the interpretation of Community law, national courts applying EC law in cases of doubt request an interlocutory ruling, in the meantime halting all proceedings pending the outcome of the reference. At present, the European Court's ruling can be expected within 21 months.

The reference procedure is to prevent national judges from declaring EC law invalid and to ensure its uniform interpretation throughout the Community. The Community institutions concerned, all member states, and the parties to the action before the national court may submit observations in writing and at an oral hearing. The idea of preliminary rulings was developed from analogous procedures in member states, such as the French reference from civil to administrative courts and the German and Italian references from ordinary courts to special Constitutional Courts.

In the early years, only an occasional reference reached Luxembourg. Today, the European Court has begun to suffer from an overload of cases, and it restricts its docket by refusing to accept hypothetical questions and by rejecting questions as manifestly inadmissible when the national judge fails to describe the factual and legal background of the national proceedings in sufficient detail.

For a long time, no national Constitutional Court ever referred a question to the European Court of Justice. In 1999 the Austrian Constitutional Court made its first reference. When a court or tribunal of last resort wrongly decides not to refer, the parties have no right of appeal to the European Court. Theoretically, the Commission could bring an action against the member state under article 226 TEC (ex art. 169). But there is evidence that national courts increasingly view themselves as Community courts as well.[23]

The preliminary ruling of the European Court must be accepted by the national judge as the authoritative and final determination of Community law. As to its prejudicial quality with regard to future cases, one should note that the European Court generally abides by its own previous decisions, but also does not hesitate to depart from them when necessary. The Court permits national courts to resubmit questions rather than forcing them to follow its previous rulings in other cases as precedents.

Generally speaking, the European Court has welcomed preliminary references as opportunities to develop Community law. Some of the most important doctrines of European law were developed in the context of this procedure.

---

[23] After Austria's accession to the EU, Austrian courts quickly and extensively used the reference procedure, bringing two cases in 1995, six in 1996, 35 in 1997, 16 in 1998, and no fewer than 56 in 1999 (total: 115). Sweden and Finland, the other new members, have made a total of 28 and 15 referrals, respectively.

According to article 220 TEC (ex art. 164), the Court must ensure that "the law" is observed when interpreting and applying the EC Treaty. The Court has used this provision to extend its jurisdiction and the competencies of the Community beyond those expressly listed in the Treaty.[24] The Court's "integrationist jurisprudence" rests on twin pillars: The supremacy doctrine and the doctrine of direct effect.[25] Equally significant are the general principles of law articulated by the Court, i.e., the right of legitimate expectations, the right to be heard, the duty to respect fundamental human rights, the right to equality of treatment, and the duty to employ means that are proportional (not excessive) to the end sought. These are higher sources of law capable of over-riding Community acts. Other general principles include contractual certainty, legal certainty,[26] the right to engage in labor union activity, and the attorney-client privilege of confidentiality.

V. The Process of Austria's Accession to the EU

On July 17, 1989, Austria submitted three applications for accession to the European Communities. Each of them contained a reservation concerning Austria's neutrality. Despite Austria's increasingly relaxed attitude towards neutrality, a large number of Austrian citizens continue to perceive the neutral status of their country as a positive value or even a defining element of their national identity. As a result, the Austrian government insisted on accession to the European Communities as a neutral member. In December 1992, Austria formally consolidated its three applications into one, for admission to the European Union. The EU was in the process of being created under the Maastricht Treaty and became effective on November 1, 1993. On November 1, 1994, Austria, still a member of the EFTA, as such became a member of the European Economic Area (EEA) formed by the EFTA and the EU.

The EEA Treaty extended the Four Freedoms of the EC's internal market to EFTA partners. In this free trade area of 19 countries, approximately 40% of world trade takes place. The EEA goes far beyond a traditional free trade arrangement in that it also establishes a system of free competition based on EC rules and contains provisions related to the Four Freedoms in areas such as social policy, consumer protection, and the environment. The Treaty also provides for "flanking" policies, e.g., in the fields of research and development, education, and tourism. EFTA states adopted approximately two-thirds

---

[24] E.g., it subjected the European Parliament to judicial review under article 230 TEC (ex art. 173), cf. Case 294/83, Parti Ecologiste 'Les Verts' v. European Parliament (1986); it even extended the international treaty-making powers of the Community beyond those listed in the Treaty, cf. Case 22/70 Commission v. Council (ERTA) (1971).

[25] Case 26/62, Van Gend en Loos v. Nederlandse Administratie der Belastingen (1963); Case 6/64, Flaminio Costa v. ENEL (1964).

[26] Legal acts must be clear, precise, and predictable to those who are subjected to them; retroactive legislation is usually barred.

of the *acquis communautaire*,[27] in all about 1,400 legal enactments of the EC. But the EEA does not include such important matters as a customs union, agriculture, economic and monetary policy, taxes, and regional policy. The EEA Treaty also omitted the two new "pillars" erected by the Treaty of Maastricht, namely, a Common Foreign and Security Policy (CFSP) and Cooperation in Justice and Home Affairs. Furthermore, the EFTA members may merely take part in EC decision-shaping, but not in decision-making; they must essentially "implement autonomously" relevant EC law.

During negotiations with the EU, the Austrian government reduced the concept of permanent neutrality to its "military core," as it had been formulated in the Constitutional Law on Neutrality in 1955. The provisional statement of the European Commission (*avis*) was issued on July 31, 1991. In this *avis*, the Commission suggested that Austria's neutral status may not be compatible with the future EU's Common Foreign and Security Policy. It recommended that Austria either notify an appropriately redefined neutrality status to its partners or apply for an exemption in the Act of Accession.

The Treaty of Maastricht separated the CFSP from Community law. Whereas according to the EEC Treaty, economic sanctions could be imposed by a qualified majority,[28] the relevant article 18 TEU (ex art. J(8)2) requires unanimity for a resolution on a "joint action" in the sense of a framing measure of common defense policy. Such a resolution is the precondition for the Council to take the "necessary actions,"[29] such as imposing an embargo. This legal position allows Austria a veto in the case of a conflict with its neutral status.

Furthermore, article 14 TEU (ex art. J(4)) envisages the integration of the Western European Union (WEU) into the development of the EU. But since at the moment this provision contains no specific obligations for EU member states, but merely states a programmatic objective, there is no contradiction with obligations arising from neutrality.

The EU was initially suspicious about neutral applicants, especially Austria, which was the only state to expressly include the maintenance of its neutrality in its application. By 1994, however, the EU dropped its opposition in favor of a profitable enlargement.

In many countries, accession to the EU led to a discussion whether such an important decision was to be made by elected representatives in parliament or should rather be submitted to a popular vote. In the case of Austria, the latter approach was mandated under constitutional law. Article 44 (3) of the Constitution provides for a mandatory referendum in the case of a total revision of the Constitution. Austrian constitutional doctrine provides that the elimination or serious modification of one of the fundamental structural principles of the Constitution amounts to a total revision. According to the official view, Austria's accession to the EU affected four of these principles: the democratic principle due to the massive transfer of legislative powers to EU

---

[27] In other words, the existing legislation of European Community organs.
[28] Art. 133 TEC (ex art. 113).
[29] Art. 301 TEC (ex art. 228a).

organs; the rule of law principle (*Rechtsstaat*), *inter alia*, because the European Court of Justice of the EC will have ultimate authority to judge the conformity of Austrian law with superior EU law; the separation of powers principle due to a distribution of functions among the organs of the Union which differs from the classical (state-oriented) model underlying the Austrian Constitution; and the federal principle because European Union membership reduces the powers of the Austrian *Länder*.

On June 12, 1994, a referendum regarding Austria's membership in the EU was held. Accession was opposed by the Freedom Party, the Greens, the Communists, several tabloids, and various grass-roots movements. They claimed that membership would produce negative effects on Austrian agriculture and food processing, transit, and the environment. These groups believed that Austrian sovereignty, neutrality, and national identity would be threatened by an undemocratic, centralized, and bureaucratic monster in Brussels. Nevertheless, a two-thirds majority voted in favor of the EU and approved the Austrian Accession Law,[30] which authorized the competent constitutional organs to conclude the Treaty of Accession.[31] On June 24, 1994, Austria signed the accession agreement with the EU, which became effective on January 1, 1995.[32] Austria ceased to be a member of the EFTA.[33]

VI. Legal Effects of Austria's EU Membership

A. Austrian Representation in Organs of the EU

In the Accession Treaty,[34] Austria obtained a number of positions in the decision-making and consultative bodies of the EU. Depending on the matter under discussion, Austria will be represented by the Federal Chancellor or the competent minister in the Council.[35] Franz Fischler, former Minister of Agriculture, was appointed Commissioner for Agriculture and Rural Develop-

---

[30] *BVG über den Beitritt Österreichs zur Europäischen Union, BGBl* 1994/744.

[31] Article 1: "With the consent of the people of the Federation to this Federal Constitutional Law the constitutionally competent organs are authorized to conclude the Treaty concerning Austria's accession to the European Union according to the results of negotiations formulated by the accession conference on April 12, 1994."

[32] At that date, Austria also acquired observer status at the WEU.

[33] Since Sweden and Finland joined the EU together with Austria, only Norway, Switzerland, Liechtenstein and Iceland remain in the EFTA. In a referendum on May 21, 2000, 67% of Swiss voters approved seven bilateral agreements aiming at closer cooperation between Switzerland and the EU in the spheres of free movement of persons, air and overland transport, agriculture, technical barriers to trade, public procurement markets, and research.

[34] OJ 1995 Nr. L 1, 1; *BGBl* 1995/45.

[35] Austria has four of a total of 87 votes in a weighted voting process. The initial dispute, whether the Federal President or the Federal Chancellor had the right to participate in the European Council, was decided in favor of the Chancellor.

ment,[36] while an Austrian judge was appointed to the Court of Justice and to the Court of First Instance, respectively.[37] Austrian members were appointed to the Court of Auditors and to the Board of Governors of the European Investment Bank. Twenty-one Austrian deputies serve in the European Parliament,[38] twelve members each represent Austrian interests in the Economic and Social Committee (ECOSOC)[39] and in the Committee of the Regions (COR).[40]

Austria's Permanent Representative to the EU participates in COREPER II, while his deputy is active in COREPER I.[41] The Permanent Representative is an ambassador who receives his instructions from the Minister of Foreign Affairs, the Federal Chancellor (who coordinates EU affairs overall) or from individual ministers. The Permanent Mission in Brussels has a staff of approximately 100 persons. Every Austrian ministry is represented by one or more officials. All *Länder*, except Vorarlberg, have opened their own liaison offices in Brussels for the purpose of information gathering and lobbying. Tirol maintains a joint mission with the Italian provinces of South Tirol (Alto Adige) and Trentino.

While quotas for administrative personnel are not determined by law, EU staff regulations call for "geographical balance." Therefore, applicants for staff positions from the three new members admitted in 1995 received preferential treatment in the past years. As far as the sizeable civil service of the Commission is concerned (approximately 20,000 employees), the informal goal to have approximately 400 Austrians in place by the year 2000 has been accomplished.[42]

---

[36] Fischler was reappointed in 1999 as Commissioner for Agriculture, Rural Development and Fisheries.

[37] Dr. Peter Jann, a former member of the Austrian Constitutional Court, was appointed to the Court of Justice. He was reappointed in 2000. Dr. Josef Azizi was appointed to the Court of First Instance. As of October 2000, Dr. Christine Stix-Hackl will serve as Advocate General.

[38] The Parliament consists of 626 deputies. The Austrian deputies, elected on June 13, 1999, represent the following parties: *SPÖ* 7 (1996: 6), *ÖVP* 7 (7), *FPÖ* 5 (6), Greens 2 (1) and *LIF* 0 (1).

[39] They represent the following institutions: Federal Chamber of Labor (2), Austrian Labor Union Federation (3), Association for Consumer Information (1), Conference of Presidents of Chambers of Agriculture (2), Economic Chamber of Austria (3), and Federal Conference of the Liberal Professions (1).

[40] The COR has a total of 222 members. There is one representative from each of the nine Austrian *Länder*, and three representatives from the Federation of Cities and Municipalities.

[41] See *supra* II.A.

[42] As of June 2000, the total number of Austrians in the five job categories of the Commission was 415 (A: 182, B: 99, C: 107, D: 9, L: 18). The letters A, B, etc. stand for job qualification requirements, A being the highest (university education and 12 years of professional experience). L stands for linguist. In July 2000, Dr. Edith Kitzmantel was appointed one of 24 Directors General.

B. Financial Consequences

Financially, Austria is a net contributor to the EU, paying approximately one percent of its GDP or 30 billion ATS annually into the budget of the EU.[43] About one-half of this amount flows back to Austria, mainly in the form of agricultural subsidies, to a certain extent also for structural measures (social and regional), as well as for research and development.

C. Political Outlook

In the course of institutional reform of the EU, it may for efficiency reasons no longer be possible to give each state a seat on the Commission and the Court. Austria, as are other small countries, is reluctant to relinquish these presently assured positions. It is likewise afraid of a re-weighting of votes in the Council and other organs in favor of more populated states, and of losing its veto power in a growing number of areas that are proposed for transfer from present unanimous to future majority decisionmaking.

In Austria, like in Germany and some other states, people fear the effects of rapid enlargement of the EU to the East, in particular the influx of migrant workers and cheap agricultural produce, arguing for extended protection and transition periods. Yet overall Austria stands to benefit economically from enlargement due to increased export opportunities. Its government is likely to constructively support the enlargement process.

D. Specific Effects on Austria's Legal System

1. General Observations

Concerning its legal system, Austria undertook to implement the entire primary and secondary law of the EU, including the case law of the European Court of Justice and the Court of First Instance. At the time of accession, this *acquis communautaire* encompassed more than 4,000 EC regulations and more than 1,200 EC directives. This massive body of law affected all branches of the Federation and the *Länder* (legislative, executive, and judicial) regardless of national decentralization.

EC regulations became effective in Austria with its accession to the EU on January 1, 1995. They are immediately binding and override opposing national law. EC directives are to be implemented by national legislation within the specific time-frame envisaged by each individual directive. In Austria, the Federation or the *Länder* are responsible for implementing EC directives, depending on the content of the matter to be regulated. The appropriate regulatory form (statute or regulation) is also determined by the Austrian legal system.

Austria had already shared many legal rules with other European states in the past. This common European legal tradition had been reinforced

---

[43] This amounts to approximately 2.6% of the EU budget.

by legal harmonization, particularly in the areas of international trade and economic cooperation. Since its political re-orientation towards accession to the EC in 1987, the Austrian government had analyzed the need for legal adjustment and had subjected all new draft legislation to an examination concerning compatibility with EC law. For Austria to join the European Economic Area, approximately 60% of the *acquis communautaire* (thousands of legal acts) had to be incorporated into national Austrian laws. This resulted in amendments to a great number of federal statutes and regulations, but also in changes to numerous statutory and other enactments on the *Land* level.

In the years following Austria's accession to the EU, its implementation record regarding EU directives was somewhat disappointing, primarily because of Austria's federal structure.[44]

It will not be attempted to present a complete survey of Austrian law as it has been affected by EU legislation. Examples from significant areas, such as constitutional law, private law, labor law, corporate law and environmental law, should serve as sufficient illustration of the broad scope and profound impact of EU lawmaking.

2. Constitutional Law

a. Constitutional Amendments

Membership in the EU required specific changes in the Austrian Constitution. A new section headed "European Union" was inserted in 1994. It comprises articles 23a to 23f.[45] These amendments address the right to participate in European elections (Const. arts. 23a and 23b), the right of local residents from other EU member states to take part in local elections (see also Const. art. 117 (2)) and the procedure to ensure the participation of Parliament in the process of proposing Austrian nationals for positions in the EU (Const. art. 23c). Articles 23d and 23e of the Constitution provide for the timely information of the *Länder*, the *Nationalrat,* and the *Bundesrat* concerning any projects pursued within the framework of the EU, allowing them the opportunity for input. The Federal Government will be bound by *Länder* comments and may deviate from them only for compelling reasons of foreign or integration policy.

By ratifying the Treaty of Accession, Austria also adopted the Treaty of the European Union and the Treaties of the European Community, the European Coal and Steel Community and the European Atomic Energy Community into Austrian law. Furthermore, the entire existing legislation of Community organs (*acquis communautaire*) came into force in Austria on January 1, 1995. All future EU legislation will be effective in Austria.

---

[44] With an implementation rate of 94.3% by December, 1998, Austria holds rank 9 behind Ireland. Of the other newcomers, Sweden with 97.3% holds rank 1 before Denmark (97%), and Finland with 96.3% holds rank 3. The EC average is 94%; the member state with the lowest implementation rate is Italy (92.5%).

[45] *BGBl* 1994/1013.

b. Supplementary Provisions

A treaty between the Federation and the *Länder* under article 15a of the Constitution (cf. Const. art. 23d (4)) specified the participatory rights of the *Länder* and municipalities in European integration issues.[46] On June 29, 1989, the Austrian Parliament passed a law establishing a Council for Questions of Integration Policy.[47] A government regulation of January 16, 1990, contains detailed provisions concerning this Council.[48] In addition, a treaty among the *Länder* under article 15a addresses the problem of determining common positions of the *Länder* in matters of integration policy.[49]

3. Private Law

The EU Treaties do not generally authorize EU legislation concerning private law. However, such legislation may be necessary in order to ensure the functioning of the Common Market, the observation of fundamental freedoms, the protection against distortion of competition, etc. Article 153 TEC (ex art. 129a) makes consumer protection a specific goal of EU regulation.

The EC has issued directives to protect the consumer in many ways with respect to contracts negotiated away from business premises (*Haustürgeschäfte*), distance contracts, self-employed commercial agents, consumer credit, vehicular civil liability insurance, package travel, legal expenses insurance, property and life insurance, procedures for the award of public supply and public works contracts, as well as procurement procedures of entities operating in the water, energy, transport and telecommunications sector, legal protection of computer programs, unfair terms in consumer contracts, misleading and comparative advertising, etc.[50]

Austrian contract law has been affected by EU law in several respects. The Four Freedoms have led to both a broadening of and restrictions on the freedom to contract. Concerning the former, especially the freedom of movement of goods and services should be mentioned; concerning the latter, antitrust provisions and equal pay for men and women.

In the area of tort law, the EC enacted a regulation establishing common rules for a denied-boarding compensation system in scheduled air trans-

---

[46] *BGBl* 1992/775.
[47] *BGBl* 1989/368.
[48] *BGBl* 1990/53a.
[49] See, e.g., Wien *LGBl* 1992/30.
[50] See, e.g., the new provisions on package travel in *BGBl* II 1998/10 and II 1999/316; directives on consumer protection (distance contracts, comparative advertising) were implemented in the Product Liability Act (cf. *infra* note 52), the Consumer Protection Act 1979, and the Federal Law against Unfair Competition (*Bundesgesetz gegen den unlauteren Wettbewerb* 1984), all of these as amended by the Distance Contract Act of 1999 (*Fernabsatz-Gesetz, BGBl* I 1999/185).

port. Austrian legislation had to be passed[51] in order to implement the EC Product Liability Directive.[52]

The law of property is generally not subject to EU legislation (art. 295 TEC, ex art. 222), but fundamental freedoms may be invoked to prevent ownership restrictions against citizens of member states.

A special problem Austria has to address is land ownership by non-residents. In the accession treaty, Austria obtained a five-year grace period for its restrictive regulation concerning foreign ownership of vacation properties. A joint declaration authorizes member states to take measures of environmental protection and zoning (*Raumordnung*) insofar as these are neither directly nor indirectly discriminatory. The Danish model of land acquisition by foreigners only after five years of residency was not extended to Austria.

In the area of private international law, the members of the EU ratified a Convention on the Law Applicable to Contractual Obligations.[53]

4. Labor Law

Austrian labor law was affected by several rules of the EU, such as the equality principle, the free access of member state citizens to the Austrian labor market, minimum standards of safety and health in the workplace and provisions protecting workers in cases of business takeovers or insolvency.

The Austrian accession treaty includes the following three concessions:

− A joint declaration safeguarding Austria's right to react to potential labor market problems that might arise as a result of its special geographical position.
− A transition period until 2001 concerning Austria's discriminatory prohibition of night labor for women.
− Permission to exclude top management from the scope of the Insolvency Directive.

5. Corporate Law

Corporate law has become largely subject to EU regulation, mostly through directives in areas like publicity, capital protection, mergers and acquisitions, annual and consolidated accounts, single member companies, etc. These directives have led to a considerable harmonization of European corporation law. The EC regulation on the European economic interest grouping has taken a first step towards creating an immediately applicable European corporate law.

---

[51] *Produkthaftungsgesetz BGBl* 1988/99 as amended 1993/95, 1994/510 (regarding genetic engineering) and I 1999/185.
[52] OJ 1985 Nr. L 210, 29.
[53] OJ 1980 Nr. L 266, 1.

6. Environmental Law

Although Austria with its accession to the EU became subject to more demanding rules concerning water quality, noise protection, and clean air,[54] Austrian legislation in many other instances contains higher standards than the EU concerning the use of or traffic in substances affecting the environment. Austria's high level of environmental protection thus clashes with the interest of the EU in the free movement of goods in the internal market. Austria was unable to maintain exceptions in favor of its standards in the Accession Treaty, but managed to achieve a compromise. The EU undertook to review those of its environmental protection norms which were lower than the equivalent Austrian norms during the following period of four years, considering the possibility of raising the EU's environmental protection norms. After that period, it was agreed that the lower EU standards would not be changed but Austria could keep most of its stricter national norms.[55]

Nature conservation (*Naturschutz*) is exclusively within *Länder* competence. There exist nine different *Länder* nature conservation acts. Implementation of EU directives differs – sometimes considerably – from *Land* to *Land*.

In 1998, a Federal Environment Office[56] was established to monitor the enforcement of the provisions intending to protect the environment, to regularly assess Austria's environmental situation, and to cooperate with EU organs. Since 1995, 16 environmental protection projects have been partly financed by the EU's LIFE program.[57]

7. Telecommunications Law

One highly ambitious project of the European Union is the complete liberalization of the telecommunications sector in the member states. Unlike in the U.S., telecommunication services in Europe have traditionally been provided by state owned and operated companies. Liberalization not only entailed the privatization of existing companies, but also the opening of the market for private sector competition. This transition was to be completed by January 1, 1998. To achieve this goal, Austria passed a comprehensive Telecommunications Act in 1997, transforming almost all EU mandates into national law and thus opening its markets in all aspects of telecommunication services. Most

---

[54] Recently, Austria implemented EU directives concerning dangerous waste, cf. *BGBl* I 1999/36, I 1999/38, II 1999/22 and II 1999/32.

[55] In the case of fertilizers, the review process was extended to the year 2001.

[56] The *Umweltbundesamt*, established by the Environment Control Act (*Umweltkontrollgesetz*), *BGBl* I 1998/152. The Environment Information Act (*Umweltinformationsgesetz*), *BGBl* 1993/495, provides for greater public access to environment-related data according to Directive 90/313/EC.

[57] The EU financed 38% (240 million ATS), the remainder (390 million ATS) was financed by Austrian administrative bodies, environmental organizations, and private citizens.

recently, Austria implemented the EU's Open Network Provision (ONP).[58] It also passed legislation concerning electronic signature.[59]

8. Intellectual Property (*Immaterialgüterrecht*)

A goal of the EU is to create a European information society, in which information will become one of the most important economic factors. To this end, the protection of intellectual property has to be strengthened and harmonized throughout the Union. Directives have been passed to harmonize the periods of protection and in particular to extend protection to chip layouts and information databases, thus creating unique new intellectual property rights. Austria has already incorporated these directives into national law.

Literature

General Works

Bermann, G. A. et al., Cases and Materials on European Community Law (1993, 1998 Supplement)
Craig, P., de Burca, G. (eds.), The Evolution of EU Law (1999)
Dinnage, J. D., Murphy, J. F., The Constitutional Law of the European Union (1996, with Documentary Supplement including the EC Treaty and the TEU)
Fischer, P., Köck, H. F., Europarecht (3rd ed. 1997)
Folsom, R. H., European Union Law in a Nutshell (3rd ed. 1999)
Hartley, T. C., The Foundations of European Community Law (4th edition 1998)
Heidinger, F., Introduction to the Law and Language of the European Union (2nd ed. 1998)
Heukels, T. et al., The European Union after Amsterdam: a Legal Analysis (1998)
Hix, S., The Political System of the European Union (1999)
Lenaerts, K. et al., Constitutional Law of the European Union (1999)
MacLean, R. M., Law of the European Union (2nd ed. 1999)
Raisch, M. J., The European Union: A Selective Research Guide, 1 Columbia Journal of European Law 1 (1994–95) 149
Rawlinson, W., Cornwell-Kelly, M., European Community Law (1994)
Rudden, B., Wyatt, D., Basic Community Laws (7th ed. 1999)
Schweitzer, M., Hummer, W., Europarecht (5th ed. 1996)
Steiner, J., Textbook on EC Law (5th ed. 1996)
Tridimas T., The General Principles of EC Law (1999)
Weatherill, S., Beaumont, P., EC Law (3rd ed. 1999)
Weiler, J., The Constitution of Europe: "Do the New Clothes Have an Emperor?" and Other Essays on European Integration (1999)

Court of Justice

Anderson, D. W. K., References to the European Court of Justice (1995)
Arnull, A., The European Union and its Court of Justice (1999)

---

[58] Directive 98/10/EC, *BGBl* I 2000/26 and Directive 98/34/EC, *BGBl* II 2000/30.

[59] *Signaturgesetz BGBl* I 1999/190 and *Signaturverordnung BGBl* II 2000/30.

Barceló, J. J., Precedent in European Community Law, in *MacCormick, D. N.,*
Summers R. S. (eds.), Interpreting Precedents: A Comparative Study (1997) 407
Brown, L. N., Kennedy T., The Court of Justice of the European Communities (4th ed.
1994)
Edward, D., How the Court of Justice Works, European Law Review 20 (1995) 539
Grimm, D., The European Court of Justice and National Courts: The German
Constitutional Perspective after the Maastricht Decision, Columbia Journal of
European Law 3 (1997) 229
Hakenberg, W., Stix-Hackl, C., Handbuch zum Verfahren vor dem Europäischen
Gerichtshof (2nd ed. 2000)
Hunnings, N. M., The European Courts (1996)
Lasok, K. P. E., The European Court of Justice: Practice and Procedure (2nd ed. 1994)
Mac Cormick, N., Questioning Sovereignty: Law, State, and Nation in the European
Commonwealth (1999)
Mancini, G. F., Keeling, D. T., Language, Culture and Politics in the Life of the
European Court of Justice, Columbia Journal of European Law 1 (1994–95) 397
Reichelt, G. (ed.), Vorabentscheidungsverfahren vor dem Gerichtshof der Europäischen
Gemeinschaft (1998)
Schima, B., Das Vorabentscheidungsverfahren vor dem EuGH (1997)
Schima, B., Zur Wirkung von Auslegungsentscheidungen des Gerichtshofes der Euro-
päischen Gemeinschaften, in *Feldner, B., Forgó, N. (eds.)*, Norm und Entscheidung.
Prolegomena zu einer Theorie des Falls (2000) 280
Slaughter, A.-M. et al. (eds.), The European Court and National Courts – Doctrine and
Jurisprudence (1998)
Tridimas, T., The Court of Justice and Judicial Activism, European Law Review 21
(1996) 199

Austria and the EU

Breuss, F., Austria's Approach Towards the European Union (1996)
Gobel, R. J., The European Union Grows: The Constitutional Impact of the Accession
of Austria, Finland and Sweden, Fordham International Law Journal 18 (1995) 1092
Griller, S., Verfassungsfragen der österreichischen EU-Mitgliedschaft, ZfRV 36 (1995)
89
Holzinger, G., Auswirkungen der österreichischen EU-Mitgliedschaft auf das öster-
reichische Verfassungsrecht, ÖJZ 1996, 264
Hummer, W., Schweitzer, M. (eds.), Österreich und das Recht der Europäischen Union
(1997)
Jorna, M., The Accession Negotiations with Austria, Sweden, Finland and Norway: A
Guided Tour, European Law Review 20 (1995) 131
Neuhold, H., Perspectives of Austria's Membership in the European Union, German
Yearbook of International Law 37 (1995) 9
Österreichische Juristenkommission (ed.), Österreich als Mitglied der EU. Kritik und
Fortschritt im Rechtsstaat (1999)
Ofner, H., Zivilrechtsakte der EU – Stand der Umsetzung, ecolex 1994, 223
Schambeck, H., Europäische Integration und Föderalismus, ÖJZ 1996, 521
Thun-Hohenstein, C., Cede, F., Europarecht: Das Recht der EU unter besonderer
Berücksichtigung der EU-Mitgliedschaft Österreichs (3rd ed. 1999)
White Book of the Austrian Federal Government: Austria in the European Union
(1995)

Chapter 5

Legal Education and Legal Professions

I. Legal Education

A. Introduction

Legal education is very much a product of a particular legal system, based on its institutional and functional characteristics, its cultural traditions, and its perceived future needs. Yet when Americans look at European legal education or, conversely, Europeans observe American law schools, they frequently ignore this fundamental caveat.

Americans generally label European legal education misleadingly as "undergraduate." They disparagingly refer to legal education in the Civil law world as intellectually boring, because professors are said to deliver systematic lectures, leaving little room for discussion, and to force students to memorize multitudes of black letter rules, constraining them to simplistic thought patterns of logical deduction from the language of the codes. They often flaunt a sense of (justifiable) pride and (less appropriate) superiority on account of the indisputable intellectual richness of their law teachers and student bodies, the highly refined Socratic method of case analysis, the active role of the student in the learning process, the interdisciplinary involvement of legal scholarship, and the in-depth exploration of relationships between law, economics, and social policy in the classroom.

Lawyers from the world of the Civil law, on the other hand, frequently fail to appreciate the sophistication of American legal education, tending to assess the Socratic method – at least when it extends beyond the first year of law school – as a massive overkill and a waste of precious classroom time that could be put to better use. They criticize the lack of structure in American legal education after the completion of the first year, a system which permits the student to finish law school with as much or as little knowledge of the law as he pleases.

Both perceptions are exaggerated and accordingly incorrect. These views, however, may be the result of a more basic misunderstanding than that of lawyers less familiar with a foreign system using their own limited national legal experience as a frame of comparative reference. These observers tend to view foreign legal education in the abstract, neglecting its particular premises and goals, and thus unhesitatingly proclaiming its failure to meet "the test."

On an abstract level, there is indeed much to be said in favor of the American model of legal education, which addresses itself to select groups of mature students who have gone through the social integration processes (such as clubs and sports) of an American high school and have subsequently received a relatively general academic college education prior to their rigorous specialization in law school. But this system is the product of specific American social structures and needs. It may not be exportable, because it might not be functional in a different context. In other words, legal education anywhere must be viewed in the light of the secondary and non-professional education that precedes it, the professional on-the-job training that follows it, and the functions and opportunities of law graduates in a specific society.

On the secondary school level (the English grammar school, the French *lycée*, and the German or Austrian *Gymnasium*), European educational systems are much more selective and academically oriented than their American counterpart. There is no equivalent to the American college. Academically well-prepared secondary school graduates, with an ample grounding in math, sciences, humanities, and at least two foreign languages, immediately enter university specialization in fields such as law and medicine at age 18 or 19. Graduation from European secondary schools is not automatic, but subject to often very demanding and competitive final examinations. Because of this tradition of academic excellence in secondary education, many European countries do not administer university entrance exams. Thus, in Austria, any secondary school graduate may be admitted to the study of law.

B. Context and Goals of Austrian Legal Education

The Austrian approach to legal education, similar to the German and to that of many other European systems, emphasizes the notion that every future lawyer should receive a broad and uniform legal education in law school; that law should be studied in the context of history and social sciences; that method should be taught on a firm foundation of substance; that theory should precede practice; and that practice should be taught by those who know it best – the practitioners.

Instruction in law school in part is based on the lecture method, but there is no attendance requirement for these lectures (*Vorlesungen*). The Austrian notion of "academic freedom" still incorporates elements of the 19th century university ideal in which "*Lehrfreiheit*" (freedom to teach) on the part of the professor was accompanied by "*Lernfreiheit*" (freedom to choose and organize his studies) on the part of the student. However, students are not only offered the opportunity, but to some extent even forced to participate in small sections (*Übungen*) in which cases are analyzed and discussed. The European emphasis on the "professorial" or "judicial" approach to the study of law at the expense of the more advocacy-oriented training that one finds in American law schools is easily explained in terms of different cultural traditions and system requirements. A few years ago, Austria, a country of approximately eight million inhabitants, had only 2,200 practicing attorneys, but many thousands of law graduates worked as civil servants in federal, state, or municipal bureaucracies. Although the "lawyers' monopoly" in the higher level civil service positions has been weakened in the last 20 years, lawyers in government service still have ample opportunities of heading non-legal departments and recruiting more of their own.

Austria has a statute-based legal system, in which comprehensive and systematic codes have for many years provided stable rules in areas like private and criminal law, as well as for civil and criminal procedure. Austria may also be described as an "administrative state," a modern welfare state with detailed government-imposed regulations in all areas of life. According to article 18 (1) of the Austrian Constitution, all administrative activity must be based on statutory law. Administrative discretion is checked by this overambitious "legality principle" and subjected to administrative and ultimately judicial review. One of the primary aims of legal education is to train judicial and administrative personnel to operate a complex legal machinery on the basis of respect for the statutes of the legislature, the administrative regulations enacted by the executive on their basis, and the interpretation given to these legal acts by the supreme courts. Courts have no overt lawmaking function; they are to be faithful servants of the statutory law. All actors in the law-making and law-application process defer to the professional authority of the law professors, relying heavily on academic expert advice supplied *ad hoc* or enshrined in leading systematic treatises or multivolume commentaries.

At this point, one should probably add that Austrian jurisprudence and legal style, although having profited from Hans Kelsen's Pure Theory of Law (*Reine Rechtslehre*) and rigorous legalism, has not been overwhelmed by his extremely positivist and normativist approach. Legal science and legal practice show sufficient creative spirit in shaping the law according to fundamental constitutional values, particularly in the protection of civil rights.

C. Austrian Law Schools

Higher education in Austria occurs in universities operated or at least supervised by the federal government.[1] Almost all are fully financed by the state and enjoy limited autonomy. Most professors and other staff are federal civil servants or employees. Of the five Austrian law schools (*rechtswissenschaftliche Fakultäten*) which are part of this system, three have existed for centuries: the University of Vienna, founded as the second German-speaking university in 1365 (after Prague in 1348), Graz, established in 1585, and Innsbruck University, founded in 1669, and its law school in 1673. Two new law schools were founded in 1965 in Salzburg and in Linz. Approximately 42% of Austrian law students study in Vienna, 22% in Graz, 15% in Innsbruck, 10% in Salzburg, and 11% Linz.[2]

---

[1] Since 1999, it has become possible to establish privately operated universities under the supervision of a special commission and the Federal Minister of Education, Science, and Culture.

[2] In the 1999–2000 academic year, no fewer than 9,811 students were registered in Vienna; 5,216 in Graz; 3,414 in Innsbruck; 2,287 in Salzburg; and 2,512 in Linz.

Within the general context of detailed federal university legislation (particularly the statutes concerning university organization and studies, *Universitäts-Organisationsgesetz 1975* and *Allgemeines Hochschul-Studiengesetz 1966*), the study of law was over-regulated on three tiers: the Federal Law on the Study of Law (1978), the Regulation of the Minister of Science and Research concerning the Study of Law (1979) and the regulations issued by the curriculum committees of individual law schools, such as the Plan of Studies at the School of Law, University of Vienna, adopted in 1981. Since the Federal Law was extremely detailed, there remained little room for autonomous regulation at the law school level.

This situation profoundly changed under a new statute on university organization (*Universitäts-Organisationsgesetz 1993*), which gave universities and faculties more autonomy. A new statute on university studies (*Universitäts-Studiengesetz 1997*) defined a framework of eight semesters and between 100 and 125 credit hours, at least 23 of which must be reserved for electives. Everything else, including subjects of instruction, credit hours, and examination procedures, is to be determined by the curriculum committees of the individual law schools, composed of an equal number of professors, non-tenured teaching staff, and students.

D. The Vienna Law Curriculum

In March 1999, the Curriculum Committee of the University of Vienna Law School, consisting of four tenured professors, four members of instructional staff below professorial rank, and four students, approved a new curriculum. It went into effect on October 1, 1999, the Ministry of Science and Transport not having exercised its right to expressly forbid its implementation (e.g., for lack of funds or violation of legal provisions). Within the legal framework of the University Studies Act, Vienna opted for the upper limit of 125 credit hours. Vienna also opted in favor of the maximum permissible mandatory program of 102 credit hours. Of the remaining 23 hours for electives, 13 may be freely chosen from offerings in and outside the law school, 10 (again the permissible maximum) must be chosen by students from courses offered in the law school itself.

One primary goal of the reform was to reduce the time needed by average students to complete law school by radically reducing the course load, offering courses in coordinated clusters, and abolishing the partial duplication of exams. New subjects introduced are EU Law and Tax Law. Unfortunately, other important requirements had to be dropped: Management Science, Economic Policy, and Sociology have only been retained as electives.

The reform abandoned the existing structure of legal studies into two segments (of two and six semesters, respectively) and reverted to an older model of three distinct groupings of subjects, each of which is to be concluded with a "diploma examination" before the student may enter the next segment of studies.

The first segment comprises two semesters. It includes as mandatory subjects Introduction to Legal Science and its Methods (six credit hours, written exam), Criminal Law and Criminal Procedure (nine credit hours, oral exam), Roman Private Law (six credit hours, written exam) and Austrian and European Legal History (six credit hours, oral exam).

The second segment comprises three semesters. Mandatory subjects are Private Law (16 credits), Commercial, Corporate and Securities Law (seven credits), Labor and Social Law (six credits), and Civil Procedure (seven credits). Students must pass written and oral exams in Private Law. All other exams are oral only. Since Private Law provides the foundation for understanding the other subjects in this cluster, professors would have liked to impose a requirement to pass the two examinations in Private Law before students are admitted to any other exam in this segment. As a compromise with student members in the Curriculum Committee, however, students must take at least one of the two exams in Private Law before they are admitted to exams in two of the remaining subjects.

The third segment also comprises three semesters. It may be taken before entering the second at the student's choice. It includes Constitutional Law (seven credits), Administrative Law and Procedure (10 credits), Tax (three credits), European Union Law (three credits), and Public International Law (four credits). In Constitutional Law and Administrative Law, students must take one oral and one written exam at their choice. The Tax exam is written; all other exams are oral.

The new curriculum also requires a diploma thesis. It consists of two seminar papers, one of which should be interdisciplinary. To develop skills in case analysis, students are required to attend six small sections (two per segment). In EU Law and Public International Law, small sections must also be offered in foreign languages. Every student must attend at least one two-hour course in a foreign language. Moot court training and internships are to be offered. The reformers decided against permitting specialization in various branches of the law (e.g., public law) but offered no fewer than 20 "baskets" of related electives, for which students may obtain recognition in the form of special certificates.

Among the positive accomplishments of the reform one might list the reduction in the number of credit hours needed for graduation by approximately one quarter to 125, and the increase of electives included in that number from previously eight credits to the present 23. EU Law and Tax Law have been elevated to the status of mandatory subjects; the number of diploma exams in the public law area was reduced.[3] It is certainly a good idea to require students to pass Private Law before they take exams in Commercial Law, Labor Law, and Civil Procedure. It also makes sense to fulfill a diploma thesis

---

[3] Previously Constitutional Law and Administrative Law were both examined in written and oral form, now there is one written and one oral exam at the student's choice.

requirement by submitting two substantial seminar papers, one of which should be interdisciplinary.

Negative aspects include the still insufficient coordination between coursework and examination, a curriculum structure based on an obsolescent private law/public law dichotomy, a limited number of elective credits that will make it difficult for students to study one of their four years abroad, and above all a fundamental lack of funds to implement the forward-looking parts of the reform in the fields of electives and practice orientation.

Ideally, law studies last eight semesters, but few students finish within this time frame. The state provides financial aid and charges no tuition, and there is a high failure rate in the progressively more demanding course of studies. In 1997–98, Vienna graduated 707 students with the basic law degree of *Magister iuris* (*Mag.iur.*).[4] Austrian law graduates have only recently begun to face employment problems due to personnel reductions in the federal bureaucracy. Most of them serve a nine-month clerkship in different federal courts before entering into a specialized bureaucratic, judicial, or prosecutorial civil service career, becoming associates in a law firm, or taking positions in the economy. Many large corporations still hire law graduates on an equal footing with MBAs and find that law graduates generally do equally well in management careers. After several years of practice in an attorney's office, associates must pass a comprehensive and difficult bar examination. Lawyers in the judicial service take an equivalent judges' exam, and lawyers in the civil service, an administrative exam, in order to be fully qualified for their respective legal practice.

Roughly 20% of the graduates set their sights on obtaining a higher law degree, the doctorate (*Dr.iur.*).[5] This requires additional coursework (seminars) and examinations in three subjects (*Rigorosen*). The focus is on the preparation of a publishable thesis (*Dissertation*) in book form under the supervision of one or two faculty members. The doctorate is a requirement for entering a law teaching career, but not for any other legal profession.[6]

---

[4] Only about one-third of the number of entering students will eventually graduate. The following numbers were reported for 1995–96: Vienna 1829 entering (562 graduating); Graz 733 (255); Innsbruck 574 (223); Salzburg 419 (182); Linz 459 (89). In 1996–97 the numbers of entering students dropped considerably in all Austrian law schools, most dramatically (by almost one-third) in Vienna. The downward trend in first year registrations continued in 1997–998: Vienna 966, Graz 425, Innsbruck 378, Salzburg 247, Linz 281. The situation seems to have stabilized at this level. The first year figures for 1999–2000 are Vienna 1,033, Graz 418, Innsbruck 336, Salzburg 238, Linz 283. The number of graduates will, therefore, significantly decline in future years.

[5] The number of doctorates awarded in the 1997–98 academic year was 154 in Vienna, 30 in Graz, 72 in Innsbruck, 76 in Salzburg, and 26 in Linz.

[6] Since 1999, the Vienna Law School has also been offering a postgraduate program on Information Law (http://www.informationsrecht.at).

E. Problems and Prospects

One should not disguise or gloss over several flaws of the Austrian system. A government-imposed free admissions policy that rules out the administration of a law-specific aptitude test has become very wasteful from both a financial and a psychological point of view. It has ideological roots in a misconceived Socialist "equal opportunity" policy, which is likely to be discontinued in the course of the European integration process. Professors could accomplish more for a smaller number of students, when they could apply some highly successful American teaching techniques. Under the Law on University Studies 1997, law schools have more autonomy in determining which subjects they should teach, and students are given more than a merely marginal choice in their curriculum. There is, of course, a continuing debate about the best possible utilization of the first year of law school. Teaching techniques are likely to move away from massive memorization of black letter law and instead emphasize method over substance, develop interdisciplinary approaches, devote more attention to the development of advocacy skills, and become generally more practice-oriented.

Despite some obvious shortcomings, the Austrian system has been remarkably successful. The examination structure forces students to reach a level of competence in both written and oral work. They must acquire not only broad knowledge but also specific research skills in virtually all major areas of the law. They leave law school with a wealth of well-defined and carefully related legal concepts, structures, and theories that provide both a framework for future reference and ample material for creative application in subsequent national or international legal practice. Consequently, they find it easy to specialize quickly in their various professional lives. Looking back on their studies, most Austrian law graduates concede that they also profited considerably from their initially often unappreciated exposure to "cultural" subjects like legal philosophy and legal history. Perhaps they value even more the comparative law experience offered in Roman law classes that make them aware not only of the common roots of most European legal systems but also alert them to the value judgments made and techniques of legal reasoning used over the last 2000 years. When Vienna law students make use of exchange agreements with other European law schools to study abroad, taking subjects such as international law or EC law in cities like Paris, Dijon, Louvain, Utrecht, Bologna, or Madrid, they find no difficulty in communicating with foreign law professors and students. They write excellent exams and receive full credit on their returning to Austria. Austrian law graduates compete well with other Europeans in American graduate programs (which offer an invaluable experience to anyone from the Civil law world), and they succeed in American bar examinations and law firms.

Even though a cynic might observe that the brightest minds can cope with any system, there should be little doubt that the Austrian system of legal education has been capable of producing well-qualified legal personnel to satisfy all practical needs in Austria and elsewhere. In 1995, Austria became a member of the European Union, in which countries operate under Council directives concerning mutual recognition of diplomas and admission to professional practice in a European market of 380 million people. The Vienna law faculty arranges courses in legal English, French, Spanish, and Italian, mindful of the stated European goal that every future professional have a working knowledge of two foreign languages. The faculty also regularly invites foreign law professors to teach courses about their legal systems in English or French. As the European Court of Justice in Luxembourg vigorously promotes the unification of European law, Austria need not fear for the future of its law graduates in the legal world of the twenty-first century.

II. Legal Professions

A. Law Teachers

1. Law School Organization

All law schools are headed by deans (*Dekane*). They are elected for four-year terms by the respective faculties (*Fakultätskollegien*) from lists of three candidates proposed by the university president (*Rektor*). They have limited administrative and financial powers. In particular, they have no influence on the hiring of professors and their salaries. The organization and evaluation of studies and examinations is supervised by a dean of studies (*Studiendekan*). The operative structure of the law schools is by departments (*Institute*), each of which is responsible for organizing teaching and research in particular areas, such as Roman Law, Private Law, Criminal Law, or International Law. Department heads are elected for two-year terms by department meetings composed of teachers and students. They have a small budget for equipment and operating expenses and some administrative control over non-professorial staff. Most departments operate with collegial consensus of the tenured professors. The latter spearhead the effective units of academic work, supervising and coordinating the teaching and administrative staff (typically one to three full-time graduate assistants and a secretary) attached to them by departmental decision.

2. Academic Qualification and Career

The road to a tenured position as professor of law is long and arduous. It begins with a requirement that does not exist for other legal professions: the graduate degree of *Dr. iur.* (*Doktor der Rechtswissenschaften*) which is based on the publication of a book, namely, a doctoral thesis (*Dissertation*) containing original research. Many law graduates aspiring to an academic career never leave the university, except perhaps to serve a judicial clerkship. They accept salaried positions as full time teaching and research assistants

(*Universitätsassistenten*)[7] and prepare for their *Habilitation* or *venia legendi* – the full academic teaching qualification as *Universitätsdozent* (roughly comparable to an American non-tenured associate professor). This step requires the publication of a substantial book reflecting high-quality research, and the evaluation of research and teaching skills by a special faculty committee with the help of outside experts. Some of these *Universitätsdozenten* remain on the law school staff and in this case receive the title of associate professor (*außerordentlicher Universitätsprofessor*), while others begin the practice of law and continue to teach as part-time lecturers.[8]

Tenured positions of full professors (*Universitätsprofessoren*) are part of the state budget and difficult to increase.[9] Appointment is subject to international advertising of the position, evaluation of applicants by a faculty committee, and the submission of three names to the university president (*Rektor*). He decides with which candidate he and the respective dean will negotiate.

Professors usually are civil servants who are subject to a fixed pay scale,[10] similar to that of high judges or administrative officials, and retire at age 65.[11] They are on average highly productive scholars and respected as experts and consultants in all fields of law application and law reform. Due to the limited Austrian "market," many of them have been promoted within their own law schools, but a fair number of them are recruited from other Austrian law schools, and some also from abroad (Germany and Switzerland).

B. Judges

As of January 2000, 1,654 judges (*Richter*) were active in the Austrian court system. In addition, 223 trainees aspired to become judges. Most of the judges work in District and Regional courts, 169 in the four Courts of Appeals, and 57 in the Supreme Court. Approximately 40% of them work in criminal courts. The number of women in the judiciary has been steadily rising. Whereas in 1969 of 1,303 judges only 20 were women, by 1989 this number had risen to 281 out of 1,575. Today approximately 35% of all Austrian judges are women; of 22 recentcly appointed new judges, 16 were women.

---

[7] There were 135 of them in Vienna in the 1999–2000 academic year, yet some of these positions are divided into half-time jobs.

[8] In 1999–2000, in Vienna the respective numbers were 23 and 14.

[9] The following numbers of tenured professors worked in Austrian law schools in 1999–2000: Vienna 49; Graz 32; Innsbruck 28; Salzburg 34; Linz 25.

[10] The starting salary of a tenured professor is approximately 45,000 ATS (supplements included, 14 times a year), the final salary is approximately 100,000 ATS per month.

[11] Exceptionally at age 68.

1. Requirements for Appointment

A candidate for judicial appointment in Austria must graduate from law school with the basic law degree of *Mag.iur.* and complete a subsequent nine-month clerkship ("*Gerichtsjahr*") in three different types of courts. Up to this point, requirements are equal for prospective judges and attorneys. But future judges must then pass an examination to be proposed by the President of the Court of Appeals to the Minister of Justice for appointment as judicial trainee (*Richteramtsanwärter*). The Minister is not bound by this nomination and does not always heed it.

Appointment as judicial trainee is followed by an additional training period in different courts, the prosecutor's office, a law firm, and a penal institution.[12] After a total traineeship of four years (including the initial judicial clerkship), the judges' examination (*Richteramtsprüfung*) may be taken. It consists of a written part which covers civil and criminal law, and an oral part including eight subjects.[13] An examination commission functions at every Court of Appeals (*Oberlandesgericht*). A failed exam may be repeated once. After the examination, the trainee is to be employed, as far as possible, in independent work until he has competed successfully for appointment to a judicial position.

2. Judicial Appointment

Judges are appointed on the basis of applications submitted by them for open positions. These applications are screened by personnel panels (*Personalsenate*) which subsequently make nominating proposals to the Minister of Justice. Personnel panels exist at the Regional Courts, the Courts of Appeals and the Supreme Court. They consist of the President and the Vice-Presidents of the respective courts *ex officio* and additional members elected by their peers in a secret vote. The number of these elected members must be greater by one than the number of the *ex officio* members. A proposal for a vacant position should contain at least three names. If several vacancies are to be filled at the same time, the number of candidates must be at least twice the number of openings. The nomination must be based on qualifications, and in case of equal qualifications, the law requires preferential treatment for women; otherwise the decision is based on seniority. The proposals must be substantiated by reasons. Although they are not binding on the Government or the Minister, in practice they are invariably respected.

Proposals for nomination of judges in District and Regional Courts are made by the personnel panels in the Regional Courts; for presidents and

---

[12] Obligatory training stations include at least one year at a District or Regional Court, five months each in the prosecutor's office and in a law firm, and three weeks in a penal institution. Optional stations are other courts, the Ministry of Justice (no more than six months), and a parole office (no more than four weeks).

[13] Private law including labor law; commercial law (including corporate, securities, and competition law); civil procedure; criminal law; constitutional law; judicial service law; judicial process; and the structure and organization of courts.

vice-presidents of Regional Courts and judges of Courts of Appeals, proposals are submitted by the personnel panels in the Courts of Appeals. The personnel panel of the Supreme Court proposes presidents and vice-presidents of Courts of Appeals and judges of the Supreme Court. No proposals by personnel panels are made for the positions of president and vice-presidents of the Supreme Court. The most highly qualified judges may reach the Court of Appeals level before the age of 40, and the Supreme Court in their mid-40s.

Judges are appointed by the Federal President upon the proposal of the Federal Government. Both the President and the Government may delegate their respective functions to the Minister of Justice.[14]

3. Independence and Supervision

In the exercise of their judicial office, judges are independent and are not bound by any instructions. In principle, they may not be removed, except by order of a criminal, service, or disciplinary court. But all judges must retire at age 65.

Courts of Appeals function as disciplinary courts (*Disziplinarge-richte*) of one of their adjoining circuits (e.g., Vienna for Graz and vice versa) for all judges below the rank of president and vice-president of a Regional Court. For the latter as well as for all judges on Courts of Appeals and the Supreme Court, the Supreme Court functions as disciplinary court. The disciplinary court consists of a five member panel. It becomes active in cases of breach of duty (e.g., violation of official secrecy, acceptance of gifts, and absenteeism) and imposes penalties ranging from admonition to dismissal. In 1995, a total of 27 disciplinary cases were handled by the five disciplinary courts.[15] Like other civil servants, judges are dismissed if they are sentenced to more than one year of imprisonment for an intentional crime.

The service court (*Dienstgericht*) has the same composition as the disciplinary court. It may become active when a judge is suspected of being physically or mentally incapable of performing his duties or when a judge's work has been evaluated as "insufficient" for three consecutive years. This evaluation is made by a personnel panel and ranges from "excellent" to "very good," "good," "sufficient," and "insufficient." Judges are evaluated annually until their performance is rated at least "good" (meaning average). In either of the two situations mentioned, the service court will ask the judge to apply for retirement. If the judge refuses, proceedings will be initiated that may result in the judge's forced retirement (with full pay).

4. Judicial Salary

A judge's income consists of his salary (*Gehalt*), a (nominal) expense allowance (*Aufwandsentschädigung*) and in some cases, for example as a court president, a service supplement (*Dienstzulage*). At the trial court level, begin-

---

[14] See article 67 (1) of the Constitution and *BGBl* 1995/54.
[15] Most cases concerned excessive procedural delays.

ning salaries are currently 38,000 ATS per month (fourteen times a year), with maximum salaries at 71,000 ATS per month. The expense allowance is 500 ATS, and the additional monthly supplements range from 1,561 to 5,306 ATS.[16]

5. Continuing Education

More than 60 continuing legal education opportunities are available to judges every year. Some of them are organized exclusively by institutions within the realm of the Ministry of Justice, some in collaboration with others. They cover a broad range of topics. For instance, there is an annual criminal law seminar, and there are regular seminars for judges specializing in labor and social law, lease law, and family law. Annual international seminars are held for judges, lawyers, and experts in the fields of construction and traffic accidents. Increasingly, European Union law is featured in continuing legal education programs. Interest of judges in these offerings is generally high.

C. Prosecutors

The Prosecutor's Office is a separate authority independent from the court. Its main function is that of public prosecution in criminal trials. Unlike judges, prosecutors (*Staatsanwälte*) are not independent but subject to instructions of their superiors. Just like judges, however, prosecutors are under a duty to be objective and explore substantive truth. They are obligated to take circumstances that exonerate the defendant into account.

Only judges with at least one year of judicial experience may be appointed as prosecutors. The Prosecutor's Offices at various levels of the court structure form personnel panels that submit proposals to the Minister of Justice for the appointment of prosecutors. In June 2000, the number of prosecutors was 209.[17]

The salary scheme for prosecutors is similar to that for judges. Monthly salaries range from 40,000 to 107,000 ATS, with an expense allowance of 500 to 620 ATS.

D. Attorneys

1. Training and Examination

Prior to 1992, law graduates had to submit to a seven-year training period before being permitted to practice on their own. At least five of these

---

[16] The salary range for judges on the Courts of Appeals is 60,000 to 85,000 ATS, with an expense allowance of 620 ATS and possible supplements of 9,000 ATS. Supreme Court judges receive between 81,000 and 107,000. The President of a Court of Appeals receives a total monthly compensation of 118,000 ATS, the President of the Supreme Court receives 131,000 ATS.

[17] Another 50 prosecutors are working in administrative positions in the Ministry of Justice.

seven years had to be spent working in a law firm in Austria. Since this apprenticeship considerably exceeded the European average, in 1992 it was shortened to five years that included a minimum of nine months clerkship at the courts and three years in an Austrian law firm.[18]

After at least three years of practice in Austria[19] and some continuing legal education supervised by the Bar,[20] candidates may sit for the bar examination (*Rechtsanwaltsprüfung*). It consists of a written part covering private, administrative, and criminal law, and an oral part covering nine subjects.[21] The examination is administered by the Court of Appeals, with each examination panel composed of two high-ranking judges and two attorneys.

Foreign attorneys generally may not practice in Austria. Attorneys who are citizens of European Economic Area countries but who do not reside in Austria may perform legal services on a limited scale.[22] If, however, they successfully pass an examination, they will be fully admitted to the Bar in Austria.[23]

Under Council Directive 98/5/EC as implemented by the Act on the Provision of Services and the Establishment of European Lawyers in Austria,[24] lawyers from EEA countries may establish themselves in Austria under their home country professional titles by registering with the Austrian Bar Association.[25] After three years of practice in Austrian and EU law, they may be admitted as regular members of the Austrian Bar without examination.[26]

---

[18] The remaining 15 months may be served in a notary's office, in the Solicitor General's Office (*Finanzprokuratur*), or, if such employment seems useful towards a future activity as an attorney, the time may be spent in an administrative authority, as research assistant in a law school, with a tax counsel or CPA, or in corresponding institutions abroad. Increasingly, Austrian trainees spend this time in foreign law firms.

[19] Including a nine-month judicial clerkship and two years in a law firm.

[20] Eight weekend seminars (24 half-days).

[21] Private law and principles of labor and social law; civil procedure; criminal law; commercial law (including corporations, securities, competition law); constitutional and administrative law; tax; drafting contracts and instruments; and the law regulating the legal profession and legal ethics, and recently also EU law.

[22] Under the Directive on Attorneys' Services 77/249/EC, they may provide cross–border services except legal representation in courts where this is mandatory. By November 1997, approximately 70 foreign attorneys (mostly from Germany) were registered in Austria.

[23] Under the First Diploma Recognition Directive 89/48/EC, their foreign law degrees are recognized, but they have to take a bar equivalency exam administered by the Court of Appeals. In Vienna, two German attorneys had taken the exam prior to July 2000.

[24] *Bundesgesetz über den freien Dienstleistungsverkehr und die Niederlassung von europäischen Rechtsanwälten in Österreich* (EuRAG), *BGBl* I 2000/27.

[25] They are enrolled in a special list of established European lawyers (*Liste der niedergelassenen europäischen Rechtsanwälte*). As of July 2000, two German attorneys and one English solicitor had been entered in this list in Vienna.

[26] Proof of practice in Austrian law having been submitted. Otherwise the aptitude test under Directive 89/48/EEC may be taken.

2. Functions

Whereas the English legal system distinguishes between barristers and solicitors, and other systems (like the German) between attorneys and legal advisers, there is only one type of attorney (*Rechtsanwalt*) in Austria. He enjoys a monopoly in comprehensive professional (regular and profit-oriented) legal representation before all courts and administrative authorities, and in all non-contentious legal matters. Notaries, tax accountants and organizations of employers are granted only limited rights of legal representation. Unauthorized legal representation (*Winkelschreiberei*) is penalized. Attorneys may not accept salaried civil service positions (except as teachers of law) and may not exercise the function of a notary. Every attorney must carry professional liability insurance. Continuing legal education (in the form of lectures, workshops, and seminars, etc.) is offered, but is not mandatory.

3. Law Firms

In January 2000, the number of Austrian attorneys was 3,857 (1525 of them working in Vienna), among them 431 (225) women. In addition, there were 1606 (781) associates, among them 505 (257) women. Most Austrian attorneys still work as single practitioners. A few "large" Vienna law firms have between 10 and 20 partners and up to 42 associates.[27]

Larger firms handle all areas of commercial and corporate law. Even in them, lawyers are often generalists with some areas of specialization. There is a growing trend to recruit young associates with international experience (LL.M. and/or law practice abroad). A number of solo practitioners are specialized and considered leaders in their fields. Several Vienna law firms have satellite offices in Brussels or cities in central and eastern Europe. Some have recently joined large international networks (German, English, and American). Very few internationally-oriented law firms exist outside Vienna (but there are some in Linz, Salzburg, and Innsbruck).

The forms of cooperation of attorneys in a law firm vary from simple overhead-sharing arrangements to various types of equity partnerships. Organization as a limited liability company became permissible in 1998.[28] Since 1994 it has also become possible to work as a salaried attorney.

4. Income

Starting salaries of associates are comparatively low (lowest in the west and south, highest in Vienna). In 1993, the Vienna Bar recommended a starting salary of 20,000 ATS per month;[29] other regional bar associations

---

[27] The largest Austrian law firm has 15 partners and 42 associates; the four firms next in size have 50, 48, 47 and 38 lawyers, respectively.

[28] Cooperation of attorneys and accountants (*Wirtschaftstreuhänder*) in one firm is not yet permitted.

[29] In 2000, top firms in Vienna paid at least 25,000 ATS to beginning associates.

followed this example. Particularly outside of Vienna, many more graduates seek positions than are offered.

No official data are available concerning attorneys' incomes. On average, they are below expectations and below incomes of comparable professions, for instance, doctors in private practice.

Lawyers' fees are negotiable. In the absence of a private agreement, the Attorney Tariff Act (*Rechtsanwaltstarifgesetz*) applies to litigation, while Bar Guidelines (*Autonome Honorarrichtlinien*) apply to non-contentious matters. They are based on considerations of case value, complexity, and time. Private fee arrangements are frequently based on billable hours, up to 3,000 ATS for an associate, 4,000 ATS or more for a partner. Lump sums are likely to be agreed on in litigation, but contingency fees (*quota litis* agreements, i.e., compensation computed as a fraction of the award) are prohibited because they are considered unethical. It is permissible, however, to negotiate a fee in advance of a fixed percentage of the claim or a bonus of up to 50% of the honorarium.

In Austrian civil procedure, the loser pays the winner's costs, including court approved lawyer's fees. There is no civil jury, and there are no punitive damages awards. Under a federally organized and financed system, legal aid is provided to indigents in civil and criminal matters. In principle, all attorneys provide *pro bono* service when appointed to specific cases by the Bar. The Austrian state, in recognition of this service, provides an annual lump sum to the Bar's retirement fund.

5. Supervision

Under a special federal statute regulating the profession (*Rechtsanwaltsordnung*), Austrian attorneys are organized in nine regional Bar Associations (*Rechtsanwaltskammern*), one for each *Land*. They are self-governing public law corporations with obligatory membership. They register attorneys, appoint bar examiners, and supervise the ethical conduct of their members under a strict code of professional responsibility.[30] Together the nine Associations form an All-Austrian Bar Association (*Rechtsanwaltskammertag*) that may enact general rules concerning professional conduct, continuing education, and fees. It has the right to comment on every government bill prior to its introduction in parliament.

Until recently, attorneys were not allowed to advertise, and the only specialization they could announce was "defender in criminal cases." Today they may list "preferred areas of activity," and advertising is permitted, subject to guidelines and disciplinary supervision.

---

[30] In 1999, 289 new disciplinary cases were brought against attorneys by the Vienna Bar alone. In the 288 cases considered in 1999, the charges were dropped in 178 instances, and 33 defendants were fully acquitted. Of the 77 guilty verdicts, 32 resulted in fines between 5,000 and 80,000 ATS. In three cases, attorneys were conditionally suspended for periods of two months to one year. One attorney was disbarred.

E. Notaries

Notaries perform an important function in the area of "preventive law." Their profession is regulated in the *Notariatsordnung* (Rules on the Notariate) of 1871 as that of "independent and impartial officers" (protecting the interests of both parties) to aid the population in the regulation of their private law affairs. Notaries must be Austrian citizens. They exercise a public office without being civil servants and bear the economic risks of their office. The number of notariates and their geographical distribution are regulated by the Ministry of Justice. As of December 31, 1999, Austria had 435 notariates. There is one notary per notariate. Each of them may employ one or more "candidates." There are 341 candidates training or waiting to become notaries. The first woman obtained a notariate in Vienna in 1989. Since then, the number of female notaries has risen to nine.

1. Training

After the completion of legal studies, future notaries must pass the notaries' examination administered by the Court of Appeals. They serve an apprenticeship of seven years, three of which must be served after the notaries' exam as "candidates" (*Notariatskandidaten*) in a notary's office. The exam has two parts – the first may be taken after 18 months of practice, the second part one year later. After completing the apprenticeship, candidates may apply for a free notariate. Openings must be advertised. Applicants are evaluated by the regional Chamber of Notaries and the personnel panels of the Regional Court and Court of Appeals. Seniority usually prevails in the ranking order on the list of three nominees submitted to the Minister of Justice, who usually appoints the first-ranking applicant. The average waiting period for a notariate is currently 13 years. Thus, upon appointment most notaries are between 39 and 47 years old. They must retire at age 70.

2. Functions

Notaries exercise a broad range of functions:

- They certify signatures and copies of many kinds of documents and attest to factual events (such as lottery drawings).
- They create documents that enjoy public trust and thus have special probatory force. They may prevent litigation or facilitate law enforcement. Notaries, therefore, have to observe special forms and are under special duties of instruction and diligence.
- In some matters the involvement of a notary is obligatory, for example, the conclusion of marital property agreements, contracts of sale, barter or credit among spouses, gifts in contemplation of death, or gifts without actual delivery, inheritance agreements, establishment of corporations, and decisions of shareholder meetings.

– Notaries frequently assist in drafting private legal documents, in particular contracts and wills. They represent parties in matters of succession, and in the registration of transactions concerning land and corporations.
– Notaries function as court-appointed commissioners in matters of non-contentious jurisdiction, in particular in probating estates.

Compensation for notarial services is regulated in the *Notariatstarifgesetz* (Notarial Tariff Act) of 1993.

3. Supervision

Notaries exercise professional self-administration. They are organized in *Notariatskammern* (Notarial Chambers) on the *Land* and federal levels. The Federal Notarial Chamber (*Bundesnotariatskammer*) submits legislative drafts and has the right to render opinions concerning draft laws. It also operates a computerized registry of Austrian wills. Disciplinary jurisdiction over notaries is exercised in the first instance by the Court of Appeals and ultimately by the Supreme Court. The disciplinary panels include notaries. Mere misdemeanors are dealt with by the Notarial Chambers. Notaries may not advertise.

F. Government Lawyers

1. Federal Bureaucracy

Article 20 of the Constitution provides for public administration by appointed professional civil servants. Their special public law relationship with their employer, the state, is characterized by special employment provisions and rights, including tenure, protection against transfer to other positions, and special pension rights. They also owe special duties of loyalty, obedience, and confidentiality.

During recent years, the Austrian civil service and its perceived privileges[31] have been under vigorous discussion. The number of public employees has been considerably reduced by the government, mainly by privatisation of state funtions and agencies (such as the mail service and railroads), but also by not replacing retiring civil servants. The present government is planning a further reduction by 9,000 civil servants immediately and a total of 30,000 (about 15%) in the near future.

a. Training and Career

Many law school graduates enter public service on the federal, *Länder* or municipal level. Training occurs mostly on the job, including limited instances of job-rotation. Since 1975, a Civil Service Academy of the Federation has operated under the Federal Chancellor's Office. Its full-time and part-time faculty are recruited from universities and administrative agencies and

---

[31] Such as tenure and pensions, see *supra* Chapter 3 (The Political System), IV.B.5.

teach basic and special administrative skills. A twelve-week course prepares candidates for the professional examination they must pass after several years of contractual employment (as *Vertragsbedienstete*) prior to obtaining tenured positions as civil servants (*Beamte*). The Academy also provides continuing education and special training courses on higher career levels.

There are five categories of employment (*Verwendungsgruppen*) ranging from E (auxiliary service) to A (higher service). Young law graduates start on level III of the higher service and may be promoted up to level IX. Within these levels, which reflect ranges of responsibility, slight salary increments occur every other year. Promotion guidelines are based on seniority and evaluation of performance, but often merit is overshadowed by political patronage. Leading positions must be advertised, but advertisements are often tailored to the qualifications of a specific desirable candidate.

The starting salary of law school graduates in the ministerial bureaucracy is 23,000 ATS per month; the top salary is 107,000 (including supplements, fourteen times a year). The retirement age is 65.

b. Functions

Lawyers in the federal ministries are involved in drafting statutes, regulations, and rules of their own department, as well as commentary on those of others. They supervise the legality of decisions taken by subordinate authorities and work in personnel, organization, and budget departments. They also exercise substantive leadership functions in technical, social, and economic policy areas. In 1990, 1749 law school graduates accounted for 55% of all university graduates working in Austrian ministries. The concentration of lawyers rises towards the higher positions – 95% of the top civil servants have law degrees.

2. *Land* Administration

In 1990, 1321 law school graduates held 47% of all positions filled with university graduates on the *Land* administration level. In district and *Land* authorities, many lawyers function as hearing officers in various administrative proceedings. Almost all leading positions are *de facto* reserved for law school graduates. Their tasks, status, and salaries are similar to those of the federal bureaucracy.

3. Municipal Administration

Whereas small municipalities usually employ no legally-trained administrative personnel, larger municipalities (with over 10,000 inhabitants) do. Cities that enjoy autonomy on the level of administrative district authorities (*Bezirksverwaltungsbehörden*) have an elaborate bureaucratic structure in which a number of law school graduates are active.

G. Lawyers in the Economy

1. The Semi-Public Sector

Chambers of business, agriculture, labor, and other representative bodies are organized as public law corporations with obligatory membership. They are established for the purpose of political interest representation and the autonomous administration of their members' economic interests. Due to these functions, many of their employees are university graduates, most of them (including all leading personnel) with legal education. Similar employment opportunities for law school graduates exist in the extensive social security system.

2. Corporations

During the last twenty years, business school graduates have increasingly superseded law school graduates in executive positions, as well as in areas like management, marketing, and public relations, which law school graduates had dominated in the past. Lawyers are still prevalent in legal and personnel departments. Many contenders for top executive positions have law and business degrees. Assets brought by law graduates to their work in the economy (including managerial positions) include their analytical approach and problem-solving capability, strategic thinking, flexibility, and communication skills.

H. Outlook

Until 1994, law school graduates had few problems finding satisfactory employment. Since then, hiring restrictions in courts and public administration, as well as saturation in law firms and notaries' offices, have made job placement difficult for the approximately 1,300 graduates of the five Austrian law schools each year. In June 2000, 460 unemployed law school graduates were registered with the Labor Market Service.[32] Unfortunately, this situation is not likely to change in the near future, but enrollment in law schools has already dropped significantly in recent years.[33]

Literature

Chalupsky et al. (eds.), Österreichischer Juristenkalender 2000 (1999)
Cuber, E., Cuber, A. (eds.), Rechtsanwaltsrecht (2nd ed. 2000)
Dimmel, N., Juristische Berufsbilder (1992)
Dimmel, N., Noll, A., Das Juristenbuch (1991)
Funk, B. et al. (eds.), Studienreform und die Zukunft der Juristenausbildung (1998)
Hauser, W. (ed.), Hochschulrecht (2000)
Heiss, H., Rungg, I. (eds.), Der Jurist in EWR/EU (1994)

---

[32] 159 of them in Vienna.
[33] See *supra* note 4.

Heller, F. H., Peck, J. C., American Law Teachers in an Austrian University, Kansas Law Review 42 (1994) 507

Hempel, K., Die rechtsberatenden Berufe im Europarecht (1996)

Krejci, H. et al. (eds.), Jus in Wien: Studieneingangsphase und Studienplan (1999)

Liu, F. R., The Establishment of a Cross-Border Legal Practice in the European Union, Boston College International & Comparative Law Review 20 (1997) 369

Mayr, P. G., Die österreichische Juristenausbildung (2nd ed. 1998)

Mayr, P. G., Neuerliche Änderung der Rechtsanwaltsausbildung, JAP 1992/93, 186

Öhlinger, T., Öffentlicher Dienst zwischen Tradition und Reform (1993)

Rechberger, W., Fuchs, H., Juristenberufe (1986)

Schneeberger, A., Qualitätsanforderungen und Weiterbildungsbedarf von Wirtschaftsjuristen (1991)

Thiele, C., Anwaltskosten (2000)

Wagner, K., Knechtel G., Notariatsordnung und alle einschlägigen Rechtsvorschriften (5th ed. 2000)

Wenger, K., Juristen, Berufsbilder und Berufsaussichten (1984)

Chapter 6
The Courts

I. Separation of Powers

The modern principle of separation of executive and judicial powers was not fully realized in Austria, then still the Austro-Hungarian Monarchy, until 1867.[1] Since that time, independent courts have handled all civil and criminal matters, whereas conflicts between citizens and administrative authorities are to this day neither adjudicated by ordinary courts (as in the U.S.) nor by special administrative courts (as in Germany or France). Until 1991, administrative law cases were first and foremost addressed within the administrative hierarchy itself. Only after all administrative appeals had been exhausted could illegal administrative action be appealed to a court of last instance, the *Verwaltungsgerichtshof* (Administrative Court).[2] This court exercises a purely cassational function – it quashes the illegal administrative decision and remands the case to the respective authority. The latter is bound by the opinion of the Administrative Court in further proceedings, in order to decide the case correctly.

In 1991, Independent Administrative Panels in the *Länder* (*Unabhängige Verwaltungssenate in den Ländern*) were established.[3] They are administrative bodies of the *Länder*, not courts (all of which are federal institutions).[4] Panel members are appointed by the *Land* governments for at least six years. Technically, they are not judges; yet the length of their term of office supposedly guarantees their independence in the exercise of the quasi-judicial functions delegated to them. They hear appeals regarding administrative rulings and penalties. In these areas, the jurisdiction of the Administrative Court has become restricted to that of a second level of appeal above the Independent Administrative Panels.

II. The Ordinary Court System

Concerning the structure, institutions and procedures of the judiciary, the Austrian Constitution of 1920 contains only basic principles and delegates the elaboration of details to the legislature. According to article 82 of the Con-

---

[1] But see article 94 of the Austrian Constitution of 1920, which provides for a complete separation of ordinary courts and administrative authorities on all levels.

[2] See *infra* Chapter 7 (Administrative Adjudication), IV.

[3] See *infra* Chapter 7, II.

[4] But the Panels qualify as "tribunals" under the European Human Rights Convention. See *infra* Chapter 9 (Fundamental Rights), IV.F.3.

stitution, all courts are federal institutions.[5] Their organization and jurisdiction may be established only by federal statute (art. 83). Furthermore, no military tribunals may be established in peacetime (art. 84).

The Constitution itself establishes a Supreme Court as the highest tribunal in civil and criminal matters (art. 92). A system of lower-level trial and appeals courts functions on the basis of a Law on Court Organization (*Gerichtsorganisationsgesetz*). Ordinary jurisdiction is exercised on four levels. On the lowest level, there are 191 District Courts (*Bezirksgerichte*); above them we find 21 Regional or Land Courts (*Landesgerichte*) functioning as courts of first instance in the more important cases and also acting as appeals courts *vis-à-vis* the District Courts; four Courts of Appeals (*Oberlandesgerichte*) in Graz, Linz, Innsbruck and Vienna hear appeals from cases decided by *Landesgerichte* as trial courts, and at the top of the judicial pyramid there is one Supreme Court (*Oberster Gerichtshof, OGH*) in Vienna.[6]

Ordinary courts do not have the power of judicial review regarding decisions or rulings issued by administrative authorities (*Bescheide*). The Constitution assigns this power to the above-mentioned Administrative Court. Judicial review of the legality of administrative regulations (*Verordnungen*) and the constitutionality of statutes (*Gesetze*) is reserved to a special Constitutional Court.[7]

A. Civil Courts

Bezirksgerichte (District Courts) have jurisdiction in civil cases involving amounts up to 130,000 Austrian Schillings (ATS) and handle all matters of family law (paternity, matrimonial and alimony matters) regardless of the value involved. All cases are heard by single judges. In petty cases, i.e., claims involving sums up to 26,000 ATS, appeal is strictly limited.

---

[5] This is different from most other federal states, like the U.S., where fully developed judicial systems exist in the states and in the federal system, or Germany, where state court systems operate under federal supreme courts. It should be noted that Austrian civil and criminal law (and the respective procedural law) are exclusively federal matters, whereas in the U.S. much private and criminal law is state law.

[6] The German Basic Law (art. 95 (1)) establishes five parallel court systems in the *Länder* under the supervision of five federal supreme courts: ordinary courts exercise jurisdiction in civil and criminal matters on three levels (*Amtsgericht, Landgericht, Oberlandesgericht*) under the *Bundesgerichtshof* (Federal Supreme Court in Karlsruhe), labor disputes are adjudicated on two levels of labor courts under the *Bundesarbeitsgericht* in Erfurt, administrative review is exercised by two levels of administrative courts in the *Länder* and the *Bundesverwaltungsgericht* in Berlin, unless they are assigned to special administrative courts, such as the social courts under the *Bundessozialgericht* (Kassel) and tax courts under the *Bundesfinanzhof* (Munich). The German Federal Constitutional Court (*Bundesverfassungsgericht*) is considered to be a special constitutional organ outside of the regular court structure (cf. Basic Law art. 92).

[7] See *infra* Chapter 8 (Constitutional Review).

Landesgerichte (Regional Courts) function as trial courts in matters concerning sums above 130,000 ATS. Cases are usually heard by a single judge. They sit in panels of three judges if the amount is over 650,000 ATS and one of the parties so requests.[8] *Landesgerichte* also function as appellate courts (sitting in panels of three) in matters decided by *Bezirksgerichte* as trial courts.

Oberlandesgerichte (Courts of Appeals) function as courts of appeal in matters decided by *Landesgerichte* as trial courts. They hear cases in panels of three judges.

The *Oberste Gerichtshof* (Supreme Court) is the highest court in civil and criminal matters (Const. art. 92).[9] It consists of a president, two vice-presidents, 13 panel chairmen, and 41 judges (including seven women) usually sitting in panels of five.[10] Three-member panels may decide certain formal matters. An enlarged panel of eleven judges deals with legal questions of fundamental importance that may result in a departure from an established line of decisions. In civil cases, decisions of appeals courts are subject to appeal for error to the Supreme Court.[11] The Supreme Court issues official reports of its decisions regarding civil matters.[12] These reports, however, contain only the most important opinions.

B. Special Jurisdiction

Special courts or special panels of regular civil courts are established to deal with matters of commercial law and of labor and social law issues. They usually involve the participation of (expert or informed) lay judges sitting on panels together with professional judges. In commercial cases, expert lay judges are appointed for three-year terms by the Ministry of Justice in collaboration with the Ministry of Economic Affairs. In labor and social cases, informed lay judges are elected for five years by employers' and employees' associations. In matters regulated by the Cartel Act 1988, the Vienna Court of Appeals (*Oberlandesgericht*) functions as Cartel Court (*Kartellgericht*), sitting as trial court for all of Austria. Panels consist of one professional judge and two "expert" lay judges nominated by the Economic Chamber Austria and the Federal Chamber of Labor.[13] Appeals are decided by a special panel of the Supreme Court (one professional judge, four lay judges).

---

[8] This happens only rarely.

[9] Cf. the *Bundesgerichtshof* in the German system, *supra* note 6. The Austrian Supreme Court also deals with matters of labor and social law, which in Germany are adjudicated by two special supreme courts.

[10] In the Supreme Court, ten panels deal with civil matters (including two panels that handle primarily labor and social law cases) and five with criminal matters. One panel deals with appeals against decisions of the Cartel Court (antitrust matters).

[11] See *infra* Chapter 11 (Civil Procedure).

[12] *SZ* = *Entscheidungen des österreichischen OGH in Zivil- und Justizverwaltungssachen.*

[13] Cf. Chapter 3 (The Political System), II.D

C. Criminal Courts[14]

Depending on the length of the sentence, a criminal act is categorized as a *Verbrechen* (felony) or as a *Vergehen* (misdemeanor). *Verbrechen* are intentional crimes which are punishable by deprivation of liberty for more than three years, all other criminal acts are *Vergehen*.

Bezirksgerichte (District Courts) have – with few exceptions – jurisdiction concerning all *Vergehen* punishable by not more than one year of imprisonment.[15] Trials are conducted by single judges. Their sentences are subject to full appeal (concerning all factual and legal aspects, including the determination of guilt, length of sentence and serious procedural flaws) to the *Landesgericht* (see Appendix 4).

Landesgerichte (Regional Courts) are courts of first instance for all felonies and serious misdemeanors. Depending on the gravity of the offense, they sit as *Einzelrichter* (single judge), when the defendant may be sentenced to not more than five years imprisonment; *Schöffengerichte* (two judges and two lay assessors), when the maximum sentence may exceed five years and in several other cases enumerated by law, or *Geschworenengerichte* (three judges and eight jurors). The latter function in felony cases involving a potential sentence of more than ten years (and a minimum of five)[16] and in all political crimes.[17]

Landesgerichte also function as appellate courts for decisions of the *Bezirksgerichte*. As such, they sit as panels of three professional judges.

Oberlandesgerichte (Courts of Appeals) sit in panels of three judges and function as courts of appeal for decisions of the *Landesgerichte*. Appeals may be brought for error, assessment of guilt, and extent of punishment. In cases of gross procedural error by a *Landesgericht* sitting as *Schöffengericht* or *Geschworenengericht*, an appeal for annulment goes directly to the Supreme Court, bypassing the Court of Appeals.

The *Oberste Gerichtshof* (Supreme Court) sits in panels of five judges and hears nullity appeals. Unlike Austrian civil procedure and German criminal procedure, Austrian criminal procedure is restricted to one level of appeal.

In 1992, the protection of civil rights in criminal procedure was strengthened by the introduction of a special fundamental right complaint (*Grundrechtsbeschwerde*) to the Supreme Court in cases where the order of a criminal court violated the basic right of "freedom of the person." This remedy is similar to a writ of *habeas corpus*. The complaint is filed directly with the Supreme Court. It has the purpose of reducing the number of complaints against Austrian criminal courts to the European Court of Human Rights in

---

[14] For a more detailed description of criminal courts and criminal procedure see *infra* Chapter 9.

[15] Misdemeanors in this category range from shoplifting (art. 127 Criminal Code) to negligent homicide (art. 80).

[16] E.g., murder (art. 75 Criminal Code), or rape resulting in death (art. 201 (3)).

[17] E.g., high treason (art. 242), or collecting weapons for combat (art. 280).

Strasbourg, France.[18] In recent years, the Supreme Court has developed case law and guidelines for pretrial arrest and detention.

The Supreme Court no longer issues an official report of its decisions regarding criminal matters.[19] The most important decisions are regularly published in the leading law journals.[20]

III. Organs of the Judicial Process

Under the Constitution, judicial power is delegated to judges (*Richter*, Const. art. 86), magistrates (*Rechtspfleger*, who are specially trained non-judicial civil servants handling specific matters of civil litigation, art. 87a), and participants drawn from the general public (art. 91).

Judges are the main actors in the judicial process.[21] They form a special branch of the civil service, and are appointed by the Federal President (who may delegate this power to the Minister of Justice) on the proposal of the Federal Government (which may also delegate this authority to the Minister of Justice). Judicial selection panels composed of judges propose at least three names for every vacant position to the Minister of Justice (art. 86).

In the exercise of their judicial authority, judges are independent (art. 87), they are not bound by any instructions, general or specific. They are subject to a legal retirement age (65 years), but may otherwise not be removed from office or transferred against their will to another position, except in cases provided by law and on the basis of a judicial decision (art. 88).

In criminal procedure, popular participation in the administration of justice (art. 91) may take two forms. In cases involving the most serious crimes, jurors (*Geschworene*) alone decide the guilt of the defendant. They subsequently join the professional judges in determining the punishment. In other felony cases, lay assessors (*Schöffen*) sit with judges and jointly determine guilt and punishment. Where the maximum penalty provided by law does not exceed a certain limit, a single judge handles the case without lay participation.

In civil procedure, "expert" lay judges sit on panels with professional judges in commercial cases, "informed" lay judges in labor and social cases.

---

[18] Cf. *infra* Chapter 10 (Fundamental Rights), IV.B.3.

[19] *SSt = Entscheidungen des österreichischen OGH in Strafsachen und Disziplinarangelegenheiten*, one volume per year; ends with volume 60 (1989).

[20] E.g. *JBl, ÖJZ*. The most important journals and court opinions are also available via the internet (*Rechtsdatenbank*), see Appendix 6.

[21] See *supra* Chapter 5, II.B for more detail.

IV. Procedure

A. Constitutional Principles

The Constitution establishes two fundamental procedural principles: 1) civil and criminal proceedings are to be oral and public; 2) criminal proceedings are to be governed by the principle of "accusatory procedure." In other words, there must be a separation between the role of the prosecutor and the role of the judge (art. 90). The dockets of judges have to be determined in advance and may be changed only in the event of a judge's disability (art. 87). This provision is to ensure a person's right to come before his "lawful judge" (art. 83).

The Constitution also contains one provision of substantive criminal law, namely, an absolute prohibition of the death penalty (art. 85).

Judges are obligated to apply all statutes, regulations, and international treaties. Any judge suspecting a regulation (*Verordnung*) he would have to apply in the case before him to be illegal (violating a statute) or unconstitutional must interrupt the proceedings and request the Constitutional Court[22] to nullify it. Only appellate courts and the Supreme Court have the right to petition the Constitutional Court to examine the constitutionality of a statute (*Gesetz*) they would have to apply. Trial courts must apply statutes as they find them unless they appear to be incompatible with EU law. (See *infra* C).

B. European Human Rights

The European Convention for the Protection of Human Rights and Fundamental Freedoms of 1950 (effective in 1953) was ratified by Austria in 1958 and has the rank of constitutional law, as expressly enacted in 1964. A number of its provisions affect criminal law and criminal and civil procedure, but also the system of administrative adjudication.[23]

C. European Law Issues

All courts may, and courts of last resort must, ask the Court of Justice of the European Communities for a preliminary ruling if they have doubts concerning the interpretation of immediately applicable European Community law.[24]

Literature

See Chapters 5 (Legal Education and Legal Professions), 7 (Administrative Adjudication), 8 (Constitutional Review), 10 (Criminal Procedure) and 11 (Civil Procedure).

---

[22] See *infra* Chapter 8.

[23] See *infra* Chapter 7.

[24] On this preliminary reference procedure see *supra* Chapter 4 (Austria and the EU), IV.D.4.

Chapter 7
Administrative Adjudication

I. History

Whereas in Germany or France there exist complete systems of administrative courts including several levels of appeal,[1] Austria until 1991 had only limited judicial review of administrative rulings. There was only one (Supreme) Administrative Court (*Verwaltungsgerichtshof*), established in 1867 and operative since 1876, which could be petitioned after exhausting all internal appeals within the various administrative structures.

In these administrative structures (municipal, *Land*, and federal authorities), decisions are usually made on several levels by civil servants who do not enjoy judicial independence, but are subject to the orders and instructions of their superiors. Only as a last resort, an independent judicial authority, the Administrative Court, ensured judicial control over the legality of administrative action.

Although in principle administrative authorities are bound by orders of superior organs and accountable to them in the exercise of their official functions (Const. art. 20 (1)), the Constitution itself as well as several constitutional provisions of the Federation and the *Länder* have over the years established a number of exceptions by providing for independent administrative authorities (*weisungsfreie Kollegialbehörden mit richterlichem Einschlag*). These bodies are collegial, the decisionmaking panel must include at least one judge, and their rulings may not be subject to internal administrative appeal. They may be reviewed by the Administrative Court only if the law expressly so provides. In any case, the constitutionality of administrative rulings may be reviewed by the Constitutional Court.

Examples of such independent collegial authorities are the *Kommission zur Wahrung des Rundfunkgesetzes* (Commission for the Observance of the Broadcasting Act), the *Datenschutzkommission* (Data Protection Commission), the *Telecom-Control-Kommission*, the *Grundverkehrsbehörden* (Land Transfer Authorities) of the *Länder*, and the *Vergabeämter* (Public Procurement Offices) of the Federation and the *Länder*. Because they are relatively independent from the executive, they have been accepted as "tribunals" under

---

[1] In Germany, administrative courts have jurisdiction in all public law disputes, unless special administrative courts have been established (social courts, financial courts and the Federal Patent Court), or the question concerns constitutional review, which is reserved to a special Constitutional Court. Trial and appeals courts (*Verwaltungsgerichte, Oberverwaltungsgerichte*) are *Länder* courts, the supreme administrative court is federal (*Bundesverwaltungsgericht*, Federal Administrative Court in Berlin).

article 6 ECHR.[2] Their independence has, however, been questioned in Austria because of the strong representation of interest groups in some of these bodies. The Constitutional Court recently criticized the exclusion of parliamentary control (and in some cases also the exclusion of Administrative Court review) over these areas of administrative activity. The Court will in the future make the constitutionality of such authorities depend on substantial reasons speaking in favor of their establishment.

In 1988 the Federal Constitution was amended[3] to include "Independent Administrative Panels in the *Länder*" (*Unabhängige Verwaltungssenate in den Ländern, UVS*), to be in effect as of 1991. These panels represent an important step forward in supervising the legality of administrative rulings, yet they still fall short of the quality of genuine courts. Their quasi-judicial decisions may be reviewed subsequently by the Administrative Court.

II. Independent Administrative Panels in the *Länder*

A. Tribunal Quality

When Austria ratified the European Human Rights Convention in 1959, the Austrian administrative penalty procedure was incompatible with the right to liberty as formulated in article 5 of the Convention. Thus, Austria made a reservation excluding the application of that article to measures of deprivation of freedom provided for under the Austrian Administrative Procedure Acts of 1950. Yet Austrian procedure also deviated from article 6 of the Convention, which grants everybody "in the determination of his civil rights and obligations or of any criminal charge against him" the right to a hearing before "an independent and impartial tribunal." The mere possibility of subsequent review by the Administrative Court did not satisfy this requirement because lower administrative agencies, which did not enjoy judicial independence, made determinations of fact that were binding on the Administrative Court. In addition, article 2 of Protocol Nr. 7 to the Convention, effective November 1, 1988, mandated two levels of judicial proceedings in criminal procedure: "Everyone convicted of a criminal offense by a tribunal shall have the right to have his conviction or sentence reviewed by a higher tribunal." Austrian courts and some scholars attempted to extend the reservation pertaining to article 5 to include article 6, but the very existence of the exception to article 5 had become more and more questionable in light of modern human rights doctrine. Therefore, constitutional amendments were passed to introduce Independent Administrative Panels (*Unabhängige Verwaltungssenate, UVS*) that finally implemented the rights emanating from article 6 of the Convention.

In the discussion preceding the introduction of the Panels, several models had been considered, among them the proposal to introduce real *Land* administrative courts. Another idea was to give the Administrative Court full

---

[2] See *infra* Chapter 9 (Fundamental Rights), IV.F.3
[3] Articles 129 to 129b of the Constitution.

jurisdiction over questions of fact and law. The idea of jurisdiction over questions of fact was quickly dropped because of protests by the Court itself, which feared the equally undesirable alternatives of a breakdown due to the resulting caseload or a massive increase in the number of judges needed in order to accommodate the additional burden. The idea of *Land* administrative courts was opposed by the Federal Government, which was reluctant to give up the federal monopoly of court organization and judicial appointment. Of the *Länder*, some demanded genuine *Land* administrative courts, while others were unwilling to assume the additional financial burden of judicial salaries. In subsequent discussions on the federal level, no agreement could be reached about the scope of jurisdiction of the proposed *Land* administrative courts.[4] Any decision in this matter requires a constitutional amendment and thus a political consensus of government and opposition.

B. Organization

A compromise measure of Independent Administrative Panels was finally adopted. The Panels are administrative agencies of the *Länder*, their organization is subject to *Länder* legislation. Their procedure, however, is regulated by federal legislation. Each of the nine *Länder* has one Panel. The Panels qualify as tribunals under the ECHR, but they are not courts under the Austrian Constitution. According to article 82 of the Federal Constitution, courts can only be established by federal law. The members of the Panels are not judges, although they exercise quasi-judicial functions.

With the exception of Tirol, all *Länder* advertise Independent Panel positions and require a ranking of the candidates as to their professional qualifications. The ranking is usually performed by the Panels themselves. Members must be law school graduates; one quarter of them should be recruited from federal institutions. Additional requirements, such as prior legal experience, may be imposed by law, but binding nomination rights would be unconstitutional. Members of the Panels are appointed by the *Land* government for at least six years. In Upper Austria and Vienna they are appointed for unlimited terms (i.e., until retirement at age 65). In all other *Länder*, reappointment – usually for unlimited terms – is possible. According to the European Court of Human Rights in Strasbourg, the members' terms of office sufficiently guarantee their independence. In the exercise of their quasi-judicial functions, they are not bound by any instructions.

Initially, several *Länder* attempted to economize by appointing part-time members to the Panels, who would also work in other, yet non-independent administrative positions. This practice cast a shadow on the quasi-judicial

---

[4] Whereas the *SPÖ* argued in favor of *Land* administrative courts deciding cases on the merits, the *ÖVP* wanted to restrict them to making cassatory decisions in order to maintain more administrative discretion on the part of (mostly *ÖVP* dominated) *Land* governments. A relatively new idea is the creation of an All-Austrian Administrative Court of First Instance.

independence of these persons. It was soon recognized to be incompatible with the principle that "justice must not only be done, but also seen to be done," as applied by the European Court of Justice and the European Court of Human Rights, and was subsequently abandoned.

Organizational matters of the Panels are decided by the Chairman (Deputy Chairman) or by the Plenary Meeting. Judicial decisions are taken by individual members or by small senates. In matters of general administrative procedure, senates of three hear appeals. Complaints against "immediate official compulsion"[5] are heard by a single member. In matters of penal procedure, appeals are heard by senates of three members if deprivation of liberty, or a money penalty of more than 10,000 ATS, has been imposed. Other matters are decided by single members. The workload of the single members or senates are to be distributed according to a schedule fixed in advance.[6]

C. Jurisdiction

Independent Panels have jurisdiction only after all internal administrative appeals have been exhausted. They generally do not function as tribunals of first instance. Their jurisdiction, contained in Article 129a of the Constitution, includes:

— **Procedures concerning administrative infractions** (*Verwaltungsübertretungen*). With the exception of violations of the federal tax laws, the Panels serve as appeals tribunals for these complaints. This function was central to the deliberations which led to their establishment through constitutional amendments in 1988. The proper implementation of article 6 of the European Human Rights Convention[7] was accomplished only by allowing the Independent Panels to have full jurisdiction over matters of fact and law.

Violations of federal tax law have been excepted because an agency structure meeting the "tribunal" requirement of article 6 of the Convention was already in place in this area. Regular tax appeals are handled by Independent Appellate Panels consisting of five members, three of whom are officials appointed by the Minister of Finance and two of whom are laymen delegated by the Economic Chamber and the Chamber of Labor. Penalties are imposed by Independent Panels composed of a professional judge, an administrative official of the tax service, and one or two laymen, while serious tax fraud cases are heard by regular courts. Although these structures seem to satisfy the European Court of Human Rights, their constitutionality is questionable. Advocates of genuine administrative courts have recently also demanded the creation of tax courts.

— **Complaints against acts of immediate administrative instruction and compulsion** (*Ausübung unmittelbarer verwaltungsbehördlicher Befehls-*

---

[5] Such as arrest, search and seizure, handcuffing, or searching a person.
[6] Article 129b (2) of the Constitution.
[7] See also *infra* Chapter 9, IV.F.

und Zwangsgewalt). This category of complaints is of particular importance. For example, article 5b of the Traffic Code authorizes law enforcement officers to prevent persons from driving motor vehicles if their ability to drive appears to be impaired by alcohol or drugs. The police may take possession of the car keys. If the driver was not intoxicated, he may complain to the Independent Administrative Panel, citing a violation of his liberty and property rights. A decision by the Panel that his rights have been violated will, however, have little effect other than psychological comfort. The citizen may, of course, take the difficult course of suing the state for damages in a civil action, and there may be a disciplinary action taken by the state against the policeman who abused his powers.

- **Complaints for failure to make a timely decision** (*Verletzung der Entscheidungspflicht*). These complaints may be brought in three situations: private actions in penal administrative law (e.g., minor violations of a person's honor), penal procedure under *Land* tax laws, and "other matters."
- **"Other matters"** (*sonstige Angelegenheiten*). These matters are those that are assigned to the Panels by federal or *Land* legislation. This clause covers issues in the category of "civil rights" as interpreted by the European Court of Human Rights, enabling Austria fully to implement the Convention.

If an Independent Panel is faced with applying a statute which it suspects of being unconstitutional or a regulation that appears to violate statutory law, it must refer the question to the Constitutional Court, requesting it to annul the faulty legal norm. In questions concerning the interpretation of EC law, the Panel may request a preliminary ruling by the European Court of Justice.

III. The Federal Asylum Panel

Two recent federal statutes on the granting of asylum to political refugees (*Asylgesetz* 1997) and on creating an independent Federal Asylum Panel attached to the Federal Chancellor's Office (*Bundesgesetz über den unabhängigen Bundesasylsenat*, 1997) attempt to increase procedural efficiency at the border and to lessen the burden on the Administrative Court.

The Federal Asylum Panel (*Bundesasylsenat*) consists of members nominated by the Federal Government and appointed for life by the Federal President. The Panel's decisions are normally made by single members, in certain cases by boards of three members. The Panel functions as the final appeals tribunal for decisions of the Federal Asylum Authority (*Bundesasylamt*) in a simplified procedure. Rulings of the Authority may be appealed within ten days, and the appellate decision by the Panel must be rendered within ten working days. Previously, the Federal Minister of the Interior ruled on administrative appeals from the Asylum Authority. His rulings could be appealed to the Administrative Court. Today, the Administrative Court may refuse to hear an appeal from the Asylum Panel (like an appeal from any other independent administrative panel) unless it concerns a fundamental question of law, e.g., because the Panel's decision deviates from the jurisprudence of the

Administrative Court, or such jurisprudence has not yet been developed, or is not uniform. This provision has substantially lessened the burden on the Administrative Court. But it remains to be seen whether summary proceedings of border police and the Federal Asylum Authority will be subject to sufficient legal supervision by the new Federal Asylum Panel.

IV. The Administrative Court (*Verwaltungsgerichtshof*)

The Austrian Administrative Court is the product of mid-nineteenth century political liberalism and constitutionalism. It was established in 1867, in what was then the Austro-Hungarian Monarchy, and became operative in 1876. It was to provide specialized and centralized, one-tier cassational judicial review of administrative legality. The Administrative Court was to function as a court of last resort, superimposing judicial control over a system of internal appeals in which administrative authorities were first and foremost authorized to police themselves. Since 1991, however, the Administrative Court has been functioning in several areas as a second level of appeal above the Independent Administrative Tribunals.

A. Organization

The Administrative Court consists of a President, a Vice-President and other Members, namely, 12 Presidents of Panels and 48 Councillors (including four women). The members are nominated by the Federal Government and appointed by the Federal President. Nominations of members other than the President or Vice-President of the Court must be based on proposals containing the names of three candidates per vacancy. These proposals are submitted to the Federal Government by the Plenary Meeting of the Court.

All judges of the Administrative Court enjoy constitutional guarantees of judicial independence. They must have earned law degrees and have a minimum of ten years of legal experience. At least one-third of the members must have passed the judges' examination; at least one-quarter should come from the *Länder*, preferably selected from administrative bureaucracies. The latter principle has not always been strictly applied.

The Court works in panels (*Senate*). As a rule, a panel has five members, but in matters of administrative penal law, only three members participate. Three-member panels may also decide certain formal questions (such as the rejection of inadmissible complaints) and simple questions of law (in particular questions that have already been sufficiently clarified by previous decisions of the Court). To deviate from a firm line of decisions, a reinforced panel is required. This is a nine-member panel that becomes active when a smaller panel holds that an established line of decisions should be abandoned, or that there are divergent positions taken by previous decisions of different panels of the Court.

There is a fixed distribution of subject matter among panels at the beginning of every year. A member of the Court may be assigned to several panels, and every panel must include a member with formal qualifications as a judge in the ordinary judiciary. In matters involving financial law, at least one panel member must have prior experience in financial administration. In matters concerning general administrative law, one member must have served in the civil service.

B. Jurisdiction

Under article 129 of the Constitution, the Independent Administrative Panels and the Administrative Court are the competent authorities for securing the legality of all acts of public administration. The Administrative Court examines complaints that allege illegality of individual rulings (*Bescheidbeschwerden*) and complaints alleging breach of the duty to reach a (timely) decision (*Säumnisbeschwerden*). Complaints against illegal administrative rulings may be brought by any party to an administrative proceeding (including a proceeding before an Independent Panel) that claims a violation of its rights. The party must have exhausted all available administrative appeals. The complaint also may be brought by an administrative agency in the case of an objective violation of the law, e.g., in matters of the administration of federal law by *Länder* authorities, the competent Federal Minister may bring this complaint, and in matters of the federal administration of *Land* laws, the respective *Land* government.

An overwhelming number of cases before the Court concern complaints against administrative rulings, prior to 1997 particularly in the area of immigration law. Complaints against deportation orders and the denial of petitions for asylum might have been a strong argument for the introduction of *Länder* administrative courts of first instance, at least for this limited function and for a limited period of time. The legislature, however, chose a different approach by creating a Federal Asylum Panel to function as a quasi-judicial body to hear appeals in this area as of January 1, 1998.[8]

Complaints for failure to reach a decision may be filed if the highest competent administrative authority to which the petitioner was able to appeal has remained inactive for at least six months. In penal matters, a different rule applies. If an administrative appeal in these matters has not been decided within 15 months, the decision expires.

An example for a complaint against official inaction may be taken from the area of construction law. To build a house, a construction permit must be obtained from the local mayor. If the mayor, for personal or political reasons, does not issue a permit although all substantive requirements have been fulfilled, the applicant may, after six months, request devolution of the case to the municipal council. After six more months of inactivity, the applicant may petition the Administrative Court. The Court must grant a grace pe-

---

[8] As a result, the number of new complaints to the Administrative Court dropped by 31% in 1998.

riod of an additional three months to the delaying institution before hearing the case. It may take the Court another two years or more to reach a decision.

C. Procedure

The procedural rules of the Court are contained in the Law on the Administrative Court (*Verwaltungsgerichtshofgesetz*) of 1985. Parties to the proceedings are the petitioner and the responding authority. Complaints against rulings must be brought within six weeks. They must be submitted in writing and by an attorney. A complaint against a ruling does not automatically prevent its enforcement, but the Court may grant a stay, after having weighed the interests at stake.

Oral hearings will only be held at the express request of one of the parties. These rarely occur in practice. If the complaint is legally founded, the ruling will be quashed by the Court. In cases of administrative inaction, the Administrative Court will decide on the merits. In other cases the legal opinion of the Court is binding on the administrative authority to which the case has been remanded. The losing party pays the court costs.

D. Effects of Decisions

The Court's function is in principle cassatory. In its main field of activity, the examination of rulings alleged to be illegal, the Administrative Court annuls the illegal ruling and remands the case to the respective administrative agency, which in turn is obligated to implement the opinion of the Administrative Court. If the agency fails to do so, the petitioner may again file a complaint with the Administrative Court. Ultimately, the petitioner may bring a civil suit for damages against the state.

In the case of a complaint against administrative inaction, the Administrative Court decides the case on the merits. The Court will order an administrative agency to implement its decision.

The Court's opinions are published annually in an official collection subdivided in administrative law and financial law sections.[9]

E. Perspectives

Judges traditionally complain about caseloads just as professors complain about exams. Yet the situation in the Administrative Court has taken a dramatic turn for the worse. The annual caseload increased from 4,121 in 1987 to 12,790 in 1996. In 1998, 7,661 new applications reached the Court; 10,858 decisions were taken. The backlog reached its peak in 1997 with 16,323 cases (1998: 13,126). In 1998, every Councillor (judge) prepared 226 decisions

---

[9] *Erkenntnisse und Beschlüsse des Verwaltungsgerichtshofes (Administrativrecht/Finanzrecht).*

(1987: 96).[10] If a case has to be decided on the merits, the average duration of the process reaches 17 months. In tax matters it is more than two years. The institution of the Federal Asylum Panel in 1997 brought (at least temporary) relief for the Administrative Court which had previously been overburdened with such cases.[11]

Literature

See also the constitutional law and administrative law textbooks listed in Chapter 2 (Constitution, Sources and Interpretation of Law).

General and Comparative Works

Grabenwarter, C., Verfahrensgarantien in der Verwaltungsgerichtsbarkeit: Eine Studie zu Artikel 6 EMRK auf der Grundlage einer rechtsvergleichenden Untersuchung der Verwaltungsgerichtsbarkeit Frankreichs, Deutschlands und Österreichs (1997)
Jabloner, C., Die Entwicklung der Verwaltungsgerichtsbarkeit in Österreich, ÖJZ 1994, 329
Lehne, F. et al. (eds), Die Entwicklung der österreichischen Verwaltungsgerichtsbarkeit (1976)
Ress, G. (ed.), Entwicklungstendenzen im Verwaltungsverfahrensrecht und in der Verwaltungsgerichtsbarkeit – Rechtsvergleichende Analysen zum österreichischen und deutschen Recht (1990)

Independent Administrative Panels

Davy, U., Die Asylrechtsreform, ecolex 1997, 708 and 821
Denk, S., Wie unabhängig sind die Unabhängigen Verwaltungssenate? ÖJZ 1995, 206
Grabenwarter, C., Auf dem Weg zur Landesverwaltungsgerichtsbarkeit, JRP 1998, 269
Keplinger, R. (ed.), Fremdenrecht (annotated statutes and legislative materials, 1997)
Pernthaler, P. (ed.), Unabhängige Verwaltungssenate und Verwaltungsgerichtsbarkeit (1993)
Pichler, H., Einführung einer Landesverwaltungsgerichtsbarkeit (1994)
Thienel, R., Das Verfahren der Verwaltungssenate (2nd ed. 1992)
Walter, R., Mayer, H., Verwaltungsverfahrensrecht (7th ed. 1999)

Administrative Court

Dolp, F. (ed.), Die Verwaltungsgerichtsbarkeit (3rd ed. 1987)
Fellner, K., Ein Plädoyer für Finanzgerichte. Zur notwendigen Neuordnung des Abgabenverfahrens, RdW 1998, 42
Jabloner, C., Strukturfragen der Gerichtsbarkeit des öffentlichen Rechts, ÖJZ 1998, 161
Klecatsky, H. R., Öhlinger, T., Die Gerichtsbarkeit des öffentlichen Rechts (1984)

---

[10] The average workload of a judge of the German Federal Administrative Court amounts to approximately one-third of this number.

[11] The Federal Asylum Panel took over approx. 3,600 cases from the Administrative Court. An appeal from the Asylum Panel to the Administrative Court remains possible. In 1998 and 1999, 1,269 appeals against decisions of the Asylum Panel reached the Administrative Court. In 226 of the 608 cases decided, the Administrative Court annulled rulings of the Asylum Panel.

Chapter 8
Constitutional Review

I. Two Systems of Constitutional Review

Constitutional review is the product of a modern democratic system of government that is based on the ideas of rule of law, separation of powers and the protection of fundamental rights. In this system it has two major tasks. The first of these tasks is to safeguard the functioning of democratic processes in the interplay of legislative, executive, and judicial institutions (that may be of particular complexity in a federal state). In other words, constitutional review is to prevent the arrogation of power by one branch of government at the expense of another. Closely linked to this first task of constitutional review – and no less important – is a second one, namely to protect the individual citizen against the encroachment of any state power in his private sphere of life.

Constitutional review has developed as a result of specific historical and political conditions that have differed from country to country. Generally, one may distinguish an earlier American system of uniform and decentralized ("diffuse") judicial review, in which all courts participate, from a more recent Austrian system of specialized and centralized ("concentrated") constitutional review, which is exercised outside the regular court system by a separate constitutional court.

In the American system, constitutional review is exercised only *incidenter*, i.e., in the context of a specific case litigated in the regular court system ("case and controversy approach"), and its effect is fundamentally *inter partes*. In the Austrian system, constitutional review also is conducted *principaliter*, without a specific case at issue, and its effect is basically *erga omnes*.

The Austrian system has its roots in the constitutional law discussions of the late 19th century. It was further developed by Hans Kelsen, a prominent legal theorist, constitutional law scholar and the "father" of the Austrian Constitution of 1920. After the Second World War, it was this system rather than the American that profoundly influenced the creation of constitutional courts in the new constitutions of Italy (1948) and Germany (1949). In the following years, the Austrian model of constitutional review – often as modified by contemporary German theory and experience – was adopted by most West European as well as by several Central and Latin American states. Most recently, virtually all emerging democracies in Central and Eastern Europe have established Constitutional Courts based on the Austrian and German experience.[1]

---

[1] The homepage of the German Constitutional Court (*Bundesverfassungsgericht*) (http://www.bundesverfassungsgericht.de) provides links to a number of constitutional courts all over the world.

The core area of constitutional review under the Austrian (European) system is the examination of the constitutionality of statutes. In addition to this principal function, other judicial powers such as examining the legality of substatutory acts (e.g., government ordinances or regulations), decision-making regarding jurisdictional disputes among other state organs, electoral disputes, and impeachment trials may be transferred to a constitutional court. Austria and Germany have endowed their constitutional courts with a multitude of such powers, whereas France has been more reticent.

There are several reasons why the American system was not adopted by European nations in the course of their constitutional reforms following World War II. European constitutional review is the product of a specific model of separation of powers and rule of law in continental Europe. This model emphasizes notions of the supremacy of parliament and of the product of its legislative activity, the statute. In Civil law countries, statutory regulation is comprehensive, and judges have no overt law-making function similar to that of their Common law brethren. They are faithfully to apply the statute, not to challenge it. Their activism is also curbed by the fact that they are part of a civil service hierarchy, in which they are promoted from lower to higher courts according to professional competence and seniority. Constitutional review being a quasi-legislative function, it is considered to differ substantially from "regular" judicial activity. It is not to be entrusted to ordinary courts and judges, whose task is to apply the statute as they find it, who may not superimpose themselves over the legislature, and who on account of personality and experience are not ideally qualified for this politically sensitive activity. This function is, therefore, reserved to a special procedure before a separate constitutional organ with justices specially selected for this function.

One should note in particular that in times of radical political change from a totalitarian to a democratic system, the regular judiciary is invariably tainted but cannot be replaced quickly, whereas a specialized constitutional court may be staffed with competent and reputable jurists. If sufficiently broad access is provided (like for instance in Hungary today), this court may swiftly impose constitutionality from above.

II. Structure and Functions of the Austrian Constitutional Court (*Verfassungsgerichtshof*)

The structure and functions of the Austrian Constitutional Court (*Verfassungsgerichtshof*) are regulated in considerable detail in articles 137 to 148f of the Austrian Federal Constitution of 1920, as modified in 1929, and as subsequently amended. Other legal regulations are contained in the *Verfassungsgerichtshofsgesetz* (*VerfGG*, Law on the Constitutional Court of 1953, with numerous subsequent amendments) and in the Rules adopted by the Court itself in 1946.

Regarding a number of its present functions, the Court had a predecessor in the Imperial Court of Justice (*Reichsgericht*) that heard jurisdictional disputes and acted as a special administrative court for the Austrian part of the

Austro-Hungarian Empire between 1867 (effective 1869) and 1919. Also since 1867, impeachment proceedings against government ministers for violations of the Constitution or statutes could be brought in a special State Court of Justice (*Staatsgerichtshof*). All ordinary courts were empowered to examine the legality of administrative regulations. An examination of the constitutionality of statutes did not exist in the Monarchy.[2] It was introduced in 1920 and assigned to the Constitutional Court, which was established in 1919.

A. Composition of the Court

The Austrian Constitutional Court consists of a President, a Vice-President, twelve Members (*Mitglieder*) and six Substitute Members (*Ersatzmitglieder*). All members of the Court must have law degrees and at least ten years of professional legal experience. Three Members and two Substitute Members must have their domicile outside of Vienna. Members are appointed by the Federal President, who is bound by nominations made by three other constitutional organs, namely the Federal Government (*Bundesregierung*), the National Council (*Nationalrat*) and the Federal Council (*Bundesrat*):

- He appoints the President, the Vice-President, six other Members and three Substitute Members as nominated by the Federal Government. Thus, more than one-half of the membership of the Court are *de facto* appointed by the executive branch without any checks and balances. These members of the Court must be judges, administrative officials, or law professors.
- He appoints three other Members and two Substitute Members as nominated by the National Council.[3]
- He appoints three Members and one Substitute Member as nominated by the Federal Council.[4]

Members of the Court enjoy judicial independence and retire from office at the end of the calendar year in which they turn 70. As of July 2000, five of the 14 members of the Court are law professors, four are former administrative officials of the Federal or *Land* Governments, three are attorneys, one is a judge of the Administrative Court, and one member is a former prosecutor. Three of the members are women.[5] The nomination of the members is, of course, subject to the influence of the major political parties as asserted in the

---

[2] Statutes were sanctioned by the Emperor, who was "hallowed, inviolable and unaccountable" under article 1 of the *Staatsgrundgesetz über die Regierungs- und Vollzugsgewalt* (State Fundamental Law on Governmental and Executive Power) 1867.

[3] See *supra* Chapter 3 (The Political System), III.A.2.b.

[4] See *supra* Chapter 3, III.B.2.

[5] Lisbeth Lass, an attorney from Innsbruck, was appointed in March of 1994, having served as Substitute Member since 1993. Eleonore Berchtold-Ostermann, a Vienna attorney, was appointed in 1997; Claudia Kahr, a former high ranking administrative official, in 1999. Gabriele Kucsko-Stadlmayer, a professor of constitutional law at the Vienna Law School, was appointed as a Substitute Member in 1995; Lilian Hofmeister, a judge, in 1999. Of the 16 members of the German Constitutional Court, five are women, among them Jutta Limbach, the President of the Court.

respective state organs.[6] Yet recent voting patterns in the Court show very little party loyalty, even in politically sensitive matters.

As to numbers, the membership of the Austrian Court corresponds to that of most other European constitutional courts.[7] But in some other aspects the Austrian Court differs significantly from those other courts: Its members do not work full time on the court, there are substitute members, and the retirement age of 70 years is comparatively high and thus accounts for a considerably longer term of office for Austrian constitutional judges than for their counterparts in other nations, who usually serve fixed and unrenewable terms,[8] ranging from six years in Portugal to 12 in Germany.[9]

B. Work Organization

Membership on the Constitutional Court is not considered a full-time occupation. The members may continue their regular work as judges, attorneys, or law professors; only administrative officials are relieved of their duties in order to safeguard their judicial independence. All members of the Court receive salaries depending on their respective functions.[10] Sessions of the Court are scheduled by the President of the Court according to need, which in practice means approximately three weeks every quarter of the year.[11] One-third of this time is devoted to deliberations in the "Small Senate" ("*Kleiner*

---

[6] But there are strict limitations placed on the eligibility of politicians in article 147 (4) of the Constitution: "The following cannot belong to the Constitutional Court: members of the Federal Government or a *Land* Government, furthermore members of the *Nationalrat*, the *Bundesrat*, or any other popular representative body; for members of these representative bodies who have been elected for a fixed term of legislation or office such incompatibility continues until the expiration of that term of legislation or office. Finally, persons who are in the employ of or hold office in a political party cannot belong to the Constitutional Court."

[7] The Italian *Corte costituzionale*, for instance, has 15 members, the German *Bundesverfassungsgericht* 16 (who are, however, working in a twin court of two permanent panels or "senates" of eight members each). The constitutional courts of Belgium and Spain have 12 members each, and the Portuguese court has 13. Only the French *Conseil constitutionnel* has nine members like the United States Supreme Court.

[8] Terms are unrenewable in Germany, Italy, and Spain, but renewable in France and Portugal.

[9] In France, Italy, and Spain constitutional court justices are appointed for nine-year terms; only the members of the Belgian *Cour d'arbitrage* serve the same indefinite terms (with retirement at age 70) as the Austrian Constitutional Court justices.

[10] The President of the Court receives a monthly salary of 180,000 ATS, the Vice-President and the permanent reporters receive 160,000 ATS, other members 90,000 ATS per month. If they receive additional income from public employment (e.g., as law professors or judges), their total monthly compensation must not exceed 200,000 ATS.

[11] Sessions are usually scheduled in the months of February/March, June, September/October and November/December. This and the following statistical information is contained in the (non-public) annual reports of the Constitutional Court. Pursuant to article 14 (3) *VerfGG* (Law on the Constitutional Court) these reports are to be submitted to the Federal Chancellor.

Senat"), a panel usually consisting of the President, the Vice-President and four Members, which may under article 7 (2) of the Law on the Constitutional Court dispose of certain cases in a simplified procedure.[12]

To prepare its decisions, the Court appoints a number of its members to function as "permanent reporters"[13] (*ständige Referenten*) for periods of three years.[14] Every reporter has two law clerks (*Schriftführer*) who help him prepare his draft opinions.

The President of the Court assigns opinions to the permanent reporters, attempting as a rule to assign related questions to the same reporter, to distribute the workload evenly, and also to take the prior legal experience (specialization) and the geographical background of the reporter into account. It is normally the reporter who decides whether the case should be heard in the "Small Senate" or by the full Court. The reporter's draft is circulated to all Members, even if it is proposed that it be dealt with in the "Small Senate," thus giving every member an opportunity to demand deliberation in the full Court.

Proceedings before the Constitutional Court[15] are usually initiated by a written motion, which is subsequently served on the opponent (if there is any) for a written reply. As soon as the permanent reporter of the Court submits his written report, the President schedules a public oral hearing.[16] After an oral summary by the reporter, the parties are given the opportunity to argue their case. It may be said that the oral argument rarely influences the outcome of the case. If possible, the decision of the Court is to be announced orally, together with the most important reasons, immediately following the hearing. In fact it is frequently announced at a later date or published only in written form. According to the Law on the Constitutional Court, the Court may in

---

[12] The most important of these authorizations are the rejection of obviously unfounded complaints and the satisfaction of petitions that are based on points of law that have already been sufficiently clarified by previous decisions of the Court.

[13] Article 2 (1) *VerfGG.* The Vice-President may be appointed "permanent reporter," the President may not. Whereas each of the nine reporters prepared an average of 232 opinions in 1991, this average has in recent years risen to numbers between 300 and 400 (1997: 411; 1998: 363; 1999: 306). Most of these opinions were adopted in the non-public sessions of the 'Small Senate." On the small number of cases decided after oral argument before the full Court see *infra* note 17.

[14] They may be – and in fact regularly are – reappointed.

[15] Articles 137 to 144 of the Constitution; articles 15 to 88 *VerfGG.*

[16] The Court has a quorum if the President and at least eight other members are present. If a member is unable to participate, a substitute member is invited from the same nomination category, if possible, (Federal Government, National, or Federal Council, respectively) as the member for whom he substitutes. Usually it is the President who chairs the Court, in the case of his disability, the Vice-President officiates. The President may ask the Vice-President to chair specific sessions of the Court. When he is not in the chair, the Vice-President may, if he wishes, participate in the session as an ordinary voting member. This is regularly the case.

exceptional cases decide without prior oral argument. In practice, however, these exceptions have become the rule.[17]

The secret deliberations of the Court are based on a motion by the reporter. After the discussion, the voting process follows the order of the members' ages, beginning with the oldest judge present. The presiding officer may only vote in order to break a tie.[18]

C. Powers of the Court .

There are at least eight types of powers of the Austrian Constitutional Court, all of which are extensively regulated in the Constitution.[19] Among these powers, the most significant and most typical is undoubtedly the examination of the constitutionality of statutes. In the Austrian system, examination of all general norms, i.e., statutes, regulations and international treaties, as to their constitutionality or legality is monopolized by a single institution, the Constitutional Court.[20]

1. Review of Regulations, Statutes, and International Treaties

The Austrian Constitution addresses the examination of regulations, statutes, and treaties by the Constitutional Court, in this order, in articles 139 to 140a of the Constitution. Whereas requests to declare regulations illegal or statutes unconstitutional are relatively frequent, requests to examine international treaties are extremely rare.

a. Statutes

The Constitutional Court examines the constitutionality of federal or *Land* statutes (*Gesetze*)[21] either *ex officio*, when they are prejudicial to a case before the Court,[22] or at the request of certain institutions or persons.[23] The

---

[17] In 1998, the total number of cases decided was 3,272, of which only 42 cases were admitted to oral argument. In 1999, 2,760 cases were decided. The annual report for that year does not indicate the number of cases scheduled for oral argument.

[18] Which happens, e.g., when a member has become incapacitated in the course of the proceedings concerning a specific case. This unique deprivation of voting power (art. 31 *VerfGG*) is usually explained in terms of a desirable neutrality on the part of a President whose task it is to guide difficult debates.

[19] Articles 137 to 145 of the Constitution.

[20] Cf. article 89 (1) of the Constitution: "the courts are not entitled to examine the validity of duly published statutes, regulations, and treaties."

[21] Article 140 of the Constitution. The Constitutional Court may also examine constitutional law. *Land* constitutions must be in conformity with the Federal Constitution (art. 99 (1)) and "simple" federal constitutional law must not contradict the "structural principles" of the Constitution. A substantial change in these principles ("total revision") could only be effected by popular referendum (art. 44 (3)), whereas normally constitutional amendment merely requires a two-thirds majority in the National Council.

[22] Article 140 (3) of the Constitution.

[23] These requests may be brought by appellate courts, Independent Administrative Panels, the Supreme Court or the Administrative Court in the case of prejudiciality.

most interesting route of access is undoubtedly the request by a private citizen to protect his constitutional rights.

This individual request for constitutional review was introduced in Austria in 1975, following the German example. It is subject to certain prerequisites, such as a degree of seriousness ("*Betroffenheitsdichte*") of direct interference with a person's rights (and not just interests) that must be actual (as opposed to merely potential); and there must also be a finding of unreasonableness in requiring the complainant to pursue his right by taking a circuitous route ("*Umwegsunzumutbarkeit*"), e.g., that the complainant accept a penalty in an administrative procedure in order to exhaust a line of appeal and finally have the decision reviewed in the Constitutional Court.

The statistics for 1999 and 1998 (the latter given in parentheses) show a fairly stable pattern. Of the 271 (270) cases of review of statutes initiated in 1999 (1998), for example, 245 (222) concerned federal statutes[24] and 26 (48) concerned *Land* statutes. Of these cases, 83 (68) were brought by way of individual citizens' complaints, 21 (34) were brought by the Administrative Court, 22 (41) by Independent Administrative Panels, nine (17) by regular courts and one (0) by *Land* Governments. The Constitutional Court examined *ex officio* 135 (90) cases. In 1998, 20 cases were brought by the Federal Asylum Panel; none were brought in 1999.

The Court may repeal an entire statute or parts of it. The statute expires at the moment of publication of the Court's decision in the *Bundesgesetzblatt* (Federal Law Gazette) or in the official publication series (law gazette) of the respective *Land*. The Court may, however, postpone this effect for up to 18 months to grant the legislature an opportunity to repair the faulty law. The Court grants no grace period if the statute violates civil rights or the Court considers the repealed provision dispensable. As opposed to the legal situation after the repeal of an illegal ordinance, the annulment of a statutory provision revives the older legal provision that had been in effect prior to the unconstitutional law. But the Court may expressly exclude this consequence.

b. Regulations

Under article 139 of the Constitution, regulations (*Verordnungen*) of federal or *Land* authorities may be declared illegal at the request of certain institutions or persons.[25] The Constitutional Court itself may examine a regu-

---

The Federal Government may contest *Land* statutes, and a *Land* Government or one-third of the members of the National Council may challenge a federal statute. Every person may challenge a statute if it violates his constitutional rights immediately, that is to say, when it affects these rights directly without mediation by a court decision or an administrative ruling (see Const. art. 140 (3)).

[24] In the past only *Land* governments, but not the opposition in parliament, exercised the right to challenge the constitutionality of a federal statute. After the formation of the *ÖVP/FPÖ* government, the *SPÖ* will certainly use the right of one-third of the deputies in parliament to challenge the constitutionality of a number of statutes.

[25] For instance, a court or an Independent Administrative Panel that would have to apply the regulation in a specific case (a situation of "concrete review"). The request

lation on its own initiative on account of prejudiciality, i.e., if it would have to apply the regulation in a specific case before it.[26]

The Court may repeal an entire regulation or parts of it.[27] The regulation expires at the moment of publication of the Court's decision in the *Bundesgesetzblatt* (Federal Law Gazette) or the law gazette of the respective *Land*. The Court may, however, grant the respondent a period of up to six months to repair the faulty regulation to avoid a regulatory vacuum. If legislative action is required for this purpose, the period may be extended to 18 months.

In principle, the repeal of an illegal regulation by the Court has no retroactive effect. The regulation continues to be applied to all cases that have arisen under its regime, the case in point being the exception to this rule. The Court may, however, extend this exception to similar cases that had been initiated but not finally decided prior to oral argument or non-public deliberation of the case in point.

c. Treaties

The Court examines the legality or constitutionality of international treaties (*Staatsverträge*)[28] according to their rank in the hierarchy of norms,[29] applying the rules relevant to the examination of statutes or regulations, respectively. Since the Court may not repeal rules of international law, its decisions in this respect are confined to the declaration of illegality or unconstitutionality and their non-applicability as domestic law. For such a ruling to be implemented, a period of up to two years may be established by the Court.[30]

---

may also be made by the Federal Government concerning all regulations of *Land* authorities and vice versa. Municipalities (*Gemeinden*) may contest regulations of superior organs unlawfully exercising legal supervision over municipal enactments. In these situations, the Constitutional Court exercises "abstract review" without the need for a specific case to arise. The request may furthermore be submitted by an individual citizen whose rights have been directly affected by the illegal regulation. Finally, the People's Advocate's Office (*Volksanwaltschaft*) may also request the examination of federal or *Land* regulations by the Court (Const. art. 148e).

[26] Article 139 (3) of the Constitution. Of the 104 (106) cases initiated in 1999 (1998), 39 (56) were brought by way of individual citizens' complaints, one (none) was brought by the Administrative Court, 17 (14) by Independent Administrative Panels, 9 (14) by regular courts. 35 (21) cases were raised by the Constitutional Court *ex officio*. In 1999, one case was brought by the People's Advocate's Office of Vorarlberg, three by *Land* governments.

[27] Article 139 (3) of the Constitution.

[28] Article 140a of the Constitution.

[29] The rank of international treaties in domestic law depends on the question of how their provisions would have to be enacted under Austrian constitutional law (Const. art. 50). The transformation of international treaties is therefore subject to the rules governing the enactment of constitutional or statutory law.

[30] No cases have been decided to this date.

2. Electoral Disputes

The Court may examine the legality of elections, popular initiatives, and referendums, and it may make decisions concerning the loss of a seat by a member of a popular representative body.[31] The Court nullifies an election if the process is proven to have been illegal and to have had an effect on the results.[32]

3. Impeachment Trial

The Constitutional Court may be called upon to conduct impeachment trials against the highest state officials for culpable violation of the law in the conduct of their office.[33] The sanction is loss of office, but in the case of a minor infraction, the Court may confine itself to the mere declaration that a violation has been committed.[34]

4. Special Administrative Jurisdiction

Under special conditions, the Constitutional Court functions as an administrative court which judges the legality of individual acts of administrative authorities.[35] A complaint may be brought by an individual citizen after administrative appeals have been exhausted. The complainant must demonstrate that the act either violated his constitutionally guaranteed rights or was based on an unconstitutional statute or treaty, or on an illegal regulation or treaty, and violated his rights. Such complaints concerning the violation of

---

[31] Article 141 of the Constitution. In 1998 the Court deprived a deputy to the *Nationalrat* of his seat for failure to attend meetings.

[32] Of the 18 cases before the Court in 1998, five were successful. In 1999 the Court decided 12 complaints, nullifying electoral results in four cases.

[33] Article 142 (1) of the Constitution. A joint session of the National and the Federal Council may accuse the Federal President of a violation of the Federal Constitution. The National Council may indict members of the Federal Government, and a *Land* parliament may indict members of the *Land* Government for violations of the law. The Federal Government may indict a *Land* Governor (*Landeshauptmann*) for noncompliance with a federal statute or regulation in matters of federal administration delegated to him.

[34] Article 142 (4) of the Constitution. To this date, three impeachment cases have been decided. The latest example occurred in 1984, when the *Land* Governor (*Landeshauptmann*) of Salzburg issued an illegal regulation permitting salespersons to work on Saturday, December 8, 1984, which was a legal holiday (on which all stores had to stay closed under federal law). In so doing, the Governor had intended to support the economy of Salzburg, which was hurt by customers using this free day for Christmas shopping on the other side of the border in neighboring German towns. Since the administration of the Federal Statute on Working Hours and Leisure Time (*Arbeitsruhegesetz*) was a federal matter in which the *Land* Governor was bound by the orders of the Federal Minister for Social Administration, and the Governor had disregarded the Minister's instruction to repeal his illegal regulation, he was charged by the Federal Government in the Constitutional Court. The Court stated that the Governor had violated the law, but did not sentence him to loss of office.

[35] Article 144 of the Constitution.

rights other than those protected directly by the Constitution may also be brought in the Administrative Court.

The Constitutional Court may reject the complaint in a simplified procedure in the "Small Senate," if it is unlikely to be successful or if the clarification of a constitutional issue is not to be expected.[36]

5. Other Areas of Jurisdiction

The Constitutional Court has jurisdiction regarding certain financial claims against the Federation (*Bund*), the *Länder*, or the municipalities (*Gemeinden*) that are not subject to the jurisdiction of regular courts or administrative agencies.[37] The Court may be called upon to resolve jurisdictional disputes between courts and administrative authorities, between the Administrative Court (*Verwaltungsgerichtshof*) and other courts (including the Constitutional Court itself), between individual *Länder*, and between a *Land* and the Federation.[38] The Court may also be asked for an authentic interpretation of the distribution of powers between the Federation and the *Länder* in view of future acts of legislation or administration.[39] The Court considers disputes arising from treaties between the Federation and the *Länder* and between individual *Länder*.[40] It may also clarify the powers of the Board of Audit (*Rechnungshof*)[41] and the People's Advocates' Office (*Volksanwaltschaft*).[42]

D. Enforcement of Decisions

The execution of financial claims is a matter for ordinary courts.[43] The enforcement of all other decisions of the Court, should this be necessary (and so far this has never been the case), is the duty of the Federal President.

---

[36] Article 144 (2) of the Constitution. In 1999 (1998) – fairly typical years – 210 (335) complaints were rejected because of the unlikelihood of their success, 424 (409) because they were not expected to contribute to the clarification of constitutional law, and 683 (706) for both reasons. These rejections account for 1317 (1450) of a total of 2373 (2670) decisions of the Court. The success rate was 15% (17%) or 351 (448) cases.

[37] Article 137 of the Constitution. This category mainly contains salary claims of civil servants and claims of territorial entities arising from revenue sharing legislation. The Court decided 26 cases in 1998 and 32 in 1999.

[38] Article 138 (1) of the Constitution. Such disputes are comparatively rare. 23 were adjudicated in 1997, 8 in 1998, 13 in 1999.

[39] Article 138 (2) of the Constitution. In practice, such questions have been raised primarily concerning legislative drafts of the Federation or the *Länder*, and in recent years they have become extremely rare. In 1999, the Court made one decision in this area; it made none in 1997 or 1998.

[40] Article 138a (1) and (2) of the Constitution with reference to treaties under article 15a (1) and (2).

[41] Article 126a of the Constitution. There has been no decision since 1995.

[42] Article 148f of the Constitution. There were no cases in 1993 and 1994, three in 1995, and one in 1996.

[43] Article 146 (1) of the Constitution.

The President instructs the appropriate state organ of the Federation or the *Länder*, including the armed forces, to enforce the decision.[44]

III. The Jurisprudence of the Court

A. From Formalism to Value-Orientation

For the greater part of its history, the Austrian Court was known for its extremely cautious translation of the Constitution into political reality. It never shared the exalted notion of being a "constitutional organ *sui generis*" developed by the German court, and it never exhibited any desire to take a "social policy" or "judicial activism" approach along the lines of some American courts. On the contrary, in the tradition of Hans Kelsen's Vienna School of Legal Positivism it considered itself a "prisoner of the words of the Constitution" subject to "strict construction," interpreting civil rights in a more formal sense than most other European courts. The Court generally exercised a maximum of judicial self-restraint *vis-à-vis* the democratically legitimized legislator.

In recent times, however, in response to scholarly criticism, taking courage from the example of the German court (which right from the beginning has explicitly imposed a high standard of substantive values on the legislature), and to a certain extent following the guidance of the European Commission and the European Court of Human Rights in Strasbourg, the Austrian Constitutional Court has shown a tendency towards a more value-oriented approach, particularly in the area of fundamental rights.

This new approach has become apparent in particular with respect to those fundamental rights that are subject to legislative restriction. The older jurisprudence of the Court had granted the legislature wide latitude in the pursuit of its political goals, forbidding only the total abolition or an excessive (unjustifiable) legislative interference with the essential minimum of a fundamental right. Thus, for instance, the Constitutional Court held that the nationalization of major enterprises in the areas of industry, mining, and banking constituted no violation of the fundamental freedom to pursue gainful activity.[45]

This extremely formal approach came under increasing criticism by Austrian constitutional law scholars, in particular Günther Winkler,[46] who regarded fundamental rights not as mere formal restrictions placed on the legislature but as substantive value judgments determining the contents of legisla-

---

[44] Article 146 (2) of the Constitution.

[45] See, e.g., State Fundamental Law of 21 December 1867, *RGBl.* No. 142, on the General Rights of Citizens, article 6: "Every citizen can take up residence and domicile at any place inside the boundaries of the state, acquire every kind of real property and freely dispose of the same, as well as practice every kind of gainful activity subject to the conditions of the law." See also the restrictive interpretation by the Court in *VfSlg.* 3118/1956.

[46] See his seminal work *Wertbetrachtung im Recht und ihre Grenzen* (1969).

tion. Today, the Constitutional Court subjects statutes to an examination of whether the legislature used its discretion in accordance with the value system established by the fundamental rights of the Constitution. Thus, for instance, the Court has since 1984 developed a line of decisions that only permits legislative restriction on the fundamental right to pursue gainful activity if there is a compelling public interest and if the measures chosen to protect this public interest appear to be suitable, adequate, and justified. It has, for instance, accepted the need to regulate in the public interest competition in the areas of medical supplies, funeral services, banking, and chimney sweeping. The Court, on the other hand, has rejected for lack of public interest legislative restrictions imposed on taxi enterprises, driver training schools, and personnel agencies. This new, more activist approach on the part of the Constitutional Court has predictably led to (isolated and unjustified) criticism charging the Court with arrogation of legislative power and political involvement.

B. The Influence of the European Human Rights Convention

There is no doubt that the development of European constitutional courts has been and will continue to be profoundly affected by the processes of expanding European human rights (see *infra* Chapter 9) and European economic and political integration. The European Convention for the Protection of Human Rights and Fundamental Freedoms (ECHR)[47] was ratified by Austria in 1958.[48] To clarify its domestic legal status, it was retroactively qualified as constitutional law in 1964.[49] Its scope has been further developed by 11 additional Protocols. The Convention and the Protocols add considerably to Austrian civil rights. Over the years, the European Court of Human Rights in Strasbourg has dealt with a large number of individual complaints, many of which have successfully challenged Austrian violations and have subsequently led to legislative change in Austria. The Austrian Constitutional Court has, in its interpretation of fundamental rights since the 1970s, become increasingly responsive to the standards developed and refined by the Strasbourg Court. These standards have generally reinforced the tendency towards a less formal and more value-oriented approach in the Austrian Court's jurisprudence. (See *infra* Chapter 9).

C. Public Attention, Criticism, and Acceptance

In the period of the Grand Coalition of the two major parties between 1947 and 1966, the cautious approach of the Austrian Court evoked little comment or criticism. During the Socialist government from 1970 to 1983,

---

[47] Initiated by the Council of Europe on the basis of the UN General Declaration of Human Rights (1948) and signed in Rome on November 4, 1950, the Convention has been in force since September 3, 1953. By July 2000 it had been signed by 41 European states.

[48] *BGBl* 1958/210.

[49] *BGBl* 1964/59.

however, the conservative parliamentary opposition began to accuse the Court of servile accommodation, especially after a seven to six majority of the Court had endorsed abortion during the first trimester, allowed student participation in university government, and ruled the state monopoly of radio and TV to be constitutional.

The Austrian Court came under massive media criticism for the first time in 1987, when it annulled a statute which restricted multiple pensions of former politicians. Although the Court correctly ruled that the statute violated the constitutional equal protection clause, the press viewed the decision as a protection of unwarranted political privileges. The legislature subsequently passed the same law with a two-thirds majority and thereby elevated it to the rank of a constitutional provision, making it exempt from regular constitutional review. Some constitutional law scholars consider such an act to be an abuse of legal form, and there are indications that in future cases the Federal President may refuse to certify the constitutionality of this process and withhold his signature. The Court itself has publicly criticized this questionable practice in its subsequent annual report[50] as weakening the protection of civil rights. The same problem arises, when legislative measures are taken in the form of constitutional law to avoid constitutional review in the first place.

Generally speaking, the Austrian Court continues to work largely outside the realm of media attention,[51] but its decisions are carefully scrutinized and actively discussed in the professional world, notably by constitutional law scholars in law schools and by special constitutional law services (*Verfassungsdienste*) established in administrative agencies. These services conduct preventive examinations of all legislative and regulatory drafts as to their constitutionality, thus assuring constitutional compliance at an early stage.

In civil law countries, there is no tradition of judges writing dissenting opinions. Following the example of the U.S. Supreme Court, the German Constitutional Court demanded and ultimately received in 1970 the right to publish dissenting opinions.[52] In Austria this idea was almost unanimously rejected as late as 1992. It was generally feared that dissents might weaken the authority of the Court and would invariably increase its workload. In 1992, the Austrian Federal Government introduced a bill in parliament, arguing that dissenting opinions would force the majority to reason their opinions more

---

[50] March 17, 1994, p. 12.

[51] Several years ago, Court President Ludwig Adamovich publicly deplored Austria's poor media coverage as compared to that in Germany or France. In the meantime, the Court itself has taken steps to provide more information to the public. On October 1, 1990, the Constitutional Court celebrated the 70th anniversary of the Austrian Constitution. This celebration has evolved into a regular "Constitution Day," with lectures and discussions in the presence of high-ranking representatives of the Austrian state and the legal community. Important decisions of the Court are accompanied by news releases, and there is even an occasional press conference by the President. The Court also has an internet homepage (www.vfgh.gv.at), where opinions and press releases may be found.

The Court is frequently visited by foreign delegations of politicians, judges, scholars and students, who are gracefully received by the President or his aides.

[52] Article 30 II 1 *BVerfGG*.

fully, thus increasing the rationality of decisions and making value judgments more explicit. But due to a lack of interest on the part of the Court, no further action has been taken. Discussions have recently resumed but have remained inconclusive. Judging from the German experience, dissenting opinions would, at any rate, be rare.[53] The Austrian Court would most likely continue to strive for unanimity, and individual members would only in exceptional circumstances take the time (and make the effort) to challenge in writing the permanent reporter's draft opinion.

D. The Impact of Austria's Membership in the EU

Austria's accession to the European Union, effective as of January 1, 1995, had far-reaching effects on the role of the Constitutional Court. Before that date, the Constitutional Court alone examined legal norms as to their conformity with the Constitution, nullifying those enactments that contradicted constitutional law. Prior to nullification by the Constitutional Court, all state authorities had to apply these norms. Since 1995, two legal systems have existed side-by-side in Austria, namely European Community law and autonomous Austrian law. Immediately applicable Community law (e.g., EC regulations) overrides national law, including constitutional law. In the case of a conflict, Austrian law may not be applied. According to most scholars, such national law automatically becomes invalid and can no longer be contested in the Constitutional Court. The question of whether a rule of Austrian law contradicts EU law is to be examined by the authority that is to apply the respective rule. Thus, the Constitutional Court's former monopoly of examination and nullification has been undermined. The Constitutional Court rejects complaints against the application of Austrian law instead of EU law on the grounds that no constitutional question is involved. If it is doubtful whether a rule of EU law or of national law should be applied, the Court accepts cases for review of the constitutionality of statutes or the legality of regulations if the rule of national was applied and this application was not unreasonable. Moreover, in interpreting norms of EC law, the Constitutional Court is bound by the interpretation of the European Court of Justice in Luxembourg, and it must refer questions of doubt to the latter.[54] If an Austrian court or tribunal does not request a preliminary ruling of the European Court of Justice concerning the interpretation of the treaties or the validity or interpretation of Community acts, the Constitutional Court holds this to be a violation of the right to a lawful judge (Const. art. 83 (2)). Under Const. article 144, an individual complaint may be brought if an Austrian authority grossly misinterpreted EU law, or based its decision on a rule of national law in obvious violation of EU law.

---

[53] A German observer reports 123 separate opinions (out of 1040 senate decisions) in a 22-year period (1970–1992).

[54] In 1999 the Constitutional Court for the first time requested a preliminary ruling of the European Court of Justice.

In the opinion of the Constitutional Court, conflicts with the European Court will rarely arise, because the spheres of EU law and Austrian law are, in principle, clearly defined, as are the competencies of the European Court of Justice and of the Austrian Constitutional Court. Yet problems of overlapping and conflicting jurisdiction cannot entirely be avoided.

IV. Reform Proposals

A. Appointment of Justices

In the Austrian tradition of strong party discipline, the Federal Government that is nominally responsible to Parliament has in the past exercised sweeping control over the latter. As a result, there has been little debate and a total absence of constitutional checks and balances concerning nominations to the Constitutional Court in either the executive or the legislative branch. Lawyers and politicians have repeatedly proposed changes in the appointment process to the Constitutional Court. Some have suggested that the composition of the Court should reflect the relative strength of political parties in the parliament. Others favor electing justices by a two-thirds majority in parliament. Additional suggestions for reform have included granting nomination rights to law faculties or to the Court itself, appointing full-time members to the Court, appointing justices to limited terms, etc. Currently, none of these reform proposals, which at least in part suggest the adoption of the German model, is under serious consideration. In the past, the two major parties (the Social Democrats and the conservative People's Party) reserved seven voting positions on the Court to the stronger party and conceded six positions to the weaker party, even when one of the two was in opposition to the other. Other parties, namely the Freedom Party, the Greens, and the Liberal Forum, have not yet been able to place one of their sympathizers on the Court.[55] How the new *ÖVP/FPÖ* government will affect the composition of the Court will be seen in 2002, when the terms of the President and another member will expire.

When in 1993 and 1994 two positions on the Austrian Constitutional Court became vacant, these were for the first time publicly advertised,[56] and for the first time a woman was appointed as a full member of the Court.[57]

---

[55] Although, taken together, they accounted for close to one-third of the 183 deputies in the National Council.

[56] Yet there still are no public discussions and no hearings concerning the government candidates prior to their appointment. Brief non-public hearings are held prior to the nomination of parliament candidates, see *infra* note 58.

[57] In this instance the procedure followed by the Federal President in making his selection from the list of three candidates submitted by the National Council was unusual. He interviewed the candidates (of whom the first and third-ranked were women) and subsequently departed from the custom of appointing the candidate at the top of the list, a high-ranking civil servant in the Ministry of Social Affairs, by choosing the third-ranking candidate, an attorney from Innsbruck. The Social Democratic Party, which had nominated all three candidates, was indignant that its first

Proportional political representation on constitutional courts has frequently been criticized in Germany as well as in Austria. But one should recognize the special nature of the functions of constitutional courts in the political framework of checks and balances. There is a special need to select politically sensitive judges and to endow them with a high degree of democratic legitimacy through a parliamentary selection process. It is certainly a shortcoming of the Austrian political process that the *SPÖ* and the *ÖVP* in the past barred the parliamentary opposition from having a voice on the Court; there is no doubt also that the number of women should and will increase. One might wish for a higher level of publicity and professional scrutiny of the nomination and appointment process (without necessarily adopting the American extreme of excessively politicized Senate hearings).[58] It might also be worth considering to reduce the longevity of the Austrian court to the single 12-year term of German constitutional judges. In times of rapid social change the Court should not run the risk of losing touch with reality[59]. Generally speaking, however, political practice has been rather successful in putting professionally qualified and politically responsible judges on the Austrian and German Constitutional Courts, at the same time satisfying demands for diversity as to previous professional experience and regional origin.

B. Organization and Workload

The members of the Austrian Constitutional Court have a modest staff of 71 employees, among them 27 staff attorneys.[60] The Austrian Court decides an impressive number of cases in a highly expeditious manner. In 1997, 4,029

---

choice had been passed over, and both major parties subsequently changed the Constitution by eliminating the President's right to choose (Constitutional Amendments 1994, *BGBl* 1994/1013).

[58] On January 14, 1997, the Federal Council held a brief non-public hearing examining 24 applicants for a vacant position. Attorney Michael Graff received 14 votes and attorney Eleonora Berchtold-Ostermann 36. On January 21, 1998, the National Council nominated Rudolf Müller, a member of the Administrative Court, with most of the votes of the government coalition. He obtained 87 of 161 valid votes in a secret election, 45 votes went to constitutional law professor Bernhard Raschauer, 23 to Gabriele Kucsko-Stadlmayer. There had previously been a brief hearing of 24 candidates (who appeared and were questioned in 15-minute intervals) in the judiciary committee. On December 5, 1998, the National Council nominated tax law professor Hans-Georg Ruppe by 92 of 147 valid votes. 32 votes went to Bernhard Raschauer, 9 to Gabriele Kucsko-Stadlmayer, 7 to Brigitte Hornyik, a law clerk at the Constitutional Court, and 7 to other candidates.

[59] This observation should not be read as implying criticism of the present incumbents, who have, on the contrary, shown remarkable adaptability to meet emerging needs, but as a *caveat* in terms of general policy. A new system could easily be phased in with the appointment of new members, without affecting the rights of incumbents to serve out their terms.

[60] More than two-thirds of the employees (over one-half of the staff attorneys) are women. The German Court commands a staff of 198, of which 66 have formal legal education (among them 21 women).

new cases were brought to the Court. At the end of the year, the Court had decided 14,869 cases (among them 11,167 almost identical complaints regarding a corporate tax provision);[61] 2,342 remained unresolved. In 1998, 2,897 new cases were brought. The Court decided 3,272 cases, while 1,967 remained unresolved. In 1999, 2,535 new cases were brought, the Court delivered 2,760 decisions; 1,742 cases remained open at the end of that year. It should not come as a surprise that in Austria, like in Germany, a stronger role for the "Small Senate" is being discussed.

In order to continue functioning effectively as the supreme adjudicator and promoter of civil rights, the Court must maintain its impressive record of deciding cases swiftly and persuasively. To this end, it should probably consider (and be authorized by legislation) to work concurrently in several (three member?) panels.[62] It should definitely increase the number of assistants working for each of the permanent reporters from two to three.[63] And it need hardly be afraid of entertaining the idea of publishing the number of votes for and against a particular opinion, or even have a judge or group of judges writing an occasional dissenting opinion. It is – with good reason – not contemplated to follow Germany's lead in appointing full-time justices, or in establishing two senates of the Court.[64]

One recent proposal calls for a fundamental restructuring of the entire system of the "courts of public law" by reducing the competencies of the Constitutional Court to strictly constitutional matters, whereas problems of a more or less administrative law character (Const. art. 144) should be handled exclusively by the Administrative Court, which itself should be relieved by the creation of administrative courts of first instance.

C. Judicial Referral

If a German judge becomes convinced that the statute he would have to apply in a specific case is unconstitutional, he must interrupt proceedings in order to submit the constitutional question directly to the Constitutional Court (*Richtervorlage*).[65] This procedure protects the legislature against disregard of

---

[61] Since 1996 the Court in its annual reports repeatedly asked for legislative measures to deal with such situations.

[62] Cf. article 221 (ex 165) TEC, which permits the European Court of Justice to form chambers of three or five judges to adjudicate certain categories of cases.

[63] As is the case in the German Court. It should be noted that every U.S. Supreme Court Justice employs no fewer than four law clerks. This may, of course, create problems of delegation and supervision of work. Thus, German observers jokingly refer to the law clerks as the "third senate" of the Federal Constitutional Court. There have been suggestions to establish a real Third Senate or even a separate *Staatsgerichtshof* in Leipzig for all matters of constitutional review other than civil rights (which would be retained by and fully occupy the present two senates).

[64] A number of states which have in recent years established constitutional review according to the German model (e.g., Spain, Portugal, Hungary, the Czech Republic, and Bulgaria) have refrained from adopting the two-senate solution.

[65] Article 100 (1) of the Basic Law.

its enactments on the part of the judiciary, and ensures legal uniformity and reliability by concentrating constitutional adjudication in a single institution. Two-thirds of the usually fewer than 100 requests[66] of this type per annum come from lower courts. The majority of them are rejected.[67]

The Austrian legal system does not open this route of constitutional review to trial courts.[68] Yet the German experience seems to demonstrate that there is room for improving the knowledge of constitutional law at this level without leading to a significant increase in the workload of the Constitutional Court. With Austria's accession to the EU in 1995, all judges are authorized to refer questions concerning the compatibility of Austrian law with EC law to the European Court of Justice in Luxembourg. There is no reason for denying the trial judge a function in domestic constitutional law which he has been granted (and will, no doubt, increasingly exercise) with respect to supranational legal rules.[69]

D. Citizens' Complaints

In Germany, the constitutional complaint is an extraordinary legal remedy of last resort, by which an individual citizen may protect himself against interference by public power with his civil rights. The great majority of these complaints are filed in opposition to the decisions of regular courts. Of more than 5,000 complaints submitted per year, very few reach the senate. The overall success rate from an applicant's perspective lies between three and five percent. It is based on the – generally correct – assumption that ordinary courts already offer a high level of civil rights protection, and that the Constitutional Court's primary task is to develop constitutional law. The screening function is exercised by the three-judge panels (*Kammern*) which handle 97% of the cases.

Austria does not allow constitutional complaints by citizens against the decisions of regular courts. Such complaints should be permitted, however, for reasons similar to those that suggest broadening existing rules concerning judicial referral.

---

[66] The numbers fluctuate between a low of 30 in 1989 to a high of 137 in 1992. There were 38 requests in 1998 and 40 in 1999.

[67] Since the Fifth Law Amending the Law on the Federal Constitutional Court passed in 1993, three-judge panels may examine the admissibility of these referrals – with the exception of those of Supreme Courts, which, as a matter of courtesy, are reserved for the senates.

[68] Originally only the Supreme Court and the Administrative Court enjoyed this right. In 1975, it was broadened to include all appellate courts.

[69] Of the 255 judicial references in 1999, 56 came from Austria, 49 from Germany, 43 from Italy, and so forth; approximately one-quarter of these requests was submitted by courts of last instance.

E. Other Avenues of Access to the Court

A prime opportunity to move in this direction was, unfortunately, missed in the establishment in 1992 of a *Grundrechtsbeschwerde* (Fundamental Right Complaint) in matters of pretrial detention. The complaint was introduced in response to frequently successful appeals to the European Commission and to the Court of Human Rights in Strasbourg as to the unwarranted frequency and duration of pretrial detention imposed in Austrian judicial practice. The new remedy is a complaint directly to the Supreme Court, not the Constitutional Court. One of the main reasons for this structural inconsistency (i.e., of not allowing fundamental right complaints against court decisions to reach the Constitutional Court) is that the Constitutional Court was reluctant to accept additional cases. This workload, however, could be greatly reduced if Austria introduced a genuine administrative court system which would relieve the Constitutional Court of its function as special administrative tribunal.

Legal scholars and politicians also consider granting the right to contest the constitutionality of statutes to additional organs such as professional associations, the People's Advocates' Office, the Board of Audit, one-third of the members of the Federal Council, or the Federal President. It would seem appropriate to allow the Board of Audit and the People's Advocates' Office, the two important monitoring institutions of bureaucratic efficiency and legality, direct access to the Court for the purpose of challenging apparently unconstitutional statutes. There may also be good reasons in favor of granting access to the Court to other petitioners to eliminate unconstitutional legislation as observed by them as players in the political process. Yet there appears to be no pressing need to accommodate these entities that would outweigh the legitimate concern of the Constitutional Court to avoid additional pressures on its scarce personnel resources – especially since such petitions could in many cases not be summarily rejected by the "Small Senate," but would require the attention of the full Court.

F. Enforcement of Decisions

Generally, the enforcement of Constitutional Court decisions presents no problem in either Austria or Germany – state organs as a rule voluntarily comply with these decisions. In Germany, the Court may determine in its opinion which organ is to enforce the decision and in what way this should be done.[70] This appears to be a better solution than the Austrian provision that calls on the Federal President, who himself has no executive power but must enlist other state organs for this purpose. Austria should fully adopt the German view of granting the Court full independence from any sort of executive tutelage. The Constitutional Court should neither depend on the Federal Chancellor to submit its personnel and budget requests to the Parliament, nor should it have to rely on the Federal President for the execution of its judgments.

---

[70] Article 35 *BVerfGG.*

G. Provisional Orders

Under Austrian constitutional law, the Constitutional Court has no power to issue provisional orders. In its annual reports since 1996, the Court has repeatedly pointed out that a necessity to issue provisional orders might arise under EU law to avoid Austrian state responsibility. Pointing out that EU law provided an appropriate basis for such orders, the Court – anxious to avoid the impression of arrogating powers not expressly granted in domestic law – requested the legislature to provide a clear foundation in Austrian law.

Literature

See also the constitutional law literature in Chapter 2 (Constitution, Sources, and Interpretation of Law).

General and Comparative Works

Brewer-Carías, A. R., Judicial Review in Comparative Law (1989) 195
Cappelletti, M., The Judicial Process in Comparative Perspective (1989) 136 and 161
Hausmaninger, H., Judicial Referral of Constitutional Questions in Austria, Germany, and Russia, Tulane European & Civil Law Forum 12 (1997) 25
Heller, K., Outline of Austrian Constitutional Law (1989) 17
Machacek, R., Austrian Contributions to the Rule of Law (1994)
Noll, A. J., Bibliographie zur Verfassungsgerichtsbarkeit (1991)
Schwietzke, J., in *Kavass, I. I. (ed.),* Supranational and Constitutional Courts in Europe: Functions and Sources (1992) 181
Welan, M., Constitutional Review and Legislation, in *Landfried, C. (ed.)* Constitutional Review and Legislation (1988) 63

Monographs and Articles

Adamovich, L. K., Die österreichische Verfassungsgerichtsbarkeit vor dem europäischen Hintergrund, Geschichte und Gegenwart 3 (1989) 163
Adamovich, L. K., Huppmann, R., Die Judikatur des Verfassungsgerichtshofes 1975–1995, in *Österreichische Parlamentarische Gesellschaft (ed.),* 75 Jahre Bundesverfassung (1995) 503
Adamovich, L. K., Zur aktuellen Diskussion über die österreichische Verfassungsgerichtsbarkeit, FS Matscher (1993) 1
Funk, B.-C. et al. (eds.), Staatsrecht und Staatswissenschaften in Zeiten des Wandels, FS L. Adamovich (1992), see in particular *Korinek, K.,* Betrachtungen zur österreichischen Verfassungsgerichtsbarkeit, *ibid.* 253.
Holoubek, M., Die Interpretation der Grundrechte in der jüngeren Judikatur des Verfassungsgerichtshofes, in *Machacek, R. et al. (eds.),* Grund- und Menschenrechte in Österreich (1991) 43
Machacek, R. (ed.), Verfahren vor dem Verfassungsgerichtshof und vor dem Verwaltungsgerichtshof (4th ed. 2000)
Noll, A. J., Verfassungsgerichtsbarkeit und Gewaltenteilung, ÖJZ 47 (1992) 148
Korinek, K., Zur Relevanz von europäischem Gemeinschaftsrecht in der verfassungsrechtlichen Judikatur, FS Tomandl (1998) 465
Korinek, K., Für eine umfassende Reform der Gerichtsbarkeit des öffentlichen Rechts, FS Koja (1998) 289

Öhlinger, T., Unmittelbare Geltung und Vorrang des Gemeinschaftsrechts und die Auswirkungen auf das verfassungsrechtliche Rechtsschutzsystem, FS Rill (1995) 359

Schäffer H., Verfassungsgericht und Gesetzgebung, FS Koja (1998) 101

Walter, R., Die Organisation des Verfassungsgerichtshofes in historischer Sicht, FS Hellbling (1971) 763

Wieser, B., Stolz, A., Verfassungsrecht und Verfassungsgerichtsbarkeit an der Schwelle zum 21. Jahrhundert (2000)

Chapter 9
Fundamental Rights

I. Introduction

In Austrian legal terminology, human rights are – for historical reasons – referred to as "basic rights" or "fundamental rights" (*Grundrechte*). As a technical term, "human rights" (*Menschenrechte*, rights of man) is used for basic rights which are guaranteed to everybody without regard to citizenship. The expression "civil rights" (*Bürgerrechte*) refers to basic rights which are guaranteed to nationals only. Legal scholars have developed a classification that distinguishes three "generations" of human rights:

– Human rights of the first generation are defensive rights which protect individuals against state intervention and grant them participation in public and political life. Modern constitutions, including the Austrian, contain a great number of such rights, e.g., freedom of the person, freedom of expression, and the protection of property against expropriation. The protection of these rights is one of the main functions of European constitutional courts.

– Human rights of the second generation are economic, social, and cultural rights. These rights are contained in international instruments such as the International Covenant on Economic, Social and Cultural Rights (1966), the International Covenant on Civil and Political Rights (1966), and the European Social Charter (1969). They obligate the state to take affirmative action to provide for education, social security, housing, work, etc. Most Western states like Austria do not include such rights in their constitutions, thus leaving the decision to what extent such rights should be provided by the state to (simple) legislation below the level of constitutional guarantees. The former Socialist constitutions of Central and Eastern Europe contained a number of social and economic rights, which were, however, largely ineffective in practice.

– Human rights of the third generation include the right to a healthy and clean environment, the right to peace, development, self-determination, etc. Austrian constitutional law, for instance, contains provisions in which the state declares its intent to protect the environment.[1] The state also declares its commitment to establishing "factual" equality of women and men (Const. art. 7 (2)). Provisions of this kind have a political, programmatic

---

[1] Cf. Federal Constitutional Law of November 11, 1984, *BGBl* 1984/491 Concerning the Comprehensive Protection of the Environment.

character, but do not establish individual rights. They cannot be invoked before the Constitutional Court.[2]

II. History and Sources of Basic Rights in Austria

A. History

It took almost a century for the ideas of the Virginia Bill of Rights of 1776 or the French Declaration of Human and Civil Rights of 1789 to find their way into Austrian constitutional law. During the first half of the 19th century, the Austrian Empire had no catalog of human rights. Some human rights were contained in the Austrian Civil Code (*ABGB*) of 1811 (prohibition of slavery, art. 16 *ABGB*; no expropriation without compensation, art. 365 *ABGB*). Although contained in a civil code, these provisions served as a partial substitute for a – then not existing – written constitution. It was not until the revolutions of 1848 that written constitutions containing human rights catalogs were drafted. Yet these either failed to be enacted, or were short-lived, or ineffective. Another era of monarchic absolutism followed, lasting until 1867. In 1862, however, two important statutes safeguarding the liberty of the person and the privacy of the home were enacted.[3] The turning point of Austrian constitutional development came with the lost war against Prussia in 1866. This defeat weakened the absolute monarchy and forced it to yield to nationalist demands for autonomy by the Hungarians on the one hand, and to liberal demands for a written constitution on the other hand. On December 21, 1867, the State Fundamental Law on the General Rights of Citizens (*Staatsgrundgesetz über die allgemeinen Rechte der Staatsbürger*) was enacted. It contains a number of civil and human rights[4] and is still a main source of Austrian basic rights.

The Austrian Republic which was founded after World War I, incorporated this statute into its constitutional law in 1920. The Constitution entrusted the protection of human rights to the Constitutional Court. After the collapse of the democratic republic and the establishment of an authoritarian

---

² It is debated among scholars, whether the provision of Const. article 7 (2) could serve as a constitutional foundation for "affirmative action." Austrian doctrine tends towards a cautious approach. Measures of "affirmative action" have to respect the equal protection clause. They must therefore fulfill the requirement of proportionality and allow for consideration of the individual case.

³ *Gesetz vom 27. Oktober 1862, RGBl 87, zum Schutze der persönlichen Freiheit; Gesetz vom 27. Oktober 1862, RGBl 88, zum Schutze des Hausrechtes.*

⁴ Civil rights (i.e., rights of citizens) include equality before the law (art. 2); equal access to public office (art. 3); free choice of domicile, acquisition of land, and gainful activity (art. 6) and freedom of assembly and association (art. 12). Human rights include the freedom of movement of persons and property (art. 4); property (art. 5); personal freedom (art. 8); inviolability of the home (art. 9); secrecy of correspondence (art. 10) and of telecommunications (art. 10a inserted in 1974); right of petition (art. 11); freedom of the press and opinion (art. 13); freedom of religion (art. 14), and the free choice of occupation (art. 18).

"Christian corporate state" in 1934, human rights were curtailed, and after Austria's occupation by Hitler's Germany (the *Anschluß*) in 1938, these rights were practically abolished. In 1945, after World War II, the reestablished Austrian Republic returned to its democratic Constitution of 1920 as amended in 1929. In 1958, Austria joined the European Convention for the Protection of Human Rights and Fundamental Freedoms, and gave it the status of constitutional law in 1964.

Since that time, human rights issues have played a greater role in public discussion, and the protection of human rights has become more effective than ever before in Austrian history. This is largely due to Austrian legal scholarship and the Constitutional Court. The latter's jurisprudence reflects the influence of the European Convention, and during the last fifteen years it has become less formal and more activist in dealing with human rights issues.

B. Sources

The framers of the Austrian Federal Constitution of 1920 did not insert a catalog of human rights into the text of the Constitution. Instead of drafting a new bill of rights, they integrated the State Fundamental Law on the General Rights of Citizens (*Staatsgrundgesetz über die allgemeinen Rechte der Staatsbürger*) of 1867 into the constitutional law of the new republic, because the political parties could not agree on a new catalog. The Social-Democratic Party on the one hand and the conservative parties on the other hand held irreconcilable views on important issues such as the institutions of property and marriage, the relationship between state and church, and the educational system. To this day – despite efforts aiming at codification which have been pursued since 1964 – no comprehensive statement of the basic rights recognized by Austrian constitutional law has been adopted. Instead, provisions granting human rights may be found in a variety of different sources:[5]

– within the constitutional document itself, for example, the equal protection clause (art. 7), the right to vote (art. 26) and to be elected (art. 60), the guarantee of the "lawful judge" (art. 83 (2)); the abolition of the death penalty (art. 85), and various principles of criminal procedure (art. 90);
– in the State Fundamental Law on the General Rights of Citizens of 1867;[6]
– in the European Convention for the Protection of Human Rights and Fundamental Freedoms of 1958 (ECHR) and subsequent Protocols;[7]
– in other international treaties, such as the Peace Treaty of Saint Germain (1920) or the State Treaty of Vienna (1955), which include provisions prohibiting discrimination against ethnic minorities;

---

[5] On the sources of Austrian constitutional law see *supra* Chapter 2, II.B.

[6] *Staatsgrundgesetz vom 21. Dezember 1867, RGBl 142, über die allgemeinen Rechte der Staatsbürger für die im Reichsrate vertretenen Königreiche und Länder.*

[7] For example, Prot. Nr. 1 (1952), rights of property and education; Prot. Nr. 6 (1983), abolition of the death penalty; Prot. Nr. 7 (1984), double jeopardy and equal rights of parents.

- in special constitutional laws, for example, the Federal Constitutional Law on Personal Freedom of 1988 and the Federal Constitutional Law Securing the Independence of Broadcasting of 1974;
- in constitutional provisions contained in ordinary laws, such as article 1 of the Personal Data Protection Act (1978) and article 1 of the Political Parties Act (1975).

III. The Role and Protection of Basic Rights in Austria

A. Constitutional Rank

Basic rights are those which are guaranteed by a legal norm in the rank of Federal constitutional law. They must be respected by the legislature, the executive, and the courts. The Constitutional Court is the competent organ to sanction violations of basic rights committed by the administration or the legislature. Individuals may complain against acts of administrative authorities infringing on their constitutionally guaranteed rights (art. 144). For the same reason, an individual may request constitutional review of a statute (art. 140). One cannot, however, bring a complaint against decisions of regular civil or criminal courts to the Constitutional Court.

Being constitutional law, basic rights may be changed only by the process prescribed for constitutional amendment. But it would be unconstitutional for parliament to restrict the number of basic rights, to deprive them of their effect, or to abolish them altogether. The existence of effective basic rights is considered a structural principle of Austrian constitutional law. Substantial restrictions of this principle would constitute a "total revision" of the Constitution and thus require a popular referendum (Const. art. 44 (3)).

B. The Dual Character of Basic Rights

The basic rights (*Grundrechte*) recognized by Austrian constitutional law have a dual legal character:

1. Basic rights are subjective rights (*subjektive Rechte*) of the individual. They are norms which not only prescribe or prohibit certain actions by the state, but which also entitle an individual to file a complaint if the state violates his basic rights. Many of the classical basic rights function as defensive rights (*Abwehrrechte*), barring state intervention in certain areas and thereby creating spheres of freedom for the individual, for instance, freedom of the person, inviolability of the house, and the freedom of family life. Some basic rights serve as guarantees for the existence of certain legal institutions (*institutionelle Garantien*) such as property, marriage or family. These legal institutions are considered vital for a self-determined life. Therefore, legislation may not abolish or restrict such institutions, and the administration may not interfere with these rights. In case of violation, the individual has the right to bring a constitutional complaint.

2. As parts of constitutional law, basic rights are not merely rights of the individual; they also constitute an objective value system (*objektive Wertordnung*). They obligate the legislature to actively secure those rights and create the conditions that enable an individual to make effective use of them. The equal treatment of women and men, the enjoyment of private property, universal and equal suffrage, marriage, or family depend on certain rules which provide legal structure to these guaranteed rights.

C. Limitations of Basic Rights

1. Statutory Reservations

No basic right exists that would guarantee unlimited freedom. Some basic rights are restricted by special provisions of constitutional law,[8] while some are subjected to statutory reservation. This means that a basic right may be either specified or restricted by statute. Most basic rights contained in the Austrian State Fundamental Law on the General Rights of Citizens of 1867 are subject to such statutory reservations.[9] Originally these statutory reservations were not intended as restrictions, but, on the contrary, as special safeguards against the infringement of basic rights by administrative discretion, because during most of the 19th century public administration was not yet based on statutory law. Basic rights imposed statutory limits on these more or less unrestricted powers of the executive. Administrative interference with basic rights was to be permissible only on the basis of special statutes. Today all administrative action must be based on statutory law (Const. art. 18 (1)). This has led to a change in the functions of statutory reservations, which now enable the legislature to restrict basic rights.

Some modern basic rights catalogues contain only limited statutory reservations. For instance, the German Basic Law and the European Convention on Human Rights include reservations which permit the restriction of basic rights under certain conditions only.[10] The statutory reservations in the Austrian State Fundamental Law on the General Rights of Citizens do not contain such restrictions. This approach, however, was not intended to give the

---

[8] For example, personal freedom and inviolability of the home are restricted by provisions in the same constitutional laws that grant these freedoms.

[9] Property (art. 5); free choice of domicile, acquisition of land, and gainful activity (art. 6); secrecy of correspondence (art. 10) and telecommunications (art. 10a); freedom of association (art. 12); freedom of religion (art. 15); freedom of the press and of opinion (art. 13); freedom of science and teaching (art. 17).

[10] The German Basic Law allows restrictions only to "protect the free democratic order or the existence or security of the Federation" (art. 10 (2) Basic Law). The European Convention concedes restrictions which are either "necessary in a democratic society, in the interests of national security, territorial integrity or public safety, for the prevention of disorder or crime, for the protection of health and morals or for the protection of the rights and freedoms of others ..." (art. 11 (2)) or "in the interest ... of the economic well-being of the country" (art. 8 (2)). A similar limitation is contained in article 14 (3) of the German Basic Law which permits expropriations only in the public interest.

legislature unrestricted power to undermine or to abolish basic rights. The Austrian Constitutional Court therefore adopted a German theory to determine the limits of interference with basic rights. Article 19 (2) of the German Basic Law provides that "in no case may the essence of a basic right be encroached upon." This means that statutory reservations may not be used to abolish a basic right altogether or to impose restrictions without reasonable cause. The problem, of course, is to determine what constitutes the "essence of a basic right" (*Wesensgehalt*) and when this is violated. For this purpose, the Austrian Constitutional Court refers to principles deduced from the equal protection clause (*Gleichheitssatz*) of the Austrian Constitution.[11] According to the jurisprudence of the Court, restrictions of fundamental rights must fulfill the following conditions:

– The restriction must serve a legitimate aim. Restrictions may not be imposed on fundamental rights for reasons which conflict with the value system of the Constitution. The Court holds that it is the right of the legislative branch to define policy goals such as public interest or economic welfare, yet that the Court may strike down restrictions which do not serve such goals.

– The measure must be capable of accomplishing that aim, and it must be necessary for public welfare. The state may not impose restrictions which have no positive effect or lead to excessive limitations on fundamental rights. If it is possible to serve the public welfare without restricting the fundamental right, the restriction is unconstitutional. The requirement of the "necessity of the restriction" has become a very important aspect in the interpretation of the statutory reservation to article 6 (1) of the State Fundamental Law. This article gives every citizen the right to "practice every kind of gainful activity subject to the conditions of the law" (i.e., as imposed by statute). The Court holds that statutes are unconstitutional if they impose restrictions on free competition which are not necessitated by reasons of public welfare. It has declared laws unconstitutional which restricted the number of taxis, driving schools, or medical practitioners in a certain area. These laws had been enacted in an attempt to protect the economic interests of individuals already in the business by restricting the establishment of new competitors. For reasons of public welfare, the Court upheld laws restricting the number of chimney sweeps, undertakers, and pharmacies. The Court argued that these businesses fulfill important public functions which necessitate restrictions on the number of competitors.

– There must be proportionality between the aim of the statute and the extent to which the statute is restrictive. If less restrictive measures would achieve the same purpose, the restriction is unconstitutional.

---

[11] Article 7 (1): "All Federal citizens are equal before the law. Privileges based upon birth, sex, state, class or religion are excluded."

2. The Doctrine of "Inherent Limitations"

In addition to express restrictions, basic rights are subject to inherent limitations. No basic right permits the limitation of the basic rights of others. This principle is established by article 17 ECHR: "Nothing in this Convention may be interpreted as implying for any State, group or person any right to engage in any activity or perform any act aimed at the destruction of any of the rights and freedoms set forth herein or at their limitation to a greater extent than is provided for in the Convention."

Inherent limitations also restrict the full extension of human rights to certain groups of people over whom the state exercises special powers, such as prisoners, soldiers, or civil servants. Thus, for example, the "right of respect for one's private and family life" (art. 8 ECHR) is restricted in the case of prisoners, and the freedom of expression of civil servants is restricted by their obligation to keep official secrets.

The freedom of the arts as guaranteed by article 17a of the State Fundamental Law (inserted in 1982)[12] may serve as an example of the doctrine of inherent limitations. The text of article 17a does not expressly allow any restrictions of this right. Nevertheless, the Austrian Constitutional Court has accepted a number of limitations contained in ordinary statutory law. Thus, for example, freedom of the arts cannot be invoked to legitimize violations of criminal or administrative law. Thereby the Court authorized the legislature to impose far-reaching restrictions on a basic right that the Constitution guarantees under no statutory reservation. The basic right is violated, however, if statutes contain provisions which are intended to restrict the freedom of the arts without reasonable cause.

Some rights, such as the prohibition of torture or capital punishment, do not allow for any restrictions.

D. Interpretation of Basic Rights

The Austrian Constitution contains no special rules regarding the interpretation of basic rights. Therefore the principles developed by the Austrian Constitutional Court for the interpretation of constitutional law in general also apply to the interpretation of basic rights. One of these principles is the principle of "interpretation in favor of constitutionality" (*verfassungskonforme Interpretation*). This means that ambiguous provisions in statutes must be interpreted in such a way as not to contradict constitutional law. If more than one possible interpretation of a given provision of a statute exists, the one which does not infringe upon a basic right must be employed.[13] Another principle may be called "*in dubio pro libertate.*" If doubts about the meaning of a provi-

---

[12] "Artistic creativity as well as the dissemination of art and its teaching shall be free."

[13] With regard to fundamental rights on the level of EU law, this principle is refered to as "interpretation in accordance with Community law."

sion restricting a basic right should arise, the least restrictive interpretation is to be preferred.

In recent years the Constitutional Court has changed its previously formalistic interpretation of fundamental rights in favor of a more active position, leading to a remarkable extension of the protection provided by these rights.

E. Third-Party Effect

A much discussed problem of constitutional theory is whether basic rights may have "horizontal" effect on relations between private parties. It is generally held that basic rights do not bind private individuals directly.[14] For instance, the equal protection clause of the Austrian Constitution does not oblige a salesman to sell his goods to everybody. He may choose his business partners freely without regard for the equal protection clause. Some basic rights, however, indirectly bind private individuals in so far as special statutes based on them extend their effect to relations between such individuals. For example, labor law statutes prescribe equal treatment of men and women or prohibit discrimination against women. Under Austrian law it is an offense to discriminate against persons in public, to deny them services or access to public places like restaurants, etc., because of their race, nationality or religious creed.[15]

According to some scholars, basic rights may have effects on certain fields of private law. They believe that basic rights may serve as guidelines for the interpretation of general clauses such as "good faith" (*Treu und Glauben*) or "public morals" (*gute Sitten*) in civil codes. "Public morals" may necessitate the equal treatment of private business partners under certain conditions. A monopolist who sells goods of vital importance, or power supply companies, or public transportation enterprises are indirectly bound by the equal protection clause, which restricts their freedom of contract. They are obligated to sell to anyone on the same conditions and to contract with anyone willing to fulfill their conditions. This obligation either arises from statutes which are based on the equal protection clause or from the "public morals" (*boni mores*) clause, both of which in these cases include the principle of equal protection.

In a recent decision, the Austrian Supreme Court held that critical statements in public which could be regarded as violations of a persons's honor giving rise to a claim of damages under article 1330 of the Civil Code may be protected by the constitutional freedom of expression.

Another problem is whether the state is obligated to respect basic rights when it acts on the level of private law. According to German doctrine, all state action must respect the Constitution and basic rights. The state is not allowed to open a loophole by choosing between public and private law as a

---

[14] But note the specific legislative provision concerning the direct effect of article 1 of the Data Protection Act of 2000 concerning the protection of personal data.

[15] Article IX (1) Nr. 3 *EGVG*. This provision was enacted in 1977.

basis of its activities. This means that if the state acts in its capacity as the proprietor of a public enterprise or as the buyer of supplies for the police, etc., it may not give a preference to one of its business partners for reasons inconsistent with basic rights, such as religious creed or political views.

A problem related to that of the third-party effect is the question of whether basic rights obligate the state to protect the individual against violations inflicted by third parties. This question was raised in connection with the divergent decisions of the Austrian and the German Constitutional Courts regarding abortion. In 1974, the Austrian Court upheld an article of the new Austrian Criminal Code of 1974 which allowed abortion within the first three months of pregnancy. The Court held that the basic rights of the Austrian Constitution were defensive rights, directed against the state and not against private parties. The right to life guaranteed by article 2 ECHR did not extend to unborn life. For these reasons, Austrian constitutional law did not create an obligation to protect the fetus by making abortion a crime.

One year later, the German Federal Constitutional Court faced the same problem and arrived at a result different from that of the Austrian Court. The German judges held that life begins before birth, and that basic rights are not simply guarantees against governmental intrusion. The Court extended the protection of article 2 (2) of the Basic Law ("Everyone has the right to life") to unborn life. From article 1 (1), which obliges all state authority to "respect and protect" human dignity, the Court inferred the state's duty to protect fetal life by means of criminal law. There were dissenting opinions on the latter point, but the Court majority decided that the right to life outweighed the countervailing right of the pregnant woman to choose to have an abortion, a right which could be deduced from article 2 (1) of the Basic Law (right to free development of personality).[16] This case demonstrates the "objective value" aspect of basic rights, and the state's duty to teach its citizens to respect the fundamental values laid down in the Constitution.

In 1993, the German Constitutional Court examined the new abortion law which had been enacted after German reunification. While reaffirming its position that the state had the obligation to protect life, the Court no longer required enforcement by means of criminal law. In 1993, the requirements of article 2 (2) of the Basic Law were satisfied by a statutory regulation which allowed for an abortion within the first twelve weeks of pregnancy if the woman still opted for the abortion after attending a required counseling session.

In addition to endorsing a state duty concerning abortion, the German Court affirmed state duties under the Constitution to protect against hazards associated with nuclear power plants, noise from aircraft traffic, terrorism, chemical weapons, and nocturnal work.

In 1998, the European Court of Human Rights ruled that article 2 ECHR imposes a duty on the state to protect human life against violations by

---

[16] The decision of the German Court allowed abortions for medical, eugenic, ethical, and social reasons.

third parties, e.g., to provide police protection or guarantee effective investigation of murder cases.

F. Example: The Equal Protection Clause (*Gleichheitssatz*)

Equal protection is the most important basic right in the jurisprudence of the Austrian Constitutional Court. This protection is guaranteed by several provisions of Austrian constitutional law, in particular article 2 of the State Fundamental Law on the General Rights of Citizens and article 7 of the Constitution. These articles grant equal protection to citizens only, and they apply to natural persons as well as to legal entities.

Only recently the Austrian Constitutional Court took steps to extend the equal protection clause to foreigners. Based on article 1 of the Constitutional Law on the Abolition of Racial Discrimination (1973), the Court declared unconstitutional any discrimination between foreigners of different nationalities, discrimination based on nationality only, unreasonable discrimination, and arbitrary administrative acts against foreigners. This jurisprudence, however, does not impose a duty of equal treatment of foreigners and Austrian nationals.

With Austria's accession to the EU a new problem, namely discrimination of Austrian nationals, has arisen, since rules of Austrian law, for instance, which are in conflict with EU law do not apply to citizens from other Member States of the Union, yet may still bind Austrians. Thus, higher quality standards for certain products under Austrian law may apply to producers in Austria, yet not to producers from other EU countries who sell such goods in Austria. The Constitutional Court accepts such restrictions for Austrian nationals on the condition that they are based on reasonable grounds.

The equal protection clause was designed to protect individuals against the administration. It obligates all administrative authorities to apply the laws equally to all citizens. In theory, any violation of law by the administration could be considered a violation of the right to equal protection, but the Constitutional Court considers only serious infractions of the law as violating the equal protection clause. If an administrative authority commits an illegal act, the injured party may file a complaint in the Administrative Court. In cases involving a serious breach of the law, the victim may also petition the Constitutional Court.

It is a violation of the equal protection clause if an administrative authority acts arbitrarily. Arbitrary acts include a gross misinterpretation of the law, the denial of a fair hearing, a decision without prior fact-finding, or decisions which give no reasons. The equal protection clause is also violated if a decision is based on a statute that violates the constitutional equal protection clause.

The Constitutional Court has extended the scope of equal protection to include acts of the legislature. The legislature, too, must treat like cases alike and unequal fact situations unequally. If differentiations are applied, they must be reasonable. In recent years, the Court has developed a general requirement for statutes to be reasonable. The Court has struck down as being unreasonable:

- different treatment of men and women with regard to the age of retirement or social benefits;
- different punishment for soldiers and officers for the same offense;
- different treatment of workers who are family members of the employer with regard to membership in labor organizations;
- higher social security premiums without entitlement to higher social security benefits.

The Court has upheld the following differentiations as being reasonable:

- the prohibition of prostitution by married women;
- higher liability insurance premiums for taxis;
- the prohibition of homosexual acts between men and boys younger than 18;
- special tax laws for banks.

The Court has often emphasized that the equal protection clause leaves sufficient room for legal policy. However, the clause forces the legislature to observe the principle of proportionality. A statute violates the equal protection clause if there exists no proportionality of the means employed and the ends pursued. This occurs when the legislature passes an inappropriate measure or when the prescribed measure leads to unreasonable differentiations.

The Court has struck down the following for a lack of proportionality:

- the prohibition of truck traffic during the night in an effort to eliminate noise pollution, without carving out an exception for trucks which produce a low level of noise;
- a statute imposing a penalty for tax fraud of up to fifty times the amount involved.

IV. The European Convention for the Protection of Human Rights (ECHR)

A. Background

The European Convention for the Protection of Human Rights and Fundamental Freedoms is a product of the period shortly after the Second World War.[17] Nazi atrocities had made it clear that it was imperative to develop means for the protection of human rights on an international level and to create an effective system for the protection of human rights in Europe as a first step towards European unity. The drafting of the European Convention was influenced by the General Declaration of Human Rights adopted by the

---

[17] Information regarding the ECHR, the Court and its case law are provided on the Court's homep..ge (http://www.echr.coe.int).

General Assembly of the United Nations on December 10, 1948. It was signed on November 4, 1950, in Rome, and went into force on September 3, 1953.[18]

The main purpose of the ECHR was not to offer international remedies to victims, but to require the domestic law of the contracting states to conform to the standards set by the Convention. The Convention is an international treaty. Its binding force within the framework of domestic law depends upon its incorporation into that framework. Austria and Germany used two different techniques of incorporation. Germany, like most other European states, incorporated the Convention on the level of ordinary statutory law, whereas Austria gave the Convention the rank of constitutional law.

B. Position in Austrian Domestic Law

Austria signed the Convention on December 13, 1957, and it was ratified by the Federal President on September 3, 1958. When it came into force on September 24, 1958, the Convention was generally considered to have the rank of constitutional law. This view, however, was rejected by the Constitutional Court, because neither the decision of the Austrian Parliament approving the Convention nor the publication in the Federal Law Gazette mentioned that the Convention should be regarded as constitutional law. For that reason the Convention was formally accorded the rank of constitutional law in 1964.

Since that time, the case law of the Austrian Constitutional Court has made frequent reference to the provisions of the ECHR and to the decisions of the former European Commission of Human Rights and the European Court of Human Rights in Strasbourg. The Convention contains a number of rights which had not yet been guaranteed under Austrian domestic law, and thus due to the influence of the Convention and the additional supervision provided by the Strasbourg organs, the Austrian Constitutional Court generally began to put more emphasis on the protection of basic rights. Austrian domestic law has also been changed by a number of statutory enactments in an effort to achieve conformity with the ECHR.

C. Development of the Mechanism for the Protection of the Rights under the ECHR

In 1950, when the ECHR was drafted, most governments still insisted that states maintain full control of the persons under their jurisdiction and that their sovereignty would be infringed upon if an independent international body were to be empowered to interfere with the way they treated their citizens. As a result, the supervision of the European Convention on Human Rights was entrusted to a diplomatic organ, the Committee of Ministers of the Council of Europe. A Commission of Human Rights was designed to handle the preparatory work for the Committee of Ministers – to establish the facts, to try to

---

[18] By July 2000 it had been signed by 41 states.

reach a friendly settlement, and to report to the Committee of Ministers. The competence of the European Court of Human Rights to decide conflicts between governments and individuals existed on an optional basis only. Of the three institutions of the Convention located in Strasbourg, France, the Commission and the Court functioned as the main organs. Over the years, the character of the procedure shifted from that of a political to that of a legal control mechanism. All participating states accepted the jurisdiction of the European Court of Human Rights. New states seeking to join the Convention were expected to do the same. This development led to Protocol Nr. 11 to the European Convention on Human Rights, signed in 1994, creating a permanent European Court of Human Rights. It entered into force on November 1, 1998, and the new court became operative at that date.

The Convention provides for two different kinds of applications. Under article 33, any Member State to the Convention may refer to the Commission any alleged breach of the ECHR by any other Member State. Such interstate applications are rare and in most cases politically motivated. More importantly, under article 34, victims of violations of the rights guaranteed by the Convention may make individual applications. Such complaints may be brought against decisions of courts or other authorities of the Member States.

Under the original procedure, complaints could be filed with the European Commission of Human Rights. The Commission was entrusted with conducting the first stages of the procedure. In cases with no prospect of success it could dissuade petitioners from demanding the formal registration of their complaints. In other cases it decided on their admissibility. If a case was declared admissible, the Commission gathered all necessary information by assembling documents, hearing witnesses, and collecting statements. The Commission then tried to reach a friendly settlement (payment of damages, etc.). If this attempt remained unsuccessful, a report on the Commission's opinion was sent to the Committee of Ministers, the executive organ of the Council of Europe, consisting of the foreign ministers of the Member States. The Committee decided the case by majority vote, unless steps were taken by the Commission or any Member State to submit the case to the European Court of Human Rights within three months of receiving the Commission's report. Usually the more political cases were decided by the Committee. Individual applicants had no right to bring their case before the court. All states were obligated to abide by the decisions of the Court. The Court could also award "just compensation" to the injured party.

The number of cases handled in the 40 years since the establishment of the Strasbourg organs is remarkable. The European Court of Human Rights delivered more than 1,000 opinions; during the same period more than 100,000 applications reached the Commission, approximately 44,000 of which were registered and 5,000 declared admissible. Yet the complicated procedure, the ever increasing case load, aggravated by the accession of 18 new states (mostly East European) in the 1990s, called for urgent reforms. The cases registered annually with the Commission increased from 404 in 1981 to 2,037 in 1993; the cases referred to the Court from 7 in 1981 to 52 in 1993. In 1997 (the last year of the old system), the numbers were 4,750 and 119, respectively. The average length of procedures had grown to between five and six years.

To remedy this situation, Protocol Nr. 11 provided for a merger of the European Commission of Human Rights and the European Court of Human Rights into a new permanent European Court of Human Rights. For a transitional period of one year (until October 31, 1999), the Commission continued to deal with cases which had been admitted before Protocol Nr. 11 went into force.

In 1999, 20,399 applications[19] were received by the Court, of which 8,396 were registered.[20] Of the 4,250 applications decided, 3,389 were declared inadmissible and 130 were struck from the list.[21] 731 cases were declared admissible, in 177 cases the Court delivered a judgment.[22]

D. Procedure under Protocol Nr. 11

The European Court of Human Rights consists of a number of judges equal to the number of Member States of the Convention (at present 41). They are elected by the Parliamentary Assembly of the Council of Europe for terms of office of six years from lists of three candidates submitted by the Member States.[23] Article 21 demands that judges "must either possess the qualifications required for appointment to high judicial office or be jurisconsults of recognised competence." They sit on the Court as individuals, not as representatives of states. They may not serve beyond the age of 70. The terms of office of one-half of the judges are renewed every three years. The Court elects a President,[24] two Vice-Presidents,[25] and two Presidents of the Sections for three years. The Court is divided into four Sections, whose composition is geo-

---

[19] The largest numbers came from Italy (3652), Poland (2898), France (2586), Russia (1787), and Germany (1596). 356 applications came from Austria.

[20] The list of admitted applications is headed by Italy (423), Turkey (112), France (51), and the United Kingdom (32). Nine applications from Austria were declared admissible.

[21] The Court may strike an application from its list if the applicant does not wish to pursue his application, or the matter has been resolved, or the Court finds that the examination is no longer justified.

[22] In 1999, the Court found violations in 120 cases, no violation in 11, lack of jurisdiction in four. A friendly settlement of cases before the Court was reached in 42 instances (25 of which concerned Italy). The list of violations by state is headed by Italy (44), Turkey (18), France (16), and the United Kingdom (12). Complaints against Austria were successful in three cases.

[23] In January 1998, the Consultative Assembly of the Council of Europe elected Willi Fuhrmann as the Austrian judge on the new Court. Fuhrmann had headed the list of three candidates submitted by the Austrian government. He is a former attorney and long-time leader of the Socialist caucus in the Austrian National Council, who also had served for nine years on the Human Rights Committee of the Council of Europe.

[24] At present the Swiss law professor Luzius Wildhaber.

[25] Who also serve as Section Presidents.

graphically and gender balanced[26] and takes account of the different legal systems of the Member States.

The Court sits in Committees of three judges, in Chambers of seven judges, and in a Grand Chamber of 17 judges. The Committees and Chambers are set up within each Section. The judge who is a national of the state concerned sits as an *ex officio* member of the Chamber and the Grand chamber. In the composition of the Grand Chamber, geographical balance and the different legal traditions are also taken into account.

Applications alleging the violation of a right guaranteed under the ECHR can be brought either by one of the Contracting States or by individuals, groups of individuals, or non-governmental organizations. An application to the European Court of Human Rights is admissible only if all domestic remedies have been exhausted and no more than six months have lapsed from the date of the final domestic decision.

The procedure before the Court is adversarial and public; French and English are the official languages. Applications may be brought in one of the official languages of the Member States. The use of the language of the application for the entire procedure may be granted by the Court.

Every case is assigned to a Section. The President of the Section appoints a *rapporteur* who will refer the case either to a Committee of three or to a Chamber of seven judges. Unless the Committee unanimously declares the application inadmissible, the Chamber determines admissibility and decides the merits. If a case raises important questions concerning the interpretation of the Convention, or if the Chamber intends to depart from a decision previously delivered by the Court, it may transfer jurisdiction to the Grand Chamber.

If an application is admitted, the Chamber may invite the parties to submit further evidence or written observations, and to attend a public hearing. At the same time, negotiations for a friendly settlement may be conducted by the Registrar.

Chambers decide by majority vote. Individual judges may append concurring or dissenting opinions or a simple statement of dissent to the judgment. The judgment of a Chamber becomes final three months after it has been delivered, unless a party requests that the case be referred to the Grand Chamber, and a panel of five judges of the Grand Chamber accepts this demand. Judgments of the Grand Chamber are final.

States are under an obligation to comply with the judgments of the Court. The execution of judgments is supervised by the Committee of Ministers of the Council of Europe.

At the request of the Committee of Ministers, the Court may deliver advisory opinions on the interpretation of the Convention and the Protocols.

---

[26] Eight judges (two in each Section) are women.

E. Some Effects of Strasbourg Jurisprudence on Austria

The provisions of article 6 (1) ECHR (the right to a fair and public hearing)[27] and their interpretation in the case law of the Strasbourg organs may serve as an example for analyzing and illustrating the impact of the Convention on Austrian domestic law. It also demonstrates problems created by the merging of Common law and Civil law traditions in the framing of this article.

Article 6 (1) ECHR is the provision of the Convention which is invoked in the majority of applications.[28] In the judgments delivered by the Court in 1999, the most frequent cases of violations of article 6 (1) ECHR concerned excessive length of court proceedings, lack of independence and impartiality on the part of courts or judges, lack of public hearing, and improper restrictions on access to court.

Article 6 (1), an essential provision for the administration of justice in a free and democratic society, has been interpreted broadly by the European Court of Human Rights. When the Court examines the interpretations given to article 6 by national authorities, the most important questions arising concern the meaning of the words "civil rights and obligations," "criminal charge," "tribunal," "fair hearing," and "within a reasonable time."

1. "Civil rights and obligations"

The Court has so far refused to give a definition of the contents of "civil rights and obligations." Sometimes "civil rights" are equated with "private law," but there is no sufficiently clear dividing line between private law and public law in legal theory and within the domestic law of the member countries. It is clear, though, that "civil rights and obligations" cannot be understood in the sense of Anglo-American "civil liberties."[29]

The Court tends to apply the procedural guarantees of article 6 (1) to a wide range of different proceedings. It examines the content and effect of the right in question, not its formal classification within the respective domestic law. Apart from cases which have an undisputed civil or private law character, the Strasbourg organs have considered the following cases as falling under article 6 (1):

– Disputes concerning permits which form a condition of the validity of contracts concluded with a private party. (E.g., in many parts of Austria the

---

[27] "In the determination of his civil rights and obligations or of any criminal charge against him, everyone is entitled to a fair and public hearing within a reasonable time by an independent and impartial tribunal established by law."

The majority of applications to the European Court of Human Rights allege violations of Article 6 (1) ECHR; the most frequent complaint concerns the length of proceedings.

[28] Article 6 (1) was involved in all cases that lead to judgments against Italy, Austria, and Belgium, and in most of the cases adjudicated against France and Portugal. Article 6 (1) played a role in 86 out of 120 cases of violations found by the Court in 1999 (cf. *supra* note 22).

[29] The French text has *"droits et obligations de charactère civil."*

transfer of land to foreigners or the transfer of agricultural land in general depends on permits which may be granted by administrative authorities. The Court held that these administrative authorities have to fulfill the requirements as tribunals under article 6.)

- Procedures concerning the granting or revocation of a license for practicing a particular profession or trade.
- Procedures in which a decision is made on claims for sickness benefits or a retirement pension.
- Restrictions imposed by public authorities on insurance companies.

Matters of clearly public law character, such as taxation, public planning, etc., are generally not covered by article 6, although they may affect private rights. It is not relevant whether the underlying dispute is one between individuals or one between an individual and a public authority, nor is it relevant whether the proceedings take place before a civil court or another body vested with jurisdiction.

The Austrian Constitutional Court differentiates between a "core" area of classical private law that must be entrusted to the jurisdiction of ordinary courts and a "marginal" area (still regarded as "civil law" by the European Convention) in which the supervisory jurisdiction of the Administrative Court is considered sufficient. Matters outside the core area include building permits, licenses to run schools for skiing instruction, permission to keep certain animals, and withdrawals of pharmacy concessions. Matters entirely outside of private law are, for instance, claims arising from crop damage caused by wild animals, permits for certain land transfers, and the regulation of hospital fees.

2. "Criminal charge"

The interpretation of "criminal charge" poses similar problems. National legislation is free to determine which behavior it classifies as criminal. What may be treated as a criminal offense in one state may be considered an administrative or disciplinary offense in another. The term "criminal charge" in the ECHR may include offenses lying outside the scope of national criminal law. The criteria developed by the Court include:

- the nature of the offense;
- whether the norm should be generally binding or applicable only to a specific group;
- the nature and severity of the punishment.

Criminal charges are, for instance, disciplinary offenses for which an imprisonment of considerable duration (several months) could be imposed, or administrative offenses which might be punished with fines of a considerable amount (comparable to those in criminal law).

Not included in the concept of criminal charge are procedures by which preventive detention may be imposed on the mere ground of an existing suspicion, or in which persons are prohibited from entering a country (no penalty), or extradition procedures (no determination of a person's guilt).

3. "Tribunal"

Article 6 (1) requires an independent and impartial tribunal established by law. Independence means that the deciding body may base its decision on its own free evaluation of facts and law, that the deciding body is independent of the parties and public authorities, and that its decision is not subject to any authority which is not independent in the same sense. The Court insists that even a semblance of dependence must be avoided.

In the core sector of civil and criminal law, courts of the "classic kind" are required to function at all stages of the procedure. In the administrative sector, when "civil rights and obligations" or "criminal charges" are at stake, it is sufficient that the highest instance of appeal fulfills the requirements of independence according to article 6.

The requirement of a tribunal to hear cases of a civil or a criminal law character had a profound influence on the Austrian legal system. In Austria, like in most countries on the European continent, independent courts decide matters in the core sectors of private and criminal law. But the jurisdiction of administrative authorities comprises many fields of law that in common law countries lie within the jurisdiction of courts. The jurisdiction of the Austrian administrative authorities includes numerous sectors of law for which the Convention requires the establishment of a tribunal.

In a great number of instances, Austrian administrative law provides for decisionmaking by independent administrative agencies. These special agencies consist of panels that include at least one judge and a certain number of administrative officials who are not bound by any instructions in deciding the cases. There exists a possibility of appeal against their decisions to the Administrative and/or the Constitutional Court. The Austrian Constitutional Court held that this system was in accordance with the requirements of article 6 of the Convention. The European Court of Human Rights shared this opinion for some time, but in the famous *Sramek* case (1984) it applied a stricter interpretation of the "tribunal" requirement. In this decision, the Strasbourg Court held that Austrian independent administrative authorities did not fulfill the requirements of the Convention because the independence of the members was not sufficient due to their short terms of office. Furthermore, the Court declared that the possibility of appeal to the Administrative and/or the Constitutional Court was not sufficient to bring the Austrian system in accordance with the Convention, because both courts were authorized only to quash administrative decisions and because the Administrative Court had no power to conduct independent fact finding.

In a decision delivered after *Sramek*, the Austrian Constitutional Court explicitly confirmed its previous position that the Austrian system fulfilled the requirements of the Convention and made it clear that it was not willing to accept the new approach of the European Court of Human Rights. The Court held that the evolution of the jurisprudence of the European Court had lead to a concept of "civil rights and civil obligations" quite different from that which prevailed at the time of the drafting of the Convention. When Austria signed the Convention, the Austrian constitutional system was in accordance with the requirements of article 6. The modifications to the Austrian system necessitated by the new approach of the European Court would amount to a substantial change in the Austrian Constitution, which only could be achieved through constitutional amendment. Since the Constitutional Court was bound by Austrian constitutional law, it could not follow the interpretation of the European Court, which was in contradiction to established principles of Austrian constitutional law. If the Court in Strasbourg arrogated powers to change the Austrian Constitution, the Convention itself could become unconstitutional (Const. art. 44 (3)).

The Strasbourg organs avoided this consequence. They accepted that by providing the possibility of appeal to the Administrative Court and by introducing Independent Administrative Panels (organized in a way similar to courts, see *supra* Chapter 7), Austria fulfilled the requirements of "determination by a tribunal."

4. "Fair hearing"

With regard to a "fair hearing," it is almost impossible to enumerate all necessary elements of a fair trial. Instead of developing an abstract definition, the former Comission and the Court have spelled out several principles.

In civil cases, the guarantee of a "fair hearing" implies the right of every party to present its case to the court under conditions which do not place it at a substantial disadvantage *vis-à-vis* its opponent.

In criminal cases, the principle necessitates an "equality of arms," which includes the right of the defendant to be present in court, the right of equal access to documents and records, the possibility of summoning witnesses and experts, and the right to oppose the arguments advanced by the prosecution.

The principle of a fair hearing is violated if the accused is treated in a way which lowers his physical or mental resistance during the hearing, if the accused is denied the assistance of a lawyer (including during the phase of pretrial investigation), or if the court refuses to summon or hear a particular witness. The principle is also violated if the court admits evidence obtained in ways contrary to norms of the Convention. "Fair hearing" also implies the requirement that a judicial decision must state the reasons on which it is based.

The Austrian Constitutional Court requires effective legal representation of the party concerned, the right to comment on the taking of evidence concerning disputed facts, and also that not even the appearance of a fair trial be impaired.

5. "Within a reasonable time"

The purpose of the "reasonable time" requirement is to end uncertainty as to the civil-law position of a person or uncertainty on account of a criminal charge against him. In criminal cases, this period starts when the person concerned has been substantially affected as a result of suspicion against him (e.g., from the person's first hearing as a suspect).[30]

The Strasbourg organs accept a temporary overburdening of the courts as an excuse. But if the problem is structural, the state is obligated to organize its judicial system in a way which enables the courts to conduct procedures within a reasonable time.

If the reasonable time requirement is not fulfilled, the Strasbourg organs may award monetary compensation to the injured party, and in criminal cases advise the state organs to take the length of procedures into account and reduce the penalty.

A large number of complaints have been brought against Austria in this respect. In 1999, the state was judged to be in violation of the Convention in two of these instances.[31]

6. Right of Access to a Court

The right of access to a court is not expressly mentioned in the text, but the Court of Human Rights holds that this right is inherent in article 6. States are prohibited from obstructing access and are under an affirmative duty to ensure effective access to all courts. Article 6 is violated if domestic law does not provide for judicial review or bars effective access to a higher court by imposing excessive costs.

V. Human Rights and the European Union

A. Early Limitations

In 1995, Austria joined the European Union. The EU is a supranational organization to which the Member States have transferred some of their sovereign powers. The organs of the EU have the power to take legislative, executive, and judicial actions which have direct effects within the Member States. All Community law takes precedence over national law, including national constitutional law and the national bills of rights. This supremacy of Community law includes an obligation to accept the decisions of the European Court of Justice in Luxembourg as to the meaning of Community law. The European Court of Justice is the sole organ which gives binding interpretations of Community law.

---

[30] The Court considered the following as unreasonable time: first instance proceedings of more than six years, criminal proceedings of 13 years and four months (Italy), court proceedings of more than ten and 17 years in duration, divorce proceedings of more than nine years (Germany), and 14 and 26 months before the Spanish Constitutional Court. It considered regular court proceedings of five to seven years in duration as reasonable.

[31] G.S. v. Austria (duration of disciplinary proceedings against a lawyer of seven years and four months); W.R. v. Austria (duration of proceedings for granting a license to run a pharmacy of more than seven years).

For historical reasons, European Community law does not include a bill of rights. The EC was founded mainly as an economic community, and only such economic and social rights appear in the Treaty as were fundamental to carry out the economic purpose of the European Community (freedom of movement, protection of ownership, equal pay for both sexes, prohibition of discrimination on grounds of nationality, and the right of association and collective bargaining).

The protection of basic rights on the level of European law was developed by the case law of the European Court of Justice. This development took place in two stages. Initially the Court refused to recognize human rights on the level of European law. In 1969, however, it cautiously accepted the idea that basic rights were part of those general principles of law which the Court uses to supplement the written sources of Community law.[32] This period of reticence ended with the famous *Solange-I* decision of the German Constitutional Court (1974), in which the latter claimed the authority to review EC law so long as this law had not achieved a standard of human rights protection equal to that provided by the German Basic Law. A similar step was taken by the Italian Constitutional Court.

B. The New Jurisprudence of the European Court of Justice

This serious threat led to significant changes in the European Court's position with regard to human rights. Thereafter, the European Court of Justice has accepted a number of basic rights which it derived from the following four sources of law:

— Community law itself. The Court today recognizes as basic rights of Community law the Four Freedoms contained in the EC-Treaty (free movement of goods, persons and capital and the freedom to provide and receive services across European borders), the freedom of enterprise, the freedom of competition, the principle of fair hearing, prohibition of discrimination on the grounds of nationality (art. 12 TEC), and equal pay for men and women (art. 141 TEC).

— "Constitutional traditions common to the Member States." The Court does not apply the basic rights of domestic constitutional law directly, but refers to underlying principles which it detects by comparing different constitutions. Such European basic rights may either provide more protection than domestic law (e.g., the guarantees of a fair hearing in comparison to the German Basic Law) or stay below the level of the domestic law of some member countries (e.g., the protection against searching a person's home as compared to the German Basic Law).

— "International treaties for the protection of human rights on which the Member States have collaborated or of which they are signatories" as

---

[32] This concept is based on an extensive interpretation of article 288 (ex 215) TEC, which regulates the non-contractual liability of the Community in accordance with "the general principles common to the law of all Member States."

"guide-lines which should be followed within the framework of Community Law." The most important of these treaties is the European Convention for the Protection of Human Rights and its additional Protocols. With reference to the Convention, the protection of property and the prohibition of retroactivity in criminal law were integrated into Community law.

– "Declarations of European organs with regard to human rights." These are used by the Court as indicators of consensus among the Member States in this field.

The European Court of Justice applies a number of principles concerning the interpretation of basic rights which originate in the German tradition, like the principle of proportionality (*Verhältnismäßigkeitsprinzip*) regarding restrictions of basic rights and the prohibition to alter the essential contents (*Wesensgehalt*) of a basic right. It also recognizes that Community law is generally to be interpreted in accordance with basic rights. But the Court also uses the Common law notion of reasonableness and maxims of English Equity. Impressed by this zeal to protect human rights, the German Constitutional Court reversed its position in *Solange-II* (1986) when it declared: "So long as the European communities, and in particular the case law of the European Court, generally ensure an effective protection of fundamental rights against the sovereign powers of the Communities that is to be regarded as substantially similar to the protection of fundamental rights that the Basic Law requires, ... the Federal Constitutional Court will no longer measure [Community] law against the standard of the fundamental rights contained in the Basic Law." This position adopted by the German Constitutional Court was codified in 1992 (after the Maastricht Treaty) in a revised article 23 of the Basic Law, which allowed the transfer of sovereign power to the European Union on the condition that this Union "guarantees a protection of human rights essentially comparable to that of the Basic Law."

Referring to the jurisprudence of the German Constitutional Court, several Austrian scholars argue the existence of a substantive core of the Austrian Constitution with which EU law that goes beyond the modifications accepted by Austria in its Treaty of Accession may not interfere. Such EU interference (for instance, with the liberal principle of the Austrian Constitution) would be considered null and void.

The significance of the protection of basic rights has been emphasized by other organs of the EU and has been incorporated into important documents. The Preamble of the Single European Act of 1986 reaffirms that the Members are "determined to work together to promote democracy on the basis of the fundamental rights recognized in the constitutions and laws of the Member States, in the Convention for the Protection of Human Rights and Fundamental Freedoms and the European Social Charter, notably freedom, equality and social justice." Article 6 (2) TEU (ex F/2) reads: "The Union shall respect fundamental rights, as guaranteed by the European Convention for the Protection of Human Rights and Fundamental Freedoms signed in Rome on 4

November 1950 and as they result from the constitutional traditions common to the Member States, as general principles of Community Law."

An evaluation of the efficiency of fundamental rights protection on the Community level shows an ambiguous picture. On the one hand, the European Court of Justice has given up its initial reluctance concerning protection of fundamental rights. On the other hand, critics have noted that the Court so far has only struck down general enactments of the Commission, but no enactments of the Council. It applies stricter methods of interpretation than the European Court of Human Rights, leaving a broader margin of appreciation to the legislation of Community organs than the European Court of Human Rights concedes to national legislatures. Observers also point to a growing distance of the European Court of Justice to the ECHR. The Luxembourg Court apparently seeks to avoid a total submission of European law under the Convention and the jurisdiction of the Court in Strasbourg.

C. Reform Proposals

It has been proposed that the EU join the European Convention of Human Rights. This seems to be an obvious step, since all Member States of the EU are members to the European Convention, and the European Court of Justice frequently refers to the European Convention as a source of human rights. Yet in an advisory opinion delivered on March 28, 1996, the European Court of Justice rejected this proposal. The Court declared that at present the EU has neither the power to legislate in the field of human rights nor to enter into an international agreement on human rights. Aside from the formal reasoning on which the Court based its negative opinion, there are also significant substantive arguments against taking such a step.

If the EU joined the European Convention on Human Rights – which would necessitate a change of the Convention which at present admits only states as members – serious procedural problems would arise to which neither the Convention nor the EU Treaty contains the necessary solutions. Thus, e.g., with regard to the interpretation of the Convention, both European Courts could claim the last word. And it would not be clear whether a petition to the European Court of Human Rights depended on a prior decision of the European Court of Justice in order to fulfill the requirement of exhausting domestic remedies (art. 26 ECHR). Nevertheless, Austria supported the EU's accession to the European Convention in a position paper submitted to the Intergovernmental Conference in 1996.

Another proposal suggests that the EU draft its own comprehensive bill of rights. The main argument underlying this suggestion is that the European Community is a community based on law and on certain common values which should be enshrined in a bill of rights. Such a bill of rights would demonstrate to individual citizens that the Community is based on respect for human rights and is not just a bureaucratic organization which interferes in all spheres of life. In June 1999 the European Council made a decision on the "drawing up of a charter of fundamental rights of the European Union" in advance of the European Council in December 2000. The draft will most likely mark only the beginning of a difficult process of consensus building.

Literature

Austria

Berka, W., Die Grundrechte. Grundfreiheiten und Menschenrechte in Österreich (1999)
Berka, W., Lehrbuch Grundrechte (2000)
Holoubek, M., Grundrechtliche Gewährleistungspflichten (1997)
Korinek, K., Entwicklungstendenzen in der Grundrechtsjudikatur des Verfassungs-gerichtshofes (1992)
Machacek, R. et al. (eds.), Grund- und Menschenrechte in Österreich (2 vols., 1991–92)
Novak, R., Verhältnismäßigkeitsgebot und Grundrechtsschutz, FS Winkler (1989) 39
Rill, H. P., Die Artikel 5 und 6 der Europäischen Menschenrechtskonvention, die Praxis der Straßburger Organe und des Verfassungsgerichtshofes und das öster-reichische Verfassungssystem, FS Winkler (1989) 13
Stelzer, M., Das Wesensgehaltsargument und der Grundsatz der Verhältnismäßigkeit (1991)
Stelzer, M., Stand und Perspektiven des Grundrechtsschutzes, in *Österreichische Parla-mentarische Gesellschaft (ed.)*, 75 Jahre Bundesverfassung (1995) 583

European Convention

Beatty, D. M. (ed.), Human Rights and Judicial Review: A Comparative Perspective (1994)
Gearty, C. A. (ed.), European Civil Liberties and the European Convention on Human Rights: A Comparative Study (1997)
Grabenwarter, C. (ed.), Kontinuität und Wandel der EMRK. Studien zur Europäischen Menschenrechtskonvention (1998)
Jacobs, F. G., White, R. C. A., The European Convention on Human Rights (2nd ed. 1996)
Janis, M. W. et al., European Human Rights Law: Text and Materials (1996)
Kempees, P., A Systematic Guide to the Case Law of the European Court of Human Rights 1960–1994 (1996)
Lawson, R. A., Schermers, H. G., Leading Cases of the European Court of Human Rights (1997)

European Union

Alston, P. (ed.), The EU and Human Rights (1999)
Baumgartner, G., EU-Mitgliedschaft und Grundrechtsschutz (1997)
Betten, L., Grief, N., EU Law and Human Rights (1998)
Guild E., Lesieur, G., The European Court of Justice on the European Convention of Human Rights. Who Said What, When? (1998)
Lenz, C. O., Der europäische Grundrechtsstandard in der Rechtsprechung des Euro-päischen Gerichtshofes, EuGRZ 20 (1993) 585
Loveland, I., Importing the First Amendment: Freedom of Expression in American, English and European Law (1998)
MacLean, R. M. (ed.), European Community Law and Human Rights (1996)
Neuwahl, N. A., Rosas, A. (eds.), The European Union and Human Rights (1995)
Schilling, T., Bestand und allgemeine Lehren der bürgerschützenden allgemeinen Rechtsgrundsätze des Gemeinschaftsrechts, EuGRZ 27 (2000) 3

Chapter 10

Criminal Procedure

I. Introduction

According to the common stereotype, the profound difference between Common law and Civil law criminal procedure is that the former is adversarial and the latter inquisitorial. An inquisitorial trial, as practiced in France until the 1789 Revolution and in Germany and Austria until the revolutions of 1848, is characterized by merging the judicial with the prosecutorial function and the treatment of the defendant as an object of (rather than a subject in) the process. He was under a duty to confess, if necessary under torture.[1] Criminal procedure at that time was subject to strict rules of evidence and admitted only limited rights of the defense. There was no presumption of innocence. The process was secret, written and not immediate, but based on the investigative file. Judges were not independent, but subject to the orders of the prince.

Although substantial reforms (that were largely based on English criminal procedure) were introduced into the European model, first in post-revolutionary France and then in other parts of continental Europe, significant differences between Civil law and Common law criminal procedure still exist. Yet contemporary Austrian criminal procedure is no longer simply inquisitorial in the sense that it would aim at establishing the truth at any price. It is rather a mixture of various principles designed to protect and balance competing interests, such as the enforcement of substantive criminal law and the protection of the fundamental rights and freedoms guaranteed by the Constitution. It is an investigative process, under the paternalistic guardianship of the court and intended to ensure substantive justice. It attempts to conduct a rational official investigation aimed at finding the objective truth. At the same time, the system seeks to protect an innocent defendant against arbitrary or erroneous prosecution. It includes important adversarial elements, such as the equality of the prosecution and of the defense. But it is not, as some observers have described the Common law system, a forensic duel in which truth is no more than an accidental by-product.

The continuing strong concern of the Austrian system with finding truth is expressed in the following characteristics: 1) the limited role of the jury; 2) free evaluation of evidence by the court; 3) little prosecutorial discretion; and 4) the active and exhaustive investigative role of the court. There are certainly weaknesses in this system, such as an exaggerated confidence in the

---

[1] Torture was abolished in Austria in 1776.

ability of the judge to find the truth, and an occasional tendency to view the defense attorney as impeding that process.

II. Sources of Criminal Procedure Law

Austrian criminal procedure law is exclusively federal.[2] Its most important source is the Criminal Procedure Code of 1975 (*Strafprozeßordnung, StPO*), as amended. This Code is a comprehensive statute (many essential features of which were already formulated in 1873) regulating almost all procedural aspects of criminal investigation, trial, and appeal. Some special aspects of court organization and procedure are regulated in the Law on Juvenile Courts (*Jugendgerichtsgesetz, JGG* 1988), the Court Organization Act (*Gerichtsorganisationsgesetz*), the Jurors' and Lay Assessors' Act (*Geschworenen- und Schöffengesetz*), the Judicial Service Law (*Richterdienstgesetz* 1961) and the Internal Court Rules (*Geschäftsordnung, Geo.*). Other sources for criminal procedure law are for example the Financial Penalties Act (*Finanzstrafgesetz*) and the Penal Administration Act (*Strafvollzugsgesetz*).

The Federal Constitution contains several key provisions concerning the general organization and independence of courts, as well as specific rules protecting due process and a fair trial (Const. arts. 82 to 94).[3] There are also important provisions of constitutional law outside the constitutional document itself. Limitations on the scope of criminal investigation are, for instance, included in such early civil rights legislation as the Law on the Protection of the Home (*Gesetz zum Schutz des Hausrechtes* 1862) and articles 10 and 10a of the State Fundamental Law on the General Rights of Citizens (*Staatsgrundgesetz über die allgemeinen Rechte der Staatsbürger* 1867). A significant role is played by a number of articles of the European Convention on Human Rights (ECHR), which has constitutional rank in Austrian law.[4] For example, procedural safeguards protecting the defendant are contained in articles 5 and 6 of the Convention; article 8 restricts government searches and seizures. The most recent provisions are contained in the Federal Constitutional Law on the Protection of Personal Freedom (*Bundesverfassungsgesetz über den Schutz der persönlichen Freiheit* 1988) and the Law on the Complaint to the Supreme Court Concerning Violation of the Fundamental Right of Personal Freedom (*Grundrechtsbeschwerdegesetz, GRBG* 1992).

III. Fundamental Principles of Criminal Procedure

Austrian criminal procedure is based on a number of fundamental principles. Together they provide the basic framework for the investigative

---

[2] But note that there exists a broad area of administrative penal law and administrative penal adjudication in matters pertaining exclusively to *Länder* jurisdiction (Const. art. 10 item 6).

[3] See *supra* Chapter 6 (Courts).

[4] *BGBl* 1964/59.

and adjudicative process. While all principles are valid for the entire process, they are tailored to meet specific requirements during certain phases of pretrial and trial procedure.

A. Principles Regarding the Initiation of Criminal Proceedings

1. Principle of Accusation (*Akkusationsprinzip, Anklagegrundsatz*)

According to article 90 (2) of the Constitution, the prosecutorial and judicial functions are separated and assigned to different organs. In Austrian criminal procedure, an authorized prosecutor must file criminal charges before a case can be tried in a criminal court. As far as the facts of the case – not their legal assessment – are concerned, the court is limited to the extent of the charge put before it. If in the course of proceedings the prosecutor drops the charge, the court must dismiss the case or acquit the defendant.

2. Principle of Public *ex officio* Prosecution (*Offizialmaxime*)

The state enjoys a monopoly of prosecution of criminal offenses through the public prosecutor's office. It is the official duty of the state, through the public prosecutor and the police, to investigate and to prosecute crimes. Therefore, the victim of a crime generally has no influence on the decision whether formal charges are brought against the suspect or not.

But if the public prosecutor decides not to prosecute, counsel for the victim may, if the victim so desires, assume the role of the prosecution (*Subsidiaranklage* or subsidiary prosecution). This possibility was instituted as a check against violations of the principle of compulsory prosecution by the public prosecutor. The subsidiary prosecutor is closely monitored by the presiding judge, and his rights are restricted in a number of ways to prevent the abuse of power. Also, the public prosecutor has the right to resume prosecution at any time during the pretrial or trial phase.

Other examples of prosecution by the victim are *Privatanklagedelikte* (offenses subject to private prosecution). For these offenses, characterized by a stronger private than public interest, the victim or his counsel assumes the role of prosecutor and brings a private charge. Such offenses include certain violations of a person's honor, the disclosure of business secrets, and various offenses against property if committed by a close relative.

In two other types of cases the principle of public prosecution is modified:

Antragsdelikte (offenses prosecuted only upon application by the victim) are offenses which can only be prosecuted if the victim petitions the public prosecutor to initiate proceedings, e.g., withdrawal of a minor from the control of the person having parental power.

Ermächtigungsdelikte (offenses prosecuted only if the victim consents) are, e.g., trespass, fraud committed in an emergency situation, and petty larceny or serious threats from family members. Unlike an *Antragsdelikt*, the public prosecutor may start to investigate an *Ermächtigungsdelikt* without the prior consent of the victim. However, the victim must immediately be asked for his consent. If the victim does not respond in the affirmative within 14 days, the investigation must be dropped.

In both cases (*Antragsdelikt* and *Ermächtigungsdelikt*), the victim may revoke his consent to prosecute at any time until the end of the trial. In such instances the accused must be acquitted.

3. Principles of Compulsory Prosecution (*Anklagezwang, Legalitätsprinzip*) and Prosecutorial Discretion (*Opportunitätsprinzip*)

The constitutional principle of equality before the law (equal protection clause) imposes a duty on the state to prosecute all crimes if there is sufficient evidence to expect a conviction. The principle of compulsory prosecution limits the flexibility of the public prosecutor. When the results of an investigation warrant that charges be brought, the public prosecutor must file these formal charges. He has no discretionary power to drop them. If a victim thinks that the prosecutor has dropped a charge despite sufficient evidence to the contrary, the victim may apply to become a subsidiary prosecutor and continue the prosecution, as discussed above.

That the public prosecutor is under a duty to prosecute crimes does not necessarily mean that he must file a formal charge. In specific situations, alternative forms of reaction to a criminal act are possible, which were originally developed in dealing with juvenile offenders:

- In cases involving juvenile delinquents, the public prosecutor must forego filing charges if it appears likely that the trial judge would decide to abstain from imposing a formal punishment. The prosecutor may condition this on the willingness of the suspect to assume responsibility for his act and deal with its consequences, in particular by indemnifying the victim.
- This possibility of diversion (*Diversion*) from criminal sanctions to alternative forms of reaction to a criminal act was extended to adults by a 1999 amendment to the Criminal Procedure Code. If the facts are sufficiently clear, if the act is not subject to the jurisdiction of a mixed (*Schöffen*) or jury (*Geschworenen*) court and has not led to the death of a human being, the public prosecutor – or in a later stage of the proceedings the court – may choose measures of diversion provided that the defendant's fault is not serious and punishment does not seem required for purposes of special or general prevention. Measures of diversion are only allowed if the suspect accepts them voluntarily. They may include a money penalty, community service, probation and out of court settlement with the victim (*außergerichtlicher Tatausgleich*). The suspect must be prepared to assume responsibility for his act and, as far as possible, indemnify the victim. As a rule, the victim's consent is required.
- The Austrian Drug Abuse Law (*Suchtmittelgesetz*) provides for a special form of diversion. The prosecutor must refrain, for a period of two years, from prosecuting someone against whom a complaint (*Anzeige*) has been brought for possessing or having obtained for personal use a small amount

of drugs,[5] if drug abuse treatment is possible and is desired by the defendant. Prosecution may be resumed during the two-year period if the defendant violates any condition imposed on him during drug rehabilitation.

There are exceptions to the principle of compulsory prosecution based on reasons of procedural expediency. These exceptions apply when the prosecutor, after balancing the interests involved, concludes that prosecution will not further the purpose of criminal justice. This is known as the principle of prosecutorial discretion. These exceptions are as follows:

— If the defendant is accused of having committed more than one crime, the prosecutor may abstain from prosecuting an offense which is likely to have little or no influence on the punishment, or if the defendant is to be extradited to a foreign country and the punishment that could be imposed on him in Austria is insignificant compared to the charges he has to face abroad.
— If the crime was committed abroad, the prosecutor may refrain from prosecution if the defendant has already been sentenced for these charges abroad and the punishment likely to be inflicted by an Austrian court would not be more severe.
— The prosecutor may also decide not to prosecute minor crimes committed by military personnel under specific circumstances if punishment is not required for purposes of special prevention. However, punishment still might be imposed in these cases on the basis of internal military rules.

Plea bargaining as in the U.S., where the prosecution agrees to drop a more serious charge if the defendant is prepared to confess to a less serious one, is prohibited in theory, but informal arrangements between the prosecution and the defense do occur. German criminal procedure law goes further than Austrian law by permitting plea bargains in limited circumstances as informal agreements between the prosecution, the defense and the court.

B. Principles Governing the Trial

1. Principle of Independent Investigation (*Untersuchungs- oder Ermittlungsgrundsatz, Inquisitions- oder Instruktionsmaxime, amtswegige Wahrheitserforschung*)

Unlike in the American adversarial system, in Austria it is the duty of the judge to uncover the truth. The judge must gather all information pertaining to the case, whether it incriminates or exonerates the defendant. In this capacity, the judge is not bound by motions or petitions of the prosecutor or counsel for the defense. This inquisitorial duty applies to both the pretrial investigating judge and to the trial court.

---

5 Moreover, the public prosecutor may refrain from prosecuting someone who has committed a minor drug-related crime, if it is not subject to the jurisdiction of a mixed or jury court, provided that the defendant's fault is not serious and drug abuse treatment is possible and desired by the defendant.

The prosecutor and the counsel for the defense are – at least in theory – not permitted to reach an agreement (plea bargain) on guilt or sentencing *inter partes*. Consequently, and in contrast to the American system, a guilty plea does not end the trial. The court must reach an independent opinion, regardless of any confession. Hence a guilty plea does not preclude the court from the collection of evidence.

The principle of independent investigation does not prevent the parties of a trial from petitioning the court for the discovery of evidence. Such petitions must be specific and detailed as to what kind of evidence is sought and what it is intended to prove. General facts and facts already known to the judge need not be proven in court. Requests for evidence may be denied by the court if the evidence is inadmissible, irrelevant, or inappropriate.

The principle of independent investigation requires the search for objective truth not only by the judge but also by the public prosecutor, who has a duty to ensure that all evidentiary material, including any evidence which may exonerate the defendant, is presented to the court. If such evidence has not been admitted, the prosecutor is obligated to appeal the verdict.

2. Principles of Orality and Immediacy (*Grundsätze der Mündlichkeit und Unmittelbarkeit*)

Article 90 (1) of the Austrian Constitution requires all proceedings to be public and oral. A judgment may only be based on facts established during an oral trial. Written documents may be used only in reaching a verdict if they have been read aloud during trial. Thus, parts of the pretrial case file may be read into the trial record.

The principle of orality does not extend to the pretrial investigation. During the investigation, the judge collects written evidence. If such evidence is to be used in the subsequent trial, however, it must be read aloud at that time. The lack of orality in the pretrial phase is understandable from an organizational point of view, as the investigatory process may continue for weeks or even months.

The principle of immediacy, closely related to the principle of orality, forces the court to admit – as far as possible – only primary evidence during the trial. The direct examination of evidence given by the defendant and by witnesses may only in exceptional circumstances be replaced by the reading of earlier records or written statements. This approach gives the judge as well as the defense a better chance to evaluate or rebut evidence, and to avoid misconceptions or contradictions. This principle also enables lay judges and the public to follow and understand the criminal process. Although not outlawed by any specific rule in the Criminal Procedure Code, the use of hearsay and other secondary evidence is to be minimized, and the court is obligated to consider primary, original sources, as they allow for the most accurate determination of the truth.

3. Principle of Free Evaluation of Evidence *(Grundsatz der freien Beweis-würdigung)*

In stark contrast to the rather complex rules of evidence in American criminal procedure, Austrian procedure lacks specific rules of evidence. In evaluating the evidence, the judge is not bound by formal rules or presumptions. The decisive element is his inner conviction reached after conscientious examination of all the evidence before him. The evaluation of the evidence must be explained in the verdict. If this reasoning is incomplete, a nullity appeal may be brought against the verdict.

The principle of free evidentiary evaluation stems from the idea that each case is different, and that fixed rules of evidence do not account for specific circumstances. Circumstantial and indirect evidence is, therefore, not prohibited, but is factored into the decisionmaking process by the court according to its individual weight.

4. Principle of Reasonable Doubt *(Grundsatz "in dubio pro reo")* and Presumption of Innocence *(Unschuldsvermutung)*

It is up to the prosecutor – and during the pretrial phase the investigating judge – to produce the necessary evidence. The defendant is presumed innocent until a verdict has been reached. He is given the benefit of the doubt, i.e., there can be no conviction if reasonable doubt exists. If the court is in doubt concerning a question of fact, it must take it into account if it is a mitigating circumstance and must disregard it if it is incriminating.

5. Principle of Publicity *(Grundsatz der Öffentlichkeit)*

According to article 90 (1) of the Constitution, all court proceedings are public, unless otherwise provided by statute. Thus all criminal trials are, within technical limits, generally open to all unarmed adults, including journalists.[6] But video, sound recording, and cameras are not permitted.

The public may be excluded from a trial in exceptional circumstances, e.g., for reasons of public order or decency, or to protect the privacy (e.g., of a victim of a sexual offense), or a juvenile offender. Even in situations where the public is excluded, the victim, counsel, other judges and prosecutors as well as three persons nominated by the defendant, and where applicable the intervenor, or the private prosecutor, have a right to be present at the trial. If a juvenile is on trial, his parents, legal representatives, and parole officers may also be present.

Generally pretrial investigatory proceedings are not open to the public, although sometimes court witnesses may be required to attend.[7] If it is likely, however, that a witness cannot be questioned during the trial or if the

---

[6] Journalists are not allowed to speculate on the outcome of an ongoing trial, if the report would be likely to influence the verdict, cf. article 23 of the Media Act *(Mediengesetz)*.

[7] E.g., for searches and seizures (art. 142 (3) Criminal Procedure Code).

victim of a sexual offense younger than fourteen is questioned, the investigating judge has to enable the prosecutor, the intervenor, and the defendant to be present and to put questions to the witness.[8]

C. Principles Regarding Court Organization

1. Right to an Independent Judge (*Recht auf einen unabhängigen Richter*)

According to the Austrian Federal Constitution, judges are independent in the performance of their duties (art. 87).[9] They are bound only by law, not by any administrative order. They decide according to their own legal convictions (except, of course, if a case is remanded on appeal). Judges cannot be dismissed or transferred to another court without their consent (Const. art. 88).[10]

2. Right to the Lawful Judge (*Recht auf den gesetzlichen Richter*)

Both the Austrian Federal Constitution (art. 83) and the European Convention on Human Rights (art. 6) provide that the laws of procedure determine in an abstract and general fashion which judge is to decide which case.[11] That nobody may be deprived of his lawful judge means that the state may not manipulate the assignment of individual cases to particular judges at will, and that *ad hoc* courts are prohibited.[12]

The jurisdictional rules (Const. arts. 83 (1) and 87 (3)) and arts. 8 et sqq. Criminal Procedure Code prescribe which court is authorized to hear a certain case. Courts annually set rules on assigning cases to individual judges, based on formal criteria such as the first letter of the defendant's last name.

3. Principle of Lay Participation (*Grundsatz der Laienbeteiligung*)

The Austrian Constitution provides for the participation of the people in criminal procedure in either of two forms: as lay judges or assessors (*Schöffen*) or as jurors (*Geschworene*).[13]

---

[8] The investigating judge may restrict this participation by questioning the witness in a different room, so that the parties are not present but can nevertheless follow the hearing via a video installation (in cases of sexual offenses against a minor this is obligatory). The same procedure applies to sexual offenses against persons aged fourteen or older, minor victims of other crimes, and relatives of the defendant if these persons request it.

[9] Cf. article 97 (1) of the German Basic Law.

[10] Cf. article 97 (2) of the German Basic Law.

[11] Cf. article 101 (1) of the German Basic Law.

[12] Cf. article 101 (2) of the German Basic Law.

[13] See *infra* IV.A.

IV. Participants in the Trial

A. The Judge and Lay Judges

In Austria, professional judges preside over every criminal trial. In some cases they are assisted by lay assessors or by a jury. Lay participation allows for democratic input in criminal procedure and helps to keep the process understandable to the public at large. The pretrial investigative stage is directed by a single investigating judge. In the trial itself, the composition of the court depends on the nature of the offense allegedly committed.

For minor offenses, the trial is conducted by a single professional judge, who decides on the verdict (*Einzelrichter*).[14] For more serious offenses, a mixed court consisting of two professional judges and two lay assessors presides over the trial (*Schöffengericht*).[15] Lay assessors have the same rights and responsibilities as professional judges for the duration of the trial, participating in reaching the verdict and in determining the sentence.

For the most serious offenses and for most political crimes, a jury trial (*Geschworenengericht*) is mandated. The jury consists of eight lay jurors. Three professional judges preside over the trial. The jury alone decides guilt or innocence, while the decision on sentencing is reached by the jury together with the professional judges.

Special courts with specially qualified judges, assessors, and jurors are instituted to adjudicate in cases involving juveniles.

The law lists reasons for which the impartiality of a judge, lay assessor, or juror may be impaired, and consequently excludes him from participation in the criminal process (*Ausschließung*). Reasons for exclusion have to be taken into account *ex officio*. If an excluded judge takes part in the proceedings, a nullity appeal may be brought against the verdict. If for reasons not expressly listed by the law, impartiality seems doubtful, the judge, lay assessor or juror may be challenged by the parties or must disqualify himself (*Ablehnung*). In these cases, however, no nullity appeal is possible.

B. The Public Prosecutor (*Staatsanwalt*)

In Austria, the Public Prosecutor's Office is part of the administrative organization of the Federal Ministry of Justice. Its responsibilities include the initiation of a formal criminal investigation, the advancement of the pretrial investigatory process through motions to the investigating judge, and the representation of the prosecution during the trial and the appeal. The public

---

[14] Either at the District Court (*Bezirksgericht*) level (for misdemeanors with a maximum sentence not more than one year, except for certain offenses in this category that are reserved to the jurisdiction of the Regional Court) or at the Regional Court (*Landesgericht*) level (for offenses with a maximum sentence between one and five years and for violations of the Media Act).

[15] This occurs if the maximum sentence exceeds five years and in special cases enumerated by the law.

prosecutor has the right to ask the police and other state institutions within certain limits to help him fulfill his investigatory task. As members of a hierarchically structured administrative body and in contrast to independent judges, public prosecutors may receive orders from their superiors up to the Minister of Justice. Such orders must in principle be issued in writing, must contain appropriate reasons, and must be obeyed unless compliance would constitute a criminal offense.

The public prosecutor has formal standing as a party to court proceedings, in which he represents the interests of the state. Despite this partisan function, a public prosecutor is obliged by law to maintain objectivity. He must submit both incriminating and exonerating evidence concerning the defendant.

The public prosecutor has the right to inspect the case file at any time and may submit motions orally or in writing, on which the court must rule. The prosecutor may also comment on motions from the defense.

C. The Defendant

A person who in the process of a criminal investigation becomes linked to the commission of a crime is called a "suspect" (*Verdächtiger*). Suspects must be informed as soon as provisional inquiries in court or preliminary investigations are initiated against them.

Once the public prosecutor has collected enough evidence to warrant further investigation, the process becomes more formalized. The suspect is then called a "defendant" (*Beschuldigter*). He becomes a formal party to the proceedings and may exercise a number of procedural rights, including the right to have his attorney inspect the file.

During the actual trial the defendant is called the "accused" (*Angeklagter*). He now enjoys full procedural and due process rights. These procedural rights flow from the presumption of innocence.

Most procedural rights may be exercised by the defendant at any stage of the proceedings. Such rights include the following:

– The right to be informed as soon as possible of all grounds for his being the subject of a criminal proceeding.
– The right to be heard by the investigating judge in the pretrial process and by the trial judge during the trial, including the ability to present or indicate exonerating or mitigating evidence.
– The right to access the investigation file and to receive copies of the evidentiary documents in the file. The investigating judge may, however, exclude individual documents from access by the defendant until the prosecutor has brought formal charges, if special circumstances justify the fear that the defendant's knowledge of the documents might hinder the investigation.
– The right to consult with an attorney of his choice. At the latest, he must be informed of his right to consult an attorney at his first judicial interroga-

tion. If necessary, indigent defendants are provided with counsel free of charge.

– A defendant who is under arrest has the right to speak with his attorney privately without being supervised. His correspondence and phone calls with his attorney may not be monitored. Other mail is censured by the investigating judge.

D. Counsel for the Defense (*Verteidiger*)

Counsel for the defense must be an attorney inscribed in the list of defense attorneys of one of the Courts of Appeals. It is his duty to bring to light all exonerating evidence and to ensure that it is considered in the decisionmaking process. He is to support the defendant in the exercise of his rights, both substantive and procedural. Counsel is prohibited from lying and from intentionally falsifying evidence. In contrast to the public prosecutor, he is under no duty to be objective.

The defendant must be represented by counsel during the pretrial stage if he is in pretrial detention or if the public prosecutor has applied for his confinement to a psychiatric ward. During the trial, the defendant must be represented by counsel before a *Geschworenengericht* (jury court) or before a *Schöffengericht* (mixed court with lay assessors). He must be represented before a single judge if the maximum sentence for the offense charged exceeds three years. Except in cases of minor offenses, juveniles must always be represented in court by an attorney. On appeal, counsel for the defense is required in all cases.

A defendant may choose his own counsel, and he has to pay attorney's fees (*Wahlverteidiger*). If the defendant has not chosen counsel, but counsel is required under the rules of procedure, the court must provide an attorney, who will be selected by the Bar Association (*Amtsverteidiger*). The defendant has to pay for such a defense attorney. If the defendant cannot afford counsel, he can apply for a court appointed counsel free of charge, who will also be nominated by the Bar Association (*Verfahrenshilfeverteidiger*). Moreover, if the defendant is in preliminary detention and does not yet have counsel, the investigating judge will provide him with counsel for the first hearing (*Pflichtverteidiger*).

An attorney is excluded from acting as counsel if he has been summoned to the trial as a witness.[16] If counsel has acted as a witness in the pretrial stage, a special three-judge panel decides whether the attorney is excluded from acting as counsel in the particular case. Several other reasons for exclusion are set forth in the Code of Bar Practice (*Rechtsanwaltsordnung*).

Defense counsel has the right to act on behalf of the defendant. If the latter contradicts counsel, the court will as a rule accept the statement of the defendant. Counsel has the right to consult with the defendant in private and to

---

[16] The attorney-client privilege prohibits the summoning of an attorney as witness against his client.

communicate with him in writing without interference. Some exceptions apply if the defendant is in pretrial confinement solely for fear of tampering with evidence.

Counsel may exercise two rights independent of the defendant. The attorney may inspect the files, though some restrictions apply, and may receive a copy of the arrest warrant and all court decisions which the defendant wishes to appeal. During the pretrial investigation, counsel may participate in searches and seizures and all actions which directly pertain to the establishment of facts. However, counsel has no right to participate in the interrogation of the defendant by the investigating judge and only in exceptional cases has a right to participate in the questioning of the victim and of witnesses in the pretrial stage.

E. The Intervenor (*Privatbeteiligter*)

The intervenor is a person whose rights have been violated by the criminal offense under investigation. For someone to be admitted as an intervenor, the crime committed must be an offense prosecuted by the public prosecutor, not any of the special offenses subject to trial without public prosecution. The intervenor must contend that his civil claim is linked to the crime committed, and he must not yet have obtained a writ of execution.

To become an intervenor, one must notify the court before the trial begins. In practice, this notification is possible until the end of the taking of evidence at the trial. The intervenor may revoke his notification at any time during the trial. This action does not preclude him from bringing a future civil suit against the perpetrator of the crime.

If the court eventually acquits the defendant, the intervenor may pursue his claim in a civil court. If the defendant is found guilty, the criminal court may grant the claim of the intervenor in full, may partially grant it or may refuse to grant it altogether. If the court has not granted the intervenor's claim in full, the intervenor is referred to a civil court. The criminal court may not deny an intervenor's claim on its merits.

The intervenor may submit to the public prosecutor all evidence suitable for the conviction of the defendant and the granting of the intervenor's claim. He has the right of access to the file and must be given notice of the trial. If a single judge has decided on the intervenor's claim, the intervenor may appeal the decision. The decision of a mixed or jury court may be appealed by the intervenor only if the court refers his claim to the civil court in cases where it could have reached a decision on its merits without taking substantial additional evidence. The appeal of the intervenor is, however, limited to the extent of his private law claims.

If the public prosecutor decides to drop the charges, the intervenor may take over the prosecution as a subsidiary prosecutor (*Subsidiarankläger*). In trials before the District Court, the intervenor acting as the prosecutor is not restricted by judicial control. In all other cases, however, the intervenor, after having been notified of the prosecutor's intention to drop the charges, may only act as a prosecutor under tight judicial supervision. In such cases, a formal pretrial investigation (*Voruntersuchung*) is mandatory. The intervenor may not bring a nullity appeal, nor may he apply for a resumption of the proceedings once the file has been closed.

V. Evidence

Austrian criminal procedure does not contain a system of strict rules of evidence. The court determines the probative value of evidence through free and diligent deliberation. The standard of "practical certainty of life" is considered both necessary and sufficient. There is no exclusionary rule as there is in American criminal procedure. However, certain kinds of evidence obtained in violation of the law are declared void by the Criminal Procedure Code and may not be used in the trial. If such evidence is used, a nullity appeal may be brought. Unfortunately, the Supreme Court holds that only evidence obtained by a court may be void, which means that evidence obtained by the police may always be used. Moreover, the documentation of void evidence is included in the file so that it may indeed influence the evaluation of evidence by the court. However, recent trends in the interpretation of the European Convention of Human Rights by the European Human Rights Court in Strasbourg suggest that stronger protection of the due process rights of the defendant is needed and stricter standards of admissibility of illegally obtained evidence ("fruit of the poisonous tree") will be imposed on Austrian criminal courts.

A. Witnesses

A witness is a person other than the defendant who is questioned on specific issues of the case. He is under the obligation (in some instances under oath) to tell the truth. In contrast to procedure in the U.S., in Austria one cannot act as both defendant and witness in the same trial. Perjury is a crime, whether it is committed intentionally during questioning by the police or in court. The object of judicial questioning is to uncover facts, not to seek judgments or conclusions by witnesses. Leading questions are to be avoided. Certain persons may be excused as witnesses entirely (e.g., relatives of the defendant) or with respect to privileged information (clergymen, attorneys, and journalists).[17]

If a properly summoned witness does not appear, he may be brought to court by the police and fined. If a witness refuses to take the stand or to take an oath, he may be fined or imprisoned for up to six weeks.

---

[17] A further right to refuse answering a question applies if the answer would cause the witness shame, the danger of criminal prosecution, or immediate financial loss.

B. Experts

The court expert is an impartial specialist who has been invited by the court to facilitate the collection and evaluation of facts. It is a crime for an expert to intentionally misinterpret facts or to misinform the court about these facts. Persons who may not take the witness stand, or who are close relatives of the defendant or the victim, may not be called upon as experts. Whether an expert will be called, and who this expert will be, is up to the court to decide. The court has discretion to select an expert from a published list. Experts on this list routinely work for the court and have proven to be reliable. The expert has a right to be compensated according to a fee schedule established by statute.

It is the duty of the expert to appear before the court and to take the expert oath. He has to participate in judicial inspections and must give expert testimony. If the testimony is unclear or inconclusive, or if two expert testimonies contradict one another, the experts may be recalled for questioning. If further testimony does not clarify the situation, the court may ask yet another expert to testify. If an expert does not appear in court when properly summoned, he may face similar charges as witnesses who fail to appear.

C. Testimony of the Defendant

The defendant (or the accused) has a due process right to be heard during the pretrial and trial stages. His testimony serves not only his defense but also the court's quest for truth. The accused is not only a party to the trial, but also a source of evidence, whose testimony can be freely evaluated by the court. However, a defendant may not be forced to testify, neither during the pretrial investigation nor during the trial itself. He cannot be held criminally liable for not telling the truth during his testimony. Only if the accused intentionally, and contrary to his own knowledge, accuses somebody else of having committed a crime can he in theory be held liable. In practice, the accused is granted wide latitude in his defense.

During interrogation, the accused has certain rights and privileges. The judge may ask questions, but the accused may decide not to answer them. It is prohibited in the interrogation of the defendant (accused) to use threats, deceptions, false promises, or any other kind of inducement to make him confess or testify in a certain way. It is absolutely prohibited for the police or other law enforcement agencies to attempt to entrap the accused by employing a third person who either persuades the suspect to commit a crime or makes him confess to one. All testimony given by the defendant must be through his free and rational choice. Consequently, all inquisitorial methods interfering with the free will of the defendant, like lie-detector tests, are prohibited, even if he has agreed to their use. The defendant may not be subjected to a medical examination without his permission.

D. Documentary Evidence

Documentary evidence consists of physical objects containing information, which are introduced into evidence by being read during the trial. Records of prior testimony given by a defendant, a witness, or an expert may be used in the trial only in exceptional circumstances. Such exceptions may apply, e.g., to earlier statements made by the accused or a witness, if subsequent testimony during trial substantially deviates from them, testimony of witnesses that have since died or have otherwise become incapable of appearing in court, or testimony to whose reading the prosecutor and the defendant have agreed. The accused must be given ample opportunity to comment on such testimony.

Other documents must be read out in court, unless both the prosecutor and the defendant waive this right. These documents may include records of judicial inspections, prior judgments against the defendant, and other relevant materials.

E. Judicial Inspection (*Augenschein*)

Judicial inspection is the direct sensory perception of relevant evidentiary objects by the judge. "Sensory" includes all senses. An inspection is necessary if it can help to clarify a major point in the case. The court may, and in some cases must, ask one or two expert witnesses to participate in the inspection. The record of the inspection must convey an accurate and complete impression of the inspected objects.

VI. The Stages of Criminal Procedure

A. Pretrial Proceedings

Austrian criminal procedure defines two investigatory phases during the pretrial process: the informal *Vorerhebungen* (provisional inquiries) and the formal *Voruntersuchung* (preliminary investigation).

1. Provisional Inquiries (*Vorerhebungen*)

Vorerhebungen are conducted to determine whether the initiation of a formal criminal procedure against a suspect is warranted. Thus, *Vorerhebungen* may also be initiated against an unknown perpetrator. In theory, the public prosecutor begins the process after receiving a formal complaint (by the police, another public institution or a private person), as a result of a sustained rumor which the prosecutor must investigate, or based on his own observations. In practice, *Vorerhebungen* are generally initiated and conducted by the police on their own.

Vorerhebungen may be orchestrated by the public prosecutor. However, the prosecutor is not permitted to take independent actions. He has to avail himself of the investigating judge, the District Courts, or the police authorities. He may ask the latter to question persons who may be able to shed light on a criminal act. Only in emergency situations when the investigating judge on duty cannot be reached in time[18] may the prosecutor ask the police to conduct a search or an inspection. Concerning all other actions, the prosecutor must petition the investigating judge, who will order specific actions to be carried out and inform the prosecutor of the orders given. The investigating judge may refuse a petition of the prosecutor only if its legality is in doubt.

At the conclusion of the *Vorerhebungen,* the public prosecutor has three main options. If he has found sufficient reason to initiate formal criminal proceedings against the suspect, he may petition the investigating judge to begin a preliminary investigation. If sufficient evidence is present, the prosecutor may immediately bring formal charges against the suspect and move for a trial. If there is insufficient evidence, the prosecutor will withdraw the complaint and the investigating judge must close the file.

2. Preliminary Investigation (*Voruntersuchung*)

The *Voruntersuchung* is a formal procedure to determine whether there is sufficient evidence for the filing of formal charges against a suspect. A *Voruntersuchung* usually follows *Vorerhebungen* conducted by the police and is initiated by a petition submitted by the prosecutor. He may decide to forego this procedural step and file formal charges without preliminary investigation. However, a *Voruntersuchung* is mandatory for several types of cases, such as offenses to be tried before a jury, or against an absent suspect, or if a subsidiary prosecutor is involved, or if the prosecutor has applied for the suspect to be committed to a mental institution.

Such a preliminary investigation must be formally requested by the prosecutor who usually specifies the name of the suspect and the offense charged, but no details. *Voruntersuchungen* against a "suspect unknown" are prohibited. The investigating judge decides on the prosecutor's request. The prosecutor or the defendant may appeal his decision to the Court of Appeals (*Oberlandesgericht*).

The defendant is officially notified once a *Voruntersuchung* has been initiated. He has the right to access the file and to petition the investigating judge, particularly to admit exonerating evidence. However, the preliminary investigation is not public. In cases where the investigating judge denies a motion, the defendant and other participants may appeal to a three-judge panel (*Ratskammer*).

The *Voruntersuchung* is directed by the investigating judge, who acts *ex officio,* but the parties may request specific investigating acts. The investigating judge decides on these requests. Against his decision the parties may lodge a complaint to the three-judge panel.

Once the investigating judge has determined that the preliminary investigation is complete, the file is given to the public prosecutor, who within

---

[18] Regional Courts have an investigating judge on duty at all times.

14 days has to decide whether to file formal charges (*Anklageschrift*) or to notify the investigating judge that the case will not be pursued. In the latter instance, the investigating judge notifies the defendant (and possibly the private prosecutor and intervenor) and closes the file. The private prosecutor and intervenor then have 14 days to file charges themselves and to assume the prosecution of the case.

The public prosecutor may withdraw the complaint at any time before the preliminary investigation is completed. If this occurs, the investigating judge has to close the file and notify the party affected. Also, the intervenor may decide to take over the case within 14 days after being notified.

Against the will of the public prosecutor, a file can be closed and the criminal process abandoned only by a decision of the investigating judge. The parties may appeal decisions of the investigating judge to close or not to close the file (*Einstellung*) to the Court of Appeals (*Oberlandesgericht*).

No new trial against the defendant based on the same evidence may take place once the case has been closed. However, if the investigation is interrupted because the defendant has fled or is absent, it may be reopened at any time.

B. Measures of Compulsion Against the Defendant

1. Summons

Pretrial confinement of the defendant is the exception under Austrian criminal procedure law. Ordinarily, a suspect is summoned to appear before the investigating judge during the pretrial stage and before the court during the actual trial, but otherwise remains at large. If the defendant does not comply with a summons (*Ladung*), a written order (*Vorführbefehl*) may direct the police to bring him before the court at a given date and time.

2. Provisional Custody

In special circumstances, however, the suspect may be taken into provisional custody (*vorläufige Verwahrung*). This temporary deprivation of freedom may be imposed on the suspect for any of the following four reasons:

- He has been caught in the act of committing a crime, or credibly accused of the crime immediately after the act, or found with weapons or other evidence directly pointing to the commission of the act.
- He is on the run or hiding, or there is a substantiated likelihood that he will attempt to flee or hide because of the severity of the possible sentence.
- He has already attempted (or there is a substantiated suspicion that he will attempt) to influence witnesses, experts, or codefendants, or to destroy evidence or otherwise impede the investigation.
- There is a likelihood of his committing another crime against the same object of legal protection or of his completing the attempted crime.

Provisional custody may not be applied if the purpose of detention may also be achieved through other means (e.g., the temporary confiscation of a passport or a driver's license), or if it would impose an undue burden in relation to the severity of the crime committed (principle of proportionality). A suspect must be taken into provisional custody if the crime is punishable by a minimum sentence of ten years, unless all four reasons for confinement may be positively excluded.

To take a suspect into provisional custody, the investigating judge must issue an arrest warrant, which must be handed to the suspect within 24 hours of his arrest by the police. Also, the suspect must be brought to the court's detention facility within 48 hours of his confinement.[19] In "exceptional" circumstances, the police authorities may impose provisional custody without a proper arrest warrant, if the suspect has been caught in the act. If any of the other three reasons for provisional custody exist, police authorities may impose provisional custody only if a proper arrest warrant cannot be obtained in time. Although described as "exceptional," this is the most common procedure for the imposition of custody. With the advent of modern telecommunication (especially mobile telephones), however, it has lately become easier for the police to consult with a judge on duty prior to taking a suspect into custody.

In these cases, the suspect must be immediately interrogated by the police. He has to be informed of the suspicions against him and the reasons for his custody. He must also be informed of his rights, especially his right to consult an attorney, to inform a relative, and to refuse to testify. He also must be warned that his testimony may be used against him. He must be freed immediately if after the interrogation no further grounds for detention exist. Otherwise, the public prosecutor must be informed. The suspect is released if the prosecutor refuses to file for ordinary preliminary detention (*Untersuchungshaft*).

3. Ordinary Preliminary Detention (*ordentliche Untersuchungshaft*)

Once a suspect has been brought to the court detention facility, he must be interrogated within 48 hours by the authorized investigating judge, who again will inform him of the suspicion against him and of his rights. After this interrogation and within the 48-hour limit, the investigating judge must decide whether to impose the more formal preliminary detention (*Untersuchungshaft*) or to free the suspect. The suspect must be informed of the judge's decision immediately. If preliminary detention is imposed, a formal written decision must be handed to him within 24 hours. Preliminary detention can only be imposed by the investigating judge upon a respective motion by

---

[19] In exceptional circumstances (e.g., considerable distance between the place of initial confinement and the appropriate court detention facility), this 48-hour limit may be extended by another 24-hour period.

the public prosecutor. A number of conditions, similar to those for provisional custody, must be met.[20]

In the past, Austria has been faulted for using the instrument of pre-trial confinement too liberally. In several cases, suspects were confined for many months, even years, before trial. The European Court of Human Rights in Strasbourg subsequently declared this practice to be in violation of the European Convention of Human Rights. To remedy the situation, the Austrian Parliament passed the Criminal Procedure Reform Act of 1993, which introduced a system of mandatory hearings and time limits on preliminary detention. This system sounds sensible in theory but has changed little in existing practice, as the reasons for confinement remained the same. Investigating judges, familiar with the cases, frequently attend the prescribed hearings with pre-formulated decisions to continue confinement, and hearings are often reduced to routine formalities. Attorneys for the defense rarely appeal confinement decisions. Given their low success rate, such appeals would in most cases serve only to prolong the pretrial procedure and thus not be in their clients' interests.

Confinement must not continue for a period longer than absolutely necessary. Preliminary detention must be lifted immediately once the reasons for confinement have expired or if its purpose may be achieved through lesser means. Such means may include the promise of the suspect not to flee or hide until trial, or not to relocate without the permission of the investigating judge, the promise to abstain from any attempts to obstruct the investigations, a judicial order to remain or live at a specific location, to abstain from drinking, to notify the judge of any change in circumstances, the temporary confiscation of identity papers, and the deposit of bail. The bail system has thus far had only limited application in Austrian criminal procedure. Although the Criminal Procedure Reform Act was intended to promote wider use of bail, little has changed as yet in practice.

C. The Trial

1. General Rules

The trial is the apex of the criminal procedure. At the end of a public oral hearing in the presence of the parties, i.e., after an adversarial procedure based on the prosecution's charge, the court decides on the verdict and the sentence.

Several persons must participate in the trial. The (lay) judges must be present during the entire trial, otherwise the trial is voidable. The same applies to the court reporter. The public prosecutor must be in attendance, or the trial

---

[20] Contrary to the conditions for provisional custody, preliminary detention may not be imposed for reason of the suspect's intention to flee or hide if the suspect lives in "orderly circumstances" and the maximum sentence for the crime committed is below five years of imprisonment.

will be adjourned. Finally, the defendant and his attorney (in all cases requiring defense counsel) must be present during the trial at all times. Even if they are excluded from only parts of the trial, the trial is voidable. The trial may take place without the defendant, however, if the defendant is charged only with a misdemeanor, has already given testimony in court, has received a summons to the trial, and has failed to appear. The defendant may also be excluded from parts of the trial for disrupting the proceedings despite a warning by the court and in certain other exceptional cases.

The trial is conducted by the court. If the bench is composed of more than one judge, functions are split between the presiding judge and the full bench. It is the presiding judge's duty to open, adjourn, and close the trial. Based on his prior study of the file, he examines the defendant, the witnesses and the experts. Parties in court may be heard only if the judge grants them leave to speak. The presiding judge determines the sequence of presentation of evidence and pronounces the judgment. He ensures that no evidence is produced that does not pertain to the case at hand. He may grant a motion by one of the parties if it has not been objected to by the other party.

The full bench of judges makes procedural decisions like the exclusion of the public or the adjournment of the trial, and it decides all motions by the parties to which the other side has objected or motions which the presiding judge has refused to grant. Against such decisions no separate appeal is allowed. They may be attacked only upon the conclusion of the trial in the context of a nullity appeal. The bench also determines fines levied on parties who are held in contempt of court.

According to the principles of continuity and concentration, the trial should not be adjourned, but completed at once. This ideal, however, is not always achieved.

2. Procedure Before the *Schöffengericht*

The details of trial procedure depend upon the court before which the trial takes place. The following steps outline the procedure in a mixed court (*Schöffengericht*).

- In the *Schöffengericht* (two lay judges and two professional judges, one of whom is presiding) the trial starts with the case being called by the court reporter.
- The presiding judge then questions the defendant regarding his personal background and circumstances.
- The presiding judge swears in the lay judges (unless they have already taken the oath in the current year).
- Witnesses and experts are called and informed when and where they must be available (unless they have been summoned for a later time). Witnesses may not attend the trial prior to their questioning. Absentee witnesses may be produced by the police.
- The prosecutor makes an opening statement, addressing all points of the charge. The defense may reply.

- The defendant is then interrogated by the presiding judge on the substance of the charge. He may plead guilty or not guilty. If he pleads not guilty, he may choose to make a comprehensive statement before the special interrogation by the judge begins. The defendant generally may consult with counsel, but is forbidden to do so prior to answering individual questions. The defendant may not be forced to speak, but if he remains silent, his previous statements before the investigating judge may be read into the record, and the court may weigh his silence against him. If the defendant responds, the examining judge will explore discrepancies with his earlier statements. The defendant is allowed to lie without criminal law consequences (unless he wrongfully accuses another person of a crime). Confession and cooperation in finding the truth are rewarded by being considered mitigating circumstances.
- After the defendant's testimony, witnesses are heard and other evidence is presented in the order determined by the presiding judge, who will take into account aspects of procedural efficiency. Parties may ask for the introduction of new evidence and may agree to waive the production of evidence during trial, but the court is not bound by such an agreement. The defendant must be given the opportunity to comment after the testimony of each witness. All other judges and parties may then ask questions of witnesses or experts.
- After all evidence has been submitted, first the prosecutor and the intervenor plead their case, then the defendant and his counsel present their side. The prosecutor addresses guilt and punishment, discussing evidence and points of law. The intervenor may only address questions of guilt and his private law claim. If the prosecution replies to the arguments of the defense, the defendant has the last word. The court may bifurcate pleadings as to guilt and punishment, yet in practice this rarely happens.
- The presiding judge then declares the hearing closed, and the court retires to deliberate in chambers.
- After the court has reached a verdict and has decided on the sentence, the presiding judge pronounces the verdict and the sentence together with the main reasons, and informs the defendant of his right to appeal. The judgment must be put in writing and signed by the presiding judge and the court reporter within four weeks.

3. The Jury Trial (*Geschworenengericht*):

The jury trial (three professional judges, eight jurors) is similar to a trial before a mixed court (*Schöffengericht*).[21] It differs only in the decision-making process. After the taking of evidence, the bench presents written questions to the jury. The questions must be read aloud and the parties must be given an opportunity to petition the court for amendments to these questions.

---

[21] Members of the jury are allowed to ask questions during the taking of evidence.

The questions comprise "main questions," regarding the guilt of the defendant, "additional questions," considering grounds for exemption from punishment as well as aggravating or mitigating circumstances, and so-called "alternative questions" (*Eventualfragen*), allowing a different legal qualification of the criminal offense. The parties will then plead their case and the trial is finished.

The jury is sequestered and elects a foreman. If it has not already done so, the Court drafts the jury charge (legal instructions or *Rechtsbelehrung*), which is then handed to the jury. Moreover, legal instructions are given to the jury orally by the presiding judge. Unlike in the U.S., the professional judges may participate in the jury deliberations, if they decide to do so unanimously and a majority of the jurors do not object. The jury may at any time request the presence of the presiding judge for the purpose of receiving legal advice. If such advice is given, the other professional judges and the court reporter must be present. However, no one is allowed to be present in the actual decision-making of the jury. Once a result has been reached, the foreman records the votes and the reasons given by the jury and hands this document to the presiding judge.

For a question to be answered in the affirmative, an absolute majority of the jury (five of eight jurors) is required. In exceptional cases, the court may order the jury to reassess their verdict (*Moniturverfahren*). This occurs if a jury member has accidentally selected the wrong answer on his ballot and would like the mistake to be corrected, or if the court, after listening to the prosecution and the defense, reaches the conclusion that the decision of the jury is unclear, incomplete, or contradictory. A jury decision may also be suspended by a decision of the court (*Aussetzungsverfahren*) if the court unanimously finds that the jury has erred concerning the main issue. The suspension may be limited to an individual charge or an individual defendant. The case is then brought before the Supreme Court, which orders a new trial by another court with a different jury.

If the jury decision is neither reassessed nor suspended, the court will base its verdict and punishment on it. The hearing is then reopened, and the foreman of the jury reads the jury questions and the decisions of the jury. The presiding judge announces the verdict, including the sentence which has been determined in joint deliberation with the jury, and the main reasons of the court.

4. Trial Before a Single Judge

Summary proceedings are employed in less serious cases tried before a single judge (*Einzelrichter*) in the Regional Court (*Landesgericht*). Charges are filed without detailed reasons. The prosecutor develops the case during the trial. To protect the defendant from potential judgment errors, verdicts and sentences by single judges are subject to "full" appeal (see *infra* D.4).

5. Trial in the District Court

In general, the trial procedure in the District Court (*Bezirksgericht*) is similar to that before the single judge in the Regional Court. In exceptional circumstances, a district judge may render a judgment after being presented with the charges, without summoning the parties to a separate trial. In such cases, the defendant must be present and agree to this "rapid trial." The prosecutor's presence is not required if the defendant makes a full confession; otherwise the prosecutor must appear before the judge as well, producing all relevant evidentiary material.

D. Appeal

1. General Rules

The appeal procedure allows for a partial or complete reevaluation of a judicial decision. A guilty verdict may be appealed by the defense or by the prosecution, while an acquittal may be appealed only by the prosecution. Based on a desire to uncover the truth, Austrian criminal procedure allows the prosecutor to appeal in favor of the defendant. Appeals must be filed within three days after the verdict. The brief must be submitted within four weeks of the delivery of the judgment in writing. The opposing party may respond to the filing of the appeal.

The appellate court is limited in its decisionmaking to the grounds and issues raised in the appeal – with two important exceptions. First, substantive reasons for annulling the verdict in favor of the defendant must be considered *ex officio* by the appellate court, even if not addressed in the appeal. Second, if the appellate court accepts reasons for the appeal raised by one defendant, the court must extend its decision in favor of this defendant to all codefendants, even if they have not appealed the verdict. The appellate court may not increase the severity of the punishment on appeal if only the defendant (and not the prosecutor as well) has appealed the verdict.[22] Depending on the type of appeal, it may or may not have suspensive effect.

Austrian criminal procedure provides for "ordinary" and "extraordinary" remedies against judgments of a trial court. Ordinary remedies are *Nichtigkeitsbeschwerde* (nullity appeal claiming error), *Berufung* (appeal regarding the extent of punishment), and *volle Berufung* (*de novo* appeal on questions of fact and law). Extraordinary remedies are *ordentliche Wiederaufnahme* (ordinary resumption of proceedings), *außerordentliche Wiederaufnahme* (extraordinary resumption of proceedings), *Nichtigkeitsbeschwerde zur Wahrung des Gesetzes* (nullity appeal to uphold the integrity of the law), and *nachträgliche Milderung der Strafe* (reduction of the penalty).

---

[22] It may requalify the offense as more serious, yet a subsequent new trial may not lead to a higher penalty for this different offense.

2. The Nullity Appeal (*Nichtigkeitsbeschwerde*, Appeal for Error)

Verdicts by the *Schöffengericht* (mixed court) or *Geschworenen-gericht* (jury court) may be appealed directly to the Supreme Court if the legality of the procedure or judgment is questioned by one of the parties. The nullity appeal is in principle restricted to questions of law. But grave error in the evaluation of evidence (questions of fact) may be considered in favor of the defendant. Moreover, only specific, enumerated types of legal error may be redressed through the nullity appeal. These types of error are listed in the Criminal Procedure Code and include error in procedural and substantive law: a judge, the defendant or his counsel was not present during the entire trial; other serious violations of procedural rules have occurred; the evaluation rendered by the court concerning key evidence is unclear, incomplete, contradictory, or insufficiently reasoned; etc. Other types of error include incorrect application of substantive criminal law, e.g., the imposition of punishment in excess of what the law permits.

The nullity appeal in jury trials includes (in addition to reasons analogous to those applying to the *Schöffengericht*) the incorrect formulation of questions submitted to the jury, incorrect legal instructions given to the jury by the court, an unclear, incomplete, or contradictory verdict rendered by the jury or the wrongful application or lack of application of the *Moniturverfahren* (order to the jury to reassess their verdict, see *supra* C.3).

The nullity appeal has suspensive effect. The appeal is examined by the trial court for formal defects. In the absence of such defects, the appeal is submitted to the Supreme Court for consideration. The Supreme Court may immediately reject the appeal if it is formally deficient or based on a procedural error which the Supreme Court panel unanimously considers insufficient for a successful appeal. The Supreme Court may also immediately grant the appeal and order a new trial, but only in favor of the defendant. Otherwise, the Supreme Court must accept the case. A special hearing is conducted to which only the defendant or his counsel will be summoned. Counsel must be present during the hearing, the defendant may be present. For the special hearing, the Procurator General (*Generalprokurator*) at the Supreme Court prepares an opinion to which counsel may reply. The *Generalprokurator* is not a prosecutor, but a party *sui generis* having the right to be heard and the right to bring motions. He assists the court without being able to dispose of the charge. If the Supreme Court finds the appeal to be justified, the judgment is reversed and the case is either remanded for retrial (in all cases of procedural error) or decided on the merits by the Supreme Court (in cases of error concerning the application of substantive law).

3. The "Ordinary" Appeal (*Berufung*, "*Strafberufung*")

Concerning a judgment of a *Schöffengericht* or a *Geschworenen-gericht*, all parties may appeal an incorrect type or extent of punishment. Errors in the evaluation of evidence may not be appealed. The appeal has suspensive effect (unless the defendant chooses to begin serving the sentence) and goes to the *Oberlandesgericht* (Court of Appeals). The procedure before the Court of Appeals is similar to that before the Supreme Court in a nullity appeal. The Court of Appeals decides on the merits either immediately or after a special hearing in the presence of counsel and possibly also the defendant. Additional evidence may be presented, but is restricted to the points raised on appeal.

If a defendant brings both a nullity appeal and an ordinary appeal, both appeals are heard by the Supreme Court.

4. The "Full" Appeal (*volle Berufung*)

Special rules apply to an appeal against a judgment of the District Court (*Bezirksgericht*) or a Single Judge (*Einzelrichter*) in the Regional Court (*Landesgericht*). Because in such cases the procedure is more summary and the accused is often unrepresented, the parties to the trial may not only appeal legal error and the extent of the punishment, but also the evaluation of evidence. This *volle Berufung* (*de novo* appeal) leads to a new trial concerning all questions of fact and law in the appellate court (*Landesgericht* or *Oberlandesgericht*) in which the appellant may present new evidence.

5. Ordinary Resumption of Proceedings (*ordentliche Wiederaufnahme*)

Motions for the revision of a judgment that has become final may be brought only in exceptional circumstances. Grounds for the resumption of proceedings in favor of the defendant are restricted to three circumstances: If the verdict was based on evidence or testimony which was later discovered to be falsified or incorrect; if substantial new evidence has surfaced; or if another person has been sentenced for the same crime in a different trial, and only one of them could have been the perpetrator.

Contrary to Anglo-American principles of double jeopardy in criminal procedure, the Austrian rules for revision allow a case to be reopened at the request of the prosecution to apply a more severe punishment and even after the defendant has been acquitted. The first two reasons for resumption of proceedings in favor of the defendant also justify a revision to his detriment. In addition, a later confession of the crime by the defendant constitutes a ground for revision. The underlying rationale is again the desire to uncover the truth.

6. Nullity Appeal to Uphold the Integrity of the Law (*Nichtigkeitsbeschwerde zur Wahrung des Gesetzes*).

The Procurator General (*Generalprokurator*) may appeal to the Supreme Court all decisions and procedures of criminal courts which are based on a violation or incorrect interpretation of the law, even if the parties have not appealed and the sentence has become final. He acts *ex officio* or on instructions of the Ministry of Justice, on suggestions by the prosecutors (who are obligated to bring such violations to his attention), or on information provided by private individuals (attorneys). This nullity appeal is an extraordinary remedy which aims to protect legality and due process. The Supreme Court reaches a decision after a public hearing, of which the defendant must be informed. The pronouncement by the Supreme Court that the law has been violated is in principle only declaratory and has no immediate effect on the defendant. But the Supreme Court has discretion to acquit the defendant, reduce his sentence, or order a new trial. The new trial may not impose a more severe sentence than the one which has been nullified.

7. Extraordinary Resumption of Proceedings (*außerordentliche Wiederaufnahme*)

The remedy of extraordinary resumption of proceedings allows the Supreme Court (*ex officio* or at the suggestion of the Procurator General) to correct serious shortcomings in the determination of facts by a *Schöffengericht* or *Geschworenengericht*. Extraordinary resumption of proceedings takes place before the judgment becomes final and it is admissible even in the absence of reasons for ordinary resumption. This remedy can only be used in favor of the defendant. The Supreme Court may acquit the defendant, reduce the sentence, or order a new trial. In practice, extraordinary resumption of proceedings is hardly ever applied because serious shortcomings in the determination of facts are usually dealt with in a nullity appeal.

8. Reduction of Penalty *(nachträgliche Milderung der Strafe)*

If, after a judgment has become final, mitigating circumstances are discovered that were not applicable or known at the time of the trial,[23] the trial court may, *ex officio* or upon the motion of one of the parties, reduce the penalty.

Literature

Commentaries and Textbooks

Bertel, C., Venier, A., Grundriß des österreichischen Strafprozeßrechts (6th ed. 2000)
Foregger, E., Fabrizy, E. E. (eds.), Die österreichische Strafprozeßordnung (short commentary, 8th ed. 2000)
Mayerhofer, C., Österreichisches Strafrecht II: Strafprozeßordnung (1997)
Platzgummer, W., Brandstetter, W., Fuchs, H., Österreichisches Strafprozeßrecht (9th ed. 2000)
Seiler,S., Strafprozeßrecht (4th ed. 2000)

Monographs and Articles

Császár, F., Das neue Untersuchungshaftrecht in der Praxis, FS Platzgummer (1995) 351
Eder-Rieder, M., The Rights of Defendants under Austrian Criminal Procedure, Comparative Law Yearbook 1995, 19
Grabenweger, A., Die Grenzen der rechtmäßigen Strafverteidigung (1997)

---

23 E.g., if the defendant has subsequently indemnified the victim.

Hinterhofer, H., Diversion statt Strafe. Untersuchungen zur Strafprozessnovelle 1999 (2000)

Höpfel, F., Staatsanwalt und Unschuldsvermutung (1988)

Jesionek, U., Die Stellung des Opfers im österreichischen Strafprozeß, FS Moos (1997) 239

Korinek, K., Kain, I. (eds.), Grundrechte und Untersuchungshaft (1988)

Löschnig-Gspandl, M., Die Wiedergutmachung im österreichischen Strafrecht (1996)

Moos, R., Der außergerichtliche Tatausgleich für Erwachsene als strafrechtlicher Sanktionsersatz, JBl 1997, 337

Moos, R., Polizei und Strafprozeß (2000)

Okresek, W., Die EMRK und ihre Auswirkungen auf das österreichische Strafverfahrensrecht, EuGRZ 1987, 497

Schmoller, K., Neu geregelte Beweisverwertungsverbote nach dem StPÄG 1993, FS Platzgummer (1995) 283

Schroll, V., Diversion als Ausdruck eines Paradigmenwechsels der Strafrechtsdogmatik, FS Moos (1997) 259

Schuppich, W., Soyer, R. (eds.), Haft und Rechtsschutz (1993)

Seiler, S., Die Stellung des Beschuldigten im Anklageprozeß (1996)

Steininger, H., Grundrechtsschutz im Bereich der ordentlichen Gerichtsbarkeit, FS Platzgummer (1995) 191

Wedrac, P. E., Das Vorverfahren in der StPO (1996)

Comparative Works

Damaska, M. R, Evidentiary Barriers to Conviction and Two Models of Criminal Procedure: A Comparative Study, University of Pennsylvania Law Review 121 (1973) 506

Damaska, M. R., The Faces of Justice and State Authority: A Comparative Approach to the Legal Process (1996)

Damaska, M. R., The Reality of Prosecutorial Discretion, American Journal of Comparative Law 29 (1981) 119

Dannecker, G., Roberts, J., The Law of Criminal Procedure, in *Ebke, W. F., Finkin, M. W. (eds.),* Introduction to German Law (1996)

Dubber, M. D., American Plea Bargains, German Lay Judges, and the Crisis of Criminal Procedure, Stanford Law Review 49 (1997) 547

Frase, R. S., Weigend, T., German Criminal Justice as a Guide to American Law Reform: Similar Problems, Better Solutions? Boston College International and Comparative Law Review 18 (1995) 317

Hatchard, J. et al., Comparative Criminal Procedure: France – Germany – Great Britain (1996)

Herrmann, J., The Federal Republic of Germany, in *Cole, G. F. et al. (eds.),* Major Criminal Justice Systems: A Comparative Survey (2nd ed. 1987) 106

Kühne, H.-H., Germany, in *van den Wyngaert, C. (ed.),* Criminal Procedure Systems in the European Community (1993) 137

Langbein, J. H., Comparative Criminal Procedure: Germany (1977)

Schlesinger, R. B., Comparative Criminal Procedure: A Plea for Utilizing Foreign Experience, Buffalo Law Review 26 (1977) 361

Stemmler, S., Incentive Structures and Organizational Equivalents of Plea Bargaining in German Criminal Courts (1994)

van Kalmthout, A. M., Tak, P. J. P., Sanctions-Systems in the Member States of the Council of Europe, vol. II (1992) 365

Weigend, T., Continental Cures for American Ailments: European Criminal Procedure as a Model for Law Reform, Crime and Justice 2 (1980) 381

Chapter 11
Austrian Civil Procedure

I. Introduction

The term "civil procedure" (*zivilgerichtliches Verfahren*) encompasses a variety of procedures conducted in civil courts. Civil procedure differs from criminal procedure (*supra* Chapter 10) and administrative procedure (see *supra* Chapters 6 and 7). Civil procedure typically comprises two stages, the first of which leads to a decision (judgment) by the court (*Erkenntnisverfahren*), the second to the enforcement of such decision by the court (*Vollstreckungs- oder Exekutionsverfahren*).

II. History and Sources of Civil Procedure Law

After the reception of Roman law,[1] European civil procedure was strongly influenced by Roman and Canon law notions. Judges were trained jurists in the service of the prince. The Imperial Court (*Reichskammergericht*), established in 1495 as the highest court of the Holy Roman Empire, worked under procedural rules that later also served as a model for other jurisdictions. This procedure (*Kameralprozeß*) was written and secret. Subsequent modifications in Saxony introduced elements of non-immediacy, i.e., the taking of evidence by a judge different from the one conducting the trial and deciding the case, and formal rules for the evaluation of evidence. The German common law procedure (*Gemeiner Prozeß*) that was developed by doctrine and jurisprudence on this basis culminated in the Austrian *Allgemeine Gerichtsordnung (AGO)* of 1781.[2]

The first modern civil procedure code was the French *Code de procédure civile* of 1806. It was based on the principles of orality, publicity, party control, and free evaluation of evidence. It had considerable influence on procedure reform in Germany and Austria. The Austrian Civil Procedure Code of 1895 pays close attention to the German Civil Procedure Code of 1877, perceiving the latter's liberalism as excessive, insisting on a social and protective function of civil procedure, trying to balance individual and public welfare interest by strengthening the position of the judge *vis-à-vis* the parties.

Under the Austrian Constitution, legislation on and application of civil procedure are exclusively federal matters. Several basic principles are referred to in Const. arts. 82 to 94. They were expanded by Article 6 ECHR

---

[1] See *infra* Chapter 16 (The Civil Law Tradition), V.

[2] The *Allgemeine Gerichtsordnung* of 1781 provided for a written, secret, non-immediate procedure with formal evidentiary rules. Virtually unlimited party control frequently led to excessive duration of litigation.

(containing fundamental notions of fair trial) which was adopted by Austria in the rank of constitutional law.[3]

Modern Austrian civil procedure dates back to 1895, when the *AGO* was profoundly reformed by Franz Klein, professor of law at the University of Vienna, later Minister of Justice. The three major legislative enactments passed at that time were the Jurisdiction Act (*Jurisdiktionsnorm, JN*), which determines the organization and jurisdiction of courts in contentious and non-contentious matters, the Civil Procedure Code (*Zivilprozeßordnung, ZPO*), which regulates contentious proceedings in civil courts, and the Enforcement Code (*Exekutionsordnung, EO*), regulating the enforcement of judgments and preliminary remedies. Other sources include the Non-contentious Procedure Act (*Außerstreitgesetz* 1854), the Bankruptcy Code (*Konkursordnung, KO* 1914) and the Composition Code (*Ausgleichsordnung, AO* 1914, repromulgated in 1934). A special Enterprise Reorganization Act (*Unternehmensreorganisationsgesetz, URG* 1997) provides preventive action against enterprise bankruptcy.

Reform legislation in 1983 and 1986 simplified and expedited procedure and improved access to the law by reducing formal requirements. Special jurisdiction in labor and social matters was put on a new footing in 1985. Private bankruptcy provisions were adopted in 1993. The Enforcement Code was profoundly amended in 1991 and 1995. An amendment concerning jurisdiction based on value in dispute (*Erweiterte Wertgrenzen-Novelle* 1997) affected trial and appeals courts.[4] At present, a sweeping reform of non-contentious procedure is under way.

Austria is a party to the European (or Brussels) Convention on Jurisdictions and Enforcement of Judgments in Civil and Commercial Matters (1968, implemented in 1998), the Lugano Convention on Jurisdictions and Enforcement of Judgments in Civil and Commercial Matters (1988, implemented in 1996) and other international treaties, such as the Convention on the Recognition and Enforcement of Foreign Arbitral Awards 1958 (New York Convention) and the European Convention on International Commercial Arbitration 1961.

III. Fundamental Principles of Contentious Civil Procedure

One may distinguish two groups of principles, one governing the relationship between the court and the parties (party control, limited investigative system, *ex officio* proceedings), the other comprising the fundamental aspects of a fair trial (orality, immediacy, publicity, speedy trial, right to be heard). Most of the principles concern primarily or exclusively the trial process.[5] Major differences between Austrian and U.S. civil procedure include the

---

[3] See *supra* Chapter 9 (Fundamental Rights), IV F.
[4] See *infra* Appendix 3.
[5] For similarities and differences with the principles of criminal procedure, see *supra* Chapter 10.

following aspects: In Austrian procedure, fact gathering is not left entirely to the parties but is dominated by the judge. There is no pretrial discovery. This approach is less complex and wasteful than the U.S. pretrial and trial production and examination of evidence. In Austrian civil trials, experts are court appointed. There is no jury.

A. Principles Governing the Relationship Between the Court and the Parties

1. Principle of Party Control (*Dispositionsgrundsatz*)

In civil procedure, the parties are largely in control of the lawsuit. The plaintiff files a claim, which together with the defendant's response defines the object of the proceeding, specifying the topics on which evidence is to be produced by the parties in support of their allegations of fact. The parties can end proceedings at any point by withdrawal of the action *(Klagsrücknahme)*, waiving the claim *(Verzicht)*, acknowledgment of the claim *(Anerkenntnis)*, or settlement of the case *(Vergleich)* in court. The court may not render a judgment that goes beyond the plaintiff's claim *(ultra petita)*.

2. Principle of Limited Investigative Powers *(abgeschwächter Untersuchungsgrundsatz)*

It is up to the parties to prove their respective claims and defenses, and they are under a duty to make truthful and complete statements. The judge is to ascertain the truth, and to this end he may collect additional evidence that has not been requested by the parties. He is, however, subject to two restraints: documents must be submitted only if one of the parties has referred to them, and witnesses may not be heard if both parties oppose their being called.

3. Principle of *ex officio* Proceedings (*Grundsatz des Amtsbetriebs*)

Once civil proceedings have been initiated by the plaintiff, the court will *ex officio* take the steps necessary to move the case along, e.g., service of the claim on the defendant, service of subsequent motions and notices, summoning of witnesses, etc.

B. Principles Governing the Trial

1. Principle of Orality (*Grundsatz der Mündlichkeit*)

Only what has been brought forward in an oral hearing may provide the foundation of adjudication in a civil trial. But the plaintiff's claim, the defendant's reply, the (orally pronounced) judgment, and all appeals must be in writing. The appellate process and several special proceedings are conducted mostly in writing.

2. Principle of Immediacy (*Unmittelbarkeitsgrundsatz*)

The case may be decided only by judges who have participated in the entire trial, and all evidence must be produced in the oral trial. In exceptional circumstances, another judge may take evidence, which will then be read out at trial. Results from other court proceedings between the same parties may be read into the record with their consent.

3. Principle of Publicity (*Öffentlichkeitsgrundsatz*)

Justice is in principle to be dispensed in open court. Trials are open to the public. Publicity may exceptionally be restricted to the parties at their request, if the privacy of the family or trade secrets would otherwise be threatened. The court may also exclude the general public for reasons of public safety or decency. Deliberations of the court are secret. Filming, radio or TV transmission of court proceedings is forbidden.

4. Principle of Procedural Concentration or Efficiency (*Grundsatz der Verfahrenskonzentration*)

Article 6 (1) ECHR guarantees a speedy trial. In an international perspective, Austrian civil trials are comparatively short. Questions of jurisdiction are resolved before the trial stage. New claims and defenses or new allegations of facts and evidence may not be introduced on appeal (*Neuerungsverbot*). The court may reject motions by the parties concerning facts and evidence as irrelevant or immaterial, and set a final date for the taking of evidence. Conversely, the parties may call on a higher court to set a date to speed up proceedings in a procrastinating trial court.

5. Principle of the Right to be Heard (*Grundsatz des beiderseitigen rechtlichen Gehörs*)

This principle of Article 6 (1) ECHR applies to both parties (*audiatur et altera pars*) and includes service of all documents, access to the file, and to be present and participate in oral hearings.

IV. Participants in the Trial

A. The Court and its Jurisdiction

Professional judges[6] preside over civil trials. There exists no civil jury in Austria. Lay judges function as expert assessors (*fachmännische Laienrichter*) sitting on panels together with professional judges in commercial matters and as informed assessors (*fachkundige Laienrichter*) in labor and social secu-

---

[6] On their appointment and promotion *supra* Chapter 5 (Legal Education and Legal Professions), II.B, on the structure of civil courts *supra* Chapter 6 (The Courts), II.A and Appendix 3).

rity law cases.[7] Subject matter jurisdiction (*sachliche Zuständigkeit*) depends on either the nature of the claim (*Eigenzuständigkeit*) or on the value in dispute (*Wertzuständigkeit*). Ordinary civil cases not exceeding a value of ATS 130,000 or family law or tenancy cases come before district courts (*Bezirksgerichte*). When the value in dispute is above ATS 130,000 the case resorts to the regional court (*Landesgericht*).

Venue or territorial jurisdiction (*Gerichtsstand, örtliche Zuständigkeit*) is basically determined by the defendant's domicile (*Wohnsitz*) or place of business (*Sitz*). There are, however, exceptions to this general local jurisdiction (*allgemeiner Gerichtsstand*) for cases involving land, in which the court where the land is situated has exclusive jurisdiction (*ausschließlicher besonderer Gerichtsstand*). The plaintiff may in many cases choose between the venue of general local jurisdiction and a venue of optional jurisdiction (*Wahlgerichtsstand*), e.g., the place of invoice or performance. Parties may in most cases determine jurisdiction by agreement (*Zuständigkeitsvereinbarung*).

The jurisdiction of Austrian courts may be limited by general principles of international law and by international treaties (e.g., providing immunity). Otherwise the rules concerning venue also apply to international litigation in Austrian courts. There is no *forum non conveniens* rule and no minimum contact requirement.

B. The Parties

Parties in contentious civil procedure are plaintiff (*Kläger*) and defendant (*Beklagter*). Aside from physical and legal persons, several associations, e.g., unlimited commercial partnerships (*OHG*) and estates, e.g., an estate in bankruptcy (*Konkursmasse*) are granted standing although they lack legal personality. Certain industrial and consumer associations have the exceptional right to bring an action on behalf of collective interests (*Verbandsklage*).

There is no room for interference by a procedurally unaffected party (e.g., an *amicus curiae* brief as in common law countries). The public prosecutor may enter proceedings as plaintiff, when the public interest so demands, for instance for the purpose of annulment of a marriage entered into only in order to obtain citizenship. But there is no general right of a government attorney (*ministère public* as in France) or *avocat général* (as in the Court of Justice of the European Communities) to render a legal opinion to the court.

Outside oral hearings (*Tagsatzungen*) the parties and the court communicate by means of writings (*Schriftsätze*) that must satisfy certain form requirements. Formal service is regularly effected *ex officio* by the court (by special mail delivery). A party who does not perform a procedural act by the established deadline is precluded from this act. The party may, however, move for reinstatement of the *status quo ante* (*Wiedereinsetzung in den vorigen*

---

[7] See *supra* Chapter 6, II.B.

Stand) if the delay was due to an unforeseeable and unavoidable event, and only slight negligence of the party was involved.

C. Counsel

Parties must be represented by counsel in District Court (*Bezirksgericht*) cases involving claims valued above ATS 52,000 (with the exception of subject matter jurisdiction), in all trials before a Court of First Instance (*Landesgericht*), and in all appellate proceedings. No representation by counsel is required on two levels of labor litigation, where workers are usually represented by authorized agents of labor unions. Representation by counsel is required in all appellate proceedings.

V. Legal Costs and Legal Aid

Legal costs comprise court fees and attorneys' fees. Under the Court Fees Act (*Gerichtsgebührengesetz*), the plaintiff or appellant deposits the entire fee for trial or appeal (including reimbursement of witnesses and experts) in advance. The fee depends on the amount in controversy (*Streitwert*). Every party pays for its own legal representation. The losing party pays the winner's costs (court and attorneys' fees) up to the amounts specified in the Attorneys Tariff Act. Many parties carry legal costs insurance (*Rechtsschutzversicherung*).

Legal aid (*Verfahrenshilfe*) is given to parties who cannot afford to litigate without endangering their livelihood (minimum of subsistence), provided that their litigation is not patently frivolous or without chance of success. Payment of costs is either delayed or waived, or an attorney is provided at reduced cost or free of charge. If possible, the party has to repay legal aid within three years.

VI. The Civil Trial

Austrian civil procedure provides for no pre-trial proceedings as they exist in common law countries (e.g., pre-trial discovery in the U.S. – a procedure for obtaining information from the other party for the proper conduct of the case, which may include extensive interrogatories, i.e., written questions put by one party to the other, depositions, i.e., answers to oral questioning by the other party, and requests for the production of documents).

A civil suit is initiated by a complaint (*Klage*) filed with the court. In this complaint or action the plaintiff claims a performance (*Leistungsklage*), a declaratory judgment (*Feststellungsklage*) or a change in a legal right or status (*Gestaltungsklage*). A properly filed suit interrupts the period of limitation.

The court examines the procedural prerequisites (*Prozeßvoraussetzungen*) such as jurisdiction of the court and the absence of *res judicata* or other impediments. If it considers the action admissible, the court serves the complaint on the defendant and summons both parties to a first hearing (*erste*

Tagsatzung), which has the limited purpose of verifying whether the case will be disputed. The defendant may claim the absence of procedural requirements. If the defendant fails to appear, the plaintiff may move for a default judgment.

If the defendant contests the plaintiff's claim, the court orders him to file a written response to the complaint (*Klagebeantwortung*).

The subsequent trial may consist of several hearings (*Tagsatzungen zur mündlichen Streitverhandlung*) spread over considerable time. It encompasses three stages: the decision as to proof-taking (*Beweisbeschluß*), the proof-taking (*Beweisverfahren*), and the closing of the trial. In their initial pleadings, the parties set out the facts and their requests as to the taking of evidence. The judge then decides which evidence will be taken and in which order. The proof-taking is followed by further discussion and argument with reference to its results. The court frequently applies considerable pressure on the parties to settle the case prior to judgment.

The Code regulates five types of evidence: documents (*Urkunden*), witnesses (*Zeugen*), experts (*Sachverständige*), judicial inspection (*Augenschein*) and testimony of the parties (*Parteienvernehmung*). This list is not exclusive. Other means may be considered if their use is permissible under the rules of evidence. There are very few exclusionary rules. Witnesses have the duty to appear and speak truthfully about their observations. They are questioned primarily by the court, with additional questions being asked by counsel. There is no cross-examination. Witnesses may claim reimbursement of their costs. Experts are appointed by the court. Parties are generally treated like witnesses, but they are under no duty to appear or testify. Testimony is not recorded verbatim, but in summarized form.

As a general rule, the party who makes a claim bears the burden of proof. The court may freely evaluate the presented evidence. It decides according to its independent conviction whether an allegation is true, the standard of proof being high probability (*hohe Wahrscheinlichkeit*).

When all the evidence the court considers necessary has been taken, the court closes the trial. From that point onwards, no new facts can be alleged, not even in review proceedings (*Neuerungsverbot*). Prior to the closing of the trial by the court, the parties may at any time end proceedings by settlement or withdrawal of the claim.

The normal end of proceedings is a judgment on the merits of the case (*Urteil*). The court pronounces the decision in the name of the Republic. Ideally, judgment is pronounced orally at the end of the last hearing. It must be served on the parties in writing. From this point in time, periods for performance (regularly 14 days) or appeal are computed. All decisions rendered in the course of proceedings (e.g., to admit or reject evidence offered by the parties) are orders (*Beschlüsse*).

If a judgment is not (or no longer) subject to appeal, it becomes formal *res judicata* (*formelle Rechtskraft*). This has the substantive effect that parties, the court and other agencies are bound by the decision, and the same object of dispute may not be litigated again (*materielle Rechtskraft*).

VII. Non-contentious Procedures (*Außerstreitverfahren*)

Non-contentious jurisdiction (in Germany: voluntary jurisdiction, *freiwillige Gerichtsbarkeit*) applies when the legislator specifically assigned a matter to this historically grown rather than systematically defined area. It has traditionally been a field governed by the idea of protective activity of the court in the public interest: probate, guardianship, adoption and legitimation, the keeping of the land register (*Grundbuch*, the quantitatively most important activity of non-contentious jurisdiction), and the company register (*Firmenbuch*), authentication of documents, etc. More recent additions to non-contentious proceedings are consensual divorce (1978) and several matters concerning rent control and tenant protection. The procedure is more flexible, and it frequently dispenses with orality and publicity. Parties do not have to be represented by counsel, they bear their own costs.

VIII. Special Procedures

1. The procedure before district courts (*bezirksgerichtliches Verfahren*) has the following peculiarities: Parties not represented by counsel may also orally file the action and all motions. The scheduling of a formal first hearing is left to the discretion of the judge. There is no written response to the complaint. The judge has to provide special guidance to unrepresented parties in their procedural actions (*Manuduktionspflicht*).

2. Summary proceedings for debt collection (*Mahnverfahren*) are obligatory for money claims not exceeding ATS 130,000. They must be submitted to an automated payment order procedure operated by a magistrate (*Rechtspfleger*) in the district court. On the basis of the claim filed by the plaintiff, the court issues the order without hearing the defendant. If the latter files an objection within 14 days, the order expires and the court has to initiate regular proceedings.

3. Commercial jurisdiction (*Handelsgerichtsbarkeit*, see *supra* Chapter 6, II.B) applies to litigation arising from dealings in which the defendant is a merchant and the matter in dispute is a commercial transaction on his part; to disputes involving commercial partnerships and corporations and their members; disputes concerning checks, bills of exchange, matters of unfair competition, authorship, product liability, patents, trademarks, etc. Court panels include expert lay judges.

4. Labor and social jurisdiction (*Arbeits- und Sozialgerichtsbarkeit*, see *supra* Chapter 6, II.B) applies to civil claims arising from employment contracts or disputes concerning the enterprise constitution (*Betriebsverfassung*)[8] on the one hand, and claims arising from social security legislation on the other hand. Court panels include informed lay judges. Except before the Supreme Court, parties may be represented by "qualified persons," including functionaries of labor unions or employers' associations.

---

[8] See *infra* Chapter 15 (Labor Law), IV.D.

5. Antitrust jurisdiction (*Kartellgerichtsbarkeit*) based on the Cartel Law Act 1988 applies to motions by entrepreneurs, the social partners or the Republic of Austria to approve, withdraw approval, or prohibit a cartel, and to exercise supervision over entrepreneurs who dominate the market. Jurisdiction is exercised by the Vienna Court of Appeals and the Supreme Court (see *supra* Chapter 6, II.B). Panels include expert lay judges.

IX. Review Proceedings (*Rechtsmittelverfahren*)

Within certain limits, either party may request review of a court decision by a higher court. The Civil Procedure Code provides for an ordinary appeal (*Berufung*) against a judgment (*Urteil*) of a trial court, and for a second appeal (*Revision*) against the decision of an appellate court. A complaint (*Rekurs*) or second complaint (*Revisionsrekurs*) may lie against a court order (*Beschluß*). Other requests for relief from court decisions are referred to as extraordinary remedies (*außerordentliche Rechtsbehelfe*).

A timely appeal suspends the legal validity (*res judicata* effect) and in most instances the enforceability of the judgment. In review proceedings, no new claims and defenses or new allegations of facts and evidence may be introduced (*Neuerungsverbot*).

A. Ordinary Recourse (*Ordentliche Rechtsmittel*)

1. Appeal (*Berufung*)

The appeal is a legal recourse against a judgment by a trial court. It must be filed within four weeks and suspends the validity (*Rechtskraft*) and enforceability (*Vollstreckbarkeit*) of the judgment. The appeal is heard by the next higher court, i.e., for the District Court the Regional Court, for the Regional Court the Court of Appeals (see *infra* Appendix 3). Formal defects (procedural error) include the so-called grounds for nullity (*Nichtigkeitsgründe*) and other instances of procedural error. Grounds for nullity are instances of particularly serious procedural error. They must be considered *ex officio* at every stage of proceedings regardless of their substantive influence on the outcome, e.g., if a party could not attend the trial because the claim was not properly served. Other instances of procedural error are those which hindered an exhaustive discussion and profound evaluation of the case, e.g., unjustified exclusion of evidence. Substantive defects include the incorrect application of the law and the incorrect statement of facts, for instance because of an incorrect evaluation of the evidence.

In cases involving an amount not above ATS 26,000, appeals can be filed only for nullity and incorrect application of the law (*Bagatellberufung*).

The appellate court may affirm, quash or modify the decision (i.e., exercise a cassatory or reformatory function). If it quashes (reverses) the decision, it usually remands the case to the trial court.

2. Second Appeal (*Revision*)

Revision is a legal recourse against judgments of appellate courts. It goes to the Supreme Court. In the civil procedure reforms of 1983, 1989, and 1997, its admissibility was strongly restricted in several ways. It is impermissible when the value in dispute is not above ATS 52,000. When the value in dispute is above ATS 52,000 but not above 260,000, the appeal reaches the Supreme Court only if the appellate court grants leave to appeal. This leave will be granted only if an issue of considerable importance (*Rechtsfrage von erheblicher Bedeutung*) in substantive or procedural law is involved with respect to the uniform application, reliability, or development of the law beyond the case in point. This is called *Grundsatzrevision* (appeal concerning a point of fundamental importance). When the value in dispute is above ATS 260,000, the appellate court may not block the appeal, but in this case – as in all others – the Supreme Court has discretion to accept or refuse to accept the case (similar to granting or denying *certiorari* in the U.S.). As a result of these restrictions, the role of *Revision* changed from that of a regular second appeal as of right to the exercise of a guideline function on the part of the Supreme Court.

The Supreme Court, like the appellate court, may affirm, quash, or modify the decision (i.e., exercise a cassatory or reformatory function). If it quashes (reverses) the decision of the appellate court, it remands the case to the appellate court. The Supreme Court is bound by the facts found by the lower courts.

3. Complaint (*Rekurs*)

A complaint (*Rekurs*, in Germany: *Beschwerde*) is a request for relief from a court order *(Beschluß)*. The order of the appellate court is subject to a second complaint (*Revisionsrekurs*). A complaint usually does not suspend the enforcement of the decision.

B. Extraordinary Recourse (*Außerordentliche Rechtsmittel*)

1. Action for Annulment (*Nichtigkeitsklage*)

This recourse is available to either party even after a decision has become final (*res judicata*). Article 529 of the Civil Procedure Code envisages two serious flaws of the trial for which this action may be brought: 1) the case was adjudicated by a judge who was by law excluded from participating in the case; or 2) one party was not properly represented. The action must be filed in – and will be adjudicated by – the court that rendered the decision within four weeks of gaining knowledge of the relevant fact or of the rendering of the judgment.

2. Action for Reopening of Proceedings (*Wiederaufnahmsklage*)

This action claims that a final decision is based on an incorrect or incomplete evaluation in the light of new facts or evidence which existed but were not usable before the end of the trial,[9] but could, had they been used, have led to a more favorable decision. The petitioner may also claim that a forged document or false testimony had influenced the decision. The action must be filed within four weeks of gaining knowledge of the relevant fact. It is adjudicated by the court that rendered the original decision.

X. Enforcement of Judgments (*Vollstreckungs- oder Exekutionsverfahren*)

A. Enforcement of Final Judgments (*Exekution zur Befriedigung*)

Final judgments with which the debtor does not voluntarily comply will be enforced by the courts. The procedure is generally written and governed by the investigation principle. In a first stage (*Bewilligungsverfahren*), the judgment creditor (*Exekutionsgläubiger*) files an application for enforcement, which the district court (*Bezirksgericht*) examines as to its admissibility and subsequently grants. In a second stage (*Vollzugsverfahren*), the executable judgment is enforced.

Most enforcement cases concern pecuniary claims. Execution concerning movable property of the judgment debtor is carried out by means of attachment (*Pfändung*) and subsequent sale by the court's execution officer acting on the creditor's request. Frequently claims (e.g., to wage payments) are attached and assigned to the judgment creditor by court order. Execution into immovable property may be carried out by entering a mortgage in favor of the creditor in the land register, forced administration, and ultimately forced sale in court auction.

Concerning non-pecuniary claims, objects owed by the debtor may be taken away from him and given to the creditor. Certain actions owed by the debtor may be taken by the creditor at the debtor's expense. Actions or omissions of the debtor himself may also be forced through fines or imprisonment.

The debtor is protected by provisions exempting certain assets, claims and parts of wage income (minimum of subsistence, *Existenzminimum*) from execution.

B. Preliminary Seizure for Security (*Exekution zur Sicherstellung*)

Preliminary seizure for security may be ordered by the court on the basis of a money judgment, which is not final and therefore not yet executable, provided that the creditor demonstrates a threat to the future execution (e.g., an impending insolvency of the defendant).

---

[9] Such as a newly discovered witness or document.

C. Provisional Remedy (*Einstweilige Verfügung*)

A provisional remedy is a court order obtained before, at or after the trial stage designed to stabilize the situation pending final disposition or to provide security to the plaintiff that he will be able to enforce a future decision favorable to him.

D. Recognition and Enforcement of Foreign Judgments

Recognition and enforcement of foreign judgments is regulated in the Enforcement Code (*Exekutionsordnung*) and in bilateral and multilateral treaties. The most important are the European (or Brussels) Convention on Jurisdictions and Enforcement and the Lugano Convention on Jurisdictions and Enforcement.

XI. Insolvency Procedures (*Insolvenzverfahren*)

Once a debtor has become insolvent, the individual pursuit of claims by his creditors is replaced by collective action of all creditors under court supervision. It is directed at the entire estate of the debtor and aims at equal satisfaction of the creditors. Insolvency procedures may involve liquidation and distribution of the debtor's assets (bankruptcy, *Konkurs*), but also rehabilitation efforts (composition, *Ausgleich*). Insolvency procedures are supplemented by preventive measures (enterprise reorganization, *Unternehmensreorganisation*).

A. Bankruptcy (*Konkurs*)

Bankruptcy (*Konkurs*) proceedings will be opened when a debtor is insolvent. In case of a physical person, insolvency (*Zahlungsunfähigkeit*) is defined as inability to meet one's obligations in due time. Legal persons are already considered insolvent when their liabilities exceed their assets (*Überschuldung*, overindebtedness). The primary aim of bankruptcy procedure is to liquidate the debtor's assets and distribute them (*pro rata*) among the creditors. Several provisions protect the debtor, exempting certain assets such as his minimum of subsistence from liquidation.

Bankruptcy jurisdiction is exercised by the Court of First Instance in the form of a single judge. Proceedings are governed by the investigation principle. They are not open to the public, and decisions may be taken without prior oral hearing. They are opened upon a motion filed with the court by the debtor or a creditor. This motion has to be filed without delay or at the latest 60 days after the debtor has become unable to meet his financial obligations. The court will refuse to open proceedings if the debtor's assets are insufficient to cover court costs.

With the opening of bankruptcy proceedings, the debtor loses the rights of administration and disposition of his assets to a receiver (*Masseverwalter*) appointed by the court. Under the supervision of the court, the receiver explores possibilities to continue the debtor's business. All claims against the debtor must be filed with the court within a specified period. Usually the first creditors' meeting is held within 14 days. Within 60 to 90 days, the creditors' meeting establishes the validity and extent of claims registered. Disputed claims may be litigated. The court then decides on the further fate of the enterprise. If no more favorable solution can be found, the debtor's assets will be sold and distributed by the receiver. This distribution does not discharge the debtor. Under Austrian law, he remains liable within the 30 year period of the statute of limitation.

In principle, all creditors are treated equally and receive a *pro rata* portion of their claim. However, priority (full satisfaction) is given to the claims for costs of the proceedings and costs of maintaining and administering the bankrupt's estate, including claims of employees that have arisen after the opening of bankruptcy proceedings. Certain claims of employees, privileged prior to reform legislation in 1983, are now treated as ordinary claims competing with all others. However, employees will be at least in part compensated out of special state funds.

Secured creditors have priority in the settlement with respect to assets secured by mortgage, pledge, etc. (*Absonderungsrecht*). If claims are insufficiently secured, the balance must be registered in the proceedings. Security interests established within 60 days preceding the opening of bankruptcy proceedings will not be recognized. Certain other transactions of the debtor within specific periods prior to bankruptcy (e.g., fraudulent transfers) may be contested by the receiver. Property of third parties found in the possession of the debtor (e.g., goods delivered under retention of title by the supplier) may be claimed in full (*Aussonderungsrecht*).

In the course of bankruptcy proceedings, the debtor may make a motion for compulsory composition (*Zwangsausgleich*), which would permit rehabilitation of the enterprise through partial waiver and deferment of debt. The debtor must offer his creditors payment of at least 20% of their claims within two years. Once compulsory composition has been approved by the creditors and confirmed by the court, the debtor is freed from obligations exceeding the agreed on quota.

B. Personal Bankruptcy (*Privatkonkurs*)

Special provisions applying to the bankruptcy of persons other than entrepreneurs were adopted in 1993. They provide for jurisdiction by district rather than regional courts, and they dispense with the appointment of a receiver. After the distribution of his assets, any bankrupt debtor who is a natural person (including the former entrepreneur) may apply for a special procedure that will prematurely terminate his outstanding debt. This procedure is a form of compulsory composition without a statutory minimum quota, with a payment plan (*Zahlungsplan*) based on the debtor's income during the following five years, to be fulfilled during a maximum period of seven years. If a payment plan is not approved by the creditors, the debtor may be subjected to withholding (*Abschöpfungsverfahren*) from his income for a maximum period of seven years. His remaining debt will expire after this period.

C. Composition (*Ausgleich*)

The composition procedure regulated in the Composition Code (*Ausgleichsordnung*) offers the debtor an opportunity to avoid bankruptcy by filing a petition for composition, with the purpose of achieving rehabilitation of his enterprise through a partial payment of not less than 40% to his creditors in full satisfaction of their claims. The time of payment may be extended to a maximum of two years. All creditors must file their claims with the court. If at least one-half in number of the creditors present (holding at least three–quarters in amount of the claims) agree and the court confirms the composition, the debtor may continue to operate his business under the supervision of a court appointed trustee (*Ausgleichsverwalter*). After completion of the payments, the debtor is discharged. If the debtor fails to fulfill the conditions of the composition, the claims are revived and the court will commence bankruptcy proceedings.

D. Enterprise Reorganization (*Unternehmensreorganisationsverfahren*)

Business debtors who are not yet insolvent may take preventive action by submitting to a procedure regulated in the Enterprise Reorganization Act 1997. Upon the debtor's petition, the Court of First Instance appoints a reorganization examiner (*Reorganisationsprüfer*) who approves a reorganization plan designed to substantially improve the enterprise's financial situation.

XII. Arbitration (*Schiedsgerichtsbarkeit*)

The Civil Procedure Code recognizes the private settlement of certain disputes by arbitration tribunals outside the state court system. In a written arbitration contract (*Schiedsvertrag*) or contract clause (*Schiedsklausel*) parties may submit a specific litigation or a dispute arising from a specific legal relationship to arbitration. The parties must also conclude a contract with the arbitrator(s) (*Schiedsrichtervertrag*) regulating his (their) rights and duties. Provided that minimum procedural standards are observed, state courts will enforce the arbitral award *(Schiedsspruch)*.

Literature

Commentaries and textbooks

Bajons, E. M., Zivilverfahren (1991)
Ballon, O. J., Einführung in das österreichische Zivilprozeßrecht (9th ed. 1999)
Deixner-Hübner, A., Zivilverfahren (2000)

Fasching, H. W., Kommentar zu den Zivilprozeßgesetzen (4 vols. 1959 – 1971, suppl. 1974; vol.1, 2nd ed. 2000)
Fasching, H. W., Lehrbuch des österrreichischen Zivilprozeßrechts (2nd ed. 1990)
Klicka, T., Oberhammer, P., Außerstreitverfahren (3rd ed. 2000)
Konecny, A., Schubert G., Kommentar zu den Insolvenzgesetzen (1997)
Mohr, F., Konkurs-, Ausgleichs- und AnfechtungsO (9th ed. 2000)
Rechberger, W. H. (ed.), Zivilprozeßordnung (2nd ed. 2000)
Rechberger, W. H., Oberhammer P., Exekutionsrecht (2nd ed. 1999)
Rechberger, W. H., Simotta, D.-A., Grundriß des österreichischen Zivilprozeßrechts (5th ed. 2000)

English language publications

Bajons, E.-M., Austria, in *Jolowicz, J. A., van Rhee, C. H. (eds.),* Recourse Against Judgments in the European Union (1999) 25
Homburger, A., Functions of Orality in Austrian and American Civil Procedure, Buffalo Law Review 20 (1970) 9
Lenhoff, A., The Law of Evidence – A Comparative Study Based Essentially on Austrian and New York Law, American Journal of Comparative Law 3 (1954) 313
Rechberger, W., Austria, in *Blanpain, R. (ed.),* International Encyclopedia of Laws, Civil Procedure – Suppl. 8 (1997)

Comparative Works

Fisch, W. B., Recent Developments in West German Civil Procedure, Hastings International and Comparative Law Review 6 (1982) 221
Gottwald, P., Simplified Civil Procedure in West Germany, American Journal of Comparative Law 31 (1983) 687
Kaplan, B., Civil Procedure – Reflections on the Comparison of Systems, Buffalo Law Review 9 (1969) 409
Kaplan, B., von Mehren, A. T., Schaefer, R., Phases of German Civil Procedure, Harvard Law Review 71 (1958) 1193 and 1443
Koch, H., Diedrich, F., Civil Procedure in Germany (1998)
Langbein, J., The German Advantage in Civil Procedure, University of Chicago Law Review 52 (1985) 823
Sherman, E. F., The Evolution of American Civil Trial Process Towards Greater Congruence with Continental Trial Practice, Tulane Journal of International and Comparative Law 7 (1999) 125

Chapter 12
The Civil Code

I. History

The Habsburg Monarchy was a conglomerate of territories (kingdoms, duchies, etc.) that was united merely by the person of the ruler. Each of the territories had its own law, which made centralized administration and adjudication increasingly difficult. Under the reign of Emperor Leopold I, Gottfried Wilhelm Leibniz (1646–1716), the eminent philosopher of natural law, proposed drafting a *Codex Leopoldinus*. After the establishment in 1749 of the *Oberste Justizstelle* (Supreme Judicial Authority) in Vienna as the highest organ of judicial administration of all hereditary Habsburg territories (*Erbländer*), this codification proposal became both more imperative and more feasible.[1]

In 1753, the Empress Maria Theresia (1740–80) instructed a commission to draft a uniform civil code for her hereditary territories (including Lower and Upper Austria, Styria, Tirol, Bohemia, Moravia and Silesia, but excluding Hungary and Italian possessions). She expressly demanded "that in drafting the code the commission should limit itself to private law, leaving the present law in force so far as may be, and bringing the various laws of the provinces into agreement so far as conditions permit, using the Common law and its best exponents as well as the laws of other countries, and always referring back to the common law of reason whenever correction or completion is called for." Chief reporter in that commission was the Prague law professor Joseph Azzoni, who, after his death in 1760, was succeeded by Johann Bernhard Zencker, a government lawyer.

The draft *Codex Theresianus* (in eight folio volumes) was originally meant to be published in Latin, but was ultimately written in German and submitted by Zencker in 1766. It was rejected by the State Council (headed by Chancellor Prince Kaunitz) as being too detailed, too much like a textbook, and incomprehensible without a knowledge of the Roman law in which it was too firmly rooted. The Empress ordered it to be shortened and reworked by a new commission set up in 1772 to apply the principles of brevity, clarity, simplicity and natural equity. The first part, comprising the law of persons and family law (in 300 instead of previously 1500 articles), was submitted by Johann Bernhard Horten, a high civil servant, and promulgated by Emperor Joseph II (1780–90) as the Josephinic Code in 1786 (effective January 1, 1787) for a trial run in the German territories.

---

[1] Codification progressed more swiftly in criminal and procedure law.

In 1790, Joseph's successor Leopold II (1790–92) appointed a new commission headed by Karl Anton von Martini, Professor of Natural and Roman Law at the University of Vienna, to rework the remainder of the *Codex Theresianus*. Martini has been called the most outstanding Austrian representative of Natural law, a follower in particular of Christian Wolff. His draft (*Urentwurf*) of a General Civil Code was approved by Francis II (1792–1835) in 1797, referred to Josef von Sonnenfels (professor, writer and influential imperial adviser) for the improvement of German language and style, and promulgated as the Westgalician Code (effective January 1, 1798) in a territory that had previously belonged to Poland and was considered to be in urgent need of statutory regulation. Its application was soon extended to East Galicia and Bukowina.

Beginning in 1801, a new Legislative Commission under the spiritual leadership of its reporter Franz von Zeiller (1753–1828), pupil of and in 1783 successor to Martini as Professor of Natural and Roman Law in Vienna, refined and polished the Westgalician Code. The Commission took into account the opinions of the provinces, law faculties, and judicial commissions. Whereas Martini had adhered to the older school of Natural law, Zeiller was influenced by its younger branch, in particular by the philosophy of Kant. Zeiller's draft was completed in 1806, but the General Civil Code (*Allgemeines Bürgerliches Gesetzbuch, ABGB*) was not promulgated until June 1, 1811 (effective January 1, 1812) for all Habsburg territories except Hungary, replacing Roman common law and the Josephinic and Westgalician Codes.

II. Spirit

The Austrian Code reflects the ideology of Josephinic enlightenment and rationalist Natural law in its last stage. But its fundamental principles of the equality of citizens, freedom of private legal relationships from state control, and freedom of economic activity did not reflect contemporary social conditions in Austria, which was an authoritarian, absolute monarchy with numerous privileges for the feudal classes, as well as the serf-like dependence of peasants. A turning point was provided by the revolutionary year 1848, but Austrian social and economic life did not come to match the libertarian and individualistic outlook of the Code until the 1870s and 1880s. It has been claimed that the Natural law of Kant had a profound influence on the Code through the work of Zeiller. But according to others, the ideas of Grotius, Pufendorf, Thomasius and Christian Wolff were more influential.[2]

As to its substance, the *ABGB* largely follows the pattern of Roman law reception in other German territories.[3] Especially in areas like personal property, contract law and tort law, the Code contains Roman law as under-

---

[2] Today Zeiller is generally praised for his sound practical sense which led him to omit from the Code those dogmas of Natural law that were unduly theoretical and remote from life.

[3] See *infra* Chapter 16 (The Civil Law Tradition), V.C.

stood (or misunderstood) by 18th century scholarship and as applied in the court practice of *usus modernus pandectarum*, with few regional modifications. Generally speaking, Natural law provided the principles, not the details. In most instances, Roman law rules were simply accepted as expressing Natural law. In a few cases, corrections were made in order to better reflect Natural law ideas.

The technical quality of the *ABGB* is generally considered to be excellent. It is characterized by clear structure and formulations, brevity, and an emphasis on flexible general principles that allowed for later adaptation by the courts and (Pandectist) scholarship.

III. Structure

Like the French *Code civil* of 1804,[4] but unlike the Prussian Code (*ALR* of 1794),[5] which otherwise exerted great influence on the Austrian Code, the *ABGB* is a pure civil code in 1502 articles. It contains neither public nor commercial law. Its structure is based on the Roman law system familiar from the Institutes of Justinian. The latter were based on the tripartite structure of the Institutes of Gaius (written around 160 A.D. and dividing private law into the categories of persons, property and actions). In the *ABGB*, a short introduction is followed by three parts: I. Persons, II. Property, and III. Common Provisions of the Law of Persons and the Law of Property.

The **Introduction** (articles 1 to 14) contains principles of statutory construction, including the remarkable article 7 which addresses the filling of gaps in the law: "When a case cannot be decided on the basis of the words or the natural meaning of a statute, the judge must look to the solutions laid down by the statutes for comparable cases and to the reasons underlying other related statutes. Should the matter still remain doubtful, it must be decided by the judge by applying the principles of natural law to the conscientiously collected and carefully evaluated facts of the case." Judges, however, have always hesitated to be openly creative under this authorization, preferring instead to make law behind a screen of traditional techniques.

Part I, **Persons** (arts. 15 to 284), deals with status and personal relations, marriage, rights between parents and children, guardianship, and curatorship.

Part II, **Property** (arts. 285 to 1341), contains two major subdivisions devoted to real and personal rights. It is based on the Roman distinction between actions *in rem* (having effect *erga omnes*) and actions *in personam* (available only against specific persons). Real rights include possession, ownership, pledge and mortgage, servitudes, and succession. Personal rights include contracts, matrimonial property agreements, and torts.

---

[4] See *infra* Chapter 16, VI.C.
[5] See *infra* Chapter 16, VI.B.

Part III, **Common Provisions of the Law of Persons and the Law of Property** (arts. 1342 to 1502), includes surety and guaranty, modification and termination of rights and obligations, limitation, and prescription.

IV. Radiation

The *ABGB* did not influence other legal systems as much as the French *Code civil* did. Unlike the latter, it was not the product of a successful revolution, but rather of a restoration-minded monarchy, a multinational state threatened by centrifugal political forces. As opposed to France, Austria also had no colonies that would readily absorb its legal system. The Code was only briefly in force in Hungary, longer in Croatia, Slavonia, Bosnia and Herce-govina, Serbia, and Montenegro. It was in force in Lombardy until 1866 and in Veneto until 1871. It remained in force beyond 1918 in areas of Poland, Yugoslavia and Czechoslovakia that used to be parts of the Habsburg Monar-chy. This continuity was facilitated by the existence of text and commentary in the respective national languages of the former Empire. None of the successor states replaced the *ABGB* with a new code in the inter-war period. But the emerging "Socialist" (Communist) political systems after World War II found no further use for a "bourgeois" code like the Austrian.

V. Subsequent Developments

A. The Exegetical School

As predicted in Savigny's criticism of Natural law codification (see *supra* Chapter 11, VII.A), the adoption of the *ABGB* led to the stagnation and decline of an Austrian legal science whose perspective quickly narrowed to the practical tasks of explaining the Code and making it work. Until 1848, judges and scholars largely confined themselves to a literal exposition of the Code (known as the exegetical school) against the background of the Roman com-mon law tradition. Besides, the political situation in the pre-1848 authoritarian state did not exactly encourage judicial independence nor did it induce legal science to look beyond the statute and fill gaps with reference to Natural law principles (article 7 *ABGB*). Zeiller's slender Commentary (four volumes and register, 1811–13) was broadened but hardly deepened by Nippel's (nine vol-umes, 1830–1838). The scholarly production of the period was generally un-remarkable.

B. The Pandectist School

In 1855, Minister of Education Count Leo Thun-Hohenstein intro-duced substantial reforms in legal studies along the lines of the German model and thrust Austrian legal science into mainstream German legal scholarship, specifically Savigny's Historical School and Puchta's Pandectist doctrines.[6] Thun's government suspected that the strong participation of law students in the 1848 revolution had been inspired by liberal ideas developed from their instruction in Natural law and philosophy. A sweeping reorientation of law studies seemed necessary in order not only to upgrade Austrian legal scholarship, but also to instill conservative Catholic thought in Austrian legal teaching and professional practice.

Thun's law curriculum in essence provided the framework of Austrian legal education up to, and even beyond, the Socialist reform of 1975. In a first phase of the four years of legal instruction, Roman law, German legal history, and Canon law provided the historical and theoretical foundation for the subsequent study of special areas of Austrian law. Thun created new chairs for legal history and filled them – often against the wishes of the Austrian law faculties – with promising young scholars from Germany. For the important field of Austrian private law his eyes fell on the 25-year-old Vienna law graduate Josef Unger (1828–1913), whom he appointed "associate professor of the General Civil Code" in Prague in 1853. After publishing the first volume of his trailblazing System of Austrian Private Law in 1856, Unger was promoted to full professor in Vienna in 1857. The representatives of the traditional exegetical school quickly resigned themselves to the fate of being eclipsed by a vigorous circle of new historically oriented scholars growing around Unger and supported by the government of Thun. Adolf Exner (1841–97), a pupil of Unger's, became professor of Roman law in Zurich and returned to Vienna when Rudolf von Jhering left his Vienna chair for Göttingen in 1872. Exner later declined the offer to succeed the famous Bernhard Windscheid in Leipzig in 1892. The third leading private law scholar of the time was Anton Randa (1834–1914), who taught in Prague and in addition to his important publications in German laid the foundations of a modern legal science in the Czech language. Two later pupils of Unger's who achieved prominence as scholars and teachers were Franz Hofmann (1847–97) and Leopold Pfaff (1837–1914). They jointly published a profound (but unfinished) commentary on the *ABGB* (1877–87). A practicing lawyer, Viktor Hasenöhrl (1834–1903), found time to write a leading textbook on the law of obligations.

The new Austrian Pandectist School followed the German model of unilaterally emphasizing the Roman law component of the legal tradition at the expense of its Germanic, Canon law and Natural law ingredients. The Pandectists criticized the Code for "incorrect legislative provisions based on misunderstanding the Roman law" and attempted to correct these unfortunate mistakes. In addition, Pandectist legal science aimed at achieving a systematic completeness and conceptual precision lacking in the *ABGB*.

Textbooks and legal instruction abandoned the structure of the *ABGB* and replaced it with the Pandect system. Unger introduced the highly abstract Pandectist "general part" into Austrian law, developing in particular the concept of legal personality and doctrines concerning the beginning, end, and

---

[6] See *infra* Chapter 16, VII.A.

protection of legal relationships, as well as adopting Savigny's theories on the conflict of laws.

Unger's pupils Randa and Exner published important monographs in the area of property law. They reduced the broad concept of "thing" used in article 285 *ABGB* to corporal things and also deviated from article 308 *ABGB* by emphasizing that the character of possession was factual rather than legal. Scholars denied the possibility of the horizontal ownership of floors of a house (*Stockwerkseigentum*), which had not been excluded by the Code. They severely criticized (but were unable to override) the Austrian "causal" as opposed to the Pandectist "abstract" acquisition of ownership.

The law of obligations was initially neglected because of hopes that this portion of the *ABGB* would soon be replaced by a uniform all-German law. It was only after the political events of 1866 that Austrian scholars began to focus their attention on this important area, producing greater conceptual clarity and frequently different solutions. Relatively little attention was paid to family law, while somewhat more scholarly effort was invested in correcting perceived shortcomings of the law of succession.

It is characteristic of the initial disregard of the Code by the Austrian Pandectists that it took until 1889 for Julius Ofner to publish the legislative materials and until 1898 for Pfaff to collect the Supreme Court decisions. This period marks the development of a more genuinely historical (instead of predominately conceptual) perspective and an – at least partial – "return to the *ABGB.*"

C. The Three Amending Laws (*Teilnovellen* 1914–16)

The work of Austrian scholars like Randa, Exner, Hasenöhrl and in particular Josef Unger, who as early as 1855 proposed to revise the *ABGB* on account of its many gaps and deficiencies, laid the foundation for subsequent Pandectist amendments to the Code. But it was not until 1904 that a revision commission headed by Unger was instituted. From 1914 to 1916, three amending laws (*Teilnovellen*) were enacted, changing or adding 180 provisions based on the model of the German *BGB*[7] (often literally adopting its text) and affecting especially the law of contract.

D. The Inter-War Period

In the aftermath of World War I, Socialist political influence led to reform legislation, particularly in the area of housing law. Special legislation in favor of tenants superseded the respective provisions of the *ABGB* during World War I and after. Rent control was introduced in 1917. An entirely new Lease Law (*Mietengesetz*) was enacted in 1922, revised in 1981, and has been amended frequently since. None of this legislation was incorporated into the Code.

---

[7] See *infra* Chapter 16, VII.B.

Another important area of private law regulated outside the original provisions of the Code is the law concerning labor contracts.[8] The state began to outlaw abusive practices as early as in the Trade Act (*Gewerbeordnung*) of 1859. In 1885, Austria was the first industrial nation to introduce an eleven-hour maximum working day, and it permitted the formation of labor unions in 1867. Social insurance was organized to cover sickness (1888), accidents (1889), unemployment (1920), and old age (for white-collar employees in 1906, for blue-collar workers in 1939). The labor contract itself was recognized as creating a special relationship. This included the employer's duty to continue paying wages in cases of employee illness, and to provide protection against the dismissal of employees in this situation. It contained a right to paid vacations, but also emphasized the employee's duty of loyalty to the enterprise. The relevant chapter of the *ABGB* was revised in 1916, but subsequent development occurred through special legislation outside the Code.[9]

In the area of private law scholarship in the 1920s and 1930s, Armin Ehrenzweig published an excellent treatise on private law,[10] and Heinrich Klang edited a multi-volume commentary on the Code.[11]

E. Austrian Private Law Under National Socialism

Under Hitler's occupation of Austria from 1938 to 1945, the *ABGB* remained in force. It was meant to be eventually superseded by an entirely new German People's Code (*Volksgesetzbuch*) based on National Socialist ideology, which, however, did not materialize. Only the German Marriage Act (*Ehegesetz*) of 1938 was introduced in Austria and remained in force even after 1945. It replaced Catholic legal principles of the *ABGB* with an obligatory civil wedding and the possibility of divorce. Strong ideological interests also led to a modification of the law of succession by introducing the German law of entail of farm property (*Reichserbhofgesetz*), which favored men over women. It was abolished in 1945.

In the areas of commercial and corporate law, the German Commercial Code (*HGB*) and German legislation concerning bills of exchange, checks and joint stock companies were introduced in 1938 and 1939. They are still in effect today.

F. Private Law Reform After World War II

After World War II, broad private law reform legislation was developed outside the Code. But as late as 1986, approximately 70% of the articles

---

[8] See *infra* Chapter 15 (Labor Law).

[9] E.g., in the *Angestelltengesetz* (White Collar Employees' Act) of 1921.

[10] Armin Ehrenzweig, *System des österreichischen allgemeinen Privatrechts* (1925), a thoroughly revised edition of Pfaff's posthumous edition of the two-volume treatise of Krainz (1885 and 1889).

[11] *Kommentar zum Allgemeinen bürgerlichen Gesetzbuch* (first edition, 1927–1935).

of the Code still contained the text of 1811. Since the 1960s (and with particular emphasis in the 1970s and 1980s), profound reforms of family law were effected,[12] most of which were incorporated into the Code. These reforms are based on changes in social and economic conditions, altered perceptions regarding the protection of children, as well as new principles of partnership and equality among spouses. The patriarchal family law of the *ABGB* was modernized in several legislative stages, as was the law of succession[13] – in favor of spouses and children born out of wedlock. The reforms included new rules on adoption (1960), guardianship (1967), rights of children born out of wedlock (1970 and 1989), legal capacity (1973), personal legal effects of marriage (1975), protection of child support (1976 and 1985), the relationship between parents and children (1977), marital property, inheritance rights of spouses and divorce (1978). Most recent reforms concern problems of reproductive medicine (1992), choice of name (1995) and divorce provisions (1999).

The Consumer Protection Act (*Konsumentenschutzgesetz*) of 1979 resulted in significant changes in the Code's law of contract.[14] Special liability legislation has further developed tort law[15] outside the Code. In 1940, the German Imperial Liability Act (*Reichshaftpflichtgesetz*) of 1871 had been introduced in Austria. In 1959, it was restricted to areas of enterprise liability not covered by the new Austrian Liability of Keepers of Railroads and Motor Vehicles Act (*Eisenbahn- und Kraftfahrzeughaftpflichtgesetz, EKHG* 1959). Other special liability statutes include the Official Liability Act (*Amtshaftungsgesetz* 1949) and the Employee Liability Act (*Dienstnehmerhaftpflichtgesetz* 1965). EC directives were incorporated into Austrian private law.[16] In addition, creative interpretation by the courts under the guidance of Austrian legal scholarship has strongly affected the Code's law of contract and of tort.

Literature

The Code

The General Civil Code of Austria (*trans. P. L. Baeck,* 1972)
General Civil Code for All the German Hereditary Provinces of the Austrian Monarchy (*trans. J. M. de Winiwarter,* 1866)

---

[12] See *infra* Chapter 13 (Private Law I), III.A.

[13] See *infra* Chapter 13, V.

[14] See *infra* Chapter 14 (Private Law II), II.I.

[15] See *infra* Chapter 13, III.F.

[16] E.g., directives on product liability in the Product Liability Act (*Produkthaftungsgesetz*) of 1988 (several amendments in the 1990s); directives on consumer protection (distance contracts, comparative advertising) in the Product Liability Act, the Consumer Protection Act and the Federal Law against Unfair Competition (*Bundesgesetz gegen den unlauteren Wettbewerb* 1984), all amended by the Distance Contract Act of 1999 (*Fernabsatz-Gesetz*). Cf *supra* Chapter 4 (Austria and the European Union), VI.D.3.

Bydlinski, F. (ed.), Österreichische Gesetze: Zivil-, Handels-, Straf- und Verfahrens-
recht (loose-leaf edition, 2000)
Dittrich, R., Tades, H., Das allgemeine bürgerliche Gesetzbuch (19th ed. 2000)
Dittrich, R., Tades, H. (eds.), Das Allgemeine bürgerliche Gesetzbuch (annotated text
of the Civil Code, 35th ed. 1999)

Commentaries and Textbooks

Apathy, P. (ed.), Bürgerliches Recht (6 vols., 2000)
Gschnitzer, F., Lehrbuch des österreichischen bürgerlichen Rechts (6 vols., 2nd ed. by
Faistenberger, C. et al., 1979-92)
Klang, H., Gschnitzer, F., Kommentar zum Allgemeinen bürgerlichen Gesetzbuch (6
vols. and suppl., 2nd ed. 1951–77, 3rd ed. by *Fenyves, A., Welser, R.* forthcoming)
Koziol, H., Grundriß des bürgerlichen Rechts (vol. 1, 11th ed. 2000)
Krejci, H., Privatrecht (4th ed. 2000)
Rummel, P., Kommentar zum Allgemeinen bürgerlichen Gesetzbuch (2 vols., 2nd ed.
1990–92; vol. 1, 3rd ed. 2000)
Welser, R., Grundriß des bürgerlichen Rechts (vol. 2, 10th ed. 1996)

Monographs and Articles

Bernat, E., Austria: The Final Stages of Three Decades' Family Law Reform, Journal
of Family Law 29 (1990–91) 285
Brauneder, W., Das Allgemeine Bürgerliche Gesetzbuch für die gesamten Deutschen
Erbländer der österreichischen Monarchie von 1811, Gutenberg-Jahrbuch 1987, 205
Brauneder, W., Privatrechtsfortbildung durch Juristenrecht in Exegetik und Pandek-
tistik in Österreich, Zeitschrift für Neuere Rechtsgeschichte 5 (1983) 22
Dölemeyer, B., Die Teilnovellen zum *ABGB*, in *Hofmeister, H. (ed.)*, Kodifikation als
Mittel der Politik (1986) 49
Festschrift zur Jahrhundertfeier des *ABGB* (2 vols., 1911)
Gschnitzer, F., Hundertfünfzig Jahre Allgemeines Bürgerliches Gesetzbuch, JBl 1962,
405
Kocher, G., Grundzüge der Privatrechtsentwicklung und der Geschichte der Rechts-
wissenschaft in Österreich (2nd ed. 1997)
Mayer-Maly, T., Die Lebenskraft des *ABGB*, Österreichische Notariats-Zeitung 118
(1986) 265
Ogris, W., Die Historische Schule der österreichischen Zivilistik, FS Lentze (1969) 449
Ogris, W., Die Wissenschaft des gemeinen römischen Rechts und das österreichische
ABGB, in *Coing, H., Wilhelm, W. (eds.)*, Wissenschaft und Kodifikation des
Privatrechts im 19. Jh. (vol. I, 1974) 153
Ogris, W., Zur Geschichte und Bedeutung des österreichischen *ABGB*, GS Laurent
(1989) 373
Robinson, O. F. et al., European Legal History (2nd ed. 1994) 253
Selb, W., Hofmeister, H. (eds.), Forschungsband Franz von Zeiller (1980)
Steinwenter, A., Der Einfluß des römischen Rechtes auf die Kodifikation des
bürgerlichen Rechtes in Österreich, in L'Europa e il diritto romano, Studi in
memoria di P. Koschaker I (1954) 403
Steinwenter, A., Recht und Kultur (1958) 57
Strakosch, H. E., State Absolutism and the Rule of Law: The Struggle for the
Codification of Civil Law in Austria, 1753–1811 (1967)
Weiß, E., Hundertvierzig Jahre Allgemeines Bürgerliches Gesetzbuch, JBl 1951, 249
Wesenberg, G., Wesener, G., Neuere deutsche Privatrechtsgeschichte (4th ed. 1985)
163

Wesener, G., Einflüsse und Geltung des römisch-gemeinen Rechts in den altöster-
reichischen Ländern in der Neuzeit (16.–18. Jahrhundert), 1989.
Wieacker, F., A History of Private Law in Europe (*trans. T. Weir*, 1995) 266
Zweigert, K., Kötz, H., Introduction to Comparative Law (*trans. T. Weir*, 3rd ed. 1998)
   163

Chapter 13
Private Law I: Persons, Family, Property, Inheritance

I. Introduction

Based on the system of the Institutes written by the Roman jurist Gaius, the Austrian Civil Code of 1811 has three parts: Persons, Property, and Common Provisions of the Law of Persons and the Law of Property. Modern Austrian textbooks, however, use the Pandect System of the German Civil Code of 1900: General Part, Obligations, Property, Family, and Inheritance. The General Part of these textbooks abstracts provisions applicable to all areas of the law from the more specific contexts in which they are treated in the Code. It includes the discussion of persons and their legal capacity, things, legal transactions, agency, and the legal effects of time.

An attempt to describe Austrian private law in the context of this book must remain selective. This chapter will briefly characterize the areas of persons, family, property, and inheritance. The following chapter (Obligations) will focus on contract law. Provisions of the General Part will be inserted in these chapters as appropriate. Unless otherwise noted, articles cited refer to the Civil Code (*ABGB*).

II. The Law of Persons

A. Legal Capacity (*Rechtsfähigkeit*) and Capacity to Act (*Handlungsfähigkeit*)

A legal subject (person) is someone who is capable of possessing rights and obligations (*rechtsfähig*). This may be a natural or physical person (*natürliche Person*),[1] or a legal person (*juristische Person*), i.e., an entity other than a human being to which the law grants legal capacity.[2]

Capacity to act is capacity to acquire rights and obligations by one's own acts. It comprises capacity to contract (*Geschäftsfähigkeit*) and capacity to be held liable in tort (*Deliktsfähigkeit*).

---

[1] Article 16 *ABGB* states that "every human being has inborn rights." There are no exceptions as to age, gender, race, mental facilities, etc.

[2] "Moral person," article 26.

B. Natural Persons

A human being's legal capacity (*Rechtsfähigkeit*) begins at birth, even if the baby dies immediately afterwards. The law presupposes that the child was born alive; a stillbirth has to be proven. Even the unborn child (*nasciturus*) has the right "to be protected by the laws from the moment of conception" according to article 22 *ABGB*. It is treated like a born person as far as its rights are concerned, conditioned on its subsequent live birth. Legal capacity ends with a person's death.

1. Capacity to Contract (*Geschäftsfähigkeit*)

Capacity to contract can be limited by age, by decision of the court,[3] and in cases of "loss of the use of reason."[4]

Children (*Kinder*), i.e., persons under seven years of age, have no capacity to contract (art. 865). Nevertheless, according to article 151 (3) they can accomplish those legal transactions which are considered "affairs of daily life of trivial importance."[5] All other legal transactions must be conducted for them by their legal representative.

Minors between seven and 14 years of age (*unmündige Minderjährige*) have a limited capacity to contract. They can enter into legal transactions which are exclusively to their advantage (e.g., accept a gift). If they conclude a contract which obligates them in any way, the contract becomes null and void if the minor's legal representative does not agree to it within a reasonable period of time.

Minors between the age of 14 and 19 years (*mündige Minderjährige*) can conclude service contracts (*Dienstverträge*) by themselves[6] but their legal representative can terminate the service contract for important (e.g., educational) reasons.[7] Minors over 14 can dispose freely of their own earned income and of those things which were given to them to dispose of.

Persons over 19 years of age are adults (*Volljährige*) fully capable to contract as long as this capacity is not limited for reasons other than age.

---

[3] A person's capacity to contract can be limited if the person is mentally impaired. Depending on the extent of the person's illness, the court appoints an administrator (*Sachwalter*) either for some of, or for all the person's affairs.

[4] An adult who has lost the "use of his reason" (*Gebrauch der Vernunft*, art. 865) either temporarily (e.g., drunkenness) or permanently (e.g., mental illness), but for whom no administrator (*Sachwalter*, cf. *supra* note 3) has yet been appointed may – like children, see *infra* note 5 – handle "affairs of daily life of trivial importance" but is incapacitated regarding all other transactions. Doctrine maintains that in those cases where a person's use of reason is less impaired, his capacity to contract is also less limited than in more severe cases. During a lucid interval, a mentally ill person who does not have a *Sachwalter* is fully capable to contract.

[5] The so-called "pocket money article." They can use public transport, buy hot dogs or cheap toys, etc., and accept small gifts. The respective contracts acquire validity by their fulfilment.

[6] Though not apprenticeship contracts.

[7] Cf. *infra* Chapter 15 (Labor Law), III.B.1.

2. Capacity for Tortious Liability (*Deliktsfähigkeit*)

Persons over 14 years of age are presumed to have the capacity to be held liable for fault.[8] If a person is mentally ill, mentally weak, or confused, he has no capacity for tortious liability as long as this impairment lasts.[9] For acts commited during a lucid interval, a mentally ill person is fully liable, even though his capacity to contract may be extremely limited.

For the acts of persons incapable of tortious liability, their parents or guardian are liable if they have neglected their duty of supervision (art. 1309, *Aufsichtspflicht*). Nevertheless, under certain circumstances the tortfeasor may be obliged to pay damages himself if the guardian is not liable or unable to pay (art. 1310).[10]

C. Legal Persons (*Juristische Personen*)

Legal persons exist in both public and private law. They may have either of two forms:

1. Associations of persons, such as bodies of public law *(Bund, Länder, Gemeinden, Kammern)*, registered societies (*eingetragene Vereine*), political parties, corporations, limited liability companies (*Gesellschaften mit beschränkter Haftung, GmbH*), stock corporations (*Aktiengesellschaften, AG*), cooperatives (*Genossenschaften*).
2. Property dedicated to a certain purpose, for instance, foundations (*Stiftungen*).

Private law partnerships (*Gesellschaften Bürgerlichen Rechts, GesBR*) are not legal persons. Some other bodies, such as certain business partnerships, e.g., unlimited partnerships (*Offene Handelsgesellschaften, OHG*) and limited partnerships (*Kommanditgesellschaften, KG*), registered trading firms (such as the trading company – *Offene Erwerbsgesellschaft, OEG,* and the limited trading company – *Kommanditerwerbsgesellschaft, KEG*), universities and their institutes, and the employees of a company as a group,[11] have limited legal capacity.

---

[8] Below the age of 14, persons are generally presumed to be incapable of fault. Yet an examination of the particular case may arrive at their (subsidiary) liability, see article 1310 *infra* note 10.

[9] The capacity of criminal guilt is likewise limited by age and mental illness (arts. 74, 11, and 21 of the Criminal Code), yet not necessarily by drunkenness (arts. 35 and 287 Criminal Code).

[10] Article 1310 *ABGB*: "If the person injured cannot obtain compensation in such manner, the judge must award either full compensation or at least an equitable part thereof, taking into consideration whether the author of the damage, notwithstanding his general mental incapacity, is nevertheless at fault in the particular circumstances; or whether the person injured failed to defend himself in order to spare the author of the damage; or finally, in view of the assets of the author of the damage and the person injured." Cf. *infra* Chapter 14 (Private Law II), III.B.

[11] Cf. *infra* Chapter 15 (Labor Law), IV.D.

A legal person must have a common interest, an organ empowered to make decisions (general assembly, stockholders' meeting, etc.) and an executive organ authorized to represent the legal person. Some legal persons also have a supervisory organ to look after the members' interests.

Legal persons of public law are created by the state through special legislation. Legal persons of private law are created by a private constituting act on the one hand and an act of legal recognition on the other hand. Some of them need a concession from the state (e.g., railroad and airline corporations, mortgage companies, mutual insurance companies). Others have a right to be recognized by the state if their organization complies with the laws (e.g., stock corporations, limited liability companies). They become legal persons with their registration in the commercial register (*Firmenbuch*).

Legal persons acquire legal capacity with their creation and lose it with their dissolution. The legal person's capacity to contract is exercised by its executive organs, which are the legal person's representatives.

Legal persons cannot as such be held liable in tort. If the question of tortious liability arises, either the legal person's statutory organs, its managing personnel (*Machthaber*, art. 337) or auxiliary persons (vicarious liability – *Gehilfenhaftung* according to arts. 1313a and 1315)[12] can be held liable.

III. Family Law

Under the title "Law of Persons," Part I of the *ABGB* (arts. 15–283), deals with personal status, marriage (arts. 44–46 betrothal; arts. 89–100 personal legal consequences of marriage; arts. 1217–1266 marital property), filiation and rights and duties between parents and children (arts. 137–178b), adoption (arts. 179–185a), guardianship and curatorship (arts. 186–283). Modern doctrine, however, distinguishes between the law of persons (i.e., legal status, to be treated in the General Part) and family law. Most of the *ABGB's* provisions on marriage have been superseded by the Marriage Act[13] of 1938 as amended, which contains the applicable provisions concerning marriage and the dissolution of marriage. The Civil Status Act[14] regulates the marriage ceremony.

A. Reforms in the Twentieth Century

The concept of marriage in the *ABGB* of 1811 was patriarchal: The wife and children were legally subordinated to the husband and father as head of the family. The father had duties of maintenance and legal representation.[15] The rights of children born out of wedlock were very limited.[16]

---

[12] Cf. Chapter 14, III.C.
[13] *EheG, dRGBl* I 1938, S 807, cf. *supra* Chapter 12 (The Civil Code), E.
[14] *Personenstandsgesetz, BGBl* 1983/60.
[15] Article 91 *ABGB* (1811): "The father is the head of the family. In this quality he has especially the right to manage the household; but he is also bound to

In the First Partial Amendment (1914), women were allowed to give evidence in court and to act as legal guardians, and the situation of illegitimate children and their mothers was slightly improved. In the inter-war period, Socialist attempts to reform family law were thwarted in the Parliament by the Christian-Socials.

The German Marriage Act, introduced in 1938 under National Socialist rule, replaced the Catholic legal principles of the *ABGB* with an obligatory civil wedding and the possibility of divorce. It did, however, not change the basic model of marriage, in which the role of the woman was still that of housewife and mother.

After World War II, a reform of family law has taken place in numerous small reform steps from the 1960s until today – mostly in the 1970s.[17] They were incorporated into the *ABGB*, whereas the Marriage Act remained as a separate statute outside the Civil Code.

B. Marriage

1. Conclusion and Legal Effects of Marriage

Only a civil wedding before a marriage registrar (*Standesbeamter*) has legal effect. The age of majority for marriage is 19 years for men and 16 years for women.[18] Consanguineous marriage, bigamy, and marriage between adoptive parent and adoptive child are prohibited.

---

provide a respectable maintenance for the wife, according to his means, and to represent her in all occurrences."

[16] Adequate provision, education, and maintenance, article 166 *ABGB* (1811).

[17] E.g., New Regulation of Adoption Act – *BG vom 17. 2. 1960 über die Neuordnung des Rechtes der Annahme an Kindesstatt, BGBl* 1960/58; New Regulation of the Legal Status of Children Born out of Wedlock Act – *BG vom 30.10.1970 über die Neuordnung der Rechtsstellung des unehelichen Kindes, BGBl* 1970/342; Coming of Age Act – *Volljährigkeitsgesetz, BGBl* 1973/108; Child Support Advance Act – *Unterhaltsvorschußgesetz, BGBl* 1976/250; New Regulation of Personal Effects of Marriage Act – *BG vom 1.7.1975 über die Neuordnung der persönlichen Rechtswirkungen der Ehe, BGBl* 1975/412; New Regulation of Rights of Parents and Children Act – *BG vom 30.6.1977 über die Neuordnung des Kindschaftsrechts, BGBl* 1977/403; New Regulation of Legal Succession of Spouses and Marital Property Act – *BG vom 15.6.1978 über die Neuordnung des gesetzlichen Erbrechts der Ehegatten und des gesetzlichen ehelichen Güterstandes, BGBl* 1978/280; Amendment of the Marriage Act – *BG vom 30.6.1978 über die Neuordnung des Ehegesetzes, BGBl* 1978/303; Protection of Child Support Act – *Unterhaltsschutzgesetz, BGBl* 1985/452, *BGBl* 1989/162; Amendment of Succession Provisions – *Erbrechts-Änderungsgesetz, BGBl* 1989/656; Amendment of Provisions Concerning Family Names – *Namensrechtsänderungsgesetz BGBl* 1995/25; Parents' Maternity Leave Act – *Eltern-Karenzurlaubsgesetz, BGBl* 1989/651; Amendment of Provisions Concerning Marriage – *Eherechtsänderungsgesetz 1999, BGBl* I 1999/125.

[18] Article 1 Marriage Act; *Volljährigkeitsgesetz, BGBl* 1973/108 (Coming of Age Act); the court can lower the majority for marriage to 18 for men and 15 for women.

Since 1995, each spouse can keep his or her own last name.[19] The last name of the children has to be jointly determined by the parents. If no consent can be reached, the child will bear the father's last name.

The reformed marriage law has incorporated the principles of partnership and equality among spouses.[20] Husband and wife have the same rights and duties towards each other.[21] The husband is no longer solely responsible for the children's maintenance, but both spouses have to contribute "according to their possibilities"[22] (but subject to individual arrangement). Both are obliged to share housekeeping chores, again subject to individual arrangement. If one spouse only keeps house and has no income, he or she is considered to be the legal representative of the other spouse in day-to-day transactions related to housekeeping, thus obligating only the other spouse.[23] The housekeeping spouse is also entitled to maintenance from the other spouse. The spouse who works in his or her partner's business or farm is entitled to remuneration.

The *ABGB*'s system of marital property is separation of property (*Gütertrennung*). The spouses may make a different arrangement by contract. Several older rules favoring the husband were abolished in the reform. The *ABGB*'s rules on intestate succession of the spouse had long been criticized when they were finally changed to improve the surviving spouse's position in 1978.[24] Also, a compulsory portion for the spouse was created.[25] The surviving spouse still has a subsidiary right of maintenance against the heirs.

2. Dissolution of Marriage

A marriage can be invalidated (*Nichtigerklärung*, e.g., because of
or bigamy), canceled (*Aufhebung*, e.g., because of threats before the marriage), or ended by divorce (*Scheidung*).

The possibility of divorce, independent of the spouses' religion and based primarily on the fault principle, was introduced by the German Marriage

---

[19] Prior to this provision of the *Namensrechtsänderungsgesetz BGBl* 1995/25, the couple could choose between either the husband's or the wife's last name, or the wife could use a hyphenated double name, with her own last name after the husband's.

[20] Instead of the terms "husband" and "wife," the term "spouse" is now used throughout.

[21] *BG vom 1.7.1975 über die Neuordnung der persönlichen Rechtswirkungen der Ehe, BGBl* 1975/412 (New Regulation of Personal Effects of Marriage Act).

[22] See *infra* C.

[23] The so-called *Schlüsselgewalt*, article 96 *ABGB*.

[24] *BG vom 15.6.1978 über die Neuordnung des gesetzlichen Erbrechts der Ehegatten und des gesetzlichen ehelichen Güterstandes, BGBl* 1978/280 (New Regulation of Legal Succession of Spouses and Marital Property Act). Now the spouse's portion is one-third (instead of formerly one-quarter) if the decedent leaves children and two-thirds (formerly one-half) if the decedent leaves no children, the remaining third going to the decedent's parents or their offspring. Cf. article 757 (1) *ABGB*.

[25] Articles 762 and 765 *ABGB*: one-half of what the spouse would have received on intestate succession.

Act in 1938. Grounds for divorce based on the fault principle are adultery, refusal to have children, and other grave matrimonial offenses (e.g., violence, alcohol abuse, neglect, etc.). Whereas in Germany today divorce is firmly based on the principle of irretrievable breakdown, the reform in Austria has brought about a mixed system with elements of both principles. A divorce based upon mutual consent[26] of the spouses is now also possible, and the principle of equality of man and woman is realized in the rules concerning alimony. The spouse who was not at fault or less at fault than the other spouse is entitled to reasonable and proportionate maintenance after the divorce. Since 1999, a spouse who is unable to support him or herself because he or she has to care for small children or because he or she cannot find employment due to reasons connected with the marriage is entitled to maintenance even if this spouse was at fault.

Divorce terminates all matrimonial rights and duties. A divorcee may take back the name he or she bore before the marriage. If the divorce is based on the sole or overwhelming fault of one spouse, the other spouse may forbid the spouse at fault to continue using the name of the spouse not at fault. Marital property is divided according to fairness and equity. Parental rights and duties after the dissolution of a marriage were an important issue in the family law reform. Before the reform, the care and education of the child was usually entrusted to the mother, while legal representation of the child and management of the child's property stayed with the father as the wielder of paternal authority. Today, all rights are vested in either the mother or the father, according to agreement between the parents or, if no agreement can be reached, by decision of the court. The other parent retains visiting rights and the right to express his or her opinion on important matters concerning the child.

C. Parents and Children

1. Rights and Duties

The relationship between parents and their children is governed by the principle that the preservation and furtherance of the child's welfare is paramount. If the parents are married, they have equal rights and duties concerning the child and should act as partners, exercising those rights and duties in mutual agreement. The father's former position of decisive authority was abolished. If they cannot reach an agreement in an important matter concerning the child, they can ask the court[27] to decide. A court can only be invoked if the child's welfare is in danger. The parents' right to chastise was

---

[26] In Austria, divorce on the grounds of irretrievable breakdown may be based either on mutual consent (*BGBl* 1978/280, art. 55a Marriage Act) or on the fact that the spouses have not lived together for at least three years (*BGBl* 1978/303, art. 55 Marriage Act). 85–90% of Austrian divorces are based on mutual consent.

[27] Matters of family law are in the jurisdiction of the District Courts (*Bezirksgerichte*), where special family judges are appointed. See *supra* Chapter 6, II.A.

completely abolished and the use of violence and any causation of suffering (body or mind) is now unlawful.

The amount of maintenance due to a child depends on the one hand on the child's needs, considering his or her talents, interests, and possibilities of development. On the other hand, the amount of maintenance depends on the financial means of the parents. Both parents have to contribute "according to their possibilities."[28] Children are entitled to maintenance as long as they are incapable of supporting themselves. Parents are also entitled to receive maintenance from their children, but this obligation is subsidiary to that of ancestors and (former) spouses. Often the mother who lives in the same household as the child depends on maintenance payments from the father who lives somewhere else, and has great difficultiy receiving these payments fully and in time. To facilitate matters for the parent caring for the child, advance payments by the state are possible.[29]

2. Children Born out of Wedlock

A child born out of wedlock[30] bears the mother's family name. The father must pay the costs resulting from the birth and the mother's maintenance for the first six weeks after birth. Maintenance of the child is a duty of both parents. The care and education of the child is the right and duty of the mother alone, but may be entrusted to both parents together if they live in the same household as the child. The child born out of wedlock acquired a restricted right of succession against its father (and vice versa) in 1970. In 1989, the restrictions were abolished, and children born in and out of wedlock now have the same rights of succession.

3. Adoption and Fostering

The rules about adoption as reformed in 1960 focus on the welfare of the underage adoptee. The adoptive father must be at least 30 years old, the mother at least 28. There must be an age difference of at least 18 years between the adoptive parents and the adoptee.[31] The adoption must be agreed on in a written contract and approved by the court, which examines not only whether the formal legal requirements are met but also the purpose of the adoption. The adoption of an adult must be founded on a justified interest of the adopter or the adoptee. Thus, abuse such as adoption solely for the purpose

---

[28] *Anspannungsgrundsatz*, article 140 *ABGB*. Child support must be provided, in this order, from the following sources: 1. the child's own income, 2. both the child's parents according to their possibilities, 3. the child's capital if that is appropriate and reasonable, and 4. the child's grandparents.

[29] *Unterhaltsvorschußgesetz, BGBl* 1976/250 (Child Support Advance Act); *Unterhaltsschutzgesetz, BGBl* 1985/452 (Protection of Child Support Act).

[30] A child who is born to a married woman or up to 302 days after the dissolution of the marriage is legally presumed to be the mother's husband's child, article 155 *ABGB*.

[31] In the *ABGB* of 1811, the adoptive parents had to be over 50 years old.

of acquiring a certain family name[32] is forestalled. The position of the adoptee is equal to that of a legitimate child.

Foster parents need the authorization of the person holding immediate parental power or of the youth welfare office (*Jugendwohlfahrtsträger*) to take care of a foster child. A written contract between the foster parents and the persons holding parental power over the child must be confirmed by the court, which must take into account the welfare of the child. If the child is under 16 years of age, the youth welfare office must agree to the foster relationship; this office may also remove the child from the foster parents if the child's welfare is endangered.[33]

D. Guardianship and Curatorship

Guardianship is the care for the person and property of a minor who has no parent capable of acting as his or her legal representative. If the guardian is not named in the deceased parent's will, the court appoints a suitable person, if possible a relative.

The court appoints a curator for persons who are not capable of attending to all or some of their affairs and who are not legally represented by a parent or a guardian. A curator must be appointed in particular for minors concerning business transactions between the minor and his or her parent or guardian; minors involved in litigation against each other who normally have the same guardian; mentally handicapped persons (where the scope of the curator's duties depends on the gravity of the handicapped person's impairment); unborn children; or absent persons.

E. Family Planning

1. Contraception

Contraceptives can be obtained from doctors or in drugstores, and sex education is part of the school curriculum, aiming at keeping the number of abortions as low as possible. Voluntary sterilization of a person over 25 by a medical doctor has been legal since 1975. The so-called "French abortion pill" RU 486 may be used since September 1999.

2. Abortion

The death penalty for abortion was abolished in 1787. In 1937, abortion on medical grounds – danger of death or permanent severe impairment of the mother's health – was legalized. During National Socialist rule (1938–45) the distinction between "worthy" and "unworthy" life brought about massive

---

[32] This consequence of the adoption was considered of paramount importance in 1811.

[33] The *ABGB's* provisions on fostering (arts. 186 and 186a) have been supplemented by the *Jugendwohlfahrtsgesetz*, *BGBl* 1989/161 (Youth Welfare Act).

punishment for abortion on the one hand and forced abortions on the other hand. In 1945, the rule of 1937 came back into force. From the late 1960s onwards, an extension of the legal grounds for abortion without criminal law sanctions was a hotly debated political issue. Ultimately, a Socialist government adopted a new abortion law by a narrow margin.

The new law[34] became effective in 1975, changing several articles of the Criminal Code as follows: basically, abortion is a crime,[35] but it is exempt from punishment if it is performed during the first three months[36] of pregnancy and if a doctor's advice has been sought; or, after the first three months of pregnancy, on medical grounds (danger to life or health of mother or child),[37] or if the mother was a minor at the time of impregnation. Doctors cannot be forced to perform an abortion; neither may those who refuse to do so be discriminated against in any way. If the abortion is performed against the will of the mother, it is a crime in any case.

The exemptions from punishment were introduced to abolish the grave health risk posed by illegal abortions and to avoid turning women in difficult personal or economic situations into criminals. To counteract abortion, increased monetary aid for mothers and intensified education about sex and contraception were introduced, and a network of counseling centers for pregnant women, mothers, and families in general was installed.

3. Artificial Procreation

Artificial procreation is only allowed for couples who are married or live together in an extra-marital partnership, and only if all other possible and reasonable means have proven to be hopeless.[38]

IV. Property Law

In Article 285, the *ABGB* gives a very broad definition of property (*Sache*): "Everything which differs from the person and serves for the use of men is called property in the legal sense." This definition includes not only corporal things. It encompasses everything that can be the object of a right, even claims arising, e.g., from contract or tort. However, the *ABGB* subdivides the law of property (*Sachenrecht*) into rights *in rem* (*dingliche Sachenrechte*, arts. 309–858), which include possession, ownership, pledge, servitudes, and inheritance,[39] and rights *in personam* (*persönliche Sachenrechte*, arts. 859–1341), i.e., obligatory rights, such as contracts, torts, and unjust enrichment.

---

[34] *BGBl* 1974/60.

[35] Article 96 *StGB* (Criminal Code): prison up to three years for the abortionist, up to five years if the pregnant woman dies, up to one year for the woman.

[36] Article 97 *StGB*, the so-called "*Fristenregelung.*"

[37] In these cases, public health insurance pays for the abortion.

[38] *Fortpflanzungsmedizingesetz BGBl* 1992/275 (Procreation Medicine Act). Only the methods listed in this statute may be used.

[39] Today, the right of succession is viewed as an absolute right, but not as a right *in rem*.

Property law in the narrow sense (*dingliche Sachenrechte*) refers to rights *in rem*. These are absolute rights authorizing persons to exercise immediate power over things (*unmittelbare Sachherrschaft*).[40] They apply only to corporal, i.e., tangible things (*körperliche Sachen*). Since real rights are effective against everyone, they must be generally recognizable (principle of publicity). Their number is limited (*numerus clausus*), i.e., parties cannot create new real rights beyond those provided by statute.

A. Possession

The law distinguishes between possessor and holder, cf. article 309 "Whoever has property in his power or custody is called the holder (*Inhaber*) of it. If the holder of property has the intent of keeping it as his own he is its possessor (*Besitzer*)." Possessors enjoy protection through self-help (art. 344 *ABGB*), accelerated judicial proceedings in case of disturbance (art. 454 sqq. Civil Procedure Code), and the position of defendant in a suit on ownership (art. 320 *ABGB*).

B. Ownership

1. Concept and Types of Ownership

Ownership (*Eigentum*) is the most comprehensive right *in rem*. It is defined as the right to dispose arbitrarily of the substance and fruits of property and to exclude everyone else from it (art. 354), subject to limitations imposed by statute or rights of third parties (art. 364 (1)). All other rights *in rem* are viewed as limitations on ownership. When they fall away, ownership expands to its previous scope ("elasticity" of ownership).

Ownership is usually sole ownership (*Alleineigentum*) by one person enjoying absolute title. Joint ownership (*Miteigentum*) is a concept under which each co-owner has a fractional interest in the undivided object of ownership. He may dispose of this interest as he pleases, but cannot dispose of the object without the consent of the co-owners. Decisions concerning ordinary administration of the property require a simple majority, other decisions must be taken unanimously. Every joint owner may request termination of joint ownership. If possible, the property will be divided. Otherwise the proceeds from sale in public auction will be distributed.

A special form of co-ownership may apply to apartments (condominium, *Wohnungseigentum*). It is the real right established in favor of the co-owner of real property to exclusively use and dispose of a separate apartment or room. *Wohnungseigentum* can be created only in favor of one person or a married couple. It is registered in the land register and administered under similar rules as joint ownership.

---

[40] Mortgage is an exception. It is a right *in rem* but grants no immediate exercise of power.

2. Acquisition of Ownership

The law distinguishes original and derivative modes of acquisition of ownership. Original modes are, e.g., occupation, treasure trove, adverse possession (*Ersitzung*) and, most importantly, *bona fide* purchase and delivery of movables from a non-owner (art. 367 *ABGB*). Examples of derivative modes are inheritance under statute or by will, or transfer based on a valid contractual relation (e.g., sale). With regard to the acquisition of ownership in movables, Austrian law follows the causal system of Roman law (*traditio ex iusta causa*, see art. 380 *ABGB* "Ownership cannot be acquired without cause and without legal manner of acquisition").[41] Ownership in land is acquired by registration in the land register (see *infra* D).

3. Expropriation

In the public interest, property must be surrendered to the state for compensation (art. 365). However, under article 5 of the State Fundamental Law on the General Rights of Citizens (1867), ownership is in principle inviolable, expropriation is permissible only in exceptional circumstances on the basis of a special statute (e.g., the Railroad Expropriation Act), not by an administrative act based on the general provision of article 365 *ABGB*.

4. Protection of Ownership

Ownership, like all other real rights, is protected against everyone. The most important remedies are the ownership action (*rei vindicatio*, art. 366), the action defending ownership against interference (*actio negatoria*, art. 523), and the action based on presumed ownership (*actio Publiciana*, art. 372). The ownership action is brought against the holder of the property. The bona fide possessor may keep the fruits that have already been separated, and has a counterclaim for necessary and useful expenditures. He is not liable for damage.

C. Limited Rights *in rem*

All rights *in rem* other than ownership are called limited real rights (*beschränkte dingliche Rechte*). They restrict the ownership of another person. These rights include servitudes (easements), charges on land (*Reallasten*), the building lease (*Baurecht*), and security interests (pledge, mortgage).

1. Servitudes

Servitudes or easements bind an owner to permit or omit something in regard to his property for the advantage of another (art. 472). They are defined as real rights enforceable against any possessor of the property. Real or prae-

---

[41] German law is satisfied with delivery based on an abstract agreement that ownership should pass (art. 929 *BGB*). French law requires only a contractual relation, without delivery, for ownership to pass (art. 1138 *Code civil*).

dial servitudes (*Grunddienstbarkeiten*) enable the better use of a dominant tenement at the expense of a servient tenement. They include, e.g., the right of view, of drawing water, of passage, or of grazing cattle. They cannot impose an obligation to perform a positive act (*servitus in faciendo consistere nequit*). Personal servitudes (*persönliche Dienstbarkeiten*, e.g., usufruct or habitation) serve the interest of specific persons and expire, as a rule, with their death. They may be created by contract or by adverse possession (*Ersitzung*). Servitudes concerning land need to be entered into the land register.

2. Charge on Land

A charge on land (*Reallast*) differs from a servitude in that it obligates the owner of a servient tenement to perform a positive act, e.g., to provide an *Ausgedinge* (continual yearly revenues) under article 530.

3. Building Lease

The building lease (*Baurecht*) is the real right to have a building on or below the surface of someone else's land. It provides an exception to the general principle *superficies solo cedit*, under which buildings have no separate legal existence but fall into the ownership of the owner of the land. Under the Building Lease Act (*Baurechtsgesetz* 1990), the right must be granted for a period between 10 and 90 years by contract and entered into the land register.

4. Security Interests

Claims may be secured by providing security *in personam* (surety, i.e. a third party enters into a contractual obligation by agreeing to pay the creditor in case the original debtor should fail to fulfill his obligation, art. 1346) or by providing security *in rem* (pledge, mortgage, transfer of title, etc.).

According to article 447 "The right of pledge (*Pfandrecht*) is a real right granted to a creditor to demand payment through property if the obligation has not been fulfilled at the time fixed." The right is accessory to a valid claim. The law distinguishes the pledge of immovables (mortgage, *Grundpfand* or *Hypothek*) from the pledge of movables (*Faustpfand*). Mortgages of registered immovables must themselves be entered into the land register. Pledge of movables generally requires delivery of the object to the creditor (art. 451). In exceptional cases, symbolic delivery suffices for the purpose of securing debts. Court decisions and scholarly doctrine have shaped a transfer of title in property (*Sicherungsübereignung*) or in rights (*Sicherungsabtretung*). They are subject to the same requirements and have the same economic effects as pledge and mortgage.

In commercial transactions, a widespread method of securing money debts is the retention of title (*Eigentumsvorbehalt*). The seller transfers possession of goods but withholds ownership until the price has been paid in full.

D. Land Register

Together with Germany and Switzerland, Austria has one of the most highly developed land register systems. It was developed in the tradition of medieval German registration practices. Uniform rules for all Austrian territories were introduced in 1790 and modernized in 1870. The land register (*Grundbuch*) is kept by the district court (*Bezirksgericht*) under the rules of the Land Register Act (*Grundbuchsgesetz* 1955). Its purpose is to give reliable information on ownership and other real rights, such as servitudes or mortgages, concerning land. A lease of real property may obtain the status of a right *in rem* by entering it into the land register. The same applies to rights of repurchase (*Wiederkaufsrecht*) or preemption (*Vorkaufsrecht*), or to prohibitions against sale or encumbrance. The register's information is considered correct and complete with respect to a person who relies on it in good faith. The register is kept as an electronic data base, to which everyone may have access.

V. Inheritance Law

The provisions concerning the law of succession are codified in articles 531 to 824 *ABGB* (Law of Property, Real Rights). Probate procedures are regulated in the Non-Contentious Proceedings Act (*Außerstreitgesetz* 1984, arts. 20–180), details on the inheritance tax are found in the Inheritance and Gift Tax Act (*Erbschafts- und Schenkungssteuergesetz* 1955).

Austrian law (art. 533 *ABGB*) acknowledges three – possibly coexisting – bases of the right of inheritance: last will (*Testament*), hereditary contract (*Erbvertrag*), or statute (*Gesetz*). Inheritance contracts may only be concluded between married spouses. They must be executed by notarial deed (*Notariatsakt*) and may affect only three quarters of the estate.

A. Intestate Succession (*gesetzliche Erbfolge*)

Intestate succession (arts. 727–761) occurs when the decedent has not (or not entirely) disposed of his estate by will. It is based on family relationships, including the spouse and children born out of wedlock, but not in-laws or live-in partners (*Lebensgefährten*), who, however, may assume the tenancy rights of the deceased under article 14 (3) of the Tenancy Act (*Mietrechtsgesetz*). The law grants intestate succession on four levels of kinship (*Parentelen*): (1) the descendants of the *de cuius*; (2) the testator's parents and their descendants; (3) grandparents and their descendants; (4) great-grandparents (but no descendants). Concerning these levels of kinship, the nearer excludes the more distant. Living relatives exclude their descendants and share the estate *per capita*. Relatives who have died before the testator are represented by their descendants *per stirpes*.

The spouse (art. 757) inherits one-third of the estate if there are direct descendants of the testator, two-thirds if there are only heirs of the second level or grandparents, or the entire estate if all surviving relatives are more distant. Divorced spouses have no inheritance rights. In the absence of eligible relatives or a spouse, the Republic of Austria becomes the legal heir (art. 760).

B. Wills (*Testamente*)

Full legal capacity to make a valid will is attained at the age of 18. Minors between 14 and 18 years of age and persons of limited mental capacity may make wills orally before a court or notary public. The most frequently used form is the holographic will, which must be personally handwritten and signed. It requires no witnesses. Allographic wills are typed by the testator or written by third parties. The will must be signed by the testator and then signed by three witnesses, two of which must be present at the same time. The testator must confirm before them that the document contains his last will. They do not have to know the contents. Oral wills can be declared before three witnesses. Both written and oral wills can also be made before a court or a notary public. All wills made before notaries are registered electronically with a central register of wills, into which other wills may also be entered, if the testator wishes.

C. Bequests (*Vermächtnisse*)

The law distinguishes inheritance and bequest (legacy). The heir is a person entitled by will or statute to the entire estate or a fraction of it. He assumes liability for its debts. The legatee merely has a claim against the heir (e.g., for delivery of a specific object bequeathed to him); he is not liable for debts of the estate. The spouse is entitled to a statutory pre-legacy (*gesetzliches Vorausvermächtnis*) comprising the movable property of the marital household (art. 758).

D. Forced Heirship (*Pflichtteilsrecht*)

Close relatives (children, parents) as well as the spouse are entitled to a statutory share (*Pflichtteil*) of the estate.[42] The testator may avoid this compulsory portion only by expressly disinheriting these persons for serious reasons (art. 768 lists *Enterbungsgründe*, e.g., felonies committed against the testator, or leaving the testator in distress without assistance). Children and spouses have a claim against the heir for one-half, parents for one-third of their intestate portion.

E. Procedural Aspects

The registrar's office issuing a death certificate informs the District Court at the place of residence of the *de cuius*. The court opens a file and passes it to the competent notary's office. The notary, acting as officer of the

---

[42] The spouse's compulsory portion is one-sixth if the decedent leaves children, and one-third if the decedent leaves no children. Cf. *supra* notes 24 and 25.

court (*Gerichtskommissär*) initiates probate proceedings by summoning the next of kin, inquiring about the existence of a will, listing potential heirs as well as assets and liabilities of the *de cuius*. The notary issues a preliminary document (*Todfallsaufnahme*) containing this information.

Wills are opened by the probate court. The prospective heir must prove his title and declare his intent to accept the inheritance (*Erbserklärung*). If he accepts unconditionally, he incurs full liability for all debts of the deceased. He may, however, accept the inheritance conditionally, which limits his liability to the value of assets he receives from the estate provided that he has prepared an inventory.

In the absence of contentious proceedings initiated by one of the parties, the court closes the non-contentious probate proceedings (*Verlassenschaftsabhandlung*) with the grant of probate (*Einantwortungsurkunde*). This document entitles the heir to take possession of the estate and dispose of its assets. Prior to this point, the estate is considered to be in suspension (*ruhende Erbschaft, hereditas iacens*). It has legal personality and can be sued by the creditors of the deceased.

F. Inheritance Tax

Austrian inheritance tax legislation establishes five classes, depending on the degree of family relationship and amount of assets in the estate. The lowest tax rate in class I (spouse and children) is 2%, the highest rate in class V (unrelated beneficiary) is 60%.

Literature

See the general literature in Chapter 12 (The Civil Code).

Monographs and Articles

Bainham, A. (ed.), The International Survey of Family Law (vol. 4, 1997)
Bernat, E., Austria: The Final Stages of Three Decades' Family Law Reform, Journal of Family Law 29 (1990–91) 285
Zankl, W., Right of Succession of the Spouse and the Relatives – A Comparative Analysis, in *Hausmaninger, H. et al. (eds.)*, Developments in Austrian and Israeli Private Law (1999) 255

Chapter 14

Private Law II: Obligations
(Contracts, Torts, Unjust Enrichment)

I. Introduction

The law of obligations deals with subjective rights "on account of which a person is bound to effect a performance to another person" (art. 859 *ABGB*). These rights are relative, i.e., they are not effective against everyone, but only bind a debtor (*Schuldner*) to make performance to a creditor (*Gläubiger*). Principal duties (*Hauptpflichten*) between the parties may be accompanied by ancillary duties (*Nebenpflichten*), such as care, loyalty, etc.

According to article 859, obligations are based directly on a statute, or on a legal transaction, or on damage suffered. Modern doctrine distinguishes between contractual and statutory obligations, considering "damage suffered" a subcategory of the latter.

The *ABGB* makes no clear distinction between contractual and delictual liability. Chapter 30, at the end of Part 2 of the Code, contains rules for both under the heading *Schadenersatz* (Damages).[1] Besides damages, statutory obligations include unjust enrichment and unauthorized management, as well as creditor's avoidance.[2]

II. Contracts

General provisions of contract law are contained in subdivision 2 of Part 2 of the *ABGB*, general rules concerning sales in article 1053 sqq. In article 983 sqq. the Code contains provisions for certain types of contracts: donation, deposit (bailment), loan for use, loan for consumption, mandate, barter, sale, brokerage, etc. The – open ended – list also includes matrimonial property agreements (*Ehepakte*, arts. 1217–1266).[3]

A number of contract law provisions are found outside the *ABGB*: The Consumer Protection Act 1979 (*Konsumentenschutzgesetz*) contains a broad range of protection provisions in favor of consumers.[4] Rules concerning special types of contracts are contained in the Commercial Code (*Handelsgesetzbuch, HGB*; commercial contracts in general in arts. 343–372 *HGB*, commercial sales in art. 373 sqq. *HGB*) and in special statutes concerning labor contracts, apartment lease, consumer transactions, etc. The UNCITRAL Con-

---

[1] The Austrian Code, unlike the French, does not maintain the Roman categories of delict and quasi-delict.

[2] The creditor's right to avoid fraudulent transfers made by his debtor (*Gläubigeranfechtung*) is not found in the Civil Code but in the Bankruptcy Code (*Konkursordnung*).

[3] See *infra* H and *supra* Chapter 13 (Private Law I), III.B.1.

[4] See *infra* II.I.

vention on the International Sale of Goods (CISG, also referred to as Vienna Sales Convention) of 1980 has been effective in Austria as of January 1, 1989.

A. General Principles of Contract Law

1. Freedom of Contract

Contract is defined in article 861 *ABGB*: "Whoever declares that he will transfer his rights to another, that is, that he will permit him to do something, will give him something, will do something for him, or will omit to do something on his account, makes a promise. If the other accepts the promise validly, a contract is created by the mutual consent of both parties." Private autonomy, one of the fundamental principles of Austrian private law, is reflected in the principle of freedom of contract. Everyone is free to determine whether to conclude a contract, and if so with whom, and with which content. The freedom of the parties to shape their agreements may, however, be limited by statutory provisions and public morals (*gute Sitten*).[5] Modern legislation, in particular the Consumer Protection Act (*Konsumentenschutzgesetz*), frequently protects the weaker party in a situation of imbalance of economic power.[6]

2. Form Requirements

In most cases, an informal meeting of the minds (offer and acceptance) is sufficient to create a (consensual) contract. Exceptionally, additional requirements must be met. Thus the *ABGB* treats loan for consumption, loan for use, deposit, and brokerage as "real" contracts (*Realkontrakte*) that arise only with delivery of the object. A mere promise to give a loan is considered a preliminary agreement (*Vorvertrag*) to form a loan contract. Some contracts require written form, e.g., contracts of suretyship (unless the guarantor is a merchant), some require notarial form (*Notariatsakt*), e.g., donations without simultaneous delivery, matrimonial property agreements, or sales or credit agreements among spouses. In consumer transactions, the rescission of door-to-door contracts, the formation of an installment sale, or a consumer credit agreement must be in writing.

3. Interpretation of Contracts

The German Civil Code provides in article 242 that "the debtor is bound to perform according to the requirement of good faith (*Treu und Glauben*), ordinary usage being taken into account." Austrian doctrine and jurisprudence apply the good faith principle in a much more limited context under article 863 (2) *ABGB*, "the custom and usage prevailing in honest

---

[5] Article 879 *ABGB*: "A contract which violates a legal prohibition or public morals is null and void."

[6] Cf. a number of mandatory provisions of the Consumer Protection Act, and in particular a content control with respect to standard contract terms in article 6 of the act.

dealing must be taken into consideration in determining the meaning and the effect of acts and omissions," and under article 914, "the interpretation of contracts shall not be based upon the literal meaning of the expressions used but rather upon the true intention of the parties, and the contract shall be construed in accordance with the customs of honest dealings (*Übung des redlichen Verkehrs*)."

Relying on articles 914 and 915,[7] Austrian doctrine distinguishes "simple interpretation" (*einfache Auslegung*) based on the wording of the agreement and the intentions of the parties from "supplementary interpretation" (*ergänzende Auslegung*) that goes beyond the wording. The starting point for simple interpretation is the common literal meaning of the words employed by the parties. However, bilateral contracts that fail to employ unequivocal language must be interpreted according to the "true intention" of the parties. The true meaning of a declaration of intent must be established by evaluating what the addressee could have recognized as being the intention of the person making the declaration ("recipient's horizon test"). If doubts remain, the "customs of fair dealing" must be considered. There may be a customary meaning of a declaration (*Erklärungssitte*), or there possibly exist standard practices in a profession or business according to which a certain factual behavior expresses a legally relevant intent (*Verkehrssitte*). [8]

If interpretation cannot remove the vagueness of a declaration, different principles of interpretation apply to gratuitous transfers, which are interpreted in favor of the transferor, and to transactions for consideration, which must be understood *contra proferentem*, i.e., to the detriment of the party making the declaration.

B. Formation of Contract

1. Offer and Acceptance

A contract is created by the mutual assent of two or more parties (art. 861). The "meeting of the minds" occurs through offer and acceptance. Both must be declared freely,[9] seriously,[10] precisely, and intelligibly (art. 869). An offer is binding as soon as it reaches the offeree. It remains binding for the time specified by the offeror or a reasonable period for the offeree to consider

---

[7] Article 915: "In unilaterally binding contracts it is presumed, in case of doubt, that the person bound intended to take upon himself a lighter rather than a heavier charge; in bilaterally binding contracts a vague declaration shall be interpreted to the prejudice of the person who has made it."

[8] Certain contracts may customarily contain specific clauses (*Vertragssitte*). If such terms are missing, interpretation does not generally permit the completion of the agreement according to the hypothetical intention of the parties.

[9] Certain utilities or transportation enterprises, which enjoy a monopoly in providing essential goods or services, may be legally compelled to conclude contracts with customers (*Kontrahierungszwang*).

[10] Mailing a price list or displaying goods in a store window usually fails to qualify as a serious intent to contract with anyone who might take notice.

his acceptance. The contract is concluded when the declaration of acceptance is brought to the sphere of influence of the offeror, enabling him to gain knowledge of it.

The common law notion of consideration (*quid pro quo*) does not exist in Austrian contract law (or in any other civil law system). Yet there exists a similar requirement in that the promise must be based on a valid cause (i.e., a legally acceptable economic background indicating the seriousness of the agreement). Like Roman law, Austrian law recognizes the notion of "natural" obligation. Certain obligations cannot be enforced by the creditor (e.g., claims barred by limitation, gambling and betting debts, or transactions invalid for lack of form), yet they are treated as obligations in so far as there arises no claim for restitution from an erroneous performance.

2. Precontractual Liability

In the bargaining period, parties must act in good faith. Precontractual duties developed by Austrian doctrine and jurisprudence include the disclosure of legal obstacles to the validity of the contract and the correct information concerning all attributes of the object which may be relevant to the other party's decision unless the other party could easily gain knowledge on his own. A party may not break off negotiations arbitrarily if it has created the other party's reliance on the conclusion of the contract and damage would result from this reliance. One may not pretend to represent others unless duly authorized to do so. Negligent violation of a precontractual duty (*culpa in contrahendo*) entitles the other party to claim reliance interest (*Vertrauens-schaden*).

C. Conditions of Substantive Validity

1. Legal Capacity of the Parties

See *supra* Chapter 13, II.A.

2. Defects of Consent

Declarations of intent must be free from mistake (error), deceit (fraud) or fear (duress). Deceit and duress ("illegal and wellfounded fear") invalidate the contract. Mistake may lead to avoidance (*Anfechtung*) or adaptation (*Anpassung*) of the contract, provided that certain requirements as to its character and circumstances are met.

In addition to these defects, Austrian law acknowledges *laesio enormis* (art. 934). The party to a bilateral contract who receives a counterperformance worth less than 50% of the value of its own performance may bring an action for rescission of the contract and restitution of the *status quo*. The other party may preserve the contract by making up the difference to common value.

3. Other Conditions of Validity

a. Cause

In contrast to German law, Austrian law in principle denies the binding effect of abstract obligations. It requires that the economic purpose of a contract, the cause (e.g., exchange, gratuitous transfer, securing, settlement) be transparent. Exceptions from the cause requirement are assignment, bills of exchange, checks, bearer bonds, etc.

b. Possibility

No valid contract arises if performance is *ab initio* clearly impossible. Impossibility may be *de facto* or *de iure*. If the promisor should have been aware of the impossibility, he will be liable to the innocent party for compensation of its reliance interest.

c. Permissibility

A contract which violates a legal prohibition or public morals is null and void (art. 879 (1)). Section 2 of the article gives specific examples: The stipulation of rewards for the negotiation of a marriage contract or the procurement of medically assisted procreation; an attorney's contingency fee agreement (*pactum de quota litis*) with his client; the alienation of the inheritance expected from a living person; and all usurious contracts.[11] Article 879 (3), inserted in 1979, voids unfair standard clauses in consumer contracts. A great number of additional specific prohibitions are contained in special statutes.

d. Public Morals

Public morals (*gute Sitten*) refer to unwritten principles of law that are generally accepted as binding by the courts because they result from a "correct judicial evaluation of the interests involved." Public morals are violated in the case of serious interference with legally protected interests or by a grave imbalance of interests. Thus Austrian courts void agreements that provide for excessive economic dependence.

4. Consequences of Defects of Consent or Lack of Substantive Validity

A person who was induced to enter a contract by deceit or fear has a choice to bring an action for avoidance (*Anfechtung*) of the contract, or to maintain it. A contract based on error may either be avoided or adapted, depending on the quality of the mistake and the extent to which the partner is worthy or unworthy of protection. Contracts violating legal prohibitions or

---

[11] Article 879 (2) Nr. 4: "An agreement by which any person exploits the improvidence, the strained financial situation, the lack of experience or the excited frame of mind of another person by causing him to promise or give to himself or to a third person a performance in exchange for a clearly disproportionate consideration ..."

public morals are null and void. Nullity is absolute and no declaration of avoidance is necessary if public interests are violated. If only private interests are affected by the illegal or immoral contract, nullity is relative, i.e., it may be asserted by the party suffering detriment (e.g., the party exploited by a usurious contract). Depending on the protective purpose of the violated rule, nullity may be total or partial. Partial nullity may lead to partial avoidance.

D. Contents of a Contract

1. Different Clauses

Express terms of a contract are subject to interpretation under articles 914 and 915. Terms may be implied by taking "the custom and usage prevailing in honest dealings" into account. Exemption and limitation clauses concerning liability for damage resulting from a breach of a contractual duty are valid unless they violate public morals. Thus, for instance, exclusion of liability for "crass gross negligence" (*krasse grobe Fahrlässigkeit*) would be invalid. Special rules are contained in the Consumer Protection Act. Penalty clauses fixing the amount of damages by way of a lump sum in advance are admissible without restriction. If the amount appears to be excessive, it may be reduced by the court.[12]

2. Conditions

Parties to a contract may add clauses by which the creation or extinction of a legal effect is made dependent on the occurrence of an uncertain future event. Conditions may be suspensive (conditions precedent) or resolutive (conditions subsequent); affirmative or negative; casual (aleatory), potestative, or mixed. A right granted under an impossible condition precedent is invalid. An impossible condition subsequent is inoperative. The same principles apply to illicit conditions.

A person entitled by a condition precedent has, for the period of abeyance, an expectancy (*Anwartschaftsrecht*) which becomes a full right when the conditional event occurs. While a condition is pending, nobody may intervene with the course of events in violation of good faith. If someone thwarts the occurrence of a condition that would detrimentally affect him, the condition is considered fulfilled. If someone who stands to benefit from a condition induces the event in violation of good faith, the condition is considered repealed.

---

[12] This provision does not apply to penalties promised by merchants.

E. Privity of Contract

1. Contracts in Favor of Third Parties

The Civil Code of 1811 had adopted the Roman law principle *alteri stipulari nemo potest*. Contracts created rights and duties only among the partners to the agreement. The Third Partial Amendment of 1916 introduced contracts for the benefit of third parties but denied the possibility of imposing duties on a third person (*Vertrag zu Lasten Dritter*). Contracts for the benefit of third parties (e.g., third party benefit insurance contracts) may either give the promisee the right to demand performance for the third party, or entitle the third party beneficiary to make such demand in his own right (true contract in favor of a third party, *echter Vertrag zugunsten Dritter*).

2. Transfer of Contractual Rights

A creditor may pass his right to claim performance from the debtor to a third person. This change in the person of the creditor is called assignment or cession (*Forderungsabtretung, Zession*). Certain rights, e.g., strictly personal rights, but also rights *in rem* such as an ownership claim, cannot be transferred by assignment. Assignment may also occur without the consent of assignor and assignee. "Legal assignment" – as in article 1358 *ABGB* and in other statutes – provides subrogation claims for those who have paid the debt of others. Thus private and social insurance companies making payments to insured victims have claims for damages against the tortfeasors.

As soon as the assignee is made known to the debtor, payment must be made to him rather than to the assignor. If an assignment is made for consideration, the assignor warrants the assignee that the claim is correct and will be paid on maturity (art. 1397 *Haftung für Richtigkeit und Einbringlichkeit*). Specific forms of assignment for special purposes include assignment of accounts receivable for collection, silent assignment, global assignment, and factoring.

3. Delegation of Contractual Duties

If the creditor consents, contractual duties may be delegated. In an assumption of debt (*Schuldübernahme*), the original debtor is replaced by a new one. It is also possible to add a co-debtor (*Schuldbeitritt*, collateral promise to pay a debt). In this case, the creditor's consent is not required.

F. Irregularities of Performance (*Leistungsstörungen*)

1. Non-Performance of the Other Party (*Unmöglichkeit der Leistung*)

Accidental impossibility automatically cancels the obligations of the parties. They must make restitution of benefits already received. The same rule applies to unreasonability (*Unzumutbarkeit*) and lack of economic feasibility (*wirtschaftliche Unerschwinglichkeit*) of performance. In the case of fault-based non-performance, the creditor may claim his interest in performance or rescind the contract. Austrian contract liability is fault liablity, not strict liability.

2. Delay (*Verzug*)

Failure by the debtor to perform in due time entitles the creditor to insist on specific performance or to rescind the contract, both after setting a grace period. If the delay is the debtor's fault, the creditor may also claim damages. As long as performance is still possible, a creditor may claim specific performance of the contract. A judgment ordering the debtor to perform *in specie* may be rendered, and the creditor may apply for coercive measures under the Enforcement Code (*Exekutionsordnung*).[13] Generally, however, the creditor will instead claim money damages.

3. Warranties (*Gewährleistung*)

In Austrian law, warranty applies to defective performance of non-gratuitous contracts for the delivery of goods. It has, of course, special importance for the contract of sale. Austrian law distinguishes deficiency of title (legal defects, *Rechtsmängel*), when the debtor is unable to transfer the promised right, from deficiency in quality (physical defects, *Sachmängel*), when expressly stipulated or implicitly assumed qualities are absent.[14]

With regard to physical defects, the law distinguishes removable (i.e., reparable by economically feasible means) from irremovable (irreparable), as well as essential (i.e., preventing the proper use) from non-essential defects. Essential irremovable defects generally entitle the creditor to cancel (rescind) the contract (*Wandlung*). Essential or non-essential removable defects give the creditor a choice between repair or exchange (*Verbesserung oder Austausch*) on the one hand, and reduction of the price (*Preisminderung*) on the other hand. The only remedy for non-essential irremovable defects is reduction of the price. Warranty claims must be filed within short prescription periods. They are six months from delivery of goods (or recognition of the defect of title) with personal property (chattels), three years for real property.[15]

---

[13] See *supra* Chapter 11 (Civil Procedure), X.A.

[14] Cf. the Common law notions of warranty of merchantability or fitness for a specific purpose.

[15] Special rules apply to the transfer of cattle and certain other categories of domestic animals. According to Directive 99/44/EC on certain aspects of the sale of consumer goods and associated guarantees, to be implemented by national legislation before June 2002, the seller is liable to the consumer for any lack of conformity of the product with the contract which exists at the time of delivery and becomes apparent within a period of two years.

4. Breach of Contract other than Impossibility or Delay (*andere positive Vertragsverletzungen*)

The concept of positive violation of contract as developed by German doctrine and jurisprudence was also adopted in Austria. It covers two situations: 1) negligent defective performance causing consequential damage to the partner in contract; 2) damage caused by negligent violation of collateral duties (*vertragliche Nebenpflichten*) aiming at the protection of the partner in contract. If in these instances losses exceed those recoverable by remedies available for non-performance, delay, or breach of warranty, they can be recovered by a claim for consequential damages.

5. *Laesio enormis*

See *supra* C.2.

6. Consumer Protection

Under articles 3 and 4 of the Consumer Protection Act, [16] a consumer who purchased a product from a businessman or agent in a door-to-door sale may rescind the contract within one week.

G. End of a Contract

1. Statutory Reasons for Extinction

An obligation is generally cancelled by payment (*Zahlung*) or performance (*Erfüllung*). The debtor has to pay to the creditor at the agreed time and place, and in the agreed manner. Payment cannot be forced upon the creditor by a third party without the debtor's consent. In certain circumstances (e.g., absence of the creditor), a debt may be deposited in court. Creditor and debtor may agree on a performance in lieu of payment (*Erfüllung an Zahlungs Statt, datio in solutum*). Of considerable practical importance is set-off (*Aufrechnung, Kompensation*), the mutual cancellation of claim and counterclaim, provided that these are reciprocal, homogeneous, correct, and due. A creditor may make a waiver (*Verzicht*) of his rights against the debtor, which requires the approval of the latter. A contract may also end because of merger of debtor and creditor (*Vereinigung, Konfusion*), because of lapse of time provided for in the contract (*Zeitablauf*), or notice of termination (*Kündigung*). Certain contracts such as agency create highly personal relations that expire with a party's death.

---

[16] See *infra* II.I.

2. Impossibility and Frustration

a. Impossibility

Austrian law distinguishes initial and subsequent, subjective and objective, accidental and fault-based impossibility. Evident initial impossibility prevents a contractual obligation from arising. Subsequent accidental impossibility invalidates the contract. The other party has a choice between specific performance and rescission. In the case of fault, it may also claim damages for non-performance.

b. Frustration

A fundamental unforeseeable change of circumstances on which the contract was based (*clausula rebus sic stantibus, Wegfall der Geschäftsgrundlage,* literally "disappearance of the foundation of the transaction") may lead to the avoidance or adaptation of the contract. It applies in particular to contracts of long duration.

3. Novation, Settlement, Recognition

Novation in Austrian law does not terminate, but significantly alters an obligation, e.g., transforming a deposit (bailment) into a loan. The new obligation remains dependent on the validity of the old. A settlement (*Vergleich*) is a contract containing a compromise concerning contested or doubtful rights and duties. It has the effect of final and definite adjustment. In a recognition (*Anerkenntnis*), only one party makes concessions. It is viewed as a subcategory of a settlement.

4. Limitation

Limitation does not extinguish a contract, but its actionability. The Code provides a complex system of rules on limitation (*Verjährung*) and adverse possession (*Ersitzung*) in articles 1451 sqq. The general limitation period is 30 years; for some contract claims this is reduced to three years.

H. Specific Contracts

In articles 938–1292, the Code deals with the following twelve contract types: donation (*Schenkung*); deposit (*Verwahrung*); loan for use (*Leihe*); loan for consumption (*Darlehen*); agency (*Bevollmächtigung*); barter (*Tausch*); sale (*Kauf*); lease (*Miete und Pacht*); service and work contracts (*Dienst- und Werkvertrag*); partnership (*Erwerbsgesellschaft*); marital property agreements (*Ehepakte*); gambling and wagering contracts (*Glücksverträge*).[17]

---

[17] A modern typology divides these contracts into five groups: 1) contracts for the acquisition of property (*Veräußerungsverträge,* including sale, barter, donation); 2) for the use of property (*Gebrauchsüberlassungsverträge,* such as lease and tenancy, loan for use, loan for consumption); 3) for services (*Arbeitsverträge,* such as employment contracts, contracts for work and services, deposit); 4) partnership con-

These were contracts current in 1811, and their regulation shows considerable Roman law influence. In addition, the Code regulates the contract of surety (*Bürgschaft*) in article 1346 sqq. and the contract of pledge (*Pfandbestellungs-vertrag*) in article 1368 sqq. Yet the principle of freedom of contract permits parties to create any contractual obligation in modification of or outside these types, unless specifically prohibited by mandatory statutory law or public morals (*gute Sitten*, art. 879).[18]

– **Donation** (*Schenkungsvertrag*) is a contract intending the gratuitous con-ferment of a benefit, e.g., transfer of ownership in a thing or renunciation of a claim. It requires either immediate delivery or a notarial deed. Dona-tions may be unilaterally revoked by the donor for grave ingratitude on the part of the donee.

– **Deposit** (*Verwahrungsvertrag*, bailment) arises when someone takes an-other's property into safekeeping. In the Roman law tradition, it is a "real" contract (*Realvertrag*), arising with the delivery of the thing (*res*). The de-positee (bailee) must carefully preserve the property entrusted to him, re-gardless of the gratuitous or remunerated nature of the contract. He is not allowed to use the property. The depositary (bailor) must reimburse the de-positee's expenses.

– **Loan for Use** (*Leihvertrag*) arranges for the gratuitous use of a (non-consumable) thing for a period of time. It is a "real" contract.

– **Loan for Consumption** (*Darlehensvertrag*) is the delivery by the lender of a certain amount of fungible things (usually money) into the ownership of the borrower with the obligation to return an equal amount of the same kind and quality. It is a "real" contract. Loans may be granted with or without interest. An excessive interest rate may qualify as usury under arti-cle 879 (2).[19]

– **Agency**. An agency contract (*Auftrag*, mandate) obligates an agent to per-form legal transactions for the account of a principal. The Code's terminol-ogy (*Bevollmächtigungsvertrag*) insufficiently distinguishes between *Auftrag* (mandate, the internal relationship establishing the legal duty of the agent to act for the principal) and *Vollmacht* (authority, power of attor-ney, the legal power of the agent to act in the name of the principal and bind him directly by his legal transactions). A mandate may be – but is not necessarily – combined with a power of attorney. Powers of attorney may be general or special, limited or unlimited. They may be conferred orally or in writing. In certain instances, the *ABGB* implies a conferment of author-ity, e.g., to persons administering a business, employees in stores, spouses

---

tracts (*Gesellschaftsverträge*); and 5) gambling and wagering contracts (*Glücksver-träge*).

[18] For "mixed" contracts containing elements of different contract types, the respective legal provisions may be considered in contract interpretation. To atypical contracts (e.g., guarantee, franchise, finance leasing contracts) only the Code's general provisions apply.

[19] See *supra* note 11.

in charge of the household. "The agent is bound to carry out the business zealously and honestly ... and give up all profit arising from the business of the principal" (art. 1009). The principal must reimburse the agent for necessary or useful expenses.

- **Barter** (*Tauschvertrag*) historically preceded sale. Thus the *ABGB* treats it ahead of sale as the more general contract type, of which sale is viewed as a special variant. Barter is a consensual contract aiming at transferring ownership in a thing in return for a transfer of ownership in another thing.
- **Sale** (*Kaufvertrag*) aims at the transfer of ownership in a thing in exchange for a certain amount of money. It is a consensual contract arising with the agreement on object and price. The object may be a tangible thing or a right. The price must be certain or at least ascertainable. Its determination may be left to a third party. Ownership passes with the delivery of the object. In a sale of real property, the contract of sale requires no form, but a notarized deed is required for entering the transfer of ownership in the land register (*Grundbuch*).[20]

Delivery of the goods and payment of price are concurrent acts. Concerning risk bearing, Austrian law distinguishes between risk of performance and risk of price. With respect to specified goods, the risk of accidental loss or deterioration passes with the date set for delivery, and in the absence of such determination with actual delivery. Accidental loss prior to delivery voids the sale and cancels contractual duties. With respect to goods not yet specified, the seller bears the risk of performance (*Leistungs-gefahr*) up to the act of specification at the delivery date agreed on or on actual delivery, i.e., he has to make delivery by taking another quantity of the same kind from his inventory (*genus non perit*). After delivery, the buyer bears the risk of price (*Preisgefahr*), i.e., he has to pay the full price.

If the buyer fails to take delivery, he cannot be forced to do so, but the risk of accidental loss or damage passes to him. The seller warrants title and quality.[21] In articles 1067–85, the Code contains detailed rules for the most frequent collateral agreements (*Nebenabreden*), in particular redemption (*Wiederkauf*), resale (*Rückverkauf*), preemption (*Vorkauf*), sale on approval (*Kauf auf Probe*), and sale with the option to resell at a higher price (*Verkauf mit Vorbehalt eines besseren Käufers*).

Special rules apply to sales (as well as to other transactions) between a businessman and a consumer (Consumer Protection Act 1979),[22] to commercial sales (art. 373 sqq. *HGB*), and to international sales of goods (UN Convention on Contracts for the International Sale of Goods, CISG 1980).

- **Tenancy and Lease (*Mietvertrag und Pachtvertrag*)** Austrian law distinguishes the permission to use a thing for payment of a certain amount of money (*Miete*, tenancy) from the permission to use a thing and reap its

---

[20] See *supra* Chapter 13, IV.D.
[21] See *supra* F.3. Implementing the EC Product Liability Directive of 1985, Austrian law holds manufacturers strictly liable for defective products, cf. *infra* III.E.
[22] See *infra* I.

fruits for money (*Pacht*, lease). Tenancy may apply to all non-consumable things. Tenants of apartments have since World War I enjoyed strong protection against eviction and benefited from rent control. Several excessive provisions of the Tenancy Act 1981 (*Mietrechtsgesetz*) were modified by the Lodging Law Amendment 1999 (*Wohnrechtsnovelle*). Generally, the landlord has the risk of accidental loss or destruction, and must bear maintenance and repair costs.

Tenancy of business premises is also subject to considerable protection, whereas lease of a business is not. The Agricultural Lease Act 1969 (*Landpachtgesetz*) contains protective rules in favor of the lessee.

The modern contract of leasing is a mixed contract not regulated in the Code. It combines elements of tenancy and sale, and mainly serves financing and/or tax purposes. The lessor (producer or leasing company) leases goods for a certain period. The lessee bears the risk of loss and costs of maintenance, and he may ultimately acquire the goods for a low purchase price.

– **Independent Service Contract** (*freier Dienstvertrag*). The pre-industrial service contract (*Dienstvertrag*) has for the most part been superseded by the labor contract (*Arbeitsvertrag*) regulated in the new field of labor law, which·has developed into a special branch of private law (*Sonderprivatrecht*).[23] Under an independent service contract, a person (*Dienstnehmer*) undertakes to provide services for an employer (*Dienstgeber*) for a certain period of time. The *Dienstnehmer* works under orders of his employer, but is not personally dependent. He uses his own resources and does not guarantee successful performance.[24]

– **Contract for Work** (*Werkvertrag*). The Civil Code, like Roman law *locatio conductio*, treats the contract for work next to the service contract. In a contract for work, an independent contractor undertakes to provide a precisely determined work for remuneration. Whereas in an independent service contract a person owes an effort, in a contract for work the contractor guarantees specific successful performance, yet is under no obligation to do the work personally. A work contractor is not integrated into the principal's organization, uses his own resources, and bears the entrepreneurial risk himself.[25]

– **Partnership** (*Gesellschaftsvertrag*) is a contract in which two or more persons agree to unite their services or their property for common benefit (art. 1175). This civil partnership (*Gesellschaft des bürgerlichen Rechts*) has no legal personality. It cannot sue or be sued. Its assets are co-owned; the partners are jointly and severally liable. It has lost much of its impor-

---

[23] The minimum content of the labor contract is that one party commits to work for the other, for a limited or unlimited time. The employee is personally dependent, i.e., he works under orders of his employer, is integrated into the employer's organization, and uses the employer's resources. He must do the work personally and carefully, but he does not guarantee successful performance.

[24] E.g., a freelance computer programmer, journalist, or performing artist.

[25] E.g., a carpenter contracting to make office furniture.

tance in view of newer forms of commercial partnerships and corporations regulated in the Commercial Code or in special statutes.

- **Matrimonial Property Agreements** (*Ehepakte*) are treated in the context of marriage by modern Austrian scholarship.[26]
- **Gambling and Wagering Contracts** (*Glücksverträge*) are characterized by the "promise and acceptance of the hope of an uncertain advantage" (art. 1267). Article 1269 distinguishes seven types: betting (*Wette*); gambling (*Spiel*); drawing of lots (*Los*); sale and other contracts regarding expectations or future uncertain rights (*Hoffnungskauf*); annuity (*Leibrente*); common maintenance contracts (*gesellschaftliche Versorgungsanstalten*, obsolete) and insurance contracts (*Versicherungsverträge*). With these contracts, rescission for *laesio enormis* (*supra* C.2) is not available. The sums promised in betting, gambling, or drawing of lots cannot be claimed in court (unless deposited). These contracts create "natural" obligations (*supra* B.1).

The Code maintains the Roman law distinction between *emptio rei speratae* (*Kauf einer erhofften Sache*), where a party promises a proportionate price for a determined amount of some future product, i.e., an ordinary sale) and *emptio spei* (*Hoffnungskauf*), where a party buys for a certain price the expectation of a future profit of a property, i.e., a speculative contract, where the buyer bears the risk of his expectation being frustrated.

An annuity is a promise, made for money or other property (frequently real estate), to make annual payments during the lifetime of a certain person. Insurance contracts were of little importance in 1811. In the meantime, insurance law has become a special branch of private law, see in particular the Insurance Contracts Act (*Vertragsversicherungsgesetz* 1959) and recent amendments made thereto in view of EU law.

I. Consumer Protection

The Austrian Consumer Protection Act as amended in the process of implementation of several EC directives subjects contracts concluded between a businessman and a consumer to a variety of mandatory rules concerning unfair contract terms, warranties, instalment and credit provisions.

III. Damages

A. Protected Rights and Interests

1. In article 1295 (1) the *ABGB* establishes a general rule on compensation for harm suffered.[27] It is extremely broad, embracing both contractual and delictual (tortious) liability: "Everyone is entitled to demand indemnifica-

---

[26] See *supra* Chapter 13, III.B.1.

[27] Cf. the similarly extensive rule of the French *Code civil*, article 1328: "Any act whatever of man which causes damage to another obliges him by whose fault it occurred to make reparation."

tion for the damage from a person causing an injury by his fault; the damage may have been caused either by the violation of a contractual duty or without regard to a contract."[28] Yet important differences exist between liability in contract and tort. In contract law, the burden of proof of fault is generally shifted to the damaging party (art. 1298), vicarious liability is broader (art. 1313a),[29] and pure economic loss is compensated to a greater extent.

The interests protected by article 1295 (1),[30] are primarily absolute rights, such as rights *in rem*, intellectual property rights, and personality rights. In the area of delictual (tort) liability, the *ABGB*'s chapter on damages (arts. 1293–1341) contains a number of specific tort provisions, including special rules for the situations most prominent at the time (1811): causation of bodily harm (arts. 1325 and 1326) and of death (art. 1327), damage caused by sexual abuse (art. 1328),[31] deprivation of liberty (art. 1329), insult and slander (art. 1330). Articles 1331 and 1332 cover damage to property. The protection of these and other absolute rights is amplified by legal duties to maintain safety and protect others against risks created by them (*Verkehrssicherungspflichten*).

Yet the scope of protected interests extends beyond this core area. Thus, liability arises from the violation of pre-contractual duties (*culpa in contrahendo*),[32] where the tortfeasor must compensate pure economic loss. Pure economic loss must also be compensated by an expert who negligently gives false information on which third parties have based their business decisions, and by a person wilfully misleading others without a justifiable business interest on his own part.

2. The protective umbrella of article 1295 (1) is further extended by article 1311 which establishes liability for the transgression of laws intended to guard against "accidental" injuries (*Schutzgesetze*).[33] To create liability, such protective laws do not require concrete endangerment, and fault only needs to relate to the transgression of the law and not to the harmful result.

---

[28] The German Civil Code (as well as the French *Code civil*) keeps contractual and tort liability separate; cf. articles 275 sqq. and 823 sqq. *BGB*.

[29] See *infra* C.

[30] Cf. the more specific general clause in article 823 I *BGB*: "A person who, intentionally or negligently, unlawfully injures the life, body, health, liberty, property or any other right of another person is bound to compensate him for any damage arising therefrom."

[31] This article has since been modified several times.

[32] Cf. *supra* II.B.2.

[33] Article 1311: "Mere accidents affect only the persons to whose property or person they occur. However, if another person has occasioned the accident by his fault, or if such person has acted in violation of a law endeavoring to prevent incidental injuries, or if he has interfered unnecessarily with the business of another, he is liable for any damages which would otherwise not have occurred." Cf. article 823 II *BGB*: "The same obligation is placed upon a person who infringes a statute intended for the protection of others ..."

3. Article 1295 (2) imposes liability on persons who wilfully inflict damage without violating a specific statutory provision, yet acting *contra bonos mores*.[34]

B. Fault Liability

The Civil Code's system of liability in contract and in tort is essentially based on the defendant's fault. Within this framework of fault liability, the Code first and foremost treats liability of the tortfeasor for his own faulty actions, then his (exceptional) liability for others and for dangerous objects. The *ABGB's* provisions on vicarious liability as modified in 1916 also include cases of liability for the actions of helpers without fault on the part of the principal. The later development of tort law in special statutes outside the Code contains numerous examples of vicarious or strict liability.

According to article 1294, fault (*Verschulden*) presupposes wrongfulness (*Rechtswidrigkeit*). In principle, the *ABGB's* standard of fault is subjective.[35] It is not based on an objective "reasonable man" standard, but on the personal abilities of the parties. A person is considered to be at fault if he was able to act voluntarily, if he should have acted differently, and if he himself – and not an ideal person in his situation – could have acted differently. An objective standard is, however, applied with regard to the degree of the tortfeasor's attention and diligence (arts. 1294 and 1297). The standard is also objective with regard to experts (art. 1299). Objectively faulty behavior creates liability of owners of defective buildings (art. 1319) and keepers of animals (art. 1320), with a shift of the burden of proof. Based on the idea of reliance, an objective standard of fault is generally applied in contract law.

In addressing liability for one's own behavior, the Civil Code recognizes two instances of liability despite the tortfeasor's faultless behavior. The first concerns causation of harm in an emergency (*Notstand*). Although urgent necessity rules out fault, the judge may award damages based on his evaluation of various aspects of the case.[36] The second situation concerns harm in-

---

[34] "A person who intentionally inflicts damage in a manner in a manner contrary to public morals is liable therefor ..." The article was inserted in 1916, modeled after article 826 *BGB*: "A person who intentionally causes damage to another in a manner contrary to public morals is bound to compensate the other for the damage."

[35] An objective standard of *bonus pater familias* (good housefather) was applied in ancient Roman law. It prevails in modern German law, cf. article 276 *BGB* "diligence required in commercial exchange" *(die im Verkehr erforderliche Sorgfalt)*.

[36] Article 1306a: "If in a case of emergency a person causes damage in order to avoid an immediately threatening danger to himself or another, a court must decide whether and in what amount such damage should be satisfied; in making such a determination the judge must take into consideration: whether or not the injured person himself has desisted from avoiding the danger out of regard to an injury which might occur to another person; in the relation between the severity of damage and the danger; and, the amount of property owned by the injuring and the injured party." The article was inserted in 1916.

flicted by minors under 14 years of age or insane persons.[37] Unless their supervisors can be successfully sued for neglect (art. 1309), the judge may impose liability on the tortfeasors themselves despite the absence of fault on their part.[38]

Joint tortfeasors are jointly and severally liable if they acted with malice. In the case of negligence, each is responsible for the share of damage caused by him (art. 1302). In the case of contributory fault on the part of the victim, article 1304 provides for apportionment of damages.[39] The injured party is generally obligated to minimize the damage as far as this is reasonable.

Fault liability is limited in two special cases. The keeper of a public way (including ski slopes and bridges) must keep the way in good condition, yet his liability is limited to gross negligence (art. 1319a introduced in 1975). An employee inflicting harm on his employer in the course of his work will not be liable in the case of "slightest" negligence. If he causes damage through slight negligence, the judge has discretion to reduce or deny compensation to the employer.[40]

C. Vicarious Liability

Article 1313a provides for extensive *Gehilfenhaftung* (vicarious liability) for auxiliary persons – including independent entrepreneurs – assisting in the performance of contractual or other obligations (*Erfüllungsgehilfen*). The principal is liable for the fault of the *Erfüllungsgehilfe* as for his own.

Article 1315 provides for limited vicarious liability of the principal for delicts of persons appointed to conduct any business of the principal under his instructions (*Besorgungsgehilfen*). The principal is liable in two situations: 1) The helper is unfit for the job for which he was selected, and he causes damage in carrying out this job. Fault on the part of the principal in selecting the helper is not required.[41] 2) The principal knowingly employed a dangerous

---

[37] Cf. *supra* Chapter 13,II.B.2.

[38] Article 1310: "If the person injured cannot obtain compensation in such manner, the judge must award either full compensation or at least an equitable part thereof, taking into consideration whether the author of the damage, notwithstanding his general mental incapacity, is nevertheless at fault in the particular circumstances; or whether the person injured failed to defend himself in order to spare the author of the damage; or finally, in view of the assets of the author of the damage and the person injured."

[39] The *ABGB* was the first modern code to introduce the principle of comparative negligence (as opposed to contributory negligence or *culpa* compensation).

[40] Employee Liability Act 1965 (*Dienstnehmerhaftpflichtgesetz*) article 1 (2) Nr. 1.

[41] German law is less severe: Article 831 *BGB* only reverses the burden of proof of the principal's fault in selecting the helper or in supervising him. Before the Third Partial Amendment (1916), the *ABGB* had established liability for *culpa in eligendo* (fault in the selection of the servant).

person who then caused the damage. The subrogation claim of the principal against his helper may be limited under the Employee Liability Act.

The Code contains a special liability of innkeepers for damage to the property of guests introduced to their premises (arts. 970 and 970a).[42] The possessor of an apartment is liable for damage caused by objects thrown or poured down from the apartment, whether the damage was caused by himself or by a third party (art. 1318).

Organs of the state or other public law corporations, i.e., public employees, are not directly liable to the victim for damage caused while acting in their official capacity. The Official Liability Act 1949 (*Amtshaftungsgesetz*) provides for an extensive liability of the state and other public law corporations for misconduct of their employees in the exercise of public authority. Subrogation claims are limited to cases of gross negligence on the part of the employee.

D. Liability for Dangerous Objects and Installations (*Gefährdungshaftung*)

Different types of increased liability may apply to keepers of dangerous objects. For some objects, only the duty of care is increased or the burden of proof is shifted to the keeper of the dangerous object. The *ABGB* itself addresses only two situations, namely, liability for damage caused by defective buildings (art. 1319)[43] and by animals (art. 1320).[44] Many statutes subsequently enacted outside the Code provide either for broad vicarious liability or strict liability of entrepreneurs or keepers of dangerous objects or installations, such as motor vehicles and railroads,[45] airplanes,[46] nuclear plants,[47] electrical and gas distribution networks,[48] pipelines,[49] mines,[50] and installations emitting air pollution dangerous to forests.[51] An Environmental Liability Act has been in preparation for several years.

---

[42] To avoid liability, the innkeeper must prove that the loss was neither caused by himself or his employees, nor by people entering or leaving the premises. The law limits liability to fixed maximum amounts.

[43] The *ABGB* shifts the burden of proof to the possessor of the structure. Jurisprudence still views the article in the context of fault liability, whereas doctrine construes liability without fault, based on the increased danger posed by the defective building and an objectively wrongful behavior of the possessor.

[44] Liability of the animal's keeper was originally interpreted as fault liability with reversal of the burden of proof. Since 1982, jurisprudence and doctrine have imposed strict liability.

[45] Liability of Keepers of Railroads and Motor Vehicles Act 1959 (*Eisenbahn- und Kraftfahrzeughaftpflichtgesetz, EKHG*).

[46] Air Traffic Act 1957 (*Luftverkehrsgesetz*).

[47] Nuclear Liability Act 1999 (*Atomhaftungsgesetz*).

[48] *Reich* Liability Act 1940 (*Reichshaftpflichtgesetz*).

[49] Pipeline Act 1975 (*Rohrleitungsgesetz*).

[50] Mining Act 1975 (*Berggesetz*).

[51] Forest Act 1975 (*Forstgesetz*).

Not all dangerous objects are covered by statutory regulation. It is generally accepted, however, that strict liability may be applied by analogy.

E. Product Liability

The Austrian Product Liability Act 1988 (*Produkthaftungsgesetz*) implements the 1985 EC Directive on product liability,[52] establishing liability without fault on the part of the producer in the event of damage caused by a defect in his product. The producer is liable for goods that are put into circulation. Liability is not based on a particular dangerousness of the good. Its extent is not limited by maximum amounts, yet the injured person must bear the damage up to the amount of 5,000 ATS himself.

F. Compensation

Damage must be compensated primarily by restitution in kind (art. 1323). If this is impossible or impractical, compensation in money is permissible. Restitution in kind is considered impractical if the plaintiff prefers compensation in money, and there are no prevailing higher interests of the defendant.

The extent of compensation depends on the degree of fault (art. 1324). In the case of slight negligence, the defendant is liable only for actual loss (*eigentliche Schadloshaltung*), excluding lost profits and non-pecuniary loss. Damage is assessed in terms of objective market value at the time the damage occurred (art. 1332). In the case of gross negligence or malice, the defendant is liable for full compensation (*volle Genugtuung*), including non-pecuniary damage.[53] The subjective loss to the plaintiff is calculated as the difference between his hypothetical and his actual patrimony immediately before judgment. The distinction between actual loss and full compensation has been blurred by the Supreme Court which includes a certain loss of profit in the concept of "actual loss."

There also exist important exceptions in both contract and tort law. Under the Commercial Code (*HGB*), contracting merchants are liable for full compensation even in cases of slight negligence. In cases of bodily injury, the tortfeasor must pay damages for pain and suffering regardless of the degree of his fault (art. 1325). A special rule applies to property damage. If the tortfeasor intentionally violated criminal law or inflicted damage wantonly or with malicious intent, he must pay for the sentimental value of the object (art. 1331).

---

[52] Council Directive 85/374/EEC. A subsequent Directive 1999/34/EC of the European Parliament and of the Council (implementation deadline December 4, 2000) extends its scope to primary agricultural products and game products.

[53] Article 1324: "In case of damage caused by malice or by gross negligence the person injured is entitled to demand full satisfaction, in other cases only indemnification ..."

The *ABGB's* rules on compensation envisage only fault liability. A number of later strict liability statutes limit compensation to maximum amounts. The recent legislative trend, however, is toward unlimited liability.[54] In the absence of specific legislation, scholars suggest analogous application of the gradation of compensation in article 1324, making the extent of compensation depend on the dangerousness of the object.

IV. Unjust Enrichment

Any person who acquires assets without legal justification at the expense of another, either by a performance rendered or in any other way, has the duty of restitution. The person suffering a loss may bring an unjust enrichment claim. The Civil Code distinguishes two types of such claims. The first category comprises claims based on enrichment by transfer or performance (*Leistungskondiktionen*). They are brought to recover a benefit conferred by the plaintiff on the defendant knowingly and intentionally with a specific purpose in mind, where it subsequently appears that the transfer was without legal justification. This category includes claims for restitution based on erroneous payment of a non-existing debt (art. 1431), subsequent lapse of the purpose of transfer of assets (art. 1435), failure of the intended transaction (in analogy to art. 1435), and absence of a legal cause (art. 877 if one party has already performed and the contract is void because of error, deceit, or duress).

The second category is referred to as *Verwendungsanspruch* (claim for profitable utilization) and covers enrichment in any other way (art. 1041). This claim is based on the fact that someone has used a thing belonging to another for his purposes without legal justification and has retained the benefit, but there has been no transfer of assets by the claimant. The plaintiff asks for the enrichment acquired by the defendant, consisting either in restitution of the thing or its value, together with all benefits the defendant derived from his possession of the thing.

V. Unauthorized Management (*Geschäftsführung ohne Auftrag*)

In principle, noone is authorized to interfere in the affairs of another without express or implied authorization. Someone who manages another's business in that person's (not his own) interest without authorization in an emergency (*Notgeschäftsführung*), may, however, claim expenses even if his endeavors have – without his fault – remained fruitless. Even outside an emergency, management in the clear and paramount (subjective) advantage of the other party (*nützliche Geschäftsführung*) entitles the unauthorized manager to reimbursement of his expenses. The intermeddler, however, who produces no

---

[54] See, e.g., the Forest Act 1975, the Mining Act 1975, the Product Liability Act 1988, the Genetic Engineering Act 1998 (*Gentechnikgesetz*), the Nuclear Liability Act 1999, and the Environmental Liability Act (in preparation).

such advantage (*unnütze Geschäftsführung*) has no right to claim expenses. He must restore the property to its previous state or pay damages.

VI. Creditor's Avoidance (*Gläubigeranfechtung*)

If the estate of a debtor is insufficient for satisfying the claims of the creditors, – mostly in the case of bankruptcy, but also in other cases – the creditors may challenge (avoid) transactions the debtor has conducted. Avoidance is possible: 1) if the debtor has acted wilfully to the detriment of the creditors, or the debtor is squandering his assets, and the acquiror was aware or negligently unaware of this fact; 2) if the transaction was a gift; 3) if, in the case of bankruptcy, the debtor has favored one creditor to the detriment of the other creditors; 4) if the acquiror was aware or negligently unaware of the debtor's bankruptcy. The debtor's transactions may be avoided only if the creditor has unsuccessfully tried to enforce payment from the debtor, or if the debtor is bankrupt.

Literature

See the general literature in Chapter 12 (The Civil Code).

Monographs and Articles

Blanpain, R., Herbots, J. (eds.), International Encyclopaedia of Laws. Contracts (looseleaf edition); for the contribution on Austria see *Posch, W.* (vol.1, 1996)

Bydlinski, F., A "Flexible System" Approach to Contract Law, in *Hausmaninger, H. et al. (eds.)*, Developments in Austrian and Israeli Private Law (1999) 9

David, R. et al. (eds), International Encyclopedia of Comparative Law (vol. VII, Contracts; vol. XI, Torts)

Fenyves, A., The Influence of Changed Circumstances on Contracts of Long Duration in *Hausmaninger, H. et al. (eds.)*, Developments in Austrian and Israeli Private Law (1999) 59

Hausmaninger, H., Roman Tort Law in the Austrian Civil Code of 1811, in *Hausmaninger, H. et al. (eds.)*, Developments in Austrian and Israeli Private Law (1999) 113

Hausmaninger, H., The Third Partial Amendment (1916) to the Austrian Civil Code of 1811 and its Influence on Tort Law, in *Hausmaninger, H. et al. (eds.)*, Developments in Austrian and Israeli Private Law (1999) 137

Koziol, H., Austria, in *Koziol, H. (ed.)*, Unification of Tort Law: Wrongfulness (1998) 11

Koziol, H., Characteristic Features of Austrian Tort Law, in *Hausmaninger, H. et al. (eds.)*, Developments in Austrian and Israeli Private Law (1999) 159

Koziol, H., Problems of Alternative Causation in Tort Law, in *Hausmaninger, H. et al. (eds.)*, Developments in Austrian and Israeli Private Law (1999) 177

Comparative Works

Bonell, M. J., An International Restatement of Contract Law: The UNIDROIT Principles of International Commercial Contracts (2nd ed. 1997)

Lando, O., Beale, H., Principles of European Contract Law, Part I: Performance, Non-Performance and Remedies (1995)

von Bar, C., Gemeineuropäisches Deliktsrecht I (1996), II (1999)
von Bar, C., The Common European Law of Torts I (1998)
Zweigert, K., Kötz, H., Introduction to Comparative Law (3rd ed. 1998) 323sqq.

Chapter 15
Labor Law

I. Introduction

Labor law (*Arbeitsrecht*) is special private law (*Sonderprivatrecht*) regulating the legal relationships of employed persons who work for another (the employer) on the basis of a contract and in a state of personal dependence, i.e., under the leadership and control of, and with resources belonging to the employer. A major function of labor law is to protect the – in most cases economically weaker – employee. This aspect provides for a strong input on the part of public law. Labor law also regulates the relationship between the state and the employer, between employees and their labor unions, and between associations representing employers and employees. It provides procedures for dealing with the labor market and with labor disputes.

Labor law is divided into two major parts. Individual labor law (*Individualarbeitsrecht*) concerns employment contract law and employee protection law. Collective labor law (*Kollektivarbeitsrecht*) includes standards regulating the relationship between associations representing employers and employees, rules concerning the collective creation of law (collective agreements, works agreements), and rules concerning worker participation in enterprise management.

The most important areas of Austrian labor law are regulated in detail by special statutes, applying either to special groups of employees, or affecting all employees but treating only certain aspects of employment conditions. In collective labor law, legal fragmentation was considerably reduced with the enactment of the Labor Constitution Act (*Arbeitsverfassungsgesetz*) in 1974. It regulates the collective creation of law (collective agreements, works agreements),[1] works representation, and conciliation procedures.

II. History

The development of labor law was a consequence of the industrialization process which began around 1800. The movement of agricultural workers to factory work in the cities led to an oversupply of labor, which resulted in deteriorating working conditions and pauperization of a large part of the population. These social shortcomings induced a reaction on the part of the state. An Austrian Imperial Decree (*Hofkanzleidekret*) of 1842, following the model of the British Moral and Health Act of 1802, aimed to stop child labor, avoid accidents, and improve sanitary conditions at the workplace. The Trade

---

[1] Concerning contents and legal nature of collective agreements and works agreements see *infra* IV, B. and D.

Act (*Gewerbeordnung*) of 1859, which essentially regulated the licensing of trades and businesses, also laid down rules concerning employment, outlawing abusive labor practices. Yet 19th century liberalism generally maintained the principle of unrestricted freedom of contract in labor relations, failing to take into account the economic imbalance between employers and workers.

A decisive improvement was initiated by Article 12 of the State Fundamental Law on the General Rights of Citizens in 1867, which granted freedom of association (*Vereinsfreiheit*), thus permitting the formation of labor unions.[2] The former ban on industrial action was expressly repealed in 1870. Subsequently, employers also formed their own associations. Soon these employees' and employers' organizations concluded contracts called collective agreements (*Kollektivverträge*),[3] which contained fundamental terms for all individual employment contracts, such as mandatory minimum wages, maximum working hours, length of paid vacations, etc. In the 1880s, special state authorities (*Gewerbeaufsicht*, later *Arbeitsinspektion*) were established to supervise the observance of employment regulations. Statutory health insurance (1888) and occupational accident insurance (1889) were introduced.[4]

Yet it was not until the *Handlungsgehilfengesetz* (Commercial Employees Act) of 1910, a forerunner of the *Angestelltengesetz* (White Collar Employees Act) of 1921, that the labor contract was understood as a legal relationship of a special kind. The Act recognized the need to protect the employee and provided for continued wage payments in case of illness, paid vacations, and formal recognition of the employer's duty to protect the life and health of the employee. At the same time it emphasized the employee's duty of loyalty (*Treuepflicht*) to the enterprise. The Act also brought white collar employees (*Angestellte*) advantages over the rights of blue collar workers (*Arbeiter*), some of which still exist today. The eight-hour work day was introduced for factories in 1919. Workers' representation was first regulated by statute in 1919, when the works councils (*Betriebsräte*) were given certain participatory rights and the mandatory normative effect of collective agreements was established. Unemployment insurance for all workers was introduced in 1920, retirement benefits for white collar employees in 1906, for blue-collar workers in 1939.

The chapter of the Civil Code on the pre-industrial service contract was revised in the Third Partial Amendment of 1916, but subsequent development of labor law occurred through special legislation outside the Civil Code.

---

[2] Cf. *infra* IV.A.

[3] Cf. *infra* IV.B.

[4] Today, protection against financial disadvantages created by illness, unemployment, old age, invalidity, work accidents, occupational diseases, motherhood and family burdens is provided mainly by insurance services operated or at least promoted and supervised by the state. Both employees and employers pay monthly contributions to the employees' social insurance system. About 99% of the population is covered by health insurance.

These changes[5] were effected for the most part after World War II under the influence of the *Sozialpartnerschaft* ("social partnership").[6] They included the successive shortening of the work week to 40 and 38 hours, the extension of vacations to between five and six weeks, expansion of maternity leave and job protection, general restrictions on dismissals, introduction of workers' co-determination in and beyond the enterprise,[7] and harmonization of the legal status of white and blue collar workers. Whereas collective labor law was comprehensively regulated in the Labor Constitution Act (*Arbeitsverfassungsgesetz*) of 1974, all attempts to codify individual labor law have thus far failed.

Austria's accession to the EU in 1995 also affected the area of labor law. The EU does not harmonize labor law, yet sets minimum standards in certain areas of labor law, with the possibility for each member state to set higher standards. In Austria,[8] implementation of EC labor law directives (mainly concerning the equal treatment of men and women, employee health and safety protection, free access to the labor market for EU citizens, form requirements of the employment contract, mass termination of contract, insolvency of the employer, transfer of undertakings, and pensions) has been gradual. Many rules were already implemented in Austria as a result of the EEA Agreement,[9] mostly by the Employment Contract Law Harmonization Act of 1993 (*Arbeitsvertragsrechts-Anpassungsgesetz*) and the Employee Protection Act of 1994 (*ArbeitnehmerInnenschutzgesetz*).

III. Individual Labor Law

A. Labor Relationships

Individual labor law regulates the relationship between individual employers and individual employees, in particular labor contract law, and it includes labor protection law, i.e., duties of the employer to protect employees from dangers to their life, health, and morals. Most issues are regulated by special statutes, with rules varying according to the type of work, in particular

---

[5] See in particular the Works Councils Act (*Betriebsrätegesetz*) and the Collective Agreement Act (*Kollektivvertragsgesetz*), both passed in 1947. In 1974 these fields of collective labor law were codified in the Labor Constitution Act (*Arbeitsverfassungsgesetz*). Important matters of individual labor law were regulated in the Motherhood Protection Act (*Mutterschutzgesetz*) 1957, the Employee Liability Act (*Dienstnehmerhaftpflichtgesetz*) 1965, the Working Hours Act (*Arbeitszeitgesetz*) 1969, the Employee Protection Act (*ArbeitnehmerInnenschutzgesetz*) 1994, the Continuation of Salary in Case of Inability to Work Act (*Entgeltfortzahlungsgesetz*) 1974, the Vacation Act (*Urlaubsgesetz*) 1976, the Blue Collar Workers Severance Payment Act (*Arbeiter-Abfertigungsgesetz*) 1979.

[6] Cf. *supra*, Chapter 3 (The Political System), II.D.

[7] Cf. *infra* IV.

[8] See also *supra* Chapter 4 (Austria and the European Union),VI.C.4.

[9] In force since January 1, 1994, cf. Chapter 1 (Political History),VII.C.2.

according to whether the employee is a blue collar *Arbeiter* or a white collar *Angestellter*.

The labor contract (*infra* B.1) must be distinguished from other, similar contract types. For instance, under an independent service contract (*freier Dienstvertrag*), a person undertakes to provide services for a certain period of time and does not guarantee for successful performance.[10] However, he is not, like the employee, personally dependent and integrated into the enterprise organization, and he uses his own resources. Under a contract for work (*Werkvertrag*), a precisely determined work has to be provided and specific successful performance must be guaranteed by an independent contractor, who is not integrated into the principal's organization, and under no obligation to do the work personally.[11] The contractor uses his own resources, bearing the entrepreneurial risk. Only small parts of labor law apply to these two contract types. They are predominantly regulated by provisions laid down in the Civil Code.[12] Likewise, civil servants are subject to a special regime.[13]

B. The Labor Contract

1. Content and Form

The minimum content of the labor contract is that one party, the employee, commits to work for the other, the employer, subject to the latter's instructions, for a limited or unlimited period of time. The employee is personally dependent, i.e., he works under orders, he cannot choose time and place of work, he is integrated into the employer's organization, and he uses the employer's resources. He must do the work personally and carefully, but he does not guarantee for successful performance. In the absence of specific contractual definition, employment conditions are determined by legislation, collective agreements, works agreements, or judicial interpretation based on equitable common practice.

No special form is required for labor contracts. Written form is mandatory only in special cases (e.g., for apprenticeship contracts).

2. Duties of Employee and Employer

The employee is obliged to carry out the agreed duties meticulously and according to the employer's instructions. In addition, the employee has a duty of obedience (*Gehorsamspflicht*) and a duty of loyalty (*Treuepflicht*), including the obligation to protect the employer's business interests by guarding secrets, refraining from competition, warning of dangers, etc.

The employer's most obvious obligation is to pay remuneration, the amount of which depends on the terms of a collective agreement or the indi-

---

[10] E.g., as a freelance computer programmer, journalist, or performing artist.
[11] E.g., a carpenter contracting to make office furniture.
[12] Cf. *supra* Chapter 14 (Private Law II), II.H.
[13] The Civil Servants' Employment Act (*Beamten-Dienstrechtsgesetz*) 1979.

vidual labor contract – provided that the latter offers a higher wage or salary. The basic wage (*Lohn*, in the case of *Arbeiter*) or salary (*Gehalt*, in the case of *Angestellter*) is frequently augmented by additional payments, such as a 50% overtime supplement (*Überstundenzuschlag*), 100% holiday overtime rates (*Feiertagszuschlag*), bonuses (*Prämien*), and allowances (*Zulagen*) for danger or hardship. Wages and salaries are paid 14 times a year. Employers also have a duty of care (*Fürsorgepflicht*). It includes obligations to provide safe and healthy working conditions, to protect morality and personality of workers, to treat employees equally, etc. Specific rules are laid down in the Employee Protection Act of 1994 (*ArbeitnehmerInnenschutzgesetz*) and numerous administrative regulations. A special administrative authority, the Labor Inspection Office (*Arbeitsinspektorat*), is responsible for checking the observance of these regulations.

3. Working Hours and Vacations

Provisions concerning maximum working hours are laid down in the Working Hours Act of 1969 (*Arbeitszeitgesetz*), the Hours of Rest Act of 1983 (*Arbeitsruhegesetz*) and specific provisions of collective agreements. Normal working time may not exceed eight hours a day and 40 hours a week. In most branches of the economy, weekly work time has been reduced to 38.5 or 38 hours by collective agreement. It may be extended in exceptional cases. Overtime must be paid with a premium of 50% on the regular hourly rate.

With a few exceptions, vacations are uniformly regulated for all employees by the Vacation Act of 1976 (*Urlaubsgesetz*). Paid minimum leave amounts to 30 workdays per year. Persons who have been employed 25 years or more are entitled to a leave of 36 workdays. Agreements providing for the nonuse of leave in exchange for payment are invalid. Illness during leave time is not counted as vacation time if it exceeds three days.

If an employee is prevented from working by illness or accident which is not due to gross negligence on his part, he retains his right of full wage or salary payment for a certain period. This sick leave (*Krankenstand*) is regulated for blue-collar workers[14] by the Continuation of Salary in Case of Inability to Work Act of 1974 (*Entgeltfortzahlungsgesetz*) and for white collar employees[15] by the White Collar Employees Act.[16] An employee is also enti-

---

[14] Four weeks of full compensation if the worker was employed from 14 days to four years, six weeks from five to 15 years, eight weeks from 15 to 25 years, ten weeks for more than 25 years. In case of industrial accident or industrial disease, eight weeks of full compensation are paid from the first day of employment up to 15 years, ten weeks for more than 15 years.

[15] Full compensation for six to eight weeks in the first four years of employment, eight weeks from five to 15 years, ten weeks from 15 to 25 years, 12 weeks for more than 25 years; compensation at one half of the salary for four additional weeks in all cases.

[16] In the first half of 2000, steps were taken to harmonize the legal status of white and blue collar workers regarding sick leave and protection against termination. Negotiations continue with the aim of completely abolishing all remaining differences.

tled to family and medical care leave (*Pflegefreistellung*) for one week maximum per year when he is obliged to care for a close relative living in the same household.[17]

4. Duration and Termination of the Labor Contract

In the absence of an agreement to the contrary, a labor contract is effective for an indefinite term. It can be canceled by mutual assent (*einvernehmliche Auflösung*). Unilateral forms of legal termination are notice (*Kündigung*) given by either party, or premature termination (*vorzeitige Auflösung*) for cause. If the latter is pronounced by the employer, it is called summary dismissal (*Entlassung*).[18] If it is declared by the employee, it is referred to as premature resignation (*vorzeitiger Austritt*). If a labor contract has been concluded for a limited period of time, it cannot be terminated by notice. The periods of notice are different for employers and employees, and for blue collar and white collar workers, respectively.

A worker may challenge notice in court, provided that he has been employed for at least six months. He must show that he was given notice for motives that violate good morals (e.g., his membership in a labor union, or his legal pursuit of claims arising from his labor contract), or that the giving of notice was unsocial (*sozialwidrig*), i.e., that his interests are gravely affected by it, whereas the employer had no sufficient reasons, such as inadequate behavior of the employee or a general need to reduce personnel. If the challenge is successful, the employer must reemploy the worker. The worker may instead demand damages.[19]

An employee is entitled to claim a compensation for notice (*Kündigungsentschädigung*) if he was summarily dismissed without sufficient cause, or if he prematurely resigned for legally acknowledged cause, or in the case of untimely notice. The compensation consists of the remuneration due for the period between the actual termination and the termination prescribed by law or employment contract. If upon termination of employment the employee has not yet consumed his entire annual leave, he is entitled to receive leave compensation (*Urlaubsentsschädigung*). The employee is entitled to severance pay (*Abfertigung*) if he has worked for the same employer for at least three

---

[17] In the case of children under 12, this leave may be increased by another week.

[18] If a cause for summary dismissal arises, the employer must act immediately or he is considered to have waived his right to terminate the employment without notice.

[19] An even more extensive protection against notice and summary dismissal is given to members of works councils, pregnant women, mothers of infants, draftees, and seriously disabled persons. They are subject to notice or summary dismissal only with the express approval of the labor court.

years[20] and employment is terminated neither by notice or premature resignation on his part nor by dismissal for cause on the employer's part.[21]

C. Protective Legislation for Special Categories of Employees

According to the Employment of Children and Juveniles Act of 1948 (*Kinder- und Jugendlichenbeschäftigungsgesetz*), the employment of children under the age of fifteen is generally forbidden. Employment for the purposes of instruction or education does not count as child labor. *Länder* administrations may permit the work of children in musical and theatrical performances and in motion picture productions.

Juveniles (*Jugendliche*) are minors under the age of eighteen or who have not yet completed an apprenticeship or other training period. They are subject of restrictions as to their working hours, with exceptions in certain areas of work. They may not perform work that poses special risks in view of their physical condition.

Provisions concerning apprenticeship (*Lehre*) are laid down in the Vocational Training Act of 1969 (*Berufsausbildungsgesetz*). The apprentice must have finished compulsory schooling. The apprenticeship contract is a fixed-term written contract. Unilateral termination of the apprenticeship by either party requires written form and is possible only for cause. The apprentice is entitled to receive payment, the employer undertakes to provide professional training. The apprentice is obligated to attend vocational training school. The time spent there counts as paid worktime. After the end of the apprenticeship period, the apprentice must be employed for an additional four months.

Members of a works council[22] may be subject to notice of termination or summary dismissal only with the consent of the court. Employees doing military service (*Präsenzdienst*) or community service in lieu of military service (*Zivildienst*) also enjoy special protection against termination, as do disabled persons[23] under the Employment of Disabled Persons Act of 1970 (*Behinderteneinstellungsgesetz*).

The employer must ensure that a pregnant employee does not engage in any activities posing a risk to her own health or that of her child. Expectant mothers and women who are breastfeeding may not work overtime. Maternity leave is compulsory for eight weeks before and eight weeks after giving birth. During this protection period (*Mutterschutzfrist*), the employee receives full

---

[20] The amount depends on the duration of service with the employer, from two monthly salaries for three to four years of service up to 12 monthly salaries for 25 years and above.

[21] Severance pay is also due if the employee resigns in order to draw an old age pension or to care for a newborn child.

[22] Cf. *infra*, IV.D.

[23] Every employer must hire at least one disabled person per 25 employees or pay an "equalization fee" (*Ausgleichstaxe*). The state pays employers a monthly premium for the employment of additional disabled persons.

compensation from the public system of health insurance. During pregnancy and up to four months after the birth, the mother's employment may not be terminated. The mother – or, since 1990, the father[24] – may take a voluntary leave (*Karenzurlaub*) for up to two years[25] with the guaranteed right to return to her/his job afterwards for at least four weeks. One parent may also work part-time for four years, or both parents for two years each, provided that their respective employer agrees. The parent on leave or part-time work receives monthly payments (*Karenzgeld*) under the Parental Leave Payments Act 1997 (*Karenzgeldgesetz*).

It has been a long tradition in Austria to ensure equal treatment of employees, especially of men and women at work.[26] There still exist restrictions on the employment of women, originally introduced for their protec_ tion,[27] that make it hard for women to find jobs in some professions. According to the Equal Treatment Act of 1979 (*Gleichbehandlungsgesetz*), discrimination between men and women without objective justification is forbidden. The Act implemented the far-reaching direct effect of protection provided against discrimination by the labor law of the EU. It defines various prohibited scenarios of discrimination as to the formation or termination of the labor contract, remuneration, voluntary fringe benefits, on-the-job training, promotion, and other working conditions. Men and women must receive equal pay not only for the same work, but also for work of equal value. Unlawful discrimination includes sexual harassment during employment. The male or female employee having suffered discrimination may claim damages or termination of the discriminating situation. In a lawsuit, the employee has to prove the discriminating situation. Women's interest groups have repeatedly yet unsuccessfully demanded that the burden of proof be shifted in discrimination suits.

An Equal Treatment Commission (*Gleichbehandlungskommission*) at the Federal Chancellor's Office renders opinions on all matters of discrimination. An Advocate for Equal Treatment Problems (*Anwältin für Gleichbehandlungsfragen*) advises and supports complainants and investigates their claims. Violations of the equal treatment principle may also be claimed in the labor courts, where they generally lead to the payment of damages.

---

[24] Parental Leave Act 1989 (*Eltern-Karenzurlaubsgesetz*).

[25] Since 1998, 18 months if only one parent goes on leave, but two years if at least six months are taken by the other parent.

[26] Courts have developed a general principle of equal treatment that is binding on the individual employer. The special protection against sexual discrimination (also as expressed in collective agreements and works agreements) began with the Equal Treatment Act (*Gleichbehandlungsgesetz*) in 1979 and was extended to civil service employees in the Federal Equal Treatment Act (*Bundes-Gleichbehandlungsgesetz*) 1993.

[27] E.g., the general prohibition to work at night of the Women's Night Work Act 1969 (*Frauennachtarbeitsgesetz*), to which, however, numerous exceptions exist. Cf. *supra* Chapter 4, VI.C.4.

D. Delictual (Tort) Liability of Employees

If the employee in the course of his employment culpably and unlawfully inflicts a loss on the employer or a third party involved in a business relationship with his employer, he will be personally liable for damages under the general rules of tort liability. However, the Employee Liability Act of 1965 (*Dienstnehmerhaftpflichtgesetz*) exempts employees from liability for "excusable errors," i.e., the lowest form of negligence. If the damage is caused by slight or gross negligence, the court may reduce the amount of damages to be paid by the employee.[28] The employee is fully liable for malice.

E. Employment of Foreign Nationals (*Ausländerbeschäftigung*)

For the purpose of employment, nationals of a member state of the European Economic Area or the European Union have the same status as Austrian citizens. So-called "third state foreigners," however, may commence their employment in Austria only after obtaining the necessary permits according to the Employment of Foreign Nationals Act of 1975 (*Ausländerbeschäftigungsgesetz*).

An employment permit (*Beschäftigungsbewilligung*) may be granted to an employer if certain statutory requirements[29] are satisfied. The Federal Minister of Economic Affairs and Labor issues quotas for foreign workers for several branches of business and regions of the country, thus dispensing of the need to check on the general requirements for an employment permit in individual cases.[30] The employment permit refers to a particular workplace in a particular enterprise and therefore automatically expires upon job rotation or termination of the employment. It is issued for not more than one year at a time and must be regularly renewed.

A work permit (*Arbeitserlaubnis*) may be issued to a foreign national for a term not exceeding two years if the foreign national has been lawfully employed in Austria for a total of 52 weeks during the past 14 months.

A certificate of exemption (*Befreiungsschein*) is issued for five years at a time to a foreign national who has been lawfully employed in Austria for at least eight years or who is married to an Austrian citizen and resides in Austria. It is also issued to juveniles who have at least in part grown up in Austria.

If a third state foreigner is employed by an employer from within the EEA for a temporary job in Austria, the employer must acquire an EU certifi-

---

[28] The court considers factors like the employee's training, job-connected responsibility, risk-related salary, and the general likelihood of the performed task to result in such damage.

[29] A work permit is issued in individual cases if the current state and development of the labor market allows the employment of foreigners and if there are no other important public or economic reasons precluding such employment. The foreign employee may not be hired out to another employer, the works council must be informed, and housing at usual local standards must be available.

[30] Exceptions are only possible for specific reasons (e.g., key personnel).

cate of posting (*EU-Entsendebestätigung*) from the local Austrian labor exchange office. The certificate of posting is issued for six months and can be renewed once. A non-EEA employer without a registered office in Austria who employs a third state foreigner may also acquire a certificate of posting for temporary jobs not exceeding four months. Otherwise an employment permit is mandatory.

Any employment of a non-EEA national without an employment permit, a work permit, a certificate of exemption, or a certificate of posting renders the labor contract void, and the employer must pay a fine[31] to the local administrative authority.

IV. Collective Labor Law

The other major Area of labor law is collective labor law. It comprises the law of trades representation and the law of works representation. Trades representation law concerns labor relationships above the enterprise level. It includes rules regulating the relationship between employees and their representative association (trade or labor union, chamber of labor), rules pertaining to the collective creation of law (in particular by collective agreements) and the law of industrial disputes. Works representation law concerns labor relationships in individual establishments or enterprises. It creates worker participation rights in enterprise administration.

A. Affiliations (*Koalitionen*)

Austrian constitutional law contains rules concerning the freedom of association and freedom of assembly in general, and concerning the freedom to form affiliations (*Koalitionen*) in particular.[32] There are two categories of affiliations: Voluntary trade organizations (*freiwillige Berufsvereinigungen*) and statutory representative bodies or interest groups with compulsory membership (*gesetzliche Interessenvertretungen mit Pflichtmitgliedschaft*).

Voluntary affiliations may be established as associations (*Vereine*) under the Associations Act of 1951 (*Vereinsgesetz*). They are based on voluntary membership, and they possess assets and legal personality. On the employees' side, there is only one significant trade association, the Austrian La-

---

[31] ATS 10,000 to ATS 120,000 per employee; the amount can be doubled for repeated violations.

[32] Under Article 12 of the State Fundamental Act on the General Rights of Citizens (*Staatsgrundgesetz über die allgemeinen Rechte der Staatsbürger*) 1867, Austrian citizens have the right "of peaceful assembly and freedom of association." A special Constitutional Act of 1918 states that "complete freedom of assembly and association is established." According to Article 11 of the European Human Rights Convention (1958) "everyone has the right to freedom of peaceful assembly and to freedom of association with others, including the right to form and to join trade unions for the protection of his interests."

bor Union Federation (*Österreichischer Gewerkschaftsbund, ÖGB*).[33] On the employers' side, there are voluntary trade associations in a few specific areas. The most important of these in the field of collective bargaining are the Association of Austrian Banks and Bankers (*Verband österreichischer Banken und Bankiers*) and the Association of Austrian Insurance Companies (*Verband der Versicherungsunternehmen Österreichs*).

Statutory representative bodies are associations established as legal entities with compulsory membership. They finance their activities by tax-like contributions. The two most important groups are the Chambers of Labor (*Arbeiterkammern*), representing all employees in the private sector, and the Economic Chambers (*Wirtschaftskammern*), representing all employers in the fields of trade, commerce, industry, transport, tourism, money, credit, and insurance business. They function on both federal and *Länder* levels. Additional statutory representative bodies are the Chambers of Agriculture (*Landwirtschaftskammern*) and various chambers of professionals in private practice, such as lawyers, physicians, or civil engineers.

Employers' and employees' associations cooperate within an informal structure and process referred to as the "social partnership" (*Sozialpartnerschaft*)[34] In the past, they have successfully found social and economic compromise and avoided disruptive industrial action such as strike or lockout.

B. Collective Creation of Law

Employers' and employees' associations collaborate in an important lawmaking process. The product of their collective bargaining are "collective agreements" (*Kollektivverträge*)[35] regulating working conditions. They are as a rule concluded on a national level for certain sectors of the economy, yet separately for blue and white collar workers. The usual partners in contract are the Austrian Federation of Labor Unions and the Economic Chamber. On account of mandatory membership in the Economic Chamber, all enterprises of the sector concerned are obligated by the collective agreement. Since collective agreements fully apply to non-union members as well, most of these agreements cover all employers and employees of the respective sector of the economy.

Collective agreements contain mandatory provisions which affect every single employment contract, i.e., they can neither be revoked nor restricted for the benefit of the employer by an individual labor contract or works agreement. Collective agreements thus guarantee minimum rights to all employees of a particular branch of the economy. They can be enforced in the labor courts by each individual worker affected by them.

---

[33] Contrary to its name, the Labor Union Federation is not an association of independent individual unions. It is organized as a strictly centralized body, with the individual unions acting as its organs.

[34] Cf. *supra* Chapter 3,II.D.

[35] Cf. *supra* Chapter 2,II.H.

An employers' or employees' association may ask the Federal Settlement Office (*Bundeseinigungsamt*) at the Federal Ministry of Economic Affairs and Labor to declare that a specific collective agreement will henceforth be extended to similar employment relations not yet governed by a collective agreement. Thereby the collective agreement acquires the rank of a charter (*Satzung*).[36] The Federal Settlement Office may also fix minimum wage rates for certain branches of industry.[37]

C. Industrial Action (*Arbeitskampf*)

Austrian labor law does not provide for compulsory mediation of labor conflicts. Yet in the Second Republic, strikes (*Streik*) or lockouts (*Aussperrung*) have been extremely rare. As a rule, social conflicts are resolved through informal negotiation, in which frequently leaders of interest groups and politicians are involved. This is an expression of the spirit of "social partnership" which has characterized Austrian labor relations to this date. There exist only few legal regulations concerning industrial action. They clarify that the organization of and peaceful participation in industrial action (strikes, lockouts) is neither a crime nor a tort.[38] There have been no court decisions on this topic in recent years, since the rare instances in which industrial action had been initiated invariably led to negotiated settlements outside of court. Legal doctrine holds that an employee who participates in a strike violates his labor contract and becomes liable for damages. Similarly, an employer incurs civil liability if he locks out his employees.[39] Strikes against the government or parliament (e.g., by civil servants) are considered inadmissible, yet violations of this rule have not been sanctioned.

D. Employee Participation on the Enterprise Level

Labor relationships in individual establishments or enterprises employing at least five workers above the age of 18 are governed by works representation law, which regulates employee participation in enterprise management. The works constitution (*Betriebsverfassung*) is a charter that forms the legal basis of cooperation between the company management (the owner) and the workforce. It is based on the Labor Constitution Act (*Arbeitsverfassungsgesetz*).[40] The employees of an establishment may organize themselves into an

---

[36] This happens in rare cases, e.g., when on the employers' side a voluntary organization as partner to a collective agreement does not represent all employers of the industry concerned.

[37] In cases where there exists no employers' representation, e.g., with domestic labor.

[38] The employer and the works council are prohibited from taking industrial action against each other.

[39] In the course of a strike, the employer may hire new workers. It is unclear, whether employees who are prepared to work but are prevented by strikers have a claim to wages.

[40] Note that the act is a "simple" statute, not a constitutional law.

association that has its own representative bodies, the most important of which is the works council (*Betriebsrat*). All employees together form the works assembly (*Betriebsversammlung*) which elects the works council by secret vote for a term of four years. The number of representatives to the council depends on the number of employees.[41] All employees have the right to vote, regardless of their union membership. Only workers of the enterprise have the right to propose candidates. The members of the works council must be granted paid time off to perform their duties.[42] They enjoy special protection against notice and dismissal. Although legally separate from the labor union, the works council as a rule closely collaborates with it.

The works council[43] represents the employees in maintaining and promoting their economic, social, health, and cultural interests. For this purpose it exercises a number of participatory rights ranging from information and consultation to veto rights against management decisions. The council is entitled to supervise compliance with all legal provisions relating to the employees. It has comprehensive rights to participate in social matters, to obtain information and deliberate on all matters of safety and health protection, and to be involved in matters of in-house training, education, and welfare facilities. It has particularly far-reaching rights in personnel matters. Every transfer worsening an employee's situation requires the council's approval. If approval is withheld, the employer may petition the labor court. An intended termination or dismissal must be notified to the works council. If the council agrees, the employee may not challenge it in court for being "unsocial." In general, strict limits are imposed on the works council's participation in economic affairs apart from the right to be informed and to make suggestions.[44] However, the works council is entitled to nominate one-third of the members of the su-

---

[41] One member for five to nine employees, two for ten to 19, three for 20 to 50, four for 51 to 100, etc.

[42] In companies with more than 150 employees, one member of the works council may request to be entirely released from work yet receive full pay.

[43] In enterprises consisting of several business units, the members of the works councils established in these businesses form the works council assembly (*Betriebsräteversammlung*), which is to elect the central works council (*Zentralbetriebsrat*) from among its members. The central works council represents the interests of the staff of the whole undertaking *vis-à-vis* the management. In groups of companies, a group representative body (*Konzernvertretung*) may be set up to safeguard the common interests of employees working in this group. A European works council (*Europäische Betriebsvertretung*) has to be set up for enterprises and groups of enterprises with at least 150 employees each in at least two different EU or EEA Member States and more than 1,000 employees in total, whose central management is located in Austria.

[44] If a proposed alteration within the company has significantly adverse effects on all or a considerable part of the staff, a works agreement in the form of a "social plan" (*Sozialplan*) must be concluded, which provides for longer notice periods and higher severance pay for retiring employees, retraining measures, or transfer to other establishments.

pervisory board (*Aufsichtsrat*) of stock corporations[45] and some other types of corporate entities.[46]

Works agreements (*Betriebsvereinbarungen*) are written agreements between the works council and the owner. They regulate matters specifically reserved to them by statute or collective agreement and are of great practical importance. Most agreements are voluntary. Certain matters such as an internal disciplinary code, staff questionnaires, or piece-work pay are subject to mandatory works agreements. In certain other matters (e.g., an employee code of conduct, timing of working hours and breaks, modes of calculation and payment of wages), the owner or the council may in the absence of consent concerning the conclusion or change of a works agreement apply to the Conciliation Board (*Schlichtungsstelle*)[47] to impose a binding decision. The works agreement may not violate statutory law or collective agreements. It binds employer and employees, yet does not preclude more favorable terms in individual labor contracts.

V. Labor Disputes

A. Labor and Social Courts

Matters of labor law are judged by labor and social courts. They comprise all disputes arising between employers and employees in connection with the employment relationship, as well as all disputes involving or concerning the works council.[48] The labor and social courts[49] are special courts (or panels of regular civil courts) governed by the provisions of the Labor and Social Courts Act (*Arbeits- und Sozialgerichtsgesetz*) of 1985 as amended. They sit in panels consisting of one professional judge (*Berufsrichter*) as chairman and two expert lay judges (*Laienrichter*),[50] one with employer status,

---

[45] Note the dual board structure (managing board and supervisory board) of Austrian stock corporations.

[46] The labor members of the supervisory board have the same rights as other members. However, the appointment or removal of members of the managing board, the chairperson, and the deputy chairperson requires not only the majority vote of the supervisory board as a whole but also the majority of the capital representatives. This provision limits the labor members' influence.

[47] Cf. *infra* V.B.

[48] The parties may represent themselves in first instance procedures. They may also retain an attorney or be represented by any other qualified person, especially by a member of the works council, or by authorized agents of their statutory interest group or of a voluntary trade association. Employees are entitled to legal protection and representation before court by the competent Chamber of Labor.

[49] Cf. *supra* Chapter 6,II.B. The labor and social courts' jurisdiction includes the function to review decisions of the social insurance administration.

[50] The lay judges are paid expenses but receive no remuneration for their activities.

the other with employee status.[51] The votes of the three judges have the same weight. The procedure before the labor and social courts is – with few exceptions – conducted in accordance with the provisions of the Civil Procedure Code.

Employee organizations capable of being party to legal proceedings, as well as the respective employer, have standing to sue or be sued before the labor and social court in a collective action (*Verbandsklage*) to affirm the existence or non-existence of rights or legal relationships affecting at least three employees. Employers' or employees' organizations capable of concluding collective agreements may also directly file an application with the Supreme Court (*OGH*) to confirm the existence or non-existence of rights or legal relationships independent of specifically named persons. The application must concern a point of substantive labor law which is significant for at least three employers or employees.

B. Conciliation Boards (*Schlichtungsstellen*)

A Conciliation Board must be set up on application of either party to decide a dispute concerning the conclusion, amendment, or cancellation of certain works agreements. The board consists of a presiding judge selected by the parties from among the professional judges of the respective labor and social court. Each party nominates two assessors. The Conciliation Board is an administrative authority, not a court. The procedure follows the provisions of the General Administrative Procedure Act (*Allgemeines Verwaltungsverfahrensgesetz*, as republished in 1991). Its function is to mediate between the parties and make settlement proposals.[52] If necessary, it decides the case in the first and last instance by majority vote.

Literature

Laws and Commentaries

Floretta, H., Strasser, R., Arbeitsverfassungsgesetz (3rd ed. 1999)
Resch, B., Arbeitsrecht – Die 54 praktisch relevanten Rechtsvorschriften (2nd ed. 1997)

Textbooks and Monographs

Blanpain, R. (ed.), International Encyclopaedia for Labour Law and Industrial Relations (1977 loose-leaf edition); for the contribution on Austria see *R. Strasser, infra.*

---

[51] The lay judges are nominated by the employers' and employees' organizations.

[52] Cases most frequently referred to the Conciliation Board concern failure by the owner and the works council to agree on the prevention, elimination, or alleviation of adverse effects in connection with an alteration of the establishment (e.g., the necessity to draw up a social plan, cf. *supra* note 44).

Blanpain, R. (ed.), Labour Law and Industrial Relations in the European Union (1998; country reports do not include Austria)

Blanpain, R., Engels, C., European Labour Law (4th ed. 1997)

Floretta, H. et al., Arbeitsrecht (2 vols., 4th ed. 1998)

Goldmann, H. et al., Österreichisches Arbeitsrecht, Austrian Labour Law (German and English, 2nd ed. 1999)

Köck S., Labor and Employment, in *Heller, K. et al.*, Austrian Business Law: Legal, Accounting and Tax Aspects of Business in Austria (1992, Suppl. 8, 1998)

Mayer-Maly, T., Marhold, F., Österreichisches Arbeitsrecht (vol. 1, 1987, vol. 2, 2nd ed. 1999)

Mesch, M., Sozialpartnerschaft und Arbeitsbeziehungen in Europa (1995)

Prisching, M., Die Sozialpartnerschaft – Modell der Vergangenheit oder Modell für Europa (1996)

Schwarz, W., Löschnigg, G., Arbeitsrecht (8th ed. 2000)

Strasser, R., Labour Law and Industrial Relations in Austria (1992)

Tomandl, T., A Brief Outline of Austria Labor Law (1990)

Tomandl, T., Schrammel, W., Arbeitsrecht (vol. 1, 4th ed. 1999, vol. 2, 4th ed. 2000)

Chapter 16
The Civil Law Tradition[1]

I. Introduction

It is common knowledge that a considerable part of our cultural heritage has its roots in the creative spirit of Ancient Greece, and that Rome played an important role as an intermediary of this culture. As great admirers of Greek philosophy, arts and sciences, the Romans made them their own and passed them on to the Europe of the Middle Ages. It is less well-known that Rome also made a very significant original contribution to European civilization, namely Roman law. This may well be the most important (and probably the most durable) legacy of Ancient Rome to the modern world. It provides a unifying element to European legal culture – past, present, and future.

II. Early and Classical Roman Law

A. The Twelve Tables and Subsequent Legislation

Roman law enters the light of history with the enactment of the Twelve Tables around 450 B.C. This legislation reflects an astonishing level of sophistication on the part of a small city state living on agriculture. The Laws of the Twelve Tables attest to an early and unrivaled creative legal talent, which expressed itself in precise logic, in language capable of concentration as well as abstraction, an economy of legal forms and procedures, and a carefully calibrated balance of unwritten rules and statutory regulation. After the Twelve Tables the development of Roman private law only occasionally occurred by legislation in popular assemblies. It was largely effected through delegated rulemaking by an elected official, the *praetor*.

B. Praetor and Edict

All Roman litigation was initiated before the *praetor*, a high state official who annually promulgated the Edict, a catalog of actions (similar to the former English common law writs) and other legal remedies. Although the *praetor* considered himself bound by his own Edict, in exceptional cases he would formulate a new remedy. In this respect, he assumed a role of equity jurisdiction similar to that of the English Chancellor. In any event, once the *praetor* selected a specific *actio* as the proper program of litigation, he would refer the parties to a *iudex* (lay judge) who collected evidence, heard oral ar-

---

[1] The term "Civil law" refers to the Roman law based tradition of continental Europe, from where it has spread to all parts oft the globe.

gument, and decided the case. In conducting the trial, however, the judge was bound by the instructions contained in the formula of the action originally issued by the *praetor*.

C. The Classical Jurists

The *praetor* and the judges were laymen with little or no knowledge of the law. But they were advised by jurists, who belonged to their own social class, the Roman aristocracy. The social and professional authority of the jurists gave their advisory opinions at least *de facto* force of law. Judicial decisions were not considered binding precedents and thus were not recorded. The legal writings of the jurists, however, functioned as authoritative works, preserving both leading and dissenting opinions and providing persuasive argument for future legal disputes.

Roman law of the so-called classical period, essentially the first two and one-half centuries A.D., was fundamentally jurists' law. It was also case law in that Roman jurists did not want to bind themselves to inflexible rules, preferring instead the freedom to develop their law on a case-by-case basis. No equivalent of the Common law doctrine of *stare decisis* (binding nature of previous opinions) existed, yet jurists had great respect for the authority of older opinions and would not deviate from them lightly.

The function of jurists in Roman society transcended the mere scholarly exposition of existing law. Despite their strong tendency to preserve legal traditions, Roman jurists also realized that the law must not be static and immutable, but rather responsive to new social circumstances and changing practical needs. They consciously accepted the challenge and the responsibility to create new law. This role changed only in form but not in substance when Roman Emperors drew jurists into their service to prepare legal opinions and decisions on their behalf.

The classical jurists had at their disposal a broad range of formal and substantive reasons to support and justify their decisions. Among their more formal arguments we find deductions from logic and grammar, references to legislative intent, or the contracting parties' intent, the ordinary usage of language, analogy and so forth. Among the substantive arguments there is strong emphasis on values such as *bona fides* (good faith), *aequitas* (equity or fairness), *boni mores* (public policy), and *utilitas* (practicability).

Roman law provided a framework in which Roman citizens could pursue their social and economic interests with considerable freedom and equality. Because private property and freedom to contract were recognized, citizens were able to order their private lives with a maximum of flexibility. For the exercise of this private autonomy, Roman jurists formulated and specified social and ethical standards calculated to facilitate the harmonization of public and private interest. As a result of the impressive level reached by Roman legal science in its classical period, it came to influence substantially the later development of legal systems in medieval and modern Europe, as well as in many other parts of the world.

III. Justinian's *Corpus Juris*

The fourth and fifth centuries A.D. mark a period of stagnation and decline in legal scholarship. The political center of the Empire moved from Rome to Constantinople (Byzantium; today Istanbul, Turkey). In the context of his ambitious plans to reconstitute the Roman Empire in its former splendor, the Byzantine Emperor Justinian (527–565 A.D.) pursued two challenging legal policy goals: 1) to reform the legal system in the spirit of Christian humanism and social justice, and 2) to codify the law to provide legal security and renew classical Roman legal culture.

In A.D. 528, Justinian instructed a commission to collect and publish imperial legal decisions and enactments of previous centuries in a single code. This code was published one year later (but does not survive). One commissioner, Tribonian, exhibited unusual skill and devotion. He was rewarded with a promotion to junior minister of justice and immediately embarked on a much more ambitious project – the collection and editing of the writings of the classical jurists. Tribonian began by preparing 50 imperial edicts ("constitutions") in which the Emperor was to decide disputed questions of classical legal doctrine. He then asked the Emperor to set up a new commission to prepare a Digest of classical jurists' law.

A. The Digest

The Commission began its work in 530 and finished only three years later. It was given free reign to select texts, to abbreviate and to change them in order to remove the obsolete, to eliminate controversies, and to harmonize the collection by reformulation. The Commission worked in three subcommittees, each of which excerpted a portion of classical legal literature. According to Tribonian, they read 2,000 "volumes" (i.e., papyrus scrolls of approximately 10,000 words each) and reduced them to roughly 1/20 of their former size. The remaining 9,142 excerpts were arranged in 50 volumes under 430 "titles" (i.e., subject matter headings). The collection contains excerpts from the works of 39 jurists from the late republic to the early third century A.D. It was given the name Digest or Pandects.

The Digest was published in A.D. 533 with a dual purpose. It was to be taught by professors in law schools and to be applied as law by the courts. But in practice, the use of the Digest outside the imperial capital remained confined to use in legal education. The provincial judges read no Latin and did not comprehend the sophisticated case analysis of the classical jurists. This situation improved when Greek translations and learned commentary led to the development of a Byzantine legal culture.

B. The Institutes

After the compilation of the Digest, Justinian asked a small commission consisting of Tribonian and two law professors to compose an authorized textbook (or nutshell) for beginning law students. These Institutes of Justinian in four slender volumes are based on a similar work of the classical jurist Gaius written about 160 A.D. They include excerpts from a few other jurists, but offer a continuous text without indicating the origin of these inserts.

C. The Code

The legislative activism of Justinian required a new edition of the original collection of imperial enactments made in 529. Thus in 534 a new Justinianic Code was promulgated, consisting of more than 4,600 enactments ("constitutions") arranged in twelve volumes and numerous subject matter headings similar to those of the Digest.

D. The Novels

Justinian continued to enact reform legislation after the promulgation of his Code. These additional laws, usually written in Greek, have been transmitted through private collections and are referred to as Novels (from *novellae leges*, "new laws"). Together with the three official parts of Justinian's compilation, they have been labeled as *Corpus iuris civilis* since the time of the standard print edition by the French humanist Dionysius Gothofredus in 1583.

IV. From Roman Law to a European Legal Science

After reconquering Italy from the Ostrogoths, the Emperor Justinian in 554 A.D. put his legal compilations into force in that part of his empire as well. Soon, however, Lombard invaders reduced the Byzantine presence to a few enclaves such as Ravenna, Rome, and parts of southern Italy and Sicily. Surviving traces of Roman law and legal science from that period are scarce. The Digest, the intellectually most demanding work, was soon forgotten and practically disappeared. Its rediscovery in the eleventh century coincided with a period of flourishing commerce and scholarship but great political tension. With these favorable conditions, a powerful intellectual movement developed Roman law into a European legal science and into the subsequent foundation of modern European civil codes.

A. The Glossators

Towards the end of the eleventh century, Irnerius, a professor of grammar or rhetoric in Bologna, founded the most important law school of medieval Europe, in which, for the first time, the entire *Corpus iuris* of Justinian was subjected to scholarly analysis and exposition. The law professors of Bologna are called glossators. Glosses are explanations of words, concepts and rules which a jurist writes in the margin or between the lines of text of his copy of Justinian's Digest, Code or Institutes. They are then copied together with the annotated text, and occasionally they are also published in separate collections.

Justinian's compilations consist of different types of materials (especially writings of classical jurists and imperial enactments) which extend over several centuries. They lack system and contain many contradictions. The analysis, harmonization, and systematization of these compilations posed a fascinating task for the law teachers of Bologna, who accepted this challenge equipped with the scholastic method of medieval theology and philosophy. Their exegetic-didactic procedures first explained the text at issue, then established links with other texts, and finally examined all of them from the perspective of their usefulness to practical problem solving.

The first steps toward a systematization of legal substance matter were taken in the form of *distinctiones* (distinctions). These distinctions provided structure to smaller and larger *summae* (summaries), which ultimately grew to the size of a textbook. Thus the glossator Azo's *Summa Codicis*, a summary of Justinian's Code published around 1210, successfully served as a student textbook until the 17th century. Conflicting rules in the Roman texts were explained away as imaginary rather than real contradictions. Maxims abstracted from the texts also served an important function in harmonization and systematization. The crowning achievement of the school was the *Glossa ordinaria* (standard gloss) by Azo's pupil Accursius, in which the work of all predecessors had been critically sifted and condensed. It comprises 96,940 glosses, 62,577 of them added to the Digest. This work remained the standard commentary to the *Corpus iuris* for centuries. In practical application, the importance of the texts receded behind the interpretation and commentary provided by the gloss – *quod non agnoscit glossa, non agnoscit curia* (what the gloss does not acknowledge will not be acknowledged by the court).

Bologna, the first center of scholarly instruction in Roman law, won high recognition, and thousands of students from all over Europe came to study there and in other universities founded in the course of the 12th and 13th centuries in Italy and France. These students were not motivated only by scholarly interest. Roman law became instrumental in the political struggle between the Emperor and the Pope, both of whom claimed worldly authority and legitimacy on the basis of Roman law sources and reasoning. In its jurisdiction, the Church generally applied Roman law (*ecclesia vivit lege Romana*). It employed learned judges trained in Roman law and thus forced parties who litigated in ecclesiastical courts, as well as the secular opponents raising jurisdictional claims against it, to use a Roman law type of argument. Law graduates from Bologna and other universities quickly found gainful employment as judges and advocates for Church and State, and as officials and consultants in the service of the Church, the Emperor, princes, and cities.

B. The Commentators

The successors to the Glossators are called Commentators. They were active from the middle of the 13th to the beginning of the 16th century and considerably strengthened the practical effect of Roman law by linking it with the other legal systems of the times, subjecting these systems, together with

Roman law, to their scholarly analysis and exposition. This broader perspective concerned primarily the Canon law of the Catholic Church, which had already been taught and studied parallel to Roman law under the Glossators. Many ideas of Canon law were now absorbed into the civil law (cf. *mala fides superveniens nocet*, i.e., a stricter standard of good faith in the acquisition of ownership by adverse possession, prohibitions against interest-taking and usury, the binding nature of pacts confirmed by oath, etc.). The Commentators also paid attention to Lombard feudal law as well as to local customs (*consuetudines*) and to the statutes (*statuta*) of Italian city-states. They developed rules for the conflict of laws and generally interpreted statutes restrictively in order to preserve the broad applicability of Roman *ius commune* (common law).

In their legal literature, the commentary to parts of or the entire *Corpus iuris* gained special prominence. This commentary emancipated itself from the order of the texts and took a further step towards systematic exposition. But perhaps the most important type of the Commentators' legal literature was the *consilium* or expert opinion. The *consilium* was rendered by a law professor on a question of practical importance. Addressees could be the parties to litigation, but more usually it was the judge. The latter had a right but not a duty to ask for an opinion concerning a difficult question of law. The opinion was not binding on him.

The expert opinion of the law professor played a special role in the new *podestà*-system in Italian city administration. The mutual distrust of local aristocracy led to a neutralization of city government: An outsider, either a nobleman or a jurist, was appointed as city manager for a specified period of time, such as one year, at the end of which he was subjected to an official liability procedure in which he had to account for the legality of his acts. If his official decisions were based on the *glossa ordinaria* or the *communis opinio doctorum* (common opinion of the learned jurists), he was cleared. In doubtful cases, he could defend his position by the expert opinion of a recognized legal authority.

These opinions were structured in five parts: the facts (*casus*), the problem (*quaestio*), arguments for (*pro*), arguments against (*contra*), and finally the decision (*solutio*). They often extended Roman law rules far beyond their original scope to fit social and economic situations in medieval life. In using bold analogy they adopted a creative idea wherever they found it, with no regard to original context and systemic limits. This opened the door to creative lawmaking as much as to abusive manipulation.[2]

The first noteworthy representative of the Commentators was Cinus da Pistoia (1270–1336), a friend of Dante's and Petrarch's who taught in

---

[2] Cf. Bartolus, *Consilium* 128, where the jurist based the duty of the husband to support his wife (for which no explicit rule of Roman law existed) on the observation that she was in his service and that, e.g., someone who borrowed a slave must also bear the cost of his upkeep. Bartolus thus found the appropriate rule for marital alimony in a Gaius text with respect to a contract of loan for use concerning a slave.

Perugia and Siena. His pupil, Bartolus de Sassoferrato (1314–57), taught as professor in Pisa and Perugia. In the commentaries and opinions of Bartolus the school reached its intellectual peak. His authority was unmatched by any medieval jurist, his method – referred to as *mos docendi Italicus* ("the Italian way of teaching") – was considered the standard way of legal thinking and remained exemplary for centuries (*nemo jurista nisi bartolista* or "nobody is a jurist unless he is a follower of Bartolus"). In the form practiced by Bartolus and his pupil Baldus de Ubaldis, Roman law achieved international recognition as *ratio scripta* (written reason) and underwent a process of reception as European common law.

V. The Reception of Roman Law

A. The Process

Reception is a general cultural phenomenon. The reception of Roman law, in particular, was a process embracing the entire European continent, beginning with an early reception in the context of ecclesiastic courts and reaching its apex in the 15th and 16th centuries (most notably in the German Imperial Court Rules, the *Reichskammergerichtsordnung* of 1495).

The reception of Roman law should be viewed primarily as a process affecting legal scholarship and method. First in Bologna, and later in other Italian and French universities, students from all over Europe were trained to become learned jurists. Upon returning to their countries of origin, these students entered the service of princes or cities and worked as judges and advocates. In their professional practice they employed the method and substance of *mos Italicus* as a frame of reference, deriving rules from written authorities and applying them to fact situations by means of logical reasoning. To the extent that they replaced lay judges who had applied unwritten customary law, this process had the secondary effect that native substantive law was superseded by Roman law. But even the surviving native law was amalgamated into the emerging science of *usus modernus pandectarum* (the modern usage of Justinian's Digest).

B. Early Reception and Canon Law

Long before the official recognition of Roman law as the common law of the Holy Roman Empire in 1495, ecclesiastical courts had applied Roman law to a variety of matters under their jurisdiction. *Ecclesia Romana vivit secundum legem Romanam* (the Roman church lives under Roman law) was a subsidiary rule, to be applied in the absence of special Canon law rules, but one of great importance. Roman law was studied and applied almost exclusively by clerics prior to the 15th century, at which point a secular legal profession emerged. Roman law and Canon law were taught jointly in the universities (*ius utrumque*, the two laws), one influencing the other. Thus, for instance, canon law maxims of equity were also extended to the civil law. Canon law rejected *usucapio* by a *mala fide possessor*, demanded a just price (*pretium iustum*) in sale, etc. In ecclesiastical courts, Germanic lay judges were replaced by learned jurists two centuries before this occurred in secular courts. Customary law was difficult to prove, and judges decided on its rationality.

Ecclesiastical courts had jurisdiction over all spiritual matters and in all lawsuits against clerics. They also claimed protection of (i.e., jurisdiction over) crusaders, poor people, widows, and orphans. They extended their jurisdiction to *causae spiritualibus adnexae* (secular matters annexed to spiritual ones) such as marriage, wills, agreements under oath, and usury. Even purely secular matters could come under church jurisdiction *ratione peccati* (because of sinful behavior), or they were at least subject to confession, where priests applied Roman law principles to determine ethical behavior, thus popularizing Roman law. University students, too, were subject to an ecclesiastical judge. Therefore in Cologne and Prague businessmen matriculated as students merely to enjoy this privilege. Litigation before ecclesiastical courts was often also agreed on by laymen because it was quicker, less costly, and not subject to bribery. It used a more rational evidentiary procedure and led to a more predictable result. Above all, it provided for efficient execution beyond narrow territorial confines – the Church did not hesitate to use excommunication, a spiritual sanction of great weight in a closed Christian society.

Because of political fragmentation in the Holy Roman Empire, imperial power was generally weak. Yet the Emperor's extraordinary personal jurisdiction had no limits. In the *Reichskammergerichtsordnung* (Imperial Court Rules) of 1495 an imperial court was established, one-half of whose members were to be trained jurists. The court was to apply Romano-Canonic procedural rules and substantive law. In theory, Roman common law was to be subsidiary, but in practice the court insisted that it would apply the law it knew (*iura novit curia*), unless the parties produced proof to the contrary. The parties found it difficult if not impossible to prove local law that had not been written down.

C. The Balance Sheet of the Reception

- Glossators and Commentators provided the intellectual tools of analysis and exposition of all areas of private law: abstract concepts, definitions, and distinctions. They further developed the law within and beyond the systematic framework of Justinian's Institutes.
- In the areas of persons, family and succession, native law, corresponding to firmly embedded social structures, successfully withstood the onslaught of Roman law as to its substance. But Roman law concepts, definitions, divisions and many technical details were adopted. The law of marriage came to be governed by Canon law.
- In property law, native law continued to dominate land law (immovable property), but personal property law (movables) was by and large received from Roman law.

- The Roman law of obligations (i.e., contracts, torts and unjust enrichment) was adopted in bulk. Together with Roman personal property law it formed a legal framework for commercial exchange that excelled in terms of rationality and efficiency, and quickly found acceptance as a supranational European common law.
- Outside the reception of Roman law, Commentators and Canon lawyers created new concepts and institutions based on Roman law notions. Examples are private law institutions like legal personality and also entire new disciplines like commercial law (law merchant) and private international law.

VI. The Natural Law Codes

A. Natural Law and Enlightenment

At the time of *usus modernus pandectarum,* a new intellectual movement began to develop, which would ultimately lead to the codification of private law, the rationalist Natural law of the period of Enlightenment. It extends from Hugo Grotius in the 17th to Christian Wolff in the 18th century. Other important legal thinkers and writers were Gottfried Wilhelm Leibniz, Christian Thomasius and Samuel Pufendorf.

Natural law is present during all periods of legal thought and legal development. It is the product of reflection on generally valid and applicable principles of human life in society, culminating in the assumption of immutable rules of human behavior, as well as the rights and duties of man. It serves as a critical measuring rod applied to positive law, aiming at achieving its congruence with ethical demands. We may observe different schools of natural law ranging from classical antiquity (Greek philosophers, Cicero, Gaius: *ius commune omnium, ius gentium, naturalis ratio*) to the early Christian period and the Middle Ages (Tertullian, St. Augustine, St. Thomas Aquinas *et al.*) to the secular natural law of the Enlightenment. After the Renaissance and the period of Humanism, legal scholars intensified their search for an autonomous intellectual foundation of the natural and social world. In an emerging age of mathematics (Galileo), philosophers like Hobbes, Spinoza, Pufendorf and ultimately Descartes developed systems of deductive reasoning based on axioms, verified by empirical observation. Second only to Justinian's *Corpus iuris,* Natural law has been the most powerful spiritual force in modern legal history. Based on the heritage of Greek and medieval thought, it shares with the latter a claim to universal and eternal validity, formal rationalism in legal argument, and an idealistic anthropology – man is endowed with reason, and he is a social being that requires society for his perfection. Natural law, however, emancipates itself from moral theology – law is not God-given, but the product of a logical construct, the social contract.

"Enlightened" monarchs, like Frederick II of Prussia, Napoleon I in France, and Maria Theresia in Austria, were fascinated by the idea of codification of this Natural law. With the enactment of the Prussian Code of 1794, the *Code Napoléon* of 1804, and the Austrian Civil Code of 1811 – the Natural law codes[3] – Roman law ceased to be an official source of law in these territories. Yet in many ways it merely changed its form and continued to display a powerful influence as to its substance. Despite general ideological criticism directed against Roman law and a specific emphasis on certain Natural law ideas in the new codes, the Roman law tradition still provided both their conceptual framework and most of the substantive content of their rules. In fact, many of these rules preserve the very language of the classical Roman jurists to this day.

B. The Prussian Code

First steps towards codification in Prussia were taken by King Frederick William I in 1713. His son Frederick II (the Great) modified and further developed these plans, ordering his Chancellor Samuel von Cocceji in 1746 to produce a uniform law "based on reason and on the constitution of the territory." It was to contain a prohibition of any commentary "in order to prevent the citizens being taken in by the subtleties of professors and advocates." The project was continued by Johann Casimir von Carmer and Carl Gottlieb Svarez but not completed before Frederick's death in 1786. It was promulgated by his successor Frederick William II in 1794 as *Allgemeines Landrecht für die Preussischen Staaten* (*ALR*, Universal Territorial Law for the Prussian States).

The *ALR* is not confined to private law but represents a comprehensive codification including constitutional, ecclesiastic, criminal, and administrative law in more than 19,000 articles. Each topic is treated in excessive detail. The principle that laws should govern, not men, is applied in a highly paternalistic and patronizing spirit. Natural law ideas, especially as propagated by Christian Thomasius, permeate the Code, but Roman law substance is overwhelmingly accepted as *ratio scripta* (written reason), frequently by literal reception of Roman texts.

C. The French Civil Code

1. History

Prior to Napoleonic times, France consisted of two historically developed provinces of law: North and Central France were the *pays du droit coutumier* (the customary local law of the oral Germanic tradition), the South (below the line Gironde – Geneva) was the *pays du droit écrit*, the written law of the Roman tradition as taught in the famous law schools of Orléans, Toulouse, and Montpellier.

---

[3] Some authors include the – at any rate less significant – Bavarian Civil Code of 1756.

The French *Code civil* of 1804 is a product of the Revolution, but it was written when political fanaticism had already cooled off. The codification process was personally supervised by Napoleon as the First Consul, and the Code therefore bears his name. His energy was needed to force it through the legislative process, and he personally chaired 59 of the 102 meetings in which the *Conseil d'Etat* considered the text of the drafting committee, bringing discussions to the practical and concrete.[4] The Code's system and substance are based on the work of French Roman law scholarship, in particular the writings of Pothier (1699–1772). This is most obvious in areas such as contracts, the law of neighbors, wills, and dowry. But alongside Roman law influence, there is also a strong impact of medieval customary law, especially as written down in the *Coutume de Paris*. This is reflected in areas such as family law and intestate succession.

2. Spirit

The Code (comprising 2281 brief and clearly formulated articles) went the farthest of all natural law codifications in implementing the equality of citizens before the law and in guaranteeing private freedom and autonomy in legal transactions. It loosened all bonds of feudalism, emancipated landed property, and secularized family law. On the formal side, the Code excels in its use of forceful language and its transparent structure, yet it allowed for progressive interpretation by scholars (doctrine) and judges (jurisprudence) through its enunciation of brief and broad principles requiring later elaboration (for example in tort law) and by virtue of technical faults, omissions, and imprecisions.

The *Code Napoléon* was the most successful natural law codification. Whereas the Prussian Code of 1794 and the Austrian Code of 1811 were decreed by enlightened despots, who continued to rule with paternalistic authoritarianism in societies that still exhibited many feudal elements, in France the Code was the product of a liberated bourgeoisie and thus much more in touch with social reality.

3. Radiation of the *Code civil*

The French Code profoundly influenced later private law codification in the Romanistic family: Italy, Spain, Portugal, Belgium, Holland, Luxembourg, Romania, Central and South America, and in the former French colonial empire, most notably in the Near East, Africa and East Asia, but also in Quebec and Louisiana.

---

[4] Napoleon later said: "It is not in winning 40 battles that my real glory lies, for all those victories will be eclipsed by Waterloo. But my *Code civil* will not be forgotten, it will live forever."

D. The Austrian Code

In 1753, the Empress Maria Theresia charged a commission with preparing a uniform civil code for her hereditary territories. But the draft *Codex Theresianus* submitted in 1766 was rejected as too detailed, too much like a textbook and too close to Roman law. A reworked part, the law of persons and family, was promulgated by Emperor Joseph II as the Josephinic Code in 1786. A new commission under Karl Anton von Martini then finished a civil code that was experimentally enacted as the Westgalician Code in 1798. It received its final form under Franz von Zeiller, Martini's successor as professor of Natural law and Roman law in Vienna, and became effective as the General Civil Code (*Allgemeines Bürgerliches Gesetzbuch, ABGB*) in 1812.

The *ABGB* reflects the ideology of rationalist Natural law in its latest phase, and contains much Roman law substance. It is a brief, clear, and flexible code containing general principles that permit later adaptation by scholars and judges. For a detailed description see *supra* Chapter 12 (The Civil Code).

VII. The Pandectist Codes

A. Savigny and the Historical School

After the Napoleonic Wars and prior to the subsequent political restoration, German patriots demanded an all-German civil code as a step towards the reunification of the fragmented country. A strong appeal in this direction was made by A.F.J. Thibaut (Professor of Roman law in Heidelberg and a representative of late Natural law) in his 1814 pamphlet *Über die Notwendigkeit eines Allgemeinen Bürgerlichen Gesetzbuchs für Deutschland* (On the Need for a General Civil Code for Germany), but his demand remained unheeded.

Thibaut's ideas were rejected by a powerful opponent – Friedrich Karl von Savigny (1779–1861), the most influential German (perhaps even European) jurist of his time. In his programmatic book *Vom Beruf unserer Zeit für Gesetzgebung und Rechtswissenschaft* (On the Calling of our Age for Legislation and Legal Science, 1814) he criticized Natural law as methodically flawed, as it claimed to deduce legal rules from principles, but *de facto* abstracted these very principles from existing legal material. Instead of philosophical criticism of law, as offered by the protagonists of Natural law, Savigny demanded historical appreciation in order to eliminate what ignorance for centuries had added to pure Roman law. According to Savigny, some legislation might be legitimate to correct existing problems, but most codification was either superfluous or outright harmful, because it claimed exclusive legal authority for unforeseeable future situations. Lawmaking should not be entrusted to the arbitrary will of the legislator, he argued, but left to organic development, based on the common conviction of the people. Law should primarily be customary law, growing under the influence of scholars and judges. Savigny glorified the statute-free Roman jurisprudence and sharply criticized specific shortcomings of Natural law codes (*ALR, Code civil, ABGB*). He saw law as an expression of the *Volksgeist* (Hegel's national spirit or genius). According to Savigny, Roman law was fully compatible with the German national spirit – Germany had, after all, also adopted Judeo-Christian religion and other sophisticated cultural emanations congenial with its highly developed character. Thus there was an inner need for the reception of Roman law in Germany. Jurists, as representatives of the people, were responsible for this reception and could legitimately claim a monopoly to effect gradual legal development. They were to purify Justinianic Roman law from later distortions by medieval *usus modernus* and continue to apply Roman law as German common law. On this foundation they should formulate and explain the legal system as a harmonious whole without internal contradictions.

Savigny's Historical School, or Pandectism (legal science based on Justinian's Digest or Pandects), espoused a theory of scholarly positivism. Rules and holdings were to be derived from the sum total of legal concepts and institutions. Extralegal valuations based on religion, morality, etc., were not considered to have any creative force. As Bernhard Windscheid formulated: "Ethical, political or economic considerations are not addressed to the jurist as such," but to the legislator, who alone is responsible for policymaking. The huge supply of concepts and theory provided by the preceding school of rationalist Natural law scholars permitted the decision of all imaginable cases by means of logical operations. With Savigny's pupil Friedrich Puchta, Conceptual Jurisprudence (*Begriffsjurisprudenz*) became the dominant trend. This approach was often criticized as mechanical (in particular by followers of Rudolf von Jhering's Sociological Jurisprudence or *Interessenjurisprudenz*), but it has also had its value in putting emphasis on the calculability and reliability of law, and on the neutrality of the judge which was to become so important to the emerging constitutional state of the 19th century.

B. The German Civil Code

1. History

Savigny's influential opposition considerably delayed but could not prevent the process of German codification. Some unification in the areas of bills of exchange and commercial law (*Allgemeines Handelsgesetzbuch*, General Commercial Code) was accomplished in 1848 and 1861, respectively. But the Dresden Draft of a Law of Obligations did not go into effect in 1866 because Prussia at that time did not want the German Confederation to enjoy a political success.

After Prussia's military victory over Austria at Königgrätz in 1866, the dissolution of the *Deutsche Bund* (German Confederation) and the foundation of the *Deutsche Reich* (German Empire) under Prussian leadership in 1871, the codification idea received a new impetus. In 1873, private law legislation became an exclusive power of the *Reich*. Political and scholarly opposition to codification vanished. In 1874, a First Commission elaborated five partial drafts of a civil code (the subsequent five books of the Civil Code). They were mostly based on the leading textbook of Windscheid and were submitted for public evaluation in 1887. The draft was criticized by some as being too Romanistic, doctrinaire, un-German, and unsocial. In 1890, a Second Commission under Gottlieb Planck changed little, but provided positive publicity. The Civil Code (*Bürgerliches Gesetzbuch, BGB*) was adopted in 1896 and became effective in 1900.

2. Spirit

The defining characteristics of the *BGB* are scholarly logic, abstraction, and systematization. It uses the Pandect system of current private law lectures and textbooks (which are based on the Digest or Pandects of Justinian). This system of the *BGB* consists of five "books": I. General Part (arts. 1–240); II. Obligations (arts. 241–853); III. Property (arts. 854–1296); IV. Family (arts. 1297–1921); V. Succession (arts. 1922–2385). The Code is a product of excellent legal craftsmanship exhibiting a high degree of precision, clear fundamental principles, and few basic types of legal institutions (e.g., legal subject, legal object, and the declaration of intent). It makes clear-cut either-or distinctions rather than acknowledging intermediate forms (that would reflect the nuances of real life). As the Code's systematic structure descends from the general to the specific, its didactic approach moves from the simple to the complex. The *BGB* was obviously written for the expert, not for the general public. Its cool and sober rules demonstrate a high sense of justice regardless of the person. The legislator of the *BGB* wisely provided openings for future development. Although legislative recognition of customary law could have placed an important corrective in the hands of the judiciary, this has rarely been used as a basis of argument. But the inclusion in the *BGB* of broad general clauses, such as good faith and public policy, has had a profound effect.

The *BGB* mirrors the political and social structure of the Bismarck Empire and its tension between liberal-federalist and conservative-states' rights forces. The idea of codification was promoted primarily by a liberal bourgeoisie dominating the *Reichstag* (Parliament) and providing leadership in law schools and courts. The same forces propagated the idea of the political unification of the Empire. Political unification required legal unification to ease traffic and exchange, and to foster trade and manufacturing.

The *BGB* expresses the ideas of liberty and equality of all citizens, freedom of property, contract, wills, trade, and competition. It provides for a broad scope of private autonomy to regulate one's life through legal transactions, reducing state influence to the absolute minimum. Virtually all property is subject to the rules of private law, and clear rules secure the reliability and predictability of the law, even at the expense of individual equity. The prototype of the Code is a property-owning citizen with a certain amount of business skill and legal knowledge. But the Code also projects a quaint image of the "good old times," a small-town scenario complete with flour mill, forge and brewery, and makes no reference to the industrial revolution with its new techniques, mass traffic and urban problems. Thus, one finds the small-town exclusion of *bona fide* acquisition of stolen or lost property (art. 935 I), an emphasis on agriculture, and conservative rules concerning marriage, marital property, illegitimate children and inheritance. Workers and their problems (labor contract, housing) were neglected. According to Gustav Radbruch's acute appraisal, the *BGB* is the final chord of the 19th rather than an upbeat to the 20th century. It represents a collection of existing wisdom provided by Pandectism rather than a creative accomplishment. Its method and substance are rooted in the past. The conservative Roman law professor Bernhard Windscheid decisively influenced the first draft, emphasizing system and doctrine (*Dogmatik*), and ignoring contemporary changes from agriculture to trade and industry, the emergence of big cities and big enterprises, a dramatically growing workforce of blue and white-collar employees and the resulting social tensions. The critical evaluation by professors of German legal history[5] and others[6] provided little change in the substance of the draft.

3. Subsequent Developments

After the adoption of the Code, criticism fell silent, and scholars and courts submitted, initially practicing a veritable cult of the legislative materials, suggesting that a Code without gaps lent itself to pure logic and deductive reasoning. An "exegetical school" explained the Code in terms of extreme conceptualism. The *argumentum a contrario* flourished. A wealth of descriptive monographs and dissertations emerged, Ludwig Enneccerus wrote the leading textbook, Gottlieb Planck the most influential commentary.

This period came to an end in the 1920s, when the *Reichsgericht* (Imperial Court of Justice) began to develop autonomous case law, loosening the strings which tied the judge to the statute, emphasizing that the general principles of good faith, public morals, etc., were superior to individual legislative rules. Under the influence of sociological jurisprudence (*Interessenjurisprudenz*), legal rules were viewed as solutions to social conflicts of interests. Law was required to adjust to changing needs, and judges had to gain a new perspective on their functions, which were to include the creative development of the law, instead of confinement to mechanical logical subsumption. State intervention in emergencies during World War I (1914–18) provided the roots for later labor and economic law. With the growing political influence of the Social Democrats, legal protection of the economically and socially weak gained importance; reference to the *clausula rebus sic stantibus*[7] supported judicial contract adjustment; reform legislation concerning labor contracts,

---

[5] In particular Otto von Gierke, *Der Entwurf eines BGB und das deutsche Recht*, 2nd ed. 1889.

[6] See Anton Menger, *Das bürgerliche Recht und die besitzlosen Klassen*, 1890.

[7] The doctrine that an unforeseen change in circumstances which the parties took for granted at the formation of the contract may invalidate the agreement (frustration of contract).

antitrust, and housing was adopted. Subsequent court practice increasingly placed equity before calculability and strict application of the statute. In particular, the *Reichsgericht* projected article 242 *BGB* ("The debtor is bound to effect performance according to the requirements of good faith (*Treu und Glauben*), giving consideration to common usage") into the role of a "supernorm" controlling all areas of the law.

The most spectacular judicial adaptation of the Code to changing social and economic conditions occurred in the "inflation cases" of 1922–23. Subsequent changes in ethical and religious values were frequently too profound to be translated into law by judicial adjustment. Thus, in the area of family law, strong legislative interference was required to replace the patriarchal model of the *BGB* with new rules based on the equality principle of the Basic Law of 1949. But in many other areas of the law (in particular contract and tort law), courts were forced to intervene due to the absence of legislative action. In a landmark decision in 1959 (Midwife case), the Federal Constitutional Court justified judicial gapfilling and the correction of legislative mistakes in response to a perceived "aging of codifications" and application of "the community's established general concepts of justice." This does not mean, however, that German courts have abandoned the Code. On the contrary, their attitude towards the *BGB* and legislation in general remains favorable, and they are clearly reluctant to deviate from its rules. If forced to make new law, courts follow the Code as closely as possible, and try to integrate their decisions into its framework. The Code has thus retained its value over time.

4. Radiation

The German Historical School and Pandectism extended far beyond Germany and influenced legal theory and doctrine particularly in Italy, France, and Austria. In a number of countries, however, the *BGB* was much admired, but had little practical effect, because its sophisticated structure and abstract conceptualist language were seen as typical products of German scholarship (demanding, difficult, pedantic techniques; precise, disciplined, artificial language) that were not easily transplantable. Yet the *BGB* exerted strong influence on codification and legal science in Russia and Hungary (the latter having repealed the Austrian code in 1861). In Czechoslovakia and Yugoslavia, too, Austrian legislative models were modified by German influence. The *BGB* was used as a model for codification in Siam (Thailand), China, and Japan, and had its strongest impact on the Greek Civil Code of 1940 (in effect since 1946).

C. The Swiss Civil Code

1. History

The Swiss Civil Code (*Zivilgesetzbuch, ZGB*) of 1907 is the second code based on pandectist science, and according to general opinion a superior product because of its stronger foundation in the social system. It expresses a strong and lively tradition of popular legal consciousness, and also practical realism by omitting a general part. It is the product of a learned and circumspect author, Professor Eugen Huber.

The Swiss had for centuries successfully defended their independence against the Holy Roman Empire, and thus the German speaking part of Switzerland had not experienced a comprehensive reception of Roman law. Where the reception did take place, it did not interrupt the citizens' legal consciousness and participation in the administration of justice. When democratic and national movements demanded Swiss legal unification, the European restoration of 1815 brought delay, but liberals ultimately succeeded in their demand for a uniform commercial law and law of obligations. In 1874 and 1883, federal legislative powers were enlarged, and in 1896, they were extended by referendum to the entire area of private law. A first Pandectist-inspired draft Law of Obligations was submitted by Munzinger and enacted in 1883. Eugen Huber (professor of German legal history and politician) was entrusted with a comparative analysis of Swiss private law, which he submitted in four volumes between 1886 and 1893. In 1893, he drafted a Civil Code without a law of obligations. The Code (*Zivilgesetzbuch, ZGB*) was unanimously adopted by the Swiss parliament on October 12, 1907. In 1911, the Law of Obligations (*Obligationenrecht, OR*) was revised. The *ZGB* and the *OR* both came into force in 1912.

2. Spirit

The *ZGB* is a Pandectist code containing 977 articles (the *OR* has 1,186 articles), with many parallels to the German *BGB*. The introduction (arts. 1–10) contains important maxims. The language is a model of clarity, forcefulness, and comprehensibility. The Swiss system of private law contains five major parts: 1) Law of persons, 2) Family law, 3) Inheritance, 4) Property, 5) Obligations.

Immediately upon its enactment in 1907, the Swiss Code was generally and enthusiastically admired. Even in Germany it was suggested to repeal the *BGB* (whose language and technique were so complex, whose structure was over-sophisticated, and whose conceptualism was extreme) and replace it with the Swiss Code. The Swiss had avoided all these defects, drafting their Code in popular and clear language, in an easily accessible structure, and with deliberately incomplete rules, permitting the judge to decide what is appropriate, reasonable, and equitable.[8] When, in the not too distant future, the project

---

[8] See in particular the famous article 1 *ZGB*: "If no relevant provision can be found in a statute, the judge must decide in accordance with the customary law and, in its absence, in accordance with the rule which he would, were he the legislator, adopt. In so doing he must pay attention to accepted doctrine and tradition." In the words of François Gény, "this is probably the first time that a modern legislator has given official recognition in a great formula to the fact that the judge is his indispensable auxiliary."

of a European Civil Code will be realized,[9] it will no doubt be written in the style of the *ZBG* rather than that of the *BGB*. Not because popularity will be the goal, but an open-endedness that will permit judicial amplification.

3. Radiation

Almost every subsequent legislator has profited from the Swiss experience in drafting or revising a civil code (cf. Italy or Greece). But there has been only one total reception, namely in Turkey. After Kemal Atatürk had created the Republic of Turkey in 1922 as a secular state, he had the Turkish Civil Code of 1926 enacted as an almost verbatim translation of the Swiss Code (including the *OR*). One author explains that this reception is the result of the Turkish Minister of Justice having studied in Switzerland, others point to the intrinsic merits of the Swiss Code, particularly its brevity and lucidity, as well as to the existence of a French version and commentaries in that language.

VIII. Civil Law and Common Law

After the Norman Conquest of 1066, England was organized as a strict and simple feudal system in which the King ruled as absolute monarch. The strong central authority of the crown prevented the barons from acquiring positions of power similar to that of feudal lords in Germany. Royal justice was dispensed by centralized courts staffed with professional judges. Local legal rules and customs from Anglo-Saxon times were overcome by a unified Common law. This Common law grew gradually, in an inorganic manner, marked by judicial activity and political struggles between monarchy, nobility, and commoners. It is characterized by a preponderance of pragmatic solutions over logical constructs.

Litigation in medieval English courts was founded on writs (standardized forms of action for particular complaints) issued by the Chancellor in the name of the King. Plaintiffs had to make the correct choice of writ, or they risked losing their case. To a certain extent, the Chancellor could help them by creating a new writ when existing remedies did not fit the facts of the case. But by the 14th century English courts had become rather formalistic. Many claims were rejected because of procedural errors, technicalities, or simply the lack of an appropriate writ. In these cases, plaintiffs could petition the King to order the defendant to act according to the requirements of morality. The King would then instruct his Chancellor, as the "keeper of the King's conscience," to consider granting relief as a matter of grace outside the Common law. The Chancellor would then exercise equitable jurisdiction by compelling the opposite party to appear and be examined, and he would hear evidence without a jury and decide himself all matters of fact and law "*secundum bonum et aequum.*" He could enforce his orders by imprisonment. In time, special rules,

---

[9] See *infra* IX.B.

remedies, and procedures of Equity in a special Court of Chancery were developed. Until the 16th century, Chancellors were ecclesiastics, applying (without express acknowledgment) rules and principles of Canon and Roman law. In general, Equity supplemented and occasionally corrected the Common law, but open confrontation was by and large avoided.

The development of the English Common law was greatly influenced by organized guilds of professional lawyers (the Inns of Court) in London. They controlled legal education until the 19th century, emphasizing a practice oriented, empirical approach. Since the 13th century, judges have been chosen from the ranks of lawyers admitted to the Bar by the Inns of Court. The powerful professional and social cohesion as well as the political influence of English lawyers and judges prevented any large scale reception of Roman law. The Common law was seen by them as an essential guarantee of freedom. They supported Parliament in its ultimately victorious confrontation with the Stuart and Tudor kings of the 16th and 17th centuries, who had sought to become absolute monarchs with the help of Roman law maxims that legitimized royal sovereignty.[10]

Yet from the very beginning, Roman law exercised a strong and lasting influence on the Common law. In 1143 Vacarius, a glossator from Bologna, arrived in England and from 1149 taught at Oxford as its first law professor. Ranulf de Glanville, an ecclesiastic, royal official, diplomat, and judge under Henry II, published a *Tractatus de legibus et consuetudines regni Angliae* (Treatise on the Laws and Customs of England), the oldest extant work on the Common law. This treatise was mostly procedural in its orientation and assumed a knowledge of Roman law on the part of its readers. Henry de Bracton (c. 1212–1268), an ecclesiastic and royal judge, subsequently published a *Tractatus* (1250–58) which not only dealt with procedure but also offered an expository text and commentary on the substantive law, a comprehensive work in clear and Romanist terms. Setting out English law in Roman law terms is said to have provided a "preventive inoculation" protecting its substance against the import of a foreign legal culture.

It was not only in areas of special jurisdiction (ecclesiastical courts, admiralty and mercantile law) that Civil law ideas prevailed and specially trained civilian lawyers pleaded. It can be shown that the Common law at various later stages of its development profited from Roman concepts, definitions and principles. Judges like Sir Edward Coke (1552–1634) and John Holt (1642–1709), who presided over the King's Bench from 1689 to 1709, used Roman law from Bracton for interpretive and gapfilling purposes (e.g., introducing negligence into the law of bailment in Coggs v. Bernard, 1703). William Murray Lord Mansfield (1705–1793, serving as Lord Chief Justice for 32 years), the "father of modern mercantile law," had a good knowledge of

---

[10] Cf. Digest 1,4,1 *quod principi placuit, legis habet vigorem* (a decision by the emperor has the force of a statute); Digest 1,3,31 *princeps legibus solutus est* (the emperor is not bound by the statutes).

Roman law and at one point even attempted to abolish the doctrine of consideration from English contract law (Pillans v. van Mierop).

Under the influence of Roman law, Jeremy Bentham (1748–1832) criticized the Common law and proposed codification. John Austin (1790–1848) was strongly impressed by the German Pandectist school. Many 19th century English jurists went to study Roman law in Bonn or Heidelberg in order to better understand continental legal systems.

In Europe today, Civil law and Common law show several signs of convergence. In the UK, statutory law increasingly overrides Common law traditions of judicial law-making, while on the continent, legal theory increasingly acknowledges the fact and necessity of judicial precedent and law-making. Important areas of the law are unified under international treaties like the European Convention for the Protection of Human Rights and the Treaty on the European Union. British judges faithfully implement European Union law that is based primarily on Civil law notions. The European Court of Human Rights in Strasbourg and the Court of Justice of the European Communities in Luxembourg creatively apply principles from both legal worlds. But despite refreshing input from the Common law, the dominant legal culture of the European Union and the emerging *ius commune Europaeum* remain very much in the Civil law tradition.

IX. The Civil Law Tradition and the Law of the European Union

A. Three Fundamental Contributions of Roman Law

Roman law contributed some of the most essential elements to the present European legal culture. First, a scientific approach to the law, with clear concepts and definitions, precise rules, and analytical and systematic reasoning. These technical aspects provided a Roman law input even into the former Socialist legal systems. They are independent of value systems and ideologies.

A second major element of Roman law influence are legal principles and substantive values, which Roman jurists used in their legal reasoning and which have become a common European heritage. They include the principles that all obligations must be performed in good faith (*bona fides*), that contracts against public morals (*boni mores*) are null and void, that nobody may enrich himself to the detriment of another, and so forth.

A third and also highly relevant Roman contribution to modern legal thought concerns patterns of legal sources and processes of lawmaking. Roman law was primarily case law shaped by jurists. Understanding the creative role of the Roman jurist may help appreciate the lawmaking role of the common law judge and enhance the contributory function of the legal scholar as expert adviser to legislators and courts.

B. Toward a European Civil Code

With the establishment of the European Union, one may observe a growing trend to reconstitute the former legal unity that was provided by the *ius commune* of *usus modernus pandectarum* but lost by national codification in the 18th and 19th centuries. European Union directives and the jurisprudence of the European Court of Justice progressively harmonize European legal systems. In 1989 and again in 1994, the European Parliament urged the Council, the Commission, and the Member States to unify and codify European private law. Various groups are already engaged in preparing drafts for particular areas like contracts and torts. In this grand venture, a historical understanding of the common Roman law foundations of European legal systems will greatly aid scholarly communication, comparative study, and eventual progress towards an – increasingly probable – All-European Civil Code. Existing European civil codes are based on values, principles, and rules that originate in Roman and subsequent European development. Many of them still transcend national law.

In attempting to establish European legal unity today, we should not return to *usus modernus* or Pandectist Roman law, but move forward on their foundations, recognizing them as useful starting points of a dialectical process. In this perspective, the Roman law experience will once again provide an important unifying element to an emerging supranational European legal culture.

Literature

Codes

The German Civil Code *(trans. S. L. Goren,* rev. ed. 1994)
The French Civil Code *(trans. J. H. Crabb,* rev. ed. 1995)
The General Civil Code of Austria *(trans. P. L. Baeck,* 1972)
The Swiss Civil Code *(trans. I. Williams,* 1976)

Textbooks

Coing, H. (ed.), Handbuch der Quellen und Literatur der Neueren europäischen Privatrechtsgeschichte (vols. I – III/5, 1973–1988)
Hausmaninger, H., Selb, W., Römisches Privatrecht (8th ed. 1997)
Merryman, J. H., The Civil Law Tradition (2nd ed. 1985)
Robinson, O. F. et al., European Legal History (2nd ed. 1994)
Schlosser, H., Grundzüge der Neueren Privatrechtsgeschichte (8th ed. 1996)
Watson, A., The Making of the Civil Law (1981)
Wesenberg, G., Wesener, G., Neuere deutsche Rechtsgeschichte (4th ed. 1985)
Wieacker, F., A History of Private Law in Europe *(trans. T. Weir,* 1995)
Zimmermann, R., The Law of Obligations: Roman Foundations of the Civilian Tradition (1990)
Zweigert, K., Kötz, H., Introduction to Comparative Law *(trans. T. Weir,* 3rd ed., paper 1998)

Monographs and Articles

Berman, H. J., Law and Revolution (1983)

Dawson, J., The Oracles of the Law (1968)

Hartkamp, A. S. et al. (eds.), Towards a European Civil Code (2nd ed. 1998)

Helmholz, R. H., Continental Law and Common Law: Historical Strangers or Companions, Duke Law Journal 1990, 1207

Hoeflich, M. H., Roman and Civil Law and the Development of Anglo-American Jurisprudence in the Nineteenth Century (1997)

Knütel, R., Rechtseinheit in Europa und römisches Recht, Zeitschrift für Europäisches Privatrecht 1994, 244

Legrand, P., Against a European Civil Code, Modern Law Review 60 (1997) 44

Reimann, M. (ed.), The Reception of Continental Ideas in the Common Law World 1820–1920 (1993)

Stein, P., The Character and Influence of Roman Civil Law (1988)

van Caenegem, R. C., An Historical Introduction to Private Law (*trans. D. E. L. Johnston* 1992)

Wieacker, F., Foundations of European Legal Culture, American Journal of Comparative Law 38 (1990) 1

Wieacker, F., Historical Models for the Unification of European Law, FS Summers (1994) 297

Wieacker, F., The Importance of Roman Law for Western Civilization and Western Legal Thought, Boston College International & Comparative Law Review 4 (1981) 257

Zimmermann, R., Civil Code and Civil Law – "The Europeanization" of Private Law within the European Community and the Re-emergence of a European Legal Science, Columbia Journal of European Law 1 (1994–95) 63

Zimmermann, R., Roman and Comparative Law: The European Perspective, Legal History 16 (1995) 21

Dates in Modern Austrian Political and Legal History

1804	Francis II, Holy Roman Emperor, adopts additional title "Emperor of Austria"
1806	Francis declares Holy Roman Empire of the German Nation (*Heiliges Römisches Reich deutscher Nation*) expired
1814/15	Congress of Vienna, Holy Roman Empire is replaced with German Confederation (*Deutscher Bund*)
1815	"Holy Alliance" of European states, to preserve stability and monarchic legitimacy
1848	Revolutions against absolute monarchies (Metternich's "system") in member states of the German Confederation
1849	King William IV of Prussia refuses election as "Emperor of the Germans" by a German Constitutional Convention
1848–51	Early Austrian constitutionalism
1852–67	Austrian neo-absolutism
1866	Rivalry between Prussia and Austria leads to military clash, Prussia wins at Königgrätz, German Confederation collapses
1867	Austria becomes a constitutional monarchy; "Compromise" (*Ausgleich*) with Hungary, Bill of Rights
1914	Archduke Francis Ferdinand assassinated in Sarajevo
1914–18	World War I
1916	Death of Emperor Francis Joseph (reigned 1848–1916)
1918	Disintegration of the Habsburg (Austro-Hungarian) Monarchy; revolutionary creation of *Deutschösterreich* (German-Austria) by Provisional National Assembly
1919	Peace Treaty of Saint Germain forbids Republic of Austria to join Germany and imposes economic sanctions
1920	Federal Constitution
1925	Constitutional amendments develop federal structure, expand jurisdiction of Constitutional Court
1929	Constitutional amendments strengthen Federal President and separation of powers
1934	Christian Corporate State (dictatorship)
1938	Occupation of Austria by German troops, Austria becomes part of Hitler's Germany (*Anschluß*)
1939–45	World War II
1943	Moscow Declaration of Allied Powers on the reestablishment of Austrian independence after the war
1945	Austrian political parties declare Austrian independence, return to the Constitution of 1920/29, but Austria remains under control of the Allied Council (four occupying powers)

1955	Moscow Memorandum, State Treaty, Austria regains sovereignty, declares permanent neutrality
1955/56	Austria joins UN and Council of Europe
1959	Austria joins EFTA (after Russian veto against EEC membership)
1989/90	Austrian government applies for EC membership and reinterprets State Treaty
1995	Austria joins EU (67 % pro-votes in popular referendum)

Appendix 2

Federal Legislative and Executive Organs

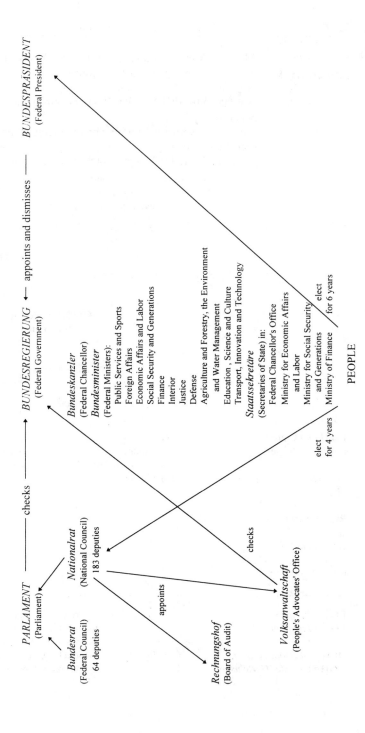

The Austrian Court System:
Civil Procedure

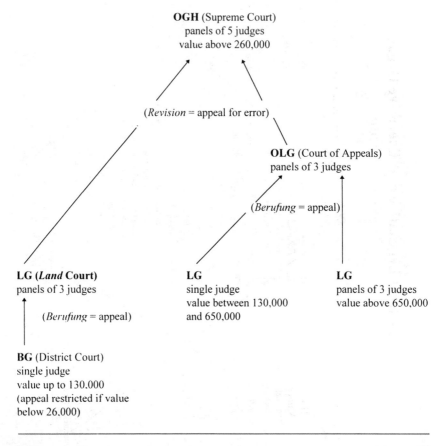

OGH (Supreme Court)
panels of 5 judges
value above 260,000

(*Revision* = appeal for error)

OLG (Court of Appeals)
panels of 3 judges

(*Berufung* = appeal)

LG (*Land* Court)
panels of 3 judges

(*Berufung* = appeal)

LG
single judge
value between 130,000
and 650,000

LG
panels of 3 judges
value above 650,000

BG (District Court)
single judge
value up to 130.000
(appeal restricted if value
below 26.000)

BG = *Bezirksgericht*	*Berufung*:	incorrect ascertainment of facts,
LG = *Landesgericht*		incorrect legal evaluation,
		serious procedural error
OLG= *Oberlandesgericht*	*Revision*:	incorrect legal evaluation,
OGH= *Oberster Gerichtshof*		serious procedural error

Appendix 4

The Austrian Court System:
Criminal Procedure

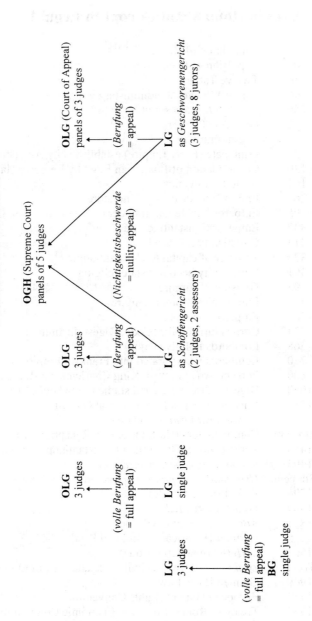

BG   = *Bezirksgericht*
LG   = *Landesgericht*
OLG = *Oberlandesgericht*
OGH = *Oberster Gerichtshof*

volle Berufung: guilt, punishment, grounds for nullity
Berufung: punishment, grounds for nullity
Nichtigkeitsbeschwerde: grounds for nullity (incorrect legal evaluation or serious procedural error)

Appendix 5

Dates in Roman and European Legal History

B.C.	753	Foundation of Rome
	509	Expulsion of Kings, Republic established
	451/450	Twelve Tables
	366	(Urban) Praetor to administer civil procedure
	286	*Lex Aquilia* (tort statute)
	242	Peregrine Praetor
	44	Caesar murdered
	27	Principate (Early Empire) established by Augustus
A.D.	130	Consolidation of Praetorian Edict by Emperor Hadrian
	161	Institutes of Gaius
	260	End of "classical" legal literature
	284–305	Emperor Diocletian, founder of Dominate (Late Empire)
	306–337	Emperor Constantine (the Great)
	313	Christianity tolerated
	326	Transfer of capital to Constantinople
	391	Christianity becomes state religion
	395	Division of Empire
	476	End of West Roman Empire
	527–565	Emperor Justinian
	528–534	Corpus iuris civilis (Code, Digest, Institutes)
	568	Lombards in Italy (Pavia)
	750	Lombards incorporated into Frankish Empire
	800	Pope crowns Frankish King Charlemagne Roman Emperor
	1050	Digest rediscovered and studied in School of Bologna
	1150	Vacarius teaches Roman law at Oxford
	1250	*Glossa ordinaria* of Accursius
	13th–16th cent.	Commentators (Bartolus *et al.*), Reception of Roman law
	1453	Turks conquer Byzantium (Constantinople, Istanbul)
	1495	*Reichskammergerichtsordnung*
	17th–18th cent.	*Usus modernus pandectarum* and Natural law
	1794	*ALR* (Prussian Code)
	1804	French *Code civil*
	1811	*ABGB* (Austrian Civil Code)
	19th cent.	German Historical School and Pandectism
	1900	*BGB* (German Civil Code)
	1907/12	*ZGB* and *OR* (Swiss Civil Code and Law of Obligations)
	1949	German Basic Law
	1953	European Human Rights Convention
	1957	Treaty of Rome (European Economic Community , EEC)
	1993	European Union Treaty (Maastricht)

Appendix 6

A Note on Legal Research

Research guides and bibliographies in English are:
- Thomas H. Reynolds, Arturo A. Flores, Foreign Law: Current Sources of Codes and Basic Legislation in Jurisdictions of the World (1991, loose-leaf, with updates. For Austria see vol. II, 2/99 release)
- Claire M. Germain, Germain's Transnational Law Research (1991, loose-leaf, with frequent updates. Austria is covered in release 4, dated 8/97)
- Ilse Dosudil, Austria, in: Jules Winterton, Elizabeth M. Moys (eds.), Information Sources in Law (2nd ed. 1997) 59
- James R. Fox, A Guide to Austrian Legal Research, 80 Law Library Journal 99 (1988).

A substantial amount of the legal literature has recently become available in electronic form and is accessible over the Internet. The commercial legal database venture *RDB (Rechtsdatenbank)*, owned by the two largest legal publishers, contains not only all primary legal sources, but also complete texts of law review articles. These materials can be reached at http://www.rdb.co.at. A valid user identification and password is required to access the databases. Fees are charged for searching, viewing and printing documents.

The site of the Austrian Government (http://www.austria.gv.at) provides information on Austria and its political system, as well as links to individual Ministries). The Federal Chancellery offers access to the complete text of federal statutes and of the decisions of the Constitutional Court and the Administrative Court, as well as the statutes of the nine *Länder*. The address is http://www.ris.bka.gv.at. The minutes of the Austrian Parliament (*Nationalrat* and *Bundesrat*) and legislative materials are also available on the Internet (http://www.parlinkom.gv.at). The online version of the the Federal Law Gazette is at http://www.verlagoesterreich.at/bgbl/ris.

The Austrian Constitutional Court offers up-to-date publication of its decisions at http://www.vfgh.gv.at. The Austrian Bar Association can be reached at http://www.oerak.or.at. It provides, *inter alia*, a database of all Austrian attorneys. The Austrian Notaries offer a similar directory at their web-site http://www.notar.or.at/. Daily legal news and hundreds of legal Internet links can be found at the Web Server of the Faculty of Law of the University of Vienna (http://www.juridicum.at). For internet sites providing information on legal history see http://www.univie.ac.at/wrg/links.htm.

The European Court of Human Rights can be reached on the Internet at http://www.echr.coe.int; the Court of Justice of the European Communities at http://curia.eu.int. The EU homepage provinding general information and links to the EU organs is http://europa.eu.int/index.htm.